F
W L

JOSEPH BRODSKY

LEV LOSEFF
Translated by Jane Ann Miller

Joseph Brodsky

A LITERARY LIFE

Yale UNIVERSITY PRESS
NEW HAVEN & LONDON

Published with assistance from the foundation established in memory of Amasa Stone Mather of the Class of 1907, Yale College.

Originally published as Lev Losev, *Iosif Brodskii: Opyt literaturnoi biografii* (Moscow: Molodaia gvardiia, 2006).

Set in FontShop Scala type by Duke & Company, Devon, Pennsylvania.
Printed in the United States of America by Sheridan Books, Ann Arbor, Michigan.

Library of Congress Cataloging-in-Publication Data
Losev, Lev, 1937–2009.
[Iosif Brodskii. English]
Joseph Brodsky : a literary life / Lev Loseff ; translated by Jane Ann Miller.
p. cm.
Originally published: Moscow : Molodaia gvardiia, 2006, under title Iosif Brodskii : Opyt literaturnoi biografii.
Includes bibliographical references and index.
ISBN 978-0-300-14119-1 (alk. paper)
1. Brodsky, Joseph, 1940–1996. 2. Authors, Russian—20th century—Biography.
I. Miller, Jane Ann. II. Title.
PG3479.4.R64Z76513 2011
891.71′44—dc22

2010024542

A catalogue record for this book is available from the British Library.

This paper meets the requirements of ANSI/NISO Z39.48-1992 (Permanence of Paper).

10 9 8 7 6 5 4 3 2 1

CONTENTS

PREFACE

There were a number of reasons for me *not* to write this book. Joseph Brodsky was a close friend of mine for more than thirty years, and I am fairly certain that he would not have been enthusiastic about anyone "writing his life." Most likely, he would have shrugged and said, "Well, if you feel like doing it . . . ," then switched the conversation to something he thought more interesting. But Brodsky's attitude toward writers' biographies was fraught with contradictions. He always insisted on the irrelevance of his life to his poetry, but he was an avid reader of other poets' lives. For example, in his Nobel lecture he said: "It is precisely their lives [Mandelstam's, Akhmatova's, Tsvetaeva's, Auden's, and Frost's], no matter how tragic or bitter they were, that often moves me—more often perhaps than the case should be—to regret the passage of time." From the beginning I set out to write a *literary biography,* not a chronicle of Brodsky's life. Being a good friend of one's subject is not necessarily an advantage: here one must strive for objectivity. But I cannot comment on Joseph's life and work dispassionately, not only because I loved him but also because I thought him a genius.

"Genius" is not a scholarly term.[1] Its common use is mainly emotive: "You're a genius!" For me, "genius" is first and foremost a cognate of "genetic." A one-in-a-million genetic makeup creates a person of unusual creative potential, willpower, and charisma. It may offend our democratic sensibilities to admit that such rare birds are so different from the rest of our common flock, but in fact they are. Marina Tsvetaeva, who was one of that rare breed herself, wrote: "Genius: being in the highest degree susceptible to inspiration first, and, second, being in command of this inspiration. The highest degree of mental disintegration, and—the highest ability to collect oneself. The highest degree of passivity and the highest degree of activity. It is letting oneself be destroyed down to some last atom, and then to re-create the world out of that atom's survival (resistance)."[2] To a Christian, Tsvetaeva's ecstatic definition of genius must sound almost sacrilegious. "Letting oneself be destroyed down to some last atom, and then to re-create the world"—is she not trying to equate her poet-genius with the Saviour? Or we can recall Pushkin's oft-quoted words: "The mob devours confessions, memoirs, etc., because in its baseness it relishes the humiliation of the supreme, the weakness of the powerful. Upon discovering any unsavory detail, it is delighted: *He is despicable, just like us; revolting, just like us!* That's a damn lie, bastards: even when despicable and revolting, he is not like you—he is different."[3]

These voices from the past confirmed my own intuition: it is impossible for me or anyone I know to lay claim to a total understanding of Brodsky, the man and the poet. A critic may successfully comment on some aspects of his poetry and a writer may well describe some event in his life, but there will be always something equally important left out—something inexplicable, indescribable, unfathomable. The lesser cannot comment upon the greater.

This last phrase I've borrowed from Brodsky. Once, when invited to give a talk about the nature of artistic creativity, he started by expressing doubt that the phenomenon could be explained at all. To explain why artists create is as impossible as explaining why cats meow (hence the title of his essay "A Cat's Meow"), and he added: "The lesser commenting upon the greater has, of course, a certain humbling appeal, and at our end of the galaxy we are quite accustomed to this sort of procedure."[4] I engaged in "this sort of procedure" when a Russian publisher commissioned me to prepare an annotated edition of Brodsky's poetry. That project implied a long, slow rereading of the texts and promised immense pleasure. I am an avid reader of good commentaries myself. Unlike interpretive analyses, which more often than not are glass-bead games or fulfillment of tenure-track requirements, a genuine commentary enhances the pleasure and the understanding of the text. Moreover, it serves a public purpose. I like the apt, albeit ingenuous, title that the eighteenth-century poet Gavrila Derzhavin gave to his commentaries on his own works: "Annotations to works as regards obscure passages within them, proper names, circumlocutions and ambiguous utterances, the true meaning whereof is known to the author alone." This is exactly the sort of commentary I wrote on approximately five hundred collected and uncollected poems by Brodsky.[5]

The time will come when someone will write a proper biography of Brodsky, wherein his life will be presented in much greater detail. The future biographer will undoubtedly make use of those of his personal papers that are currently closed to public scrutiny. Moreover, the future biographer will not be hindered by any obligation to protect the privacy of those who were intimately related to the poet at different periods in his life. This book is merely an attempt at re-creating the "noise of time," as Mandelstam called it—that is, the heterogeneous cultural background of the poet's life and work: the books he read cover to cover and the books he just skimmed; the words of people dear to him and the voices of the street; world events and personal troubles; travels, buildings, paintings, music, meals, wines, jobs, diagnoses, and so on and so forth. It does not aspire to be a biography of the poet, although it begins: "Iosif Aleksandrovich Brodsky was born on May 24, 1940, in Leningrad . . ."

This book would not have been possible without the generous care of many individuals, especially Mikhail Gronas, Yakov Klots, and Irina Kaliteevskaya. Special gratitude is also owed to the Estate of Joseph Brodsky, and to Ann Kjellberg in particular.

NOTE ON TRANSLATIONS AND SOURCES

Joseph Brodsky's poems that appear in his *Collected Poems in English* (New York: Farrar, Straus and Giroux, 2000) are quoted as they appear there, with the exception of "Portrait of Tragedy." When the peculiarities of the original Russian text are being discussed, poems appear in non-poetic (interlinear) translation. The non-poetic translations are Jane Ann Miller's, and those quotations are followed by references to the relevant collections of Brodsky's poetry in Russian.

For quotations taken from Brodsky's *Collected Poems in English,* no reference is provided. A list of abbreviations used in citing other sources appears at the beginning of the bibliography.

All quotations from Russian and other non-English texts are in Jane Ann Miller's translations unless otherwise indicated.

Solomon Volkov's *Dialogi s Iosifom Brodskim,* 2nd ed., expanded (Moscow: Nezavisimaya gazeta, 2000), quoted here, was compiled without Brodsky's participation. The Estate of Joseph Brodsky has requested access to the tapes upon which it was based, and these have not been provided or made public.

Almost all of Brodsky's papers at Yale's Beinecke Rare Book and Manuscript Library are open for public scrutiny. A portion of the papers housed at the National Library of Russia in Saint Petersburg are closed, at their author's request.

Every effort has been made to supply complete and correct credits; if there are errors or omissions, please contact Yale University Press so that corrections can be made in any subsequent edition.

The system of Russian transliteration is mostly that of the Library of Congress, with the following exceptions. Masculine family names ending in *-skii* are spelled with *-sky* to make them consistent with Brodsky's name. The vowels *ia, io, iu* are here spelled *ya, yo, yu;* the short *i* (*i-kratkoe*) is spelled *y;* the soft sign is not marked.

In the bibliography the names of non-Russian authors whose works were published in Russian appear, not in Russian transliteration, but in their original form—for example, not Ventslova but Venclova.

JOSEPH BRODSKY

CHAPTER ONE

> I was born and grew up in the Baltic marshland
> by zinc-gray breakers that always marched on
> in twos. Hence all rhymes, hence that wan flat voice.
>
> —"A Part of Speech"

HOME

IOSIF ALEKSANDROVICH BRODSKY was born on May 24, 1940, in Leningrad, at Professor Tur's clinic on the Vyborg Side.[1] This is a saint's day in the Russian Orthodox calendar, the holy day of Cyril and Methodius, creators of the Cyrillic alphabet—a fact that the poet, who grew up in an assimilated Jewish family, learned only as an adult, long after he had bound his fate to "sweet Cyrillic." While in his poems he would occasionally note that he'd been born under the sign of Gemini (which, according to astrologers, presages an inborn tendency to "profound dualism and harmonious ambiguity"), in casual conversation he would more often toss off an old Russian saying—"Born in May, suffer alway" ("V mae roditsya—vek mayatsya").

Of all the great cities in the world, Leningrad (the once and future Saint Petersburg) lies farthest north. All his life Brodsky feared the heat; in summertime he was always drawn northward, toward pines and granite, gray skies and gray water. He always wanted to live in a city on a river or an ocean.

When Russia was pulled into World War II and Brodsky's father left for military service, Brodsky's mother moved herself and her one-year-old son out of their rooms on the corner of Obvodny Kanal and Prospekt Gaza (formerly Staro-Petergofsky Prospekt) into a communal apartment nearer her own family, just opposite Spaso-Preobrazhensky Sobor (the Cathedral of the Transfiguration of Our Saviour). Here they lived until 1954 or 1955.[2] Iosif was already a teenager when they moved again, this time into the "Muruzi Building," on the other side of the cathedral square.

Commissioned by Prince Aleksandr Muruzi and designed by architect A. K. Serebryakov, the Muruzi was a large apartment house built in the Moorish style fashionable in the late nineteenth century. The lot it stood on had once been owned by Nikolay Rezanov, an architect of another kind (Russian expansion across the Pacific), now best known for his fateful voyage to California in 1803. Later, from 1890 until the Russian Revolution, the house was owned by a certain Lieutenant General Rein.[3] After the Revolution, the Muruzi became state property, and here Brodsky lived in a "room-and-a-half" until his departure from Russia in 1972. His parents lived there to the end of their days.

But whenever young Iosif looked out the window, no matter from which house, the Cathedral of the Transfiguration was always there. Designed by Mikhail Zemtsov and Domenico Trezzini in the mid-1700s and rebuilt by the famed Russian architect Vasily Stasov between 1827 and 1829, it was one of only a handful of working churches in Soviet Leningrad. "Throughout my entire childhood, there it was, just outside my window: the cupolas and crosses, the bell-ringers, the Easter processions, the funeral masses, the bas-relief centurions' torches, wreaths, and rods on its white outer walls, the light classical trim on its cornices," recalled Brodsky.[4] His mother and grandfather taught him to ride a bicycle in the church square, which was bounded by a fence made of cannon barrels seized from the Turks during Russia's victorious 1828–1829 war in the Balkans.[5] The cannon were linked by heavy iron chains,

> on which children swung wildly, enjoying both the danger of falling on spikes below and the clang. Needless to say, that was strictly forbidden, and the cathedral wardens chased us away all the time. . . . Needless to say, the fence was far more interesting to us than inside of the cathedral, with its smell of incense and much more static activity. "See those?" asks my father, pointing to the heavy chain links. "What do they remind you of?" I'm in second grade, and I say, "They are like figure-eights." "Right," he says. "And do you know what the

> figure eight is a symbol of?" "Snakes?" "Almost. It is a symbol of infinity." "What's infinity?" "That you had better ask in there," says my father with a grin, his finger pointed at the cathedral.[6]

Transfiguration Square marks one end of Saint Panteleimon Street (Pestel Street in Soviet times); at the other end is a small bridge over the Fontanka River, bordering the Summer Garden. Set into the wrought-iron railing of the bridge are Perseus's shield and Medusa's head, images from Greek myth that Russian children of Brodsky's generation would likely have known in a retelling by the poet Korney Chukovsky: the visage of Medusa the Gorgon, whose head sported writhing snakes instead of hair, was so terrible that whoever looked at her directly would instantly turn to stone. But Perseus was as clever as he was brave, and he tricked the Gorgon into looking at her own reflection in his brightly polished shield.

In childhood, myths and fairy tales read alike; that is, they're interesting, intriguing, and a little bit frightening. In adulthood, we begin to read myths differently; we discover that they suggest and even explain what lies beneath the surface of our lives: "And on a certain bridge, a black cast-iron Gorgon / seemed in those parts to me the truth's most honest version," wrote Brodsky, many years later and far from home ("The Fifth Anniversary"). By that time he would already be an established writer, and the image of the mirror, Stendhal's "mirror carried along a road," would be a constant in both his verse and his prose.[7] By that time, too, he would have learned that another Petersburg poet had called the beautiful city "a bog medusa."

> And the flesh of the medusa
> Was draped in heavy porphyry.[8]

But again, in childhood, everything is taken as a given, as the only possible order of things. So it seemed perfectly natural that the façades of the buildings and the faces on the railings of this far northern city narrated the myths of Greece and Rome, just as it seemed perfectly natural that a Christian house of worship should be ringed by cannon.

If we take Transfiguration Square as the center and cast a radius of half an hour's walk, then within that circle we will find some of Saint

Petersburg's best-known landmarks: the Summer Garden, Saint Michael's Castle, the Hermitage, the Tauride Gardens, Smolny Convent, and nearly every place that figured significantly in Brodsky's early life. The circle includes the schools he attended, the homes of his friends, the Writers' House on Shpalernaya Street, where he was first lauded and then conspired against; it reaches across Liteiny Bridge to the factory where he held his first job, and to the hospital where he held his second. There, too, just across the river, is Kresty (Crosses), the prison where he was held in 1964. Closer to home, a mere two blocks away from the Muruzi, was the KGB lockup where he spent two days after his arrest in 1962. The "Big House," Leningrad KGB headquarters, was just down the block.

This part of Petersburg is steeped in cultural history. Brodsky's friend and fellow poet Vladimir Uflyand grew up at No. 5 Saint Panteleimon, which served as home to Aleksandr Pushkin in 1833–1834. Brodsky once quoted a letter from Pushkin to his wife: "[E]very morning, in nightgown and slippers I go across the bridge for a stroll in the Summer Garden. The entire Summer Garden is my orchard."[9]

This building on the corner of Panteleimon and Liteiny, where Brodsky lived two-thirds of his Russian life, at various times also housed such literary figures as Aleksandr Aleksandrovich Pushkin, the eldest son of the poet, the novelist Nikolay Leskov (1879), and, finally, between 1899 and 1913, Zinaida Gippius, Dmitriy Merezhkovsky, and D. V. Filosofov, perhaps the most famous literary family of Russia's "Silver Age." The Merezhkovskys' flat served as a meeting place for a religious-philosophical society often attended by Aleksandr Blok and Andrey Bely. In 1919, in another flat, Korney Chukovsky ran a literary studio attached to the World Literature publishing house; among its lecturers were Nikolay Gumilyov and Evgeniy Zamyatin, and among its attendees were the Acmeist poets and a group of prose writers who called themselves the Serapion Brethren. By 1920, Chukovsky's studio had been replaced by a club called Poet's House, first headed by Blok, then later by Gumilyov. Gumilyov's famous Poets' Workshop also met here.[10]

This "sacred space" was never empty. Fyodor Dostoevsky mentions it in *The Idiot:* "General Epanchin owned a house just off Liteiny, toward Transfiguration Cathedral." In the words of the symbolist poet Vladimir Pyast, who also lived for a time in the Muruzi,

The chiseled granite of the buildings
Does not keep its people's legends.
But in it *other* beings
Leave their words.

Brodsky didn't pay much attention to the literary importance of his address. He was vague on facts and dates. He assumed that Aleksandr Blok had rented a flat in the Muruzi, but in fact Blok had never lived there. In "A Room and a Half" Brodsky writes that "from the little balcony off our room-and-a-half, larva-like Zinka [Zinaida Gippius] shouted abuse to revolutionary sailors."[11] A vivid image, but it never happened. The Merezhkovskys moved out of the Muruzi in 1913. Furthermore, they had always lived in an entirely different part of the building.

Still, while Brodsky was never a thoroughgoing expert on the city's history, his Petersburg was densely populated by literary ghosts.

again in Petersburg I see
your eternal figure.[12]

Here, in a very early poem called "A Petersburg Romance," he addresses the chief ghost of all, the hapless Evgeniy of Pushkin's "Bronze Horseman." Brodsky's verse is still clumsy here; many of his similes, metaphors, and epithets are overwrought and incoherent, and the reader is hard pressed to understand what exactly the twenty-year-old poet is trying to say—for example, in this stanza, with one possessive stacked upon another:

The river and the streets breathed love
into worn houses,
into the guesses of the eternal mind
of the volumes of daytime literature—

or in the following one, which is missing a verb:

Chased but not yet chased away,
alone, through the rattling century,
along the gutters and the cornices—
a man alive and dead.[13]

Brodsky obviously wants to express his delight at the discovery that while Pushkin the poet is long since dead, Pushkin's poor hunted Evgeniy lives on in our imagination. For someone who loves this city, its buildings and the books make up a whole; one has no meaning without the other. Not until two years after writing "A Petersburg Romance" would Brodsky read a genuinely powerful poem on the same theme: Osip Mandelstam's "Petersburg Stanzas." By that time he himself would have a far freer command of his verse.

By some standards, Brodsky became interested in poetry relatively late; he began writing at about seventeen and was already past twenty when his verse began to show signs of originality. After that he was quick to master his craft. "Procession," a long poem ("mystery play") written a few months after "A Petersburg Romance" is equally full of youthful turmoil, but presents the theme much more clearly, with Dostoevsky's idiot prince Myshkin, Blok's Harlequin and Columbina, and the Pied Piper (probably more like Aleksandr Grin's "ratcatcher" than Marina Tsvetaeva's) roaming the autumn streets of Leningrad.

By the early 1960s, these classic characters had been off the list of officially sanctioned reading for a good thirty years. So were the lyric motifs and philosophical themes that had informed Petersburg writing from Dostoevsky to the Silver Age: the city as a labyrinth where those who had lost God wandered lost themselves; the city as a place of ghosts; the city as the embodiment of earthly evil. This breakdown of an ongoing tradition came about not through literary evolution but through political revolution—the Bolshevik revolution and the ideological censorship that followed. By the middle of the 1920s, Russian high culture was at a standstill, and the post-Stalin generation of the early 1960s regarded the ensuing thirty years as a yawning gap in the country's history. Naturally, that generation rushed to bridge the gap between generations, to reconnect. Young Brodsky probably did this more intuitively than consciously. The true significance of what he was doing was more obvious to the older generation.

The poet Anna Akhmatova read "A Petersburg Romance" "long and intensely, often leafing back to pages she'd already read."[14] In Paris, the émigré literary critic Wladimir Weidle rather surprisingly ended his "Petersburg Poetics" (a long essay devoted to Gumilyov and other poets of the Silver Age) with a passage on Brodsky: "I know that he was born in 1940; he couldn't possibly remember. But still, reading him, I think—no, he does remember, through the murk of [all the] deaths and births he [somehow] remembers the Petersburg of 1921, the year of our Lord one thousand nine hundred and twenty-one, the Petersburg in which we buried Blok but could not bury Gumilyov."[15]

PARENTS

On the Soviet social scale, the Brodskys ranked somewhere in the middle; they belonged to the amorphous category of white-collar workers. Aleksandr Ivanovich Brodsky (1903–1984) was a news photographer; Marya Moiseevna Volpert (1905–1983) was a bookkeeper. Iosif Aleksandrovich was a late child, and their only one. Apparently it was not an easy pregnancy, and Marya Moiseevna gave birth in a specialized clinic instead of an ordinary maternity hospital.

They lived "just like everybody"—that is, they shared a kitchen and a bathroom with neighbors in a communal apartment. At first the three of them lived in one sixteen-square-meter room, and then in the slightly more spacious room-and-a-half.

Brodsky's parents occupied the larger, walk-through room, while their son slept at one end of the "half." At the other end, screened off by a wardrobe, Aleksandr Ivanovich developed and printed his photographs. Both rooms were crowded with old furniture, none of it matching. The family wore the same clothes year after year, constantly mended and restitched.[16] While the Brodskys never went hungry, money was always short, the family income was small ("at home, as long as I remember, there were never-ending squabbles over money").[17] In sum, Brodsky's early life was lived against the backdrop of war (1941–1945) and privation (1945–1948). He was too young to remember all the horrors of the siege of Leningrad, but like most of his peers, in childhood he led a meager, semi-starved existence.

His parents were never part of the city's intellectual elite—they were not writers, artists, musicians, or scholars—but they were relatively well read and well educated. They listened to classical music; they went to the theater when they could.[18] Both had received a solid education; both spoke clear, grammatical, standard Russian; both had an extensive vocabulary. Aleksandr Ivanovich, whose father had owned a small printing house in Petersburg, had finished high school there and gone on to earn a degree in geography from Leningrad University. Marya Moiseevna had been born in Dvinsk (now Daugavpils, Latvia), where her father worked as a salesman for the American Singer Sewing Machine Company. She had spent most of her childhood in Lithuania, near Siauliai. Like most middle-class Baltic families, hers was bilingual, and she grew up speaking both Russian and German.[19]

Iosif, however, was never taught languages at home, and he later speculated that his parents might have been trying to mask their "bourgeois antecedents," one sign of which was a knowledge of foreign languages.[20] And while Brodsky's parents themselves had never been direct victims of Stalin's purges, they were always careful of what they said.

Under normal circumstances family legends are usually absorbed at an early age and, to a great extent, define a child's sense of self. But Brodsky learned his only in bits and pieces. Later, all he could do was fantasize about his ancestors, who, judging by his surname, hailed from Galicia. About those sixteen square meters of family space, Brodsky also remembered some hallmarks of social mimicry. Over the stove stood a black plaster bust of Lenin, which in later, less dangerous times gave way to a marble bust "of some woman in a flouncy bonnet, the kind [of bust] they used to sell in antique stores," and over his bed hung a portrait of Stalin, apparently meant as a hint to the casual visitor that the boy had been named for that particular Iosif.[21]

FIRST IMPRESSIONS (WAR)

Brodsky's first and rather fuzzy childhood recollections were of Cherepovets, a town in Vologda province north and east of Leningrad. He and his mother were evacuated to Cherepovets on April 21, 1942, after the first winter of the siege. "[I] remember the way down to our basement apartment [on Lenin Street]. Three or four white steps leading from the street door to the kitchen. I barely have time to get down there before my grandma is handing me a freshly baked roll, a bird with a raisin for its eye. The bird's wingtips are burnt, but where the feathers are supposed to be, the dough is lighter. There's a table to the right, where they roll the dough; the stove is to the left. Between the stove and the table lay the way to our room, mine, grandma's, and grandpa's. My bed stood along the same wall as the stove in the kitchen. Across the room was my mother's bed; the window above it opened onto the street, just like the one in the kitchen. . . . I don't remember our landlords at all, except for their son Shurka, whose name I couldn't pronounce. I called him Khunka."[22]

As time passed, Iosif's speech defects disappeared, and all that remained was an inability to pronounce the Russian rolled *r*. But there would always be a peculiar nasal quality to his speech. And while he no longer substituted *n* for *r*, as he had in infancy, that extra sound could often be heard, especially between words, no matter how one word ended or the other began. It was particularly noticeable when he gave readings. Nadezhda Mandelstam writes that "his nose takes a decidedly active part in producing his sound. I've never seen anyone or anything like it: [his] nostrils stretch, flare, go through all sorts of flourishes that bend every single vowel and consonant. This is not a man, it's a whole wind orchestra."[23]

Iosif and his mother spent roughly a year in evacuation. The memory of Cherepovets stayed with him throughout his life, and some of those memories were horrific. Thanks to her knowledge of German, Maria Moiseevna was able to find work at a prisoner-of-war camp. "Several times she took me with her to the camp. She and I would clamber into an overloaded little boat; some old man in an overcoat was at the oars. The water was up to the gunnels, there were so many people in it. I remember asking her on the first trip, 'Mama, so we're going to drown pretty soon?'"[24]

Yet another frightening memory had to do with the train station in Cherevpovets, when it came time for the two to return to Leningrad: "Everyone was crazy to get back; the boxcars were crammed, even though you had to have a pass to get into Leningrad. People were perched on the roofs, on the couplings, on anything that gave a foothold. I remember it very well: white clouds and blue sky above a red boxcar draped with people in faded-yellow padded jackets, women in scarves. The car starts moving, and an old man starts running after it; he's limping. As he runs, he tears off his fur hat, and I see he's completely bald; he's reaching toward the car, looking for a handhold, but then a woman leans out over the railing, grabs a teakettle, and pours boiling water onto his bald head. I see the steam rise."[25]

HEREDITY

We can only guess how such frightening scenes, as well as the lack of a father for the first eight years of his life, affected the boy's psyche. Aleksandr Ivanovich had left for military service in 1941 and did not return until 1948. When he did, his relationship with his son was uneven at best.

Aleksandr Ivanovich could spend hours walking with Iosif, or talking seriously with him, and he might defend him against unfair schoolteachers—but in a fit of rage he could just as easily swing a belt.[26] "I wasn't a good student, and this irritated my father, something he never bothered to hide. My parents yelled at me so much that I became pretty well steeled against that sort of tactic."[27] Years later, in "A Room and a Half," "August Rain," and "In Memory of My Father: Australia," Brodsky's recollections of his parents would be tinged with nostalgia, as childhood became the stuff of personal myth. But the younger Iosif felt that his father's life lacked any spiritual dimension at all. In an unfinished verse portrait of his father entitled "The Photographer among the Ships" he describes a sixty-year-old man "whose speech has long since shunned all depths of soul." But this fragment also marks a watershed in the young man's relationship with his father, a first attempt by the son to understand rather than simply rebel. "Photographer" was written in 1964, a year of crisis, when Aleksandr Ivanovich had not only thrown himself wholeheartedly into the defense of his son but had also begun to take his son's literary efforts seriously, as achievements worthy of respect.

Iosif's father also taught him his own trade of photography. In practical terms it was not that useful—Brodsky did only a feature or two for Leningrad children's magazines, then some part-time work while in exile. But his verse is clearly written by a man with a trained eye, and much of that training may have come by looking through the viewfinder of a Leica.

Heredity may have been a factor, too, in Iosif's behavior as a child, and especially as a youth. He was overly impressionable; he often couldn't bear conflict or emotional situations; even in the midst of a family celebration he might simply jump up and run out of the room. He himself said this happened when "my mental batteries were running low." He suffered from various phobias, one of which was the fear of being alone. This fear and the poet's struggle with it are described with remarkable powers of self-observation in an early, uncollected poem called "In Mustard Wood." As an adult, commenting on his own psychoses (or neuroses), he liked to paraphrase Ryūnosuke Akutagawa: "I don't have convictions—I've just got nerves."[28]

Popular psychology associates this type of personality with artistic creativity, and the impression gleaned from early school reports and from the recollections of those around him is of a child and young man perhaps slightly unbalanced, thin-skinned, and easily hurt. (And like many reddish-haired Ashkenazi Jews, he was literally thin-skinned; his veins lay close to the surface, and his pale, freckled face easily broke into a blush.) As the years passed, he learned self-discipline, and later in life he would show enviable courage in the face of mortal illness. But even as a young man, when a moment of crisis came (as in his trial in 1964), he managed to find enough inner resources to maintain his composure and keep a clear head. This, his moral steadfastness, and his enormous capacity for work—the ability to see a major artistic project through not just to the end but to a very good end—all point to a personality much more complex than that of the "classic neurotic." In Brodsky, willpower won out over biological determinism.

THE LESSONS OF THE CITY

Brodsky came of age in a city ravaged by war. In one memoir he wrote: "[I]f anyone profited from the war, it was us: its children. Apart from having survived it, we were richly provided with stuff to romanticize or to fantasize about."[29] In the poet's case, these fantasies were also fueled by his father's tales of service on every front from Romania to Shanghai, by radio reports of the heroic feats performed by the Red Army and Red Navy, and by the heroic survival of the city itself. The aftermath of war was everywhere evident: in the shells of bombed-out buildings, on walls pocked by artillery fire, in the fireworks celebrating the victory, and the prisoner-of-war details clearing the rubble.

> I remember pale workers.
> I remember searchlights and POWs.
> The plashes of victory fireworks.[30]

In a block of historical buildings called Solyanoy gorodok, just a few minutes away from the Brodsky apartment, lay the short-lived Museum of the Defense of Leningrad, which featured Soviet and German military technology—everything from binoculars to tanks and planes and displays with full-size mannikins set in battle scenes.[31] After returning from China, his last posting, Brodsky's father spent two years working at the photography lab of the Naval Museum, and nine-year-old Iosif had free run of the museum after hours. "There was nothing I liked better than peering through a forest of masts and ship models at those close-shaven golden-framed admirals painted *en face* and in profile."[32]

This immediate sense of a war just fought and won merged with official Soviet and Russian imperial mythology, just as the still visible scars of war in the city merged with Petersburg's symbols of empire; at one end of the boy's street was Transfiguration Cathedral and its cannon-barrel fence; at the other end was the Church of Saint Panteleimon, built to celebrate the victory of the Russian fleet at the battle of Hango. Replicas of Roman swords and lances, spears and lictors' fasces, shields and helmets, decked the railings of a small wrought-iron bridge near the church and could also be seen on many façades in the former imperial capital.

These neoclassical trappings of empire did more than inspire a basic sense of patriotism, however: "[F]rom these façades and porticoes—classical, modern, eclectic, with their columns, pilasters, and plastered heads of mythic animals or people, from their ornaments and caryatids holding up the balconies, from the torsos in the niches of their entrances, I have learned more about the history of the world than I subsequently have from any book."[33]

Just as his first notions of the naked female body came from the marble statues of the Summer Garden, more abstract aesthetic concepts like symmetry, perspective, and proportion came from the neoclassical buildings all around him. In the child's mind and the child's world, there grew an image of an ideal country, an empire whose might and glory were founded—improbable as it might seem—on harmony and proportion rather than violence and death. Some critical speculation to the contrary, this private utopia had nothing to do with the real, historical Russian empire.[34] As a child, Brodsky gave little thought to the empire; as an adult, he regarded Russian imperialism and militarism with undisguised scorn. The flag of his imagined empire was the blue Saint Andrew's cross on a white field, the navy cross, "not that foul double-headed imperial fowl or the vaguely Masonic hammer-and-sickle."[35] It is this very conflict between his childhood utopian vision of an ideal state and the ugly realities of a prematurely decrepit Soviet empire that make for the drama that underlies such works as "Anno Domini" (*OVP*), "Post Aetatem Nostram" (*KPE*), and *Marbles*.

He imagined himself flying the skies and sailing the seas of this perfect world. As a teenager, his dreams of joining the fleet would be crushed when he was denied entrance to the naval academy, and years later, when he took flying lessons in the United States, it soon became clear that vertigo would keep him from ever becoming a pilot. But these dreams so typical of a child of the 1940s left him with a lasting love for propeller planes and Antoine de Saint-Exupéry's *Vol de nuit* and *Terre des hommes*.[36] And while he was never to find himself at the helm of a ship or alone in a cockpit, the themes and metaphors of flight and sail abound in his work.

Equally abundant are the ruins that surrounded him as a child and young man. Leningrad had been devastated by German air raids and artillery fire. Even five years after the war, the shells of bombed-out buildings still loomed, the apartments and the lives of the dead were still open to public view. In the center of the city plywood murals of the old façades were erected to screen off the rubble. The city soviet might have wanted to suggest by this that life would eventually return to normal, but the effect was quite the opposite. The streets of Leningrad looked like an abandoned stage.[37]

According to legend, when Peter the Great divorced his first wife, Avdotya, and sent her to a nunnery, she put a curse on the emperor's new city: "May Petersburg stand empty." Tsaritsa Avdotya's eighteenth-century curse took effect in the twentieth. Petersburg's population dropped drastically, first from starvation and disease during the Revolution and Civil War (1917–1921), then from the widespread purges of the 1930s (in which the cultural elite were first to be targeted for extinction), and finally from the terrible siege of 1941–1944. The destruction of the city's buildings had also begun during the Civil War, and while old Petersburg, unlike old Moscow, was never subjected to Soviet scorched-earth urban planning, World War II did its part. By 1944–1945, grass was growing over sidewalks paved with Silurian limestone. The courtyards and approaches of classical palaces and mansions—at least those that had survived the war—were planted with subsistence gardens. To anyone who grew up seeing this, Piranesi's *vedute* of goats grazing in the ruins of Rome look strangely familiar.

Peter the Great might have intended his city to be a true Third Rome, but in the minds of the Petersburg intelligentsia of the early twentieth century, the historical analogy was not Rome but Hellenic Alexandria, a refined and cultured city on the fault line between East and West, a city where Hellenism and Christianity merged, a city with a library unrivaled in all the world, a doomed city with book-burning barbarians perennially at the gates.[38] On the eve of World War I another eschatological myth was in the making: Saint Petersburg was the new Alexandria, destined to perish just as the old one had.[39] After the Civil War of 1919–1921, the barbarians were no longer at the gates; they had breached them. Surviving members of the old Petersburg intelligentsia found themselves living *post aetatem nostram* (after our era).

This is the subject of one of Brodsky's favorite novels, Konstantin Vaginov's *Goat Song* (*Kozlinaya pesn*) and would figure constantly in Brodsky's mature work: in "Post Aetatem Nostram" (*KPE*), "The Theatrical" (*PSN*), *Marbles,* "Plato Elaborated," and other works in which the future is imagined as the Nietzschean eternal return, a barbaric past redux.[40] Brodsky elaborates this theme in his essay on the remarkable modern Greek poet Constantine Cavafy, who lived and wrote in Alexandria, and also in "Guide to a Renamed City," an essay devoted to Petersburg's past and present. In "Pendulum's Song," his essay on Cavafy, Brodsky writes: "With the exception of six or seven unrelated poems, the 'literal city' does not come to the surface in Cavafy's 220-poem canon. What emerges first are the 'metaphoric' and mythical cities. . . . [U]topian thought, even when, as in Cavafy's case, it turns to the past, usually implies the unbearable character of the present."[41] All this applies equally to Brodsky's poetry. So it might not be too much to assume that growing up in the ruins of an imperial city predetermined that one genre—the elegy—would dominate his work.

SCHOOL DAYS

Brodsky started elementary school in 1947, at age seven, as was mandatory for all Soviet children. He dropped out just eight years later, in 1955.

Soviet schools, even in the best of times, were never meant to educate in the full sense of the word. The curriculum was standardized throughout the enormous USSR, and all learning was based on rote memorization. Giving children an aesthetic education or teaching them to think analytically or critically was the last thing on anyone's mind. History and literature were in absolute thrall to ideology; the task was to produce good little Soviet citizens. Textbooks on history, literature, and even geography were crudely written and full of propaganda. The official school curriculum required the study of at least one foreign language, but given the miserable textbooks and methods, the overcrowded classes, and the few class hours spent per week, virtually no one graduated from high school with even a basic command of another language.[42] And whatever the subject, teachers were generally overworked, underpaid, and irritable. Any sign of independence was seen as rebellion and immediately quashed. It was standard practice to publicly humiliate and punish children for not learning their lessons or not behaving properly in class. This extended to summer camp, where children who wet the bed could expect to have their sheets put on public display; youth organizations like the Young Octobrists (ages seven to ten) and the Young Pioneers (ten to fourteen) publicly discussed and condemned any missteps. Between 1945 and 1955, boys and girls in the larger cities attended separate schools. In the boys' schools, the atmosphere tended to be overheated and unhealthy. "In the puritanical atmosphere of Stalinist Russia even an innocent Socialist-Realist painting like 'Joining the Komsomol' (reproductions of which hung in every other classroom) was enough to arouse us. There was a little blonde girl in it; she was sitting down, with her legs crossed just high enough to reveal maybe five or six centimeters of thigh. But it wasn't so much the thigh itself as the contrast between it and the dark brown of her dress that drove me crazy and stalked my dreams."[43]

Physically, Iosif developed early and quickly, and just as quickly declined after age forty. Apparently his first sexual experience came roughly around the time he quit school. In all likelihood, one of the reasons he left at fifteen was that he felt himself more mature than his classmates.

In his eight and a quarter years of official schooling, Brodsky changed schools five times. He spent his first three years quite close to home, at School No. 203 on Saltykov-Shchedrin Street (formerly Kirochnaya), in a building that in pre-Revolution days had housed the Annenschule, a Lutheran girls' school affiliated with the nearby Church of Saint Anna (hence the old name of the street, from the German *die Kirche;* under the Soviets the church was turned into the movie theater that Brodsky recalls in the first of his "Twenty Sonnets to Mary Queen of Scots"). He attended grades four through six at School No. 196 on Mokhovaya Street, grade seven at School No. 181 on Solyanoy Lane.

There was trouble with school almost from the start. In an evaluation written at the end of fourth grade, the class supervisor notes, "The boy is obstinate, stubborn, lazy. His written homework is poorly done, or not done at all, he is rude, misbehaves during lessons, is disruptive in class.

His notebooks are messy, smudged, notes and drawings in the margins. Capable, could be a star student, but doesn't try." On moving from fifth grade to sixth, Iosif received a slightly more favorable review: "A capable and intelligent boy. Reads much. Short temper. Did not work consistently in English or arithmetic. Must retake exams in fall. Pioneer. Fulfilled community service obligations conscientiously and eagerly." By the end of sixth grade things were looking even better: "Draws well, reads a great deal, is responsible, truthful, intelligent, but short-tempered. Has changed for the better over the past year. Fulfills community obligations conscientiously and eagerly. Helped lay out his brigade's news poster. Pioneer. Excellent discipline." This may have been the last time Brodsky would get along with the school system or the social system the schools embodied. The following year he received four 2s on a scale of 5 (the equivalent of a D), three of them in the sciences and one in English, and was held back for a year. Looking back at himself as a schoolboy, Brodsky confided to a journalist in 1980: "In school, I questioned the conformity. You rebel against all that. I remained apart, more an observer than a participant. This separation had to do with certain traits of my character. Moodiness, not buying the preconceived notions, being affected by the weather, I don't really know. . . . It just so happens that I was a little more demanding, less ready to excuse banality, stupidity, or redundancy."[44]

He repeated seventh grade, but at a different school (No. 286, on Obvodny Kanal), because his father was still officially registered in that district. Eighth grade involved yet another move, to School No. 289, on Narvsky Prospekt.[45]

OUTSKIRTS

"There's a certain menacing stillness, a certain picturesque misery, to the Obvodny Kanal," wrote Konstantin Vaginov, one of Brodsky's favorite Petersburg writers.[46] On the far side of this canal lay an entirely different city, the rough old industrial edge of the former capital. Construction had only just begun beyond the Narvskie Gates on what would become the modern industrial suburb of Avtovo. Not far from School No. 289 lay one of the city's oldest parks, Ekateringof, now a neglected and dangerous spot. Nearby, too, flowed the Tarakanovka, a small river that local kids called the Prolovonyalovka (roughly, Stink Creek) where, according to local legend, there still floated skeletons of people who had perished in the blockade. These were mysterious, deserted places, close to the Gulf itself, close to Gutuevsky and Volny islands where "there was a yacht club, and a gunboat that I used to climb around on."[47] These outlying districts, with their shabby tenements, their soot-blackened factory complexes, the garbage-strewn strips of rail lines, were the stuff of modern elegy, replacing the withered parks, picturesque ruins, and village churchyards of the past. The dreary urban world of factory yards and back alleys, the joyless encounter between nature and civilization, struck a nerve in Brodsky long before he read Blok or Eliot or Auden or Miłosz in any serious way, or saw the cityscapes of Félix Vallotton, Frans Masereel, and Mstislav Dobuzhinsky.

In 1961 and 1962, when Brodsky was especially taken with jazz, he made several stabs at writing poems in the style of a jazz improvisation.

> I'm a son of the outskirts, the outskirts, the outskirts,
> in a wire cradle, dank hallways, are my door and my address,
> streetcars clanking, rattle bang ring, stone sidewalks, soles,
> girls lined against painted wood fences,
> grassy banks, oil spot, factory lights
> (Non-poetic)[48]

Whatever the variation, the basic motif was always some memory or impression of this factory district. In "Russian Gothic," the first lines of which are quoted above, we see the intersection of Staro-Petergofsky Prospekt and Obvodny Kanal, replete with weed-choked banks and oil-fouled water ("tugboats in dark slop"). Brodsky was truly a son of this shabby perimeter; he spent the first year of his life next door to two old factories, Metalworker and Red Triangle, the latter of which, for years on end, poisoned the air with the noxious fumes of burning rubber. (This perhaps explains the last line of the poem: "O sunrise clarinet, lift those triangles of life high up above this quarter.")

REAL EDUCATION

Despite poor grades, Brodsky still took in much of what Soviet schools had to offer. Primarily, this meant that he gained a thorough understanding of Russian grammar and syntax. As his early manuscripts and letters show, he wrote not only freely, expressively, and coherently but grammatically. He might deviate from standard rules, but these deviations were conscious and consistent. He spent a great deal of time pondering his native language. In a 1963 letter addressing a proposed spelling reform, this young man with little formal education tries to explain to scholars and linguists that simplifying spelling means simplifying thought: "Complexity in a language is not a fault but is rather, first and foremost, evidence of the spiritual richness of the nation that created it. And the goal of a reform should be to allow people to partake of that wealth as fully and as quickly as possible. In essence, to simplify a language is to loot it."[49]

Brodsky's solid knowledge of geography and history (especially that of ancient Greece and Rome) came more from his own reading than from school assignments. School generally bored and irritated him. Years later, in "A Part of Speech," he would write about the schedule of a typical sixth-grade day: Ancient History, Physical Education, Russian, Physics, Geometry.

> A navy-blue dawn in a frosted pane
> recalls yellow streetlamps in the snow-piled lane,
> icy pathways, crossroads, drifts on either hand,
> a jostling cloakroom in Europe's eastern end.
> "Hannibal . . ." drones on there, a worn-out motor,
> parallel bars in the gym reek with armpit odor;
> as for that scary blackboard you failed to see through,
> it has stayed just as black. And its reverse side too.
> Silvery hoarfrost has transformed the rattling bell
> into crystal. As regards all that parallel-
> line stuff, it's turned out true and bone-clad, indeed.
> Don't want to get up now. And never did.

They were all unpleasant, all the sights and sounds of school—the shoving in the coatroom, the stink of unwashed bodies in the gym, the squeak of chalk on blackboards, the electric buzzer in physics experiments.

Perhaps the most important thing Brodsky ever did for himself was quit school. This was a radical act. For all the official Soviet homage to the working class, Soviet schoolchildren were constantly told that without a higher education they would never amount to anything. Both at school and at home teenagers were told, "If you don't finish school, you'll end up hauling garbage" (or loading freight, or picking turnips, or sweeping floors). For a city boy raised in a middlebrow family, quitting school meant turning himself into a virtual outcast.

But while Brodsky left school as soon as he legally could, he still yearned for some sort of formal education. He enrolled in evening classes and audited lectures at the university.[50] The eventual breadth and depth of his knowledge, however, was ultimately due to his own tireless efforts to educate himself. As a young man, he taught himself English and Polish; later he would learn to read Latin, Italian, and French. Toward the end of his life he began studying Chinese.

Together with some of his friends at the university, he studied Otto Jespersen's classic introduction to linguistics, *The Philosophy of Grammar;* he read European and Hindu philosophy on his own. He also read a great deal of Pushkin and a great deal about the poet and his times; the family of the great Pushkin scholar Boris Tomashevsky befriended him and gave him access to Tomashevsky's private library. He was never without the "Brokhaus" (that is, the eighty-nine-volume encyclopedia published by Brokhaus and Efron at the turn of the century). Later, in America, he was equally attached to the *Encyclopedia Britannica.* By all accounts, he must have paid particular attention to the philosopher Vladimir Solovyov's remarkable Brokhaus entries on the history of philosophy and religion.

Brodsky himself half joked that he had always learned "by osmosis." But in some sense this was absolutely true. Many of his friends were outstanding linguists, literary scholars, art historians, composers, musicians, physicists, biologists—and Brodsky was known for his ability to "interrogate" his expert friends on whatever subject interested him at the time. His close friend Andrey Sergeev, himself a poet and translator, writes that "Iosif just seemed to breathe it all in. He would gulp down every new piece of information and then put it to use in his poetry. You might say that nothing ever went to waste; everything was recycled, with incredible, mind-boggling deftness."[51]

What betrays Brodsky's lack of systematic education has less to do with any gaps in his knowledge (he could always fill those in) than with his undisciplined way of thinking. That is, he was never taught formal logic, and he lacked the skills that come with it. For him, "to think" was to construct a chain of syllogisms—but without testing, either empirically or analytically, the individual links. For example, the basic theme of his Nobel lecture might be reduced to the following formula: Art is the means by which a social animal became an individual "I," and therefore aesthetics is superior to ethics. The highest form of aesthetic activity is poetry, and therefore the creation of poetry is the ultimate goal, the evolutionary goal, of the species. In formal intellectual discourse any one of these statements might be disputed, and every one would have to be proved. Was art really the one tool that turned primitive humans into individuals? Is there really any hierarchy of creativity, and if there is, what makes poetry superior to philosophy, or theater, or music? Is there even such a thing as an evolutionary goal for "humans as a species"?

Brodsky was asked these questions, and many others like them, after his speech at the Swedish Academy of Sciences. And truly, had he been presenting a philosophical treatise, he might have been accused of making unfounded assertions, using incorrect terminology, and making all the mistakes dilettantes usually do. But the "chain of logic" frequently found in Brodsky's prose and poetry is simply a device, a stylization, and a parody, just as his "syllogisms" are often paradoxes arrived at not through deduction or induction—but through intuition. As he writes in the conclusion to "Lagoon,"

> In our dim days and few,
> the speed of light equals a fleeting view,
> even when blackout robs us blind.

Here Brodsky parodies a law of physics (the speed of light is x given y) in order to suggest the absolute truth of the subjective metaphysical experience of a person thrown into an unfamiliar environment. Transferring the quality of one thing to another thing—that is, creating a metaphor, thinking by analogy—is something formal logic will not risk. But it is the very foundation of art. In his late works Brodsky almost grotesquely bares this basic artistic device, this thinking by analogy and association: some couches are called sofas; some women are named Sofa; the couches have legs; the women have legs—therefore sofa and Sofa merge into a kind of centaur ("Centaurs").

BRODSKY AS JEW

Brodsky was born and raised at a time when anti-Semitism was all but official policy, when a general distrust and dislike of Jews was resprouting and spreading among the populace. Jews like Brodsky's father—military officers, engineers, mid-level managers, college instructors, journalists—were the ones who felt the anti-Semitism most acutely, especially at work.[52] The knowledge that his opportunities were limited was something Brodsky took in with his mother's milk; this knowledge was constantly reinforced by the everyday prejudice of his peers. "In school, being 'a Jew' was something you had to defend. They called me the Russian equivalent of 'kike.' I engaged in fist fights. It was silly enough to take the "jokes" as a personal affront. That was silly, because I *am* a Jew. Now I don't think there's anything offensive about being called what you are, but that awareness came later."[53]

Still, looking at the sum of Brodsky's autobiographical references in verse, prose, and interviews, it would seem that as an adult, he suffered relatively little from anti-Semitism. This may have in part to do with the fact that he never strove for the sort of career that might present the usual hurdles for a Soviet Jew—enrollment quotas at universities and institutes, promotion quotas in the workplace. But it has much more to do with his stubborn sense of independence: even as a youth he had never stooped to argue with a government and a social system held together by a primitive ideology, only one component of which was anti-Semitism. In theory, official Soviet ideology defined *natsionalnost* (ethnicity) in fairly liberal terms; in theory, it merely meant a shared language, culture, and territory—and an entry in one's internal passport. (What group the passport holders identified themselves with was somehow never taken into consideration.) However, actual ethnic policy was based on the same "blood-and-soil" myth as popular prejudice was. Hence Stalin's strategy: kill some, uproot the rest, cut them off—Chechens, Ingushetians, Crimean Tatars—from any contact with their native land. Hence, too, the rather startling rhetoric from the heirs of the Communist International, who in 1948 declared a new "war on cosmopolitanism," a policy that would end only with Stalin's death in 1953.

How did Brodsky define himself? Who was he? He said it best himself, in a lapidary formula he repeated time and again: "I'm a Jew, a Russian poet, an American citizen."[54] Linguistically and culturally, he was Russian. By nature a stubborn individualist, he resisted any attempts at automatic association by race or ethnicity. Brodsky once told me how, one or two days after his arrest in the winter of 1964, he was brought out of his cell for interrogation. His interrogator was a certain Detective S, also a Jew. Perhaps S was simply playing good cop, perhaps he just wanted to help, but at any rate, he tried to talk the young "parasite" into confessing his sins, expressing remorse, et cetera, et cetera. "Think about your parents," said S. "I mean, *our* parents are one thing, *their* parents are another." Brodsky was disgusted by the encounter.

Zionism never attracted him, nor was he ever particularly interested in the modern State of Israel. Like all Jews leaving the Soviet Union in the 1970s, his documents stated that he was applying for permanent residence in Israel, but he never really considered settling there. And while he appreciated the culture of America, the country he finally made his home (its film, literature, music; its civil society and rule of law), he felt equally comfortable in England, in northern Europe, or in Italy, where he also lived, worked, and eventually found a family.

In other words, Brodsky was a direct descendant of a sophisticated, cosmopolitan westward-looking Russian intelligentsia. Any "Jewish element" in his verse was roughly the same "Jewish element" found in Western civilization—the Old Testament as received and interpreted by the Christian West. His long meditation on religion and philosophy, "Isaac and Abraham" is characteristic in this respect: while it alludes to the tragic fate of the Jewish people, to the Diaspora and the Holocaust, its main theme, the sacrifice of Isaac by Abraham, is quite obviously refracted through other lenses—the works of the Christian existentialist Søren Kierkegaard and the Russian philosopher (apostate Jew) Lev Shestov.

Longtime friend Shimon Markish, a literary scholar who focused on questions of Jewish identity within the larger Russian culture, wrote this about Brodsky: "I would venture to say that this unique poetic talent had not a grain of 'Jewishness' about it. Jewish themes and Jewish 'material' had nothing to do with Joseph Brodsky, nor he with them."[55]

Unlike fellow poets Osip Mandelstam and Boris Pasternak, who were first- or second-generation assimilated Jews, Brodsky's family had long been part of secular Russian culture. His great-grandfather had served in the tsarist army, thus earning the right to live outside the Pale of (Jewish) Settlement; after his army service he opened a clock repair shop in Moscow.[56] Brodsky's father had received only the scantest of religious upbringings, and in fact, except for a few years in early childhood, both parents grew up under the Soviets. By the end of World War II, Jewish religious and community life had been virtually wiped out, first by Soviet anti-religion campaigns, then by the Nazi Holocaust. And although some Jewish families in the provinces tried to preserve a traditional way of life,

Jewish families in Moscow and Leningrad were virtually indistinguishable from their gentile peers. Neither the teachings of Judaism, nor its folklore, nor its holidays figured in Brodsky's everyday life. He didn't know Hebrew and only rarely heard the occasional Yiddishism at home—which he nonetheless put to good use in the mock-German of his 1965 poem "Two Hours in a Container."

Aside from "Isaac and Abraham," only two poems in all of Brodsky's work touch on Jewish themes. "A Jewish Cemetery near Leningrad," written in 1958, is an imitation of a popular samizdat poem by Boris Slutsky entitled "About Jews" ("Jews don't sow wheat"). Brodsky never included it in any of his collections. The other, "Leiklos" (named for a street in the old Jewish quarter of Vilnius), is part of his 1971 cycle "Lithuanian Divertissement," in which he imagines himself as one of his ancestors in Lithuania.

He felt a great nostalgia for the lost world of central European culture. This was evident in his fondness for Polish language and literature, for the novels of Robert Musil and Joseph Roth, and even for *Mayerling,* a 1968 Hollywood melodrama based on the 1889 murder-suicide of Archduke Rudolf of Austria-Hungary and Baroness Maria Vetsera, his lover. The southernmost point of this lost civilization was Trieste, "deep in the wild Adriatic," once the home of another Austrian archduke, Maximilian, to whom Brodsky dedicated two poems in "Mexican Divertimento." The northernmost point was Brody, a town in Galicia on the border between Austria-Hungary and the Russian empire, territory described by Joseph Roth in his *Radetzky March.* In only a few poems does Brodsky touch on the theme of some ancestral homeland ("Hills," "Fifth Eclogue," "On Ukrainian Independence"), and only once, in an interview with a Polish journalist, did he talk about it: "[Poland] is a country that I, and maybe this sounds stupid, a country I have some feelings for, maybe more than for Russia itself. This may have something to do with . . . I don't know, maybe it's a subconscious thing, I mean, that's where all my ancestors are from. . . . I mean Brody . . . that's our name."[57] This not quite coherent confession tells us that for him "Brodsky" was not just a rather common east European surname but a sign of ancestral identity: Iosif Brodsky—Joseph from Brody.

Brodsky's sense of his Jewishness stemmed not from any sense of oppression but—however politically incorrect this might sound—from the way he looked and sounded. In one of his frankest interviews, given barely a year before his death, he told Polish journalist and longtime friend Adam Michnik that "[w]e have to be very careful talking about anti-Semitism. Anti-Semitism is, essentially, a form of racism. But we're all racists to some degree. There are some faces we just don't like. Some types of beauty." To Michnik's question, "Were you raised as a Jew or a Russian?" Brodsky gave no answer, but said instead, "When anybody asked what my ethnic background was, I of course answered Jewish. But that didn't happen often. There was really no need to ask. I can't say a Russian *r*."[58]

Jews swallow their *r*'s. Jews have beaked noses, or, in politer parlance, "aquiline profiles." So did Brodsky, and so he considered himself a Jew, although, in line with his usual tendency to lower the metaphor, in "Afterword to a Fable" he turns the eagle into a crow. Still, in defiance of orthodoxies of all stripes, he declares in the same interview that his Jewishness goes even beyond that. "I'm a Jew. One hundred percent. You can't be more Jewish than I am. Papa, mama—no question. No mixing, no intermarriage. But that's not the only reason I'm a Jew. I realize I tend to state things in absolute terms. But—if I were to define for myself some notion of a Higher Being, I would have to say that it comes down to pure force. This is the God of the Old Testament. I sense this, I feel this, in the absence of any proof at all."[59]

CHAPTER TWO

> The hammer-hugging sickle there adorns the banner.
> But nails are not struck home and weeds submerge the planner:
> into the Great Machine someone has lobbed a spanner.
>
> —"The Fifth Anniversary"

FIRST JOBS

BRODSKY'S APPLICATION to the submarine school of the Second Baltic Naval Academy was rejected, and he always assumed that he'd been turned down because he was Jewish. When he dropped out of school just short of sixteen years of age, he first found work as an apprentice machinist at Factory No. 671, better known in the city by its older and more revealing name, the Arsenal. He worked there for roughly six months.

And so it went for several years, as Brodsky traded one job for another, each lasting just a few months—morgue assistant, bathhouse stoker, lighthouse keeper, porter. In between he looked for new work, read, studied, and wrote. With the exception of the morgue, where he'd gone in search of experience that might get him into medical school, none of these jobs required anything other than rough physical labor—shoveling coal, pounding nails, digging holes, hauling packs. In those days he seemed perfectly hale and hearty, and in the words of a chance acquaintance, he was "a pretty big guy, a redhead, freckled all over, with shoulders yea wide."[1] His friend and fellow poet Andrey Sergeev writes about opening his apartment door and "seeing this strapping redheaded kid. Broad-shouldered, husky . . ."[2]

Healthy as Brodsky might have seemed at the time, he was probably already suffering from congenital heart disease. His parents first noticed something wrong after he returned from a trek through the mountains of Central Asia in 1960, and in 1962 he was exempted from compulsory military service "as per articles '8c' and '30c' (neurosis, heart disease)."[3]

What he remembered most about his first job was how badly everything was organized, how much everyone drank, and how little anyone worked.[4] He would get up at dawn and pile into an already packed city bus for his commute to the plant, where endless cigarette breaks and arguments over soccer were only occasionally punctuated by feverish attempts to meet some deadline. The boredom and idiocy of such a life are reflected in the not entirely joking lines of "Rubai":

> In the morning I take the bus to where
> the ugly mug of labor comes to greet me.
>
> . . . in late November, into the dark and slush and mud,
> ride sleepy, sullen crowds with rotten teeth,
> afraid of guards with time cards.
> The wind whips round and laughs with evil glee.
> (*Uncollected;* non-poetic)

EXPEDITIONS

Much more suited to young Brodsky's character and temperament was the seasonal work he first took on in 1957: geological expeditions ranging from the far north of European Russia to the Soviet Far East, to Yakutia, to the steppes north and east of the Caspian Sea.[5] The fact that he chose this sort of grueling, "unregulated" physical labor rather than a regular eight-to-four factory job is telling: "Working on these expeditions freed the young man from bureaucratic supervision and control; he was outdoors, under the open sky; he was also part of a close-knit group."[6] The work also satisfied a certain youthful *Wanderlust*. Even after Stalin's death the USSR was a closed country, but it was still an enormous one, with many wild places left to explore.

It was no accident, therefore, that the best-known student poetry circle in late-1950s Leningrad was an informal group run by Gleb Semyonov at the Mining Academy. Among the "miners" (geologists) were some gifted poets, including Leonid Ageev, Vladimir Britanishsky, Lidiya Gladkaya, Aleksandr Gorodnitsky, Elena Kumpan, and Oleg Tarutin. Non-geologists like Gleb Gorbovsky and Aleksandr Kushner were also invited to join. The first of the group to publish was Vladimir Britanishsky, whose *Exploration* emphasized physical hardship and male camaraderie on the trail.

> We've done our work,
> Torn and smeared the charts
> That showed enormous swamps
> So elegantly drawn. . . .
>
> The road follows the river, bending round icy banks
> Never stopping, leading on . . .
> Half snow-covered, half seen.
> (Non-poetic)[7]

Years later Brodsky was to say that these poems by Britanishsky were what first spurred him to write: "The title of the book was *Exploration*. This was a play on words: exploring in the geological sense and exploring in general—for the meaning of life and all that . . . and I thought it might be possible to do this theme better."[8]

And he tried to do better in 1957 poems like "Goodbye," "Work," and "A Toast," which open the samizdat collection that Vladimir Maramzin put together between 1972 and 1974.[9] Here, he has clearly absorbed much of the "miners'" style but hasn't yet mastered technique.

> Break through the jams.
> Drag through the swamps.
> Scramble up passes.
> Go.
> That's your job.
> (Non-poetic)[10]

At the time, rough treks like these were seen as a rite of passage, a way to "find oneself." In a letter to a former schoolmate, Eleonora Larionova, written August 7, 1958, from the village of Persha-Ozero, in the far northern reaches of Arkhangelsk region, "exploration," or "search," is the pivotal word.

> There are people on this earth who are trying to make the future more tolerable than the past. Real writers, real doctors, real teachers. By real I mean that they create [something] worthwhile. I would like to become someone worthwhile.

> To do that, you need to know a lot. If you want to create [something], you have to figure out for yourself just whom you're doing it for. . . . You need to find a foundation, something you can lean on; you need to see whether it will hold or not. You need also to find people who believe in the same idea, people who will help. That's essentially what it all comes down to. And overall you have to search for a long time.
>
> I really regret that I started what you call "traveling" so late. These last two years obviously have not gone to waste. But I could have gotten the same results in a much shorter time. Still, actually, I'm just starting. I'm just starting to do what I need to do. I'm just starting my journey. . . . Yes, I'm too self-absorbed. I just rolled out a page-and-a-half hymn to my own opinions, but I want you to understand exactly what I'm saying. You say, you write again and again, that I flit around like some migratory bird, that I'm a dilettante. But Norka, please understand that this is a real quest. Yes, I'm juggling my life around, but not because I'm looking to find something fixed or stable. That is, I've got no intention of picking some career ladder and climbing it to the top. . . . I made my decision about ends a long time ago. Now I'm trying to decide about the means. I think I'm making the right decision.
>
> This sounds both stupid and pompous. But that's because I'm simplifying the issue. I want you to understand me. What I'm doing now is searching. Exploring new ideas, new images, and mainly new forms.[11]

SOCIAL STATUS

Recalling these expeditions (the exhaustion, the dirt, the "monstrous swarms of mosquitoes"), Brodsky also speaks about his younger self: "At that age you take everything in, you absorb it with tremendous greed and tremendous intensity. And everything that happens to you seems incredibly interesting."[12] One companion on the Yakutia trek, geologist Eduard Blumshtein, recalls: "In the field, Iosif was one of us; that is, he understood his job, his responsibilities as a collector or geologist's assistant. He had a great respect for our profession. He hauled backpacks, often very heavy ones; he was never bothered by the endless hikes from one place to another, however risky or difficult they might be. The big rivers in the taiga we had to either ford or cross by small boat. And it was often very cold. The fishing was always great, and so was the hunting, so we didn't go hungry. There were times, though, when we had to eat tinned meat for weeks on end."[13]

Nor later, during his exile in Arkhangelsk region, was hard work like splitting wood or clearing rocks ever a burden; it was, in fact, the best part of those days. His recollections of that northern village stand in stark contrast to his recollections of the dark factory days in Petersburg described in "Rubai": "When I would get up at dawn and clock in at six in the morning to get my work order for the day, I realized that all over this so-called great land the same thing was happening; the nation was going to work. And I truly felt that I belonged to that nation. It was a tremendous feeling."[14]

Brodsky was the only major Russian poet of the twentieth century to begin his working life as an unskilled laborer.

The irony here was that the USSR would eventually make the same accusation against him as it did against the "usual suspects," like writers, artists, and musicians: that he was a parasite on the body politic, that as the rather hellish cliché had it, he refused "to stew in the working-class boilerpot."

But work he did, and probably literally inside boilers. This is hinted at in one unfinished draft from the early sixties (1963?), where he describes the inside of a boiler in great detail:

> V. G. Petrov, sprightly, bald,
> was senior engineer at BoilInspect
> I plied my trade at that same joint,
> working as his rat.
>
> . . . .
>
> We made our rounds to boiler rooms
> by streetcar—when we felt like it.
> On the Sabbath I forgot that it was Sabbath.
> I beheld the boilers in all their inner beauty.
>
> . . . .
>
> And I was narrow-shouldered and big-headed
> (with all that stuff inside my skull)

and, given such a build, what can you say
(that most important complex notwithstanding),
I was quite the find for BoilInspect,
and scrabbled through its furnaces and ashpits.[15]
(Non-poetic)

When Brodsky was charged with "parasitism" in 1964, the indictment stated that he had never had any regular work, that he had constantly jumped from one job to another (in the eight years between 1956 and 1963 he had held thirty different part-time jobs, which came down to two years and eight months of full-time work).[16] The charge had little to do with law and everything to do with ideology. Nothing in Soviet law banned changing jobs so often. But high worker turnover was bad for manufacturing, and "hoppers" like Brodsky were officially reviled in the Soviet press. There was another nuance to these accusations: How could someone like Brodsky, who worked a mere few weeks or months at a time, become part of a team, a collective; how could he gain any true understanding of the working class; and therefore, how could he possibly express its spirit in his verse? The unspoken rule was that to understand working people, "you had to spend a year or two on the floor." This rule never took into account that gifted artists are gifted precisely in that they are more intuitive than others; when they find themselves in a new place, they are quicker to catch on, quicker to sense how one is expected to behave, how everyone else behaves, and why.

But in the final analysis, it wasn't that Brodsky never worked long or hard enough, or that he had changed jobs too often, or even that he didn't understand working-class life. It was that he broke the rules of initiation into Soviet society. Young men either went off to college, the army, or the factory. It was assumed that those who went to the factories would become faithful and enthusiastic builders of Communism. Hundreds of young aspiring poets went through this ritual and turned out the requisite sort of poems. For example—a boy comes to work at a plant, and the foreman gives him his first assignment. He is to make a key.

"Do it"
sings the file meekly.
"Do it"

the metal is clumsy
and rough.
Great things
are born in pain,
Your first test
is the key!
You hear
"The boy's no slacker!"
You see
your key
a-turning,
A burnished stem
with clean-cut grooves,
It gleams in the foreman's hand.

Next, the poet explains the symbolic meaning of the act:

To youth
this key
we give.
Accept it,
make it your destiny.

The initiation complete, the boy is not obliged to stay at the factory; he can also become a professional writer.

Awkwardly,
I take a step
and leave forever.
New overalls
smelling of freedom
and the fires of labor.
(Non-poetic)[17]

So young Brodsky, for all his range of cultural interests, never was part of what Osip Mandelstam termed the "hothouse youth"; the endless self-absorption and self-analysis typical of many Russian intellectuals were not his style. Nor was he, as ideological watchdogs claimed, "alienated from the people." He was neither cynical about "simple working folks," nor was he sentimental. In many ways he felt that he was one of them.

EARLY READING

Iosif learned to read very early, perhaps as early as four. Brodsky's mother recalled one day in Cherepovets in 1943, when she walked in to find her three-year-old son with a book in his hands. She took it from him to see what it was. It was Nietzsche's *Thus Spake Zarathustra.* She handed it back, upside down, and Iosif immediately turned it right side up. Her story wasn't meant to suggest that the three-year-old boy was reading Nietzsche but that he had some sense of how a book was put together.

Like all children of his age in a country where practically everyone was literate and television was a rarity, he read a great deal. The knowledge that he gleaned from his reading, combined with a naturally rich imagination, took him to different countries, epochs, and cultures. But he rebelled against the hierarchy of values imposed by an odious school curriculum, and for the rest of his life he treated Leo Tolstoy (who was at the top of the official hierarchy) with a certain irony: to Nikolay Nekrasov and Anton Chekhov (just a few rungs down) he was relatively indifferent. Tolstoy suffered in comparison not only to Brodsky's beloved Dostoevsky (who was not taught in Soviet schools at the time) but also to Ivan Turgenev. Brodsky loved the stories in Turgenev's *Notes of a Hunter,* especially "Prince Hamlet of Shchigrov," "Chertopkhanov and Nedopyuskin," and "The End of Chertopkhanov." His attitude toward Pushkin also betrays a tinge of youthful iconoclasm, although he never disputed the pivotal role that Pushkin played in Russian culture. "[I]n school we read . . . *Eugene Onegin* aloud, acting out the scenes. . . . I really enjoyed the whole thing. One of the nicest memories I have of my school years."[18] The last letter Brodsky ever wrote was devoted to a discussion of Pushkin's prose.[19] He could recite many of Pushkin's short poems and all of "The Bronze Horseman" from memory. He once said that a single line from Pushkin's "Recollection"—"And reading my life with disgust" gave birth to Dostoevsky's prose and to Russian prose in general.

At the same time, he wanted Russian readers to reconsider their traditional worship of Pushkin and Pushkin alone, to pay homage to the other fine poets in the so-called Pushkin pleiad: Batyushkov, Vyazemsky, Katenin, and, above all, Baratynsky. He also knew and loved the eighteenth century—from Kantemir and Tredyakovsky to Derzhavin and Karamzin. He had his favorites among the minor writers of the Russian nineteenth century, too: he especially liked Aleksandr Veltman's romantic novel *The Wanderer* (1832) and the acutely observed memoirs of Elena Shtakenshneider (1854–1886).

After the Russian and European classics that Brodsky read catch-as-catch-can in childhood and youth came the literature of modernism, most of it read in translation. Young Russians in the latter half of the 1950s were particularly interested in what was going on outside the USSR; this was a generation that after the final, cruel round of Stalinist oppression was eager to join the rest of the world. Books salvaged from both private and public libraries were passed from hand to hand: prerevolutionary editions of Nietzsche, Bergson, Freud; prewar Soviet translations of Aldous Huxley, John Dos Passos, Louis-Ferdinand Céline, Ernest Hemingway, Thomas Mann. There were anthologies, too: *French Lyrical Poetry of the Nineteenth and Twentieth Centuries,* translated by Benedikt Livshits; Mikhail Zenkevich and Ivan Kashkin's *American Poets (Twentieth Century);* D. S. Mirsky's *Anthology of Modern English Poetry*—as well as old copies of *Internatsionalnaya literatura* (International Literature), a journal that had once upon a time published chapters from James Joyce's *Ulysses.*[20]

In 1956 this journal reemerged under a "more Russian" name—*Inostrannaya literatura* (Foreign Literature)—and featured both prose and poetry. It was the poetry that especially caught young Brodsky's eye; many of his early poems are written in free verse, a form very rare in Russian poetry up to that time but quite common on the pages of *Inostrannaya literatura.*

He could not abide most modernist Russian prose: Bely, Zamyatin, Babel, Pilnyak, Rozanov. In the case of the first four, his objection was stylistic; in the case of Rozanov, it was moral. But there were notable exceptions: he considered the recently rediscovered Andrey Platonov one of the major writers of the twentieth century; he loved Mikhail Zoshchenko. Somewhat later he read and like Leonid Dobychin, Anatoly Mariengof, and Konstantin Vaginov. In the fall of 1961 he had his first chance to read hard-to-find works by such émigré writers as Nabokov, Tsvetaeva, Khodasevich, and Georgy Ivanov—all part of a private samizdat library put together by a young scholar named Sergey Shults (photocopies and carbon copies of manuscripts, and the occasional article from the Paris émigré journal *Sovremennye zapiski*). Schults's library also included translations from Samuel Beckett, Jean Anouilh, and Franz Kafka.[21]

Oddly enough, Brodsky's first acquaintance with Russian "high modernism"—Pasternak, Mandelstam, Akhmatova, Khlebnikov, the Oberiuty—came relatively late. He read most of these poets in the early 1960s, several years after he began to write on his own. The only exception might be Tsvetaeva, whose "Poem of the Mountain," "Poem of the End," and "Ratcatcher" he read in samizdat versions in the late 1950s. She made the greatest impression of all, and to the end of his life she was his poet of poets.[22]

WINDS FROM THE WEST

While *Inostrannaya literatura* provided some notion of intellectual and aesthetic trends in the West, Polish periodicals and books provided even more. Although "capitalist" Western European publications were unavailable in the USSR, "socialist-democratic" Polish magazines and newspapers were sold freely. One could even subscribe. "I probably read half of modern Western literature in Polish translation," Brodsky recalled.[23] One reason he learned Polish in the first place was to read Kafka and Camus.

Like many of his friends in Leningrad, he was a regular follower of *Przekrój* (The Review). This was a rather odd publication, an intellectual, avant-garde magazine masquerading as a tabloid. It served up gossip on the squabbles and divorces of movie stars East and West; it also offered remedies for hangovers. At the same time, it reported and reviewed new trends in philosophy (mostly existentialist) and art (mostly absurdist). In these lines from Brodsky's "Sketch"—

> The moon shines [bright],
> it hurts my eyes,
> and underneath it floats a brain, a cloud

—longtime *Przekrój* readers would immediately recognize Daniel Mróz's surrealist prints, which often depicted a brain-shaped cloud floating over a night landscape. The style and range of *Przekrój* ran from the tragic absurd of Samuel Beckett to the psychedelic lyrics of the Beatles, and this was reflected in much of Brodsky's work.

Still, it was Polish poetry that played an especially important part in the development of Brodsky's own style. This was a poetry written in a Slavic language closely related to Russian, but more deeply and organically connected to western European traditions—down to and including its Latin roots. One of the high points of Polish poetry was its baroque period (1600s–1700s), and that worldview was something the young Brodsky found very attractive. He translated such sixteenth-century poets as Mikołaj Rey and Mikołaj Sęp Szarzyński. (Russia never really had a literary baroque, although Brodsky detected some baroque elements in Kantemir, Tredyakovsky, and Derzhavin.) All this prepared him to read and understand John Donne and the English metaphysical poets.

He translated the great Polish romantic poet Cyprian Norwid, who anticipated Tsvetaeva not only in his sense of the tragic but also in his ecstatic poetic style, which abounded in unusual rhythms and bold ellipses. Brodsky translated older contemporaries—Polish modernists like Konstanty Ildefons Gałczyński, Zbigniew Herbert, and Czesław Miłosz—and would eventually strike up a friendship with the last. He also became friends with the slightly younger Wiktor Woroszylski and later, in America, with a poet of his own generation, Adam Zagajewski.

A love of Poland and Polish poetry remained with him throughout his life, and it was amply requited. The Poles were translating Brodsky as early as the 1970s; in 1979, Stanisław Barańczak published a marvelous set of translations with an underground press called NOW. *Zeszyty literackie,* Poland's leading literary journal, published translations of Brodsky's poetry in twenty-eight of its fifty-five issues from 1983 to 1996. During the poet's life, fifteen books of his prose and poetry were published in Polish—more than in any other language, including his own. Professor Zofia Ratajczak, a psychologist whom Brodsky met during her student years in the USSR and to whom he dedicated several poems, invited him to read in Poland in the 1960s, but the Soviet regime did not allow him to cross even this border.

But he eventually managed to visit Poland twice: first in October 1990 and then in June 1993. These were something like victory laps; they were also warm encounters with old friends and new readers, although Brodsky rather sadly noted on his return that he had gotten to Poland "too late, and from the wrong side."[24]

MODERNISM

What do Proust and Tsvetaeva have in common? What does Dos Passos have to do with the Polish baroque? The stylistic range of the works that young Brodsky read is colossal—but the common thread is modernism. Granted, terms like "romanticism," "realism," "modernism," and "postmodernism" mean different, sometimes very different, things to different people, but still, there is little doubt that Brodsky learned his trade from the modernists.

Modernism, which should not be confused with the avant-garde (an entirely different artistic phenomenon), dominated European literature and art from the last quarter of the nineteenth century through the middle of the twentieth. For all their obvious differences, modernist writers had one great principle in common. All of them tended to build on ancient mythological archetypes, to see reality not sequentially but discretely, to expose the triumph of chaos and absurdity where their predecessors had sought to reveal harmony and logic. And for all the modernists, the central philosophical and narrative issue came down to the problem of time. T. S. Eliot was one of the first to point out this similarity between modernist and metaphysical poets; he saw modernism as a contemporary manifestation of baroque sensibility.

We should also note that Brodsky at eighteen and nineteen was reading not only Western fiction and poetry but also the Bhagavad Gita, the Mahabharata, and the *Daodejing*. Later he would often say that through them he had glimpsed the furthest reaches of the human mind.[25]

POETRY

As a child, Iosif read no poetry other than what was assigned in school. He laughingly recalled that the first real book of poetry he had read on his own was Saadi's *Gulistan,* which he took out of the library on his mother's advice. This was at age sixteen![26] The wooden Russian translations of didactic verse by a Persian poet particularly impressed the teenage Brodsky. Later he "really liked" Samuil Marshak's translations of Robert Burns. Still, "I wasn't writing anything myself, the thought of writing had never even occurred to me."[27]

By age seventeen, however, he was constantly reading poetry and easily committing it to memory; he could recite both short passages and whole works by heart: Derzhavin ("On the Death of Prince Meshchersky"), Baratynsky ("Autumn," "Desolation," "To My Italian Tutor"), Aleksey Tolstoy ("Popov's Dream"), and poems by his contemporaries.

In 1988, Brodsky wrote a foreword to a small anthology of nineteenth-century Russian poems translated into English by Alan Myers. He also wrote brief notes about each of the eleven poets included. (The poets were all the translator's choice. Had Brodsky been putting together his own anthology, he might have included Ivan Krylov, another poet he admired greatly.) Each note includes a brief biography, followed by a review of each poet's particular strengths and each one's contributions to Russian literature. These notes are a good indicator of Brodsky's preferences and idiosyncrasies. He writes enthusiastically about Batyushkov ("a master of the extended elegy that covers in its progress much cultural, historical, and psychological ground, with a somber, often ecclesiastically toned coda"), Vyazemsky ("a superb yet underestimated poet . . . , a 'critical realist'"), Pushkin ("There was nothing of greater consequence to Russian literature and the Russian language than this thirty-seven-year-long life"), Baratynsky ("often seems superior to his great contemporary in the genre of the philosophical poem"), Yazykov ("the most ringing, most vigorous verse of the period, similar to but sometimes besting Pushkin's"), Lermontov ("A poet of immense lyric intensity"), and Aleksey Tolstoy ("a poet of unique facility and versatility. . . . Given the record of the country in the century that followed his death . . . what seemed to his contemporaries to be escapist or nostalgic musings has acquired the quality of cautionary and largely prophetic tales").

The rest of the reviews are rather tepid. Vasily Zhukovsky deserved mention because he introduced the western European ballad to Russia, Afanasy Fet because he was "a lyrical poet of the highest acumen" and wrote miniatures *à la japonaise*. Nikolay Nekrasov had acute powers of observation; he was an indifferent poet, but managed to infuse his civic poetry with a certain lyricism. Tyutchev's "philosophical verse" was no match for Baratynsky's; Tyutchev wrote a great deal of servile poetry; his later love poems were memorable in that he managed "to infuse his keen philosophical insights with a natural, half-haphazard air." The note on Tyutchev ends with the ironic reminder that he was one of Lenin's favorite poets.[28]

These likes and dislikes point to the very roots of Brodsky's art, to the genesis of his poetic self. Literary criticism often focuses on how poets modify or change inherited modes of expression in an attempt to remain true to themselves and their own time. Yet what they inherit forever remains an organic part of their work. The genesis of Brodsky's style, the "uncommon visage" he talked of in his Nobel lecture, sets him apart from the rest of his generation, other poets who came of age in the 1950s and 1960s. Osip Mandelstam once wrote a poem in which "more than one treasure, perhaps / Bypassing the grandsons / Comes down to the great-grandsons." That is, Mandelstam believes that his poetics hark back at least two generations; they take little from Russian symbolism or the poets of the late nineteenth century but instead stem directly from Pushkin and his peers. If for Mandelstam this was at least partly true, it was certainly not true of Akhmatova or Pasternak, whose poetics could be traced (albeit by a winding road of influences and counterinfluences) to those of their immediate predecessors (Annensky, Blok, Kuzmin, Vyacheslav Ivanov) and through these poets back to Sluchevsky, Fet, Polonsky, Nekrasov, and even further back to Tyutchev, Benediktov, Pavlova.

LENINGRAD POETRY, LATE 1950S

The young Leningrad poets of the late 1950s were taught the same rules as the generation that immediately preceded them—and here we are of course talking about real poetry rather than official versifying. One of their most popular mentors was the talented and apolitical (therefore rarely published) Gleb Semyonov (1918–1982), who did not believe in any sort of leaps across generations:

> But it's Pushkin's stars that sparkle
> through my frozen window.
> But it's Tyutchev's undertone
> that pierces heart and soul.
>
> But it's Blok's madness that can
> torment me forever.
> Nothing but this fine thread spun
> can keep me up at night.
> (Non-poetic)[29]

After Blok came Khodasevich and the Acmeists, and after them, Semyonov's generation—the Leningrad poets of the 1930s and 1940s. By this time the fine-woven thread stretching from the past to the present was very thin indeed. The basic tendency throughout these two decades was to choose those parts of the Russian poetic legacy that best approached the ideal of "concise, bare speech" (an expression coined by

Vladimir Mayakovsky, whose style was neither particularly concise nor simple and whose poetic pedigree had skipped a few generations itself, harking back to the ode writers of the eighteenth century). Nikolay Gumilyov and Vladislav Khodasevich (the first was executed in 1921, the second emigrated in 1922) were never mentioned in public, although the names of their students and imitators (Nikolay Tikhonov, for example) sometimes were used as surrogates. The style of the day dictated concrete imagery, close observation, emotional restraint, laconicism, aphorism. These verses by N. N. Ushakov were often trotted out as an example and admonition to young poets:

> I know
> the hard joy,
> the unfrivolous peace
> of crushing thick bunches of grapes
> with a stubborn hand.
>
> The wine is silent.
> And years will sleep
> in a gloomy cellar, like smoke,
> until the nectar of hot berries
> flares
> into golden heat.
>
> Wine merchants—they're chatty,
> they'll make your head spin.
> But I, the patient writer,
> keep words, like music.
>
> I've learned to hoard their sound
> in the cellar, to preserve it.
>
> The longer the silence,
> the more surprising the speech.
> (Non-poetic)[30]

This style was hardly suitable for composing panegyrics to the Party, the Soviet state, or the Soviet people, let alone for writing diatribes against American capitalism and the West. On the other hand, since it avoided difficult tropes "incomprehensible to the [Soviet] people" and stayed within the lexical bounds of literary language, it didn't raise the ire of the censors. Vadim Shefner (1915–2002), a talented lyric poet who worked mainly in this vein, was a favorite with the Leningrad intelligentsia in the years immediately after the war. His poem "Things" was written in 1957:

> The owner dies, but his things remain.
> They don't care, these things, for human troubles.
> At the hour of your passing, not a teacup on the shelf will break.
> Nor will sparkling rows of glasses melt like ice.
>
> Maybe for things it's just not worth the effort—
> So the mirrors resignedly let others look,
> The chairs, indifferent, crowd the room like gawkers,
> The table's faceted legs won't creak or shudder.
>
> And just because you've left this world,
> Electric meters won't run backward,
> Telephones won't die, film will not be exposed,
> The fridge won't march behind your coffin, sobbing.
>
> Be their lord—don't give yourself in sacrifice.
> Be their fair impartial master—
> He who lives for things will lose them as he breathes his last;
> He who lives for people will live on.
> (Non-poetic)[31]

This is neither Shefner's best poem nor his worst. The eternal theme of the transience of human life is offered up to the reader in the form of a precise and sadly humorous description of a house bereft of its owner. Shefner was in general a master of the deft ending, but in this particular poem he cannot quite resolve the theme poetically. So he does it rhetorically. In Shefner's best poems, "Mirror" (1942) and "By the Picture" (1971), the imagination takes off from some closely observed detail; in "Things" it starts with a generalization: people die, their things remain.

I bring up Shefner's poem because the antithesis between the short life of humans and the long life of their things was to become a constant in Brodsky's poetry. If we compare Shefner's "Things" to Brodsky's "Nature Morte" (1971), it is easy to see the difference between the poetic world of serious Leningrad poets during Brodsky's youth and the poetic world that Brodsky was in the process of creating. In "Nature Morte" Brodsky rebels against all the rules that govern "Things": its poetics, its lexicon, its observance of good taste.

Like Shefner, he begins with an utterly obvious statement about common concepts. There are people and there are things: "People and things crowd in." But in the following lines, the reader is slapped with the misanthropic declaration that since both people and things can bruise and hurt the eye, "[i]t's better to live in the dark." From here on, we are riding what feels like a train of thought constantly switching tracks—things, objects, my life, life in general—and then the whole angry and sometimes crude poem ends with a scene from the Gospels.

If we judge Brodsky's poem by the standards of Shefner's generation, it is both too long and too vulgar; it mixes literary and substandard language; it lacks emotional restraint when discussing "ultimate questions of being." In 1967, Shefner wrote a letter to the Leningrad branch of the Sovetsky Pisatel publishing house, urging it to publish a collection by the young poet. He had the very best of intentions, so he couched his criticisms in the mildest of terms. But they are revealing. About "Isaac and Abraham," for example, he writes that he "perhaps didn't fully understand it, but it didn't excite me, it was too elaborate. In the Bible itself, the tale is much shorter and richer in meaning."[32] In Shefner's eyes, excessive elaboration was a fault. Shorter equaled better. The older poet's eye, trained in a different school, could not quite take in the complicated but congruous and balanced structure that Brodsky had built for his own poetic ends.

Why did Brodsky never absorb the lessons of the Leningrad school of poetry? Simple: he never attended that school. As we already know, he neither read nor wrote poetry until he was in his late teens. For a "Leningrad poet" this was already unusual. The usual route in those days led through the Leningrad school system, Houses of Culture, and Young Pioneer Houses. That is, the people who became poets were generally the boys and girls who had started reading and writing poetry at an early age. Schools, Houses of Culture, and Young Pioneer Houses sponsored more than just photography or model airplane clubs; they ran poetry clubs as well. The most gifted of these children were chosen to attend a studio at the central Young Pioneer Palace, which was housed in the Anichkov Palace on Nevsky Prospekt. In the first years after the war, Gleb Semyonov headed the studio, and pupils as young as thirteen quickly learned to compose in iambic, trochaic, anapestic, amphibrachic, and dactylic meters and to come up with more or less exact rhymes for their line endings in various patterns. Once the children were a little older, it was explained to them that correct versification was not an end in itself but merely a form in which to put content. Content was thought—not abstract thought but thought expressed through the description of a specific real-life state or situation. The basis of all such descriptions was detail, closely observed. In other words, what the highly cultured Gleb Semyonov was teaching consciously and deliberately, and what his less well-educated colleagues in other less prestigious "litclubs" were teaching out of general stylistic inertia, were the basics of Acmeism—this in the aftermath of the 1946 literary pogroms organized by Stalin's commissars of ideology, in a time when the very word "Acmeism," much less the very name of its finest exemplar, Anna Akhmatova, was never spoken aloud. Nonetheless, the Acmeist aesthetic was becoming the cornerstone of these future poets' education.

What Russia termed "Acmeism" Anglo-American poetic culture called "Imagism." In 1919, following in the footsteps of Ezra Pound, who insisted that poetry should avoid any hint of symbolism, allegory, or abstraction in general, T. S. Eliot proposed his now-famous definition of the "objective correlative": the expressive force of the poetic text is greater if emotions are not expressed directly but rather through the description of an object—a thing, a situation, an event. This is one of the golden rules of modernist poetics. In 1968, Brodsky wrote in "Candlestick" that

> Probably, art gets to us because
> it just explains, it never lies,
> because its basic law
> is, undoubtedly, the independence of the detail.
> (*OVP;* non-poetic)

At least to some extent, this emphasis on an objective correlative steered young poets away from the official canon of an oppressive and highly ideological regime and toward much more tempting experiments "à la Mayakovsky." But the Leningrad school had its negative side as well. In practice, its "realism" all too often turned into mere formalism—that is, if a poem clearly demonstrated the author's powers of observation, it was deemed a success. The mentors of these young poets were unable to impart to their students (or perhaps they themselves had forgotten) that even keenly perceived detail is valuable less in itself than as an expression of sorrow, hope, fear, despair, love; as an expression of an intellectual or metaphysical quest. (This is precisely why Eliot chose the word "correlative.")

One example held up for general admiration and imitation was a neatly rhymed and perfectly metered composition dating back to the 1930s, written by a schoolboy named Seryozha Orlov. It describes a pumpkin:

> [It] lies next to the rutabaga,
> And you think that any minute
> It will oink out loud, from happiness,
> And wag its [piggy] tail.
> (Non-poetic)[33]

This is a perfectly harmless little poem written by a child. But it is symbolic of a tradition come to a dead end. A pumpkin looks like a pig, a pig looks like a pumpkin. Anything beyond that is the devil's work.

BRODSKY'S EARLY VERSE

Brodsky never went through this official mill. No one ever beat it into his head that confronting issues of life and death directly was somehow in bad taste, or that writing on historical or cultural themes was somehow pretentious. He began not as a good little boy striving to follow the rules and earn a pat on the head but as a young man entering into adulthood, seriously preoccupied with what that really meant: the inevitability of suffering and death; the beauty and ugliness of sex; the ever-present threat of poverty and unfreedom; and, last but not least, the question of one's place in the world. Born into a society in which literature, and especially poetry, had immense prestige, he chose poetry as his way of proving himself and finding answers to all the "accursed questions of existence."

Brodsky, by nature, always wanted to be first and best. He was also naturally charismatic. His peers were drawn to him by his sincerity, his wide range of interests, his genuine inability to conform; by the intensity that marked his relationships, his conversations, his attitudes to abstract ideas and to mundane events. This charisma was combined with a certain naïveté, in that Iosif at eighteen or nineteen was unacquainted with the etiquette of poetry circles. Instead of humbly submitting a first draft for everyone else to hear and review, he came ready to read, convinced that he was done. As a rule, his performances at such readings were the loudest and most emotional of all (granted, loud and emotional were in vogue at the time).[34] He often left early—sometimes alone, sometimes with friends—but in any case without listening to the rest of the readings. All this could not help but annoy, and alarm, the mentors of the up-and-coming literary establishment.

One memorable scandal surrounded Brodsky's appearance at a poetry contest held at the Gorky Palace of Culture on February 14, 1960. Brodsky read "A Jewish Cemetery," and as usual, most of the young people in the audience liked his performance. But then up stood Gleb Semyonov, who had helped organize the contest; he took the microphone and loudly expressed his outrage and indignation. Yakov Gordin, another participant in the contest, explains Semyonov's reaction in his memoirs: "An accomplished poet who over the long-suffering course of his life had schooled himself in maintaining a proud reserve and silent resistance, Gleb Sergeevich was outraged at the naive rebelliousness that Iosif exuded; he was outraged by a freedom that seemed to him unearned and unfounded in any gift."[35] In reply, Brodsky recited "Poem with an Epigraph," the epigraph in question being "Quod licet Jovi non licet bovi"—"What is permitted to Jupiter is not permitted to the ox." This brief confrontation turned into a major "incident," contributing to Brodsky's reputation both among young rebels in Leningrad and among those charged with keeping an eye on them.

PERSECUTION-PROSECUTION

Brodsky first collided with the Soviet police and security services in 1960. In 1959 a journalism student at Moscow University named Aleksandr Ginzburg had launched a samizdat journal called *Sintaksis* (Syntax). In Ginzburg's "Leningrad issue," the magazine's third, there were five poems by Brodsky, including "A Jewish Cemetery" and "Pilgrims."

Sintaksis was the first samizdat journal to gain widespread fame both in the USSR and abroad.[36] Copies were passed from hand to hand in Moscow and Leningrad and eventually made their way to the West, at which point the Soviet press went on the offensive, led by an *Izvestia* lampoon entitled "The Parasites Crawl Up Parnassus."[37] As a result, in July 1960 Ginzburg was arrested. He was eventually sentenced to two years in a work camp. The formal charge on which he was convicted was using false identification papers. And indeed he was guilty of that crime—once upon a time he'd sat in for a friend at an exam, and used the friend's I.D.

While the poems published in *Sintaksis* were ideologically unacceptable to Soviet censors (too individualist, too pessimistic), none of them contained any direct criticism of the regime. Still, many of the young people called in for questioning by the KGB were told that their lives might be ruined, that they might even go to prison, if they didn't come to their senses and straighten up.[38] From this time forward, Brodsky was always somewhere in the KGB's line of sight. He himself explained the interest of the security police in him as a simple need to justify their own existence: "Since they're security, they set up a systematic way for citizens to report. On the basis of these reports they come up with some sort of information. And on the basis of this information they then have to do something. It's particularly convenient way to deal with a writer . . . [b]ecause for all messieurs there are dossiers, and the dossiers get fatter with time. And if you're a writer, your dossier grows even faster, because all your manuscripts—poems, novels, whatever—go into it."[39]

On January 29, 1962, Brodsky was arrested and held for two days in the KGB lockup on Shpalernaya Street. A pretrial investigation was under way, with charges pending against Aleksandr Umansky and Oleg Shakhmatov, two of Brodsky's friends. Brodsky faced serious charges himself.

UMANSKY AND HIS CIRCLE

Oleg Shakhmatov, a former military pilot, an accomplished musician, and a man with a decidedly wild streak, was six years older than Brodsky. They first met in 1957, at the editorial offices of *Smena,* a newspaper affiliated with the Komsomol. Both young men had come to submit their poems. Iosif was still fascinated by flying, and he and Shakhmatov struck up a friendship. Shakhmatov, in turn, introduced Brodsky to Aleksandr Umansky.[40]

Umansky himself was a dilettante, but a truly gifted one: he wrote piano sonatas, essays on elementary particles, treatises on political philosophy; he dabbled in the occult; he studied Hindu mythology and practiced hatha yoga quite seriously. Judging by the memoirs of his contemporaries, he always had a following—not only young, nonconformist artists and musicians but also young people who simply wanted to discuss "eternal questions" outside any official ideological framework. Some of these were full-time students, and others eked out a living at part-time jobs, but whatever their circumstances, their real lives mainly consisted of ferreting out hard-to-find books on Eastern philosophies and esoteric learning and then discussing what they'd read. Drugs were still relatively rare in Umansky's circle, but there was a good deal of alcohol, and not a few drunken escapades. (Brodsky never used drugs. He did drink, but, by that group's standards, only moderately.)

One member of this purely informal circle, Georgy ("Garik") Voskov-Ginzburg, became Brodsky's friend for life. But Umansky himself didn't particularly take to Brodsky and refused to believe that this would-be poet had any particular gift. What had attracted Brodsky to Umansky's group in the first place was the opportunity to discuss metaphysics, but by the time of his arrest he was already somewhat skeptical of the guru. He had come to believe that Umansky's obsession with Hindu philosophy, which was already "too much based on negation," was degenerating into a sterile nihilism—essentially, into unbelief. If in "Isaac and Abraham" we find traces of the esoterica learned in Umansky's circle, in Brodsky's late 1960s works we find pointed criticism of the sort of mysticism practiced there:

> [A] friendship with the abyss
> is a purely local interest
> in our day. Besides,
> this trait is incompatible
> with fraternity, equality, and, obviously,
> nobility of spirit,
> [it is] intolerable in true men.
> . . . .
> Otherwise—the telepaths,
> the Buddhists, spirits, nostrums,
> the Freudians, neurologists, and psychopaths will win.
> The euphoria, the high,
> will dictate its own laws.
> The addicts will pin stars upon their shoulders,
> instead of icons of the Virgin and the Saviour,
> they'll hang up their syringes [on a wall]
> They'll shroud the soul in a great veil.
> ("A Speech about Spilt Milk," *KPE;* non-poetic)

There's mysticism, there is faith, and there is God.
There's a difference between them. And there's a unity.
("Two Hours in a Container," *OVP;* non-poetic)

INCIDENT IN SAMARKAND

Shakhmatov, meanwhile, had been doing jail time for a brawl in the women's dormitory of the Leningrad Conservatory of Music, and after serving out his sentence, he left for Samarkand to enroll in the conservatory there.[41] In December 1960, Brodsky went to visit him, and Umansky gave him his latest philosophical treatise to pass along.[42]

The few weeks that Brodsky spent in Samarkand with his reckless friend were to bring about some serious consequences. One day, in the foyer of a Samarkand hotel, they spied Melvin Belli, the celebrated American attorney who had represented a variety of Hollywood stars, including Brodsky's childhood hero Errol Flynn. (Three years after this Samarkand episode, Belli was to defend Jack Ruby.) Brodsky recognized Belli; he had seen him in a film.

So Shakhmatov and Brodsky improvised. They asked Belli to smuggle Umansky's manuscript out of the country. But Belli, apparently out of caution, turned them down.[43]

Next, the friends concocted a fantastical plan to jump the Russian border. Many years afterward, Brodsky described it thus: They would buy tickets for a flight, any flight. After takeoff they would knock out the pilot. Shakhmatov would sit down at the controls and fly the plane to Afghanistan.[44]

Shakhmatov's version of the plan sounded somewhat more realistic. Shakhmatov owned a pistol, so when the pilot began to taxi down the runway, Shakhmatov would threaten him with the gun, shove him out onto the tarmac, then take over the controls. The young fugitives would not head for Afghanistan, where the local authorities would hand them back to the Soviets, but fly instead to Iran, to the American base at Meshhed.[45]

The two went so far as to buy tickets for the regular flight from Samarkand to Termez, but as Brodsky tells it, he began having qualms about hurting some perfectly innocent pilot, so he and Shakhmatov abandoned their plan. In Shakhmatov's version, the flight itself was cancelled.

A year later, Shakhmatov was arrested in Krasnoyarsk for illegal possession of firearms. Under questioning, to avoid a second and possibly much longer stretch in jail, he gave a statement about the "underground anti-Soviet Umansky group" and named dozens of people who had some acquaintance with Umansky. He also talked about the aborted plan to jump the border. Brodsky was detained, but since no crime had actually been committed, and the only proof of any intent to commit one was Shakhmatov's statement, Iosif was released after two days. However, the Samarkand escapade would resurface at the 1964 trial, and Brodsky would be under surveillance by the KGB until he was turned out of the country in 1972. And perhaps even afterward.[46]

CHAPTER THREE

> Since the stern art of poetry calls for words . . .
>
> —"The End of a Beautiful Era"

THE BEGINNINGS OF A STYLE

BY THE AGE OF TWENTY-TWO, when his more privileged peers were just barely graduating from university and embarking on adult life, Brodsky had already traveled the country, lived among ordinary people, and survived political persecution. He had learned to separate fact from fantasy and to cast a critical eye on his fellows.

He had also learned how to write poetry.

Thanks to his native energy and imagination, there are good lines to be found even in the work he wrote at age eighteen or nineteen. But these poems are mainly youthful stabs at writing "deathless verse." Like others his age, Brodsky was fascinated by grandiose abstractions and romantically contemptuous of the mundane world around him. He liked the sound of Latinate words and sometimes, to the Russian ear, almost seemed to be speaking in tongues.

> . . . to completely lose one's way
> in the liquid shrubbery of ambitions,
> in the wild mud of prostrations,
> associations, and conceptions,
> and—simply in emotions.
> ("Verses on the Acceptance of the World,"
> 1958; non-poetic)[1]

Out of a mishmash of exotic books and films his imagination builds grand but incoherent allegories:

Past stadiums and temples,
past shrines and bars,
past elegant graveyards,
past great bazaars,
past the world and sorrow,
past Mecca and Rome,
burnt by a dark blue sun,
over this earth go pilgrims.
("Pilgrims," *Uncollected;* non-poetic)

Here we have Mecca and Rome, bars that seem to symbolize some mysterious and luxurious life outside the borders of the USSR, a blue sun straight out of science fiction, and sunburnt pilgrims straight out of a poem that Soviet schoolchildren were routinely forced to memorize—"Reflections at the Entrance to the Palace," by the nineteenth-century civic poet Nikolay Nekrasov, whom Brodsky claimed to dislike. In Brodsky's notorious "Poem with an Epigraph" (1958), the narrator may be either godlike or beastly (Jupiter or the bull), but in any case the human is left out.

In youth everyone, or practically everyone, writes like this. At this age Mikhail Lermontov declared that he was "either God—or no one!" There was nothing strange in the popularity of poems like this among teenage romantics of the day, especially when the voice reading them sounded like some stringed instrument. What *was* unusual was that Brodsky's early success among his peers never tempted him to rest on his laurels, that he soon abandoned the stilted romanticism of these poems and struck out in a different direction. By age nineteen he had begun to suspect that poetry was not the stuff of dreams (especially egomaniacal ones) but the stuff of life "as it is." When he was first hauled into the offices of the KGB for interrogation, he already knew how to behave:

To remember the view . . .
    from the agents' office windows . . .
To remember
    opaque streams of rain on glass
    distorting the proportions of the buildings opposite

as it's being explained to us just what we have to do.
("Definition of Poetry," 1959; non-poetic)[2]

Brodsky was learning the lyricism of daily life, the potential of the vernacular; he was finding the metaphysical that underlies the ordinary. By 1962 serious poems of this sort began to outnumber all his abstract-romantic ones. In this, too, he had his teachers. He himself mentioned his slightly older contemporaries Evgeniy Rein and Vladimir Uflyand. There were other poets of this generation who also had an influence: Stanislav Krasovitsky, Gleb Gorbovsky, and Vladimir Britanishsky. It was Britanishsky's verse that nudged young Iosif into writing his own. But without a doubt his chief lessons came from Boris Slutsky.

BORIS SLUTSKY: METER, RHYME, COMPOSITION, INTONATION

Boris Slutsky (1919–1986) was the most significant and original poet of the World War II generation. This brave and stalwart man was a lifelong, convinced Communist, but his mercilessly realistic poems had absolutely nothing to do with official socialist realism. He published almost nothing until the post-Stalinist thaw of the middle 1950s, and even then his more politically charged pieces circulated only in samizdat. Despite his orthodox Marxist convictions, in Slutsky's poems there was always a common thread of universal humanism and metaphysical justice. His creative peak came at the end of the decade, and nearly all the young poets of the time felt his influence in one way or another—Brodsky perhaps more than most.

In April 1960, Brodsky traveled to Moscow to meet Slutsky, and apparently Slutsky had some kind words for him. Brodsky's poem "I slept best at Savelovsky station" ends with an expression of gratitude to the elder poet:

Good-bye, Boris Abramych.
Good-bye. Thanks for your words.
(Non-poetic)[3]

Konstantin Kuzminsky recalls showing his first poems to Brodsky in 1959. Instead of commenting on them or giving any advice, Brodsky read him Slutsky's "Cologne Pit," a brutal poem about Soviet POWs thrown into a pit and left to die of starvation by the Germans. Then he said, "This is how you write."[4]

Brodsky never forgot Slutsky, and whenever the conversation turned to the elder poet, he would recite his "Music over the Market" by heart:

I grew up at the Kharkov market
Where the only clean thing was the trash urn
Because running by, you'd hawk up fast
And miss the mark.
I grew up in a place spit-stained,
Grime-smeared, thief-ridden,
Sworn-at, sworn-over,
And damned six ways to hell.

The pedlars and the vendors drank
And ate, and showed their gut no mercy.
A step away, all business, they'd be
Beating up some boy-thief "to make a man of him."

That's how men got made here.
And the boy would reel from hit to hit,
And then an old and heavy coin
Would be laid on each dead eye.

But time moved on and faster every day.
And then—
above the sleaze and filth of the bazaar,
Far higher than the fire-station tower,
A pole was raised
and there on top was music.

Those speeches blasting from the pole,
The song that sounded from the pole,
the crowd would hear, and haggle less,
And listen as if studying the sound.

And my heart pounded cheerfully and sweetly.
Think this music gives a crap for these bourgeois?
Calisthenics on the radio
Flogged the pedlars
like a lash.

(Non-poetic)[5]

While Brodsky himself was never averse to bashing the bourgeoisie, what attracted him to Slutsky was not the latter's socialist thematics but the power of his verse. Slutsky had opened up new territory between the defunct poetic forms of the nineteenth century and the rarefied experimentation of the twentieth. He could take strict-form rhyme and meter, change here, tweak there, and, lo and behold, the poetic line did not break down. It became more flexible. Following Slutsky's lead, Brodsky began to mine the hidden depths of classic Russian verse.[6] Gradually he began to change a foot, an accent, slip in an extra syllable. Thus, in "A Part of Speech," a cycle written between 1974 and 1976, the doleful and overused Russian anapest takes on an entirely different sound. Slutsky had shown him that *not all* rhymes in Russian had been exhausted, that there were more subtle ways to connect sounds, that the rules taught in poetry class ("never use grammatical rhyme") were not absolute. Slutsky's own poetry, which sounds deceptively like prose, is in fact a tightly woven fabric of alliteration, assonance, anaphora, paronomasia, and pun.

The first lines of Brodsky's "Isaac and Abraham" (1962) are a sort of homage to the teacher who taught him that wordplay could be more than just a game; it could address very serious themes. In these lines, Brodsky plays on the difference between the biblical Isaac and the Russian Isak: "In Russian, Isaac loses one sound. . . . Isak is the stub of the candle once called Isaac." Slutsky wrote a short poem on the same theme. It begins:

> Everywhere Isaac is praised,
> He is hailed from all the altars.
> But Isak, he's treated different,
> He can't even get through the door.
> (Non-poetic)[7]

One of the important lessons that Brodsky learned from Slutsky was how to build a poem, how to structure it semantically. Slutsky begins "Music over the Market" with a raw scene described in raw language; he ends it, without changing style, with a barely disguised reference to the Gospels: like a whip, the music broadcast through the loudspeaker lashes at the vendors in the market just as Christ drove the moneylenders from the temple. Brodsky, too, would combine the vulgar physical with the abstract philosophical and metaphysical. In "The Funeral of Bobo" (1972), his new Dante creates a world ex nihilo by putting words on paper. But then in the last stanza he rhymes "word" (*slovo*) with "screwed" (*kherovo*).

He often begins a poem with a snapshot of some ugly reality—a squalid interior, his own inner misery—and ends with the discovery of some spiritual order, even though this order might offer little comfort or hope. In the 1962 poem "I threw my arms" and a much longer one written in 1971, "Nature Morte," this move from bottom to top is straight and clear, but in many other poems the way is much more complicated.

But the main thing that Brodsky took from Slutsky, consciously or not, was an overall key, a tone. Brodsky talked about this very thing in 1985: "It is Slutsky who has almost singlehandedly changed the diction of post-war Russian poetry. His verse is a conglomeration of bureaucratese, military lingo, colloquialisms and sloganeering. . . . This poet indeed speaks the language of the twentieth century. . . . His tone is tough, tragic and nonchalant—the way a survivor normally talks, if he cares to, about what, or into what, he survived."[8]

LENINGRAD LITERARY CIRCLES

Brodsky had managed to escape the mind-numbing "verse control" of school poetry clubs. He had studied, if not yet mastered, Russian literature on his own. But like any novice, he was looking for a teacher. Aleksandr Umansky's circle included many talented dilettantes but no truly gifted poets. So in the late 1950s and early 1960s, aspiring writers tended to lean either toward the "miners" that Brodsky had trekked with, or toward a loosely organized group more or less associated with Leningrad University's School of Philology. The miners had good mentors like Gleb Semyonov and the fiction writer David Dar to advise and influence them; the "philologists"—Leonid Vinogradov, Vladimir Uflyand, Mikhail Eremin, Sergey Kulle, Aleksandr Kondratov, and this author—had instead a set of official watchers, and any real talk about poetry went on at home, outside the university.[9] But there was no particular antagonism between the two groups, and poets from one often sat in on readings by the other.

The real difference lay in their aesthetics. Semyonov schooled his students in a relatively conservative verse tradition; the philologists had no teacher. They saw themselves as restorers and practitioners of an avant-garde tradition quashed in the 1930s. This difference also determined how these two groups were perceived by the previous generation: the miners were taken seriously by the Leningrad intelligentsia, published whenever possible, supported. The philologists were not; their work was generally considered childish, a game. Even so, a few poems by Vladimir Uflyand and Sergey Kulle found favor by dint of their quirky and original humor.

Brodsky was never entirely welcome in the miners circle, especially after his spat with Semyonov. But in 1959–1960 he became acquainted with Vinogradov, Uflyand, and Eremin. Brodsky and Uflyand were to become close friends, and to the end of his life Brodsky loved Uflyand's poetry, with its odd lyrical fusion of parody and sentiment and its unobtrusive but tremendously inventive technique. When Brodsky later named Uflyand as one of his mentors, we should take this quite literally: Brodsky's own rhyme technique echoes and builds upon what Uflyand wrote in the late 1950s. But even here, among the philologists, Brodsky was not taken particularly seriously. Both his poetry and his conversation struck them as juvenile and overblown. He was welcomed, but taken with a grain of salt.

There was yet another singular character on the Leningrad literary scene, a poet named Evgeniy Rein, who belonged to neither group and who saw signs of genius in the enthusiastic ramblings of the young redhead.

EVGENIY REIN: THE ART OF THE ELEGY

When Brodsky writes about other poets, he makes no particular effort to understand what constitutes a unique and unrepeatable "other." He proceeds from the assumption that there are certain lyric constants, certain universals that inform the work of lyric poets from Virgil to Tsvetaeva to Auden to himself and those contemporaries for whom he would write so many prefaces in the last years of his life. And so, in his essays on other poets, he blithely projects his own experience, stylistic preferences, and prejudices onto them.

This results in two types of essay. One, written out of inner need, tells us how Brodsky read and perceived Virgil, Tsvetaeva, Auden, and other poets dear to him; the other, represented by many of these prefaces, tells us more about Brodsky himself than about the subject of the essay. But his short essay on Evgeniy Rein, written in 1991 as a preface to the latter's *Selected Verse*, is a special case.[10] Nowhere is Brodsky's identification with his subject more fitting.

First of all, Brodsky notes that elegy not only dominates but defines

Rein's verse: "Elegy is a retrospective genre, the most common of all poetic genres. The reason for this, in part, is the natural human feeling that our life becomes [truly] real only after the fact, that moving a pen across a piece of paper is, strictly chronologically, also a retrospective process."[11] Indeed, this elegiac quality is what separated Rein from other aspiring Leningrad poets of the time, whose preferred genre was the "short poem," the "miniature" —the record of a brief impression, emotion, observation, or thought.

Many talented poets were working in that genre, but they wrote very different poems and so are hard to compare: there was Leonid Ageev, a miner, who painted grimly naturalist pictures of Soviet life; there was Mikhail Eremin, a philologist, who wrote esoteric eight-liners; there was Aleksandr Kushner, who encased complex thoughts in lapidary lines. Still, it was one genre and one focus, a direct impression, a psychological nuance, a sudden emotion articulated through specific detail. Overly general words like "joy" or "sorrow" were to be avoided.

Rein, who was five years Brodsky's senior, nudged his younger friend toward a philosophical rather than a formal choice. The elegy is an essentially nostalgic genre; it has more to do with the past than with the present, that is, it has to do with time, with life under the eye of death. Poetry becomes necessary when other forms of discourse do not suffice. In this sense the elegy's raison d'être flows from Wittgenstein's famous remark that we cannot reason about death because "[d]eath is not an event in life. It is not a fact of the world."[12] Where reason is helpless, a song may provide. And song, or lyric, has yet another layer, which is the irresolvable problem of language and time, because writing is by definition a "retrospective process." This truth troubled the nineteenth-century romantics; no written text could sufficiently describe direct experience because the text always came after it. Brodsky, however, was less concerned with the "inexpressibility of emotions" than with the impossibility of stopping time.

> Stop, moment! You are not so
> lovely as you are unrepeatable.
> ("A Winter Evening in Yalta," *OVP;*
> non-poetic)

By happy coincidence, just as Brodsky was getting to know Evgeniy Rein, he was also discovering Evgeniy Baratynsky, a magnificent nineteenth-century elegist forever overshadowed by his great contemporary, Pushkin.

When Brodsky and Rein finally met again in 1988, sixteen years after Brodsky was exiled, Rein asked, "What made you write poetry?" and Brodsky answered, "Somewhere around 1959, I flew into Yakutsk and got stuck there for about two weeks because of bad weather. I remember walking around that awful city, and stopping in at a bookstore, and stumbling onto Baratynsky—the Poet's Library edition. There wasn't much else to read, and once I found this little book and read it through, I realized—this is what I had to do."[13] What he "had to do," his notion of the contemporary elegy, is explained in this note on Baratynsky: "[He] is never subjective and autobiographical, but tends toward the general, toward psychological truth. His poems are denouements, conclusions, postscripts to dramas already played out; they are not the plot itself so much as the wrap-up. . . . Baratynsky's verse pursues its theme with almost Calvinist zeal, and this theme is the far from perfect soul, which the author creates in his own image."[14]

AKHMATOVA

It was Rein who introduced Brodsky to Akhmatova, on August 7, 1961.[15] Brodsky was twenty-one years old, and Rein was all of twenty-five, when they went to visit Anna Akhmatova's dacha in Komarovo, a resort town thirty miles from Leningrad where many writers and artists had summer homes.

Such pilgrimages were nothing new to Akhmatova. Even in the late Stalin years, when anyone associating with her might expect to pay a heavy price, admirers sought her out; by Khrushchev's time, young visitors bearing flowers and notebooks full of poetry were a fairly common occurrence. Brodsky's visit was actually rather accidental; he had not read much of Akhmatova's work and was fairly indifferent to what little he had. Having just discovered Tsvetaeva, he was still under her very strong influence. On that day in August he was simply accepting an invitation from a friend and getting out of the city for a while. But the trip turned out to be much more interesting than he had expected; he later made another visit or two to Komarovo, and "one fine day, in a jam-packed commuter train on my way back from Akhmatova's, I suddenly realized—you know, somehow the veil suddenly lifts—just who or rather just what I was dealing with."[16]

We do not have very many documented statements by Akhmatova about particular pieces by Brodsky.[17] We do know that she singled out

"The cocks will start to crow," written in 1962 for her birthday, as a piece more profound than one might expect from a piece of occasional verse; she used a line from it ("You write about us slantwise") as an epigraph for her poem "The Last Rose." We know that she paid a great deal of attention to "Isaac and Abraham" and to the line about the sound of *A* (ah)—"In essence this is an infant's cry / sorrowful, awful, lethal"—which she took as an epigraph for the first variant of her quatrain "Name."[18] Her remark after hearing a reading of "Grand Elegy to John Donne"—"You have no idea what you've written!"—was to become part of Brodsky's personal myth, his moment of initiation.[19]

Nonetheless, Brodsky's own style was already taking shape. It was not only different from Akhmatova's but in many ways its direct opposite. Hers was grounded in suggestion, understatement, and deliberately modest diction. Brodsky was fully aware of this and later explained:

> We didn't go to her for praise, or for acknowledgement, or for approval of our "oeuvre." . . . We went to her because she set our souls in motion, because in her presence it was as if you renounced yourself, renounced the emotional, spiritual—I don't know what to call it—level you were on at the time, renounced the "language" in which you conversed with reality in favor of the "language" she used. Of course we talked about literature, of course we gossiped, of course we ran [to the store] for vodka, listened to Mozart, and mocked the government. But looking back, that's not what I hear or see; what comes to mind is a line from her "Sweetbriar": "You do not know just what you've been forgiven." This, this line, does not so much break out of the context as break away, because it is said by the soul itself—for those who forgive are always greater than what or who needs to be forgiven. For this line, addressed to a person, is really addressed to the entire world; it is the soul's response to existence. This—not versification—was what we were learning from her.[20]

Akhmatova was fond of all the young writers who surrounded her—Natalya Gorbanevskaya, Dmitriy Bobyshev, Mikhail Meilakh, and her secretary, Anatoly Naiman—but her attitude toward Brodsky, as both a person and a poet, was entirely different. Certainly, she was the first to recognize his potential as a poet, the yet unrealized scope of his talent. "Brodsky, after all, was her discovery, her pride and joy," writes Lidiya Chukovskaya in her diary.[21] First and foremost, Akhmatova addressed Brodsky as an equal: "Iosif, you and I know every rhyme in the Russian language."[22] She and Nadezhda Mandelstam alike were struck by "Osya junior's" resemblance in outward appearance and manner to his great namesake Osip Mandelstam (Osip and Iosif are variants of the same name).[23] Apparently, Akhmatova saw the resemblance as more than skin-deep. In one of her diary entries from 1963 we read that "something about the other Iosif's attitude toward me reminds me of Mandelstam."[24] This was what in fact determined Akhmatova's rather unexpected (given the fifty-year difference in their ages) treatment of Brodsky as an equal whose judgments carried a great deal of weight. In her diaries and letters she often returns to Brodsky's thought that the chief thing in poetry is the "magnitude of the idea": "And once again, those words of salvation come to mind: What's most important in poetry is the magnitude of the idea." "I think constantly [about the magnitude of the idea and] about our last meeting, and thank you"; "Your words of last year are as valid as ever: 'The main thing is the magnitude of the idea.'"[25]

In another entry Akhmatova writes: "For an epigraph to 'Pages from a Diary' take [this] from I. B[rodsky]'s letter: 'What does he [Man] consist of—Time, Space, Spirit? A writer, I think, in striving to re-create Man, must in fact write Time, Space, and Spirit.'"[26] In a moment of deep doubt she wonders: "And where is this salutary 'magnitude of the idea' that has saved Iosif?"[27] (We should note here that Brodsky's "magnitude of the idea" has a literary antecedent, a famous passage in chapter 104 of *Moby-Dick* that speaks of the "magnifying virtue of a large and liberal theme." "We expand to its bulk," writes Melville. "To produce a mighty book, you must choose a mighty theme.")[28]

These years in which Brodsky and Akhmatova were close were some of the most difficult in the young man's life; he went through a turbulent romance, a betrayal by a close friend, a suicide attempt, a stint in a mental hospital, prison. Everything transpiring with him touched Akhmatova to the quick. In September 1965 she writes:

> Iosif was just released by order of the Supreme Court. This is pure and utter joy. I saw him a few hours before the news

> [came out]. He looked terrible—seemed on the verge of suicide. He was saved from it (I think) by Admoni, who ran into him on the streetcar on the way back from my house.[29] He had just read me his "Hymn to the People." Either I know nothing at all, or this is genius, both as poetry and as the sort of moral path that Dostoevsky speaks of in *The House of the Dead:* there is not the slightest shade of that bitterness or arrogance that F[yodor] M[ikhailovich Dostoevsky] warns against. This [bitterness] is precisely what has undone my son. Once he began to despise and hate people, he ceased to be a person. Lord teach him Thy ways! My poor Levushka.[30]

In this entry, made after all Brodsky's trials (literal and figurative) of 1964 and 1965 were over, the comparison between Brodsky and Akhmatova's son is telling. She appreciates not only the poem itself but the morality and the steadfastness that made such a poem possible. Brodsky, for his part, always felt that he was merely trying to follow Akhmatova's example as best he could: "[H]ow much she went through, and still there was no hate, no reproach, no attempt to settle old scores. She simply had a lot to teach. Humility, for example. I think, and maybe I'm fooling myself, that I'm obliged to her in great part for those human qualities that are best in me. If it hadn't been for her, it would have taken a great deal more time for them to develop, if in fact they ever appeared in the first place."[31]

The lessons Brodsky took from Akhmatova had to do not only with private morality but with the poet's moral calling. A staunch individualist, a "private party" on principle, he understood that poets who take their calling seriously could not help but be a voice of the people whose language they spoke and wrote. Soviet ideology demanded *narodnost,* a virtually untranslatable word that fuses primitive aesthetics with political correctness. One consequence of that demand was that over the years, the intelligentsia developed a severe allergy to the very combination of the words "poet" and "people" (*narod*); many among them took earlier literary manifestos about "pure art" and "ivory tower poetics" all too seriously. For her part, Akhmatova never deigned to argue with "agitprop." The dominant motif in her late work, most importantly in "Requiem," is the poet as representative and witness. She understands her mission: through her voice, "a hundred million cry out." This is precisely what

Brodsky affirms in his poem "On Akhmatova's Centenary": through her, the native land finds its voice, thanks to her it is given the "gift of speech amidst a deaf-and-dumb universe."

MARINA BASMANOVA AND *NEW STANZAS TO AUGUSTA*

Overall, Brodsky's life was an eventful one: he was given the blessing of two great poets, Anna Akhmatova and W. H. Auden; he was arrested, then tried in a courtroom straight out of Kafka; he was jailed, committed to a mental hospital, sent into exile twice over; he was praised and celebrated worldwide; he was struck by a mortal illness. For all that, the central event of his life was Marina (Marianna) Pavlovna Basmanova. In Pushkin's "Prophet," a six-winged seraph descends from on high and gives the poet-prophet miraculous sight, hearing, and voice. Brodsky believed that in his case, this transformation came about through love for one particular woman. Years after the relationship ended, he wrote:

> It was you, on my right,
> on my left, with your heated
> sighs, who molded my helix,
> whispering at my side.
>
> It was you by that black
> window's trembling tulle pattern
> who laid in my raw cavern
> a voice calling you back.
>
> I was practically blind.
> You, appearing, then hiding,
> gave me my sight.
> ("Seven Strophes")

Brodsky was not yet twenty-two when on January 2, 1962, he first met Marina Basmanova, a young artist almost two years his senior. The intelligent and beautiful young woman made an impression on everyone she met; Akhmatova, for example, wrote that she was "[s]lender . . . smart . . . and wears her beauty so well! . . . No makeup . . . she's like [clear] cold water."[32] To Brodsky she seemed the very image of a Renaissance maiden à la Lucas Cranach (he may have had in mind Cranach's *Venus with Apples* at the Hermitage).[33] The relationship between Brodsky and Basmanova, a stormy one marked by frequent breakups and equally frequent reconciliations, lasted for roughly six years, finally ending in 1968, shortly after the birth of their son. The drama came to a head in late 1963 and early 1964.

Throughout the fall of 1963, Brodsky had been subjected to ever greater official harassment, and by the end of the year, fearing arrest, he left Leningrad for Moscow. While he was bringing in New Year, 1964, at a Moscow psychiatric hospital, back in Leningrad an affair had sprung up between Basmanova and Dmitriy Bobyshev, someone whom Brodsky had considered a close friend.[34] The double betrayal shook Brodsky to the bone, and that January he slit his wrists in an attempt at suicide.[35]

The poems dedicated to "M.B." are central to Brodsky's poetry not because they are his best. They are not, although there are some masterpieces among them. They are central because these poems and the inner experience they reflect are the furnace in which his poetic identity was forged. Late in life Brodsky was to say that they "were the main thing I did."[36] When he was explaining how and why it occurred to him to gather everything dedicated to M.B. into a single collection, he compared his *New Stanzas to Augusta* not to such classic examples as Tyutchev's Denisyeva cycle or Akhmatova's "Sweetbriar" nor to any other cycles of love lyrics. Instead, he compared it to Dante's *Divine Comedy:* "Unfortunately, I didn't write a 'Divine Comedy.' And apparently I never will. But here I've turned out something like a book with a plot of its own."[37]

The plot he speaks of is a "sentimental education," a coming of age. The beginning is a relatively serene stage of love and bliss (lyrics written in 1962 and 1963, elsewhere collected into a cycle called "Songs of a Happy Winter"), in which he sees himself and his love in terms of nature: ("You, my girl, are the wind. And I'm your forest").[38] The relationship between the lovers is inevitable in that it is inseparable from natural processes like the changing of night to day, the changing of the seasons, the changing of the tides. The woods, the water, the air and the birds in it, are all part of the lovers' life, but until the lovers are forced to part in "Like a lock on a prison door" (1964), nowhere is there any mention of another human being. Even those poems written from Norenskaya in 1964–1965 are still grounded in metaphors of nature, although the natural order of things has already been invaded by an unnatural force that tears the lovers apart:

So here I stand, my coat flung open,
and the world flows into my eye through a sieve,
through a sieve of unknowing.
I'm halfway deaf. Dear God, I'm halfway blind.
I hear no words, and the moon burns
at exactly twenty watts.
(*New Stanzas to Augusta,* in *OVP* and *NSKA;* non-poetic)

His 1965 poem "Prophecy" marks the end of this period; it depicts a desperately personal utopia, in which the world of nature has shrunk to a slip of land on the edge of the sea, a small plot with a garden next to the beach (oysters on the beach were also mentioned in early, serene lyrics like "A Riddle for an Angel" and "A Slice of Honeymoon"). The lovers have separated themselves from the world of "others"; they have walled themselves off from the post-apocalyptic world of a civilization that has destroyed itself.

The next stage in the development of this lyric plot is described in poems composed between 1969 and 1972, just after the final break with Basmanova. There are no more meditations on love and *Naturphilosophie:*

From the drab carousel that
Hesiod sings and chides
you get off not where you got
on, but where night decides.
("Strophes")

The elegiac "Six Years Later" (1968) and "Love" (1971) belong to this group. Here, human relationships are not filtered through metaphors of nature but are instead presented directly as memories of a failed union. Here, too, Brodsky begins to recast his personal drama in terms of classical and Christian culture, sometimes in the form of a direct comparison, as in "To Lykomedes, on Skiros" (1967)—

I quit the city, as Theseus
quit his labyrinth, leaving the Minotaur
to rot, Ariadne to coo
in Bacchus's arms

—or "Almost an Elegy," from 1968,

> I waited for one beauty in the foyer
> like Jacob at the bottom of the ladder,

other times more allegorically, as he reworks classical stories in "Anno Domini," "Dido and Aeneas," and "Odysseus to Telemachus."

In poems to M.B. written in his first years abroad, the preoccupation with a lost love feeds into the larger sense of nostalgia: "I'm howling 'youuu' through my pillow dike / many seas away" ("From Nowhere with Love"). The poems from the late 1970s that eventually became part of *New Stanzas* were more meditative in nature, and those written much later—"My dear, I left the house tonight" (1989) and "Sweetheart, losing your looks" (1992)—read like an ironic afterword to a long-finished drama.

But what would have prompted Brodsky to call this compilation of poems to M.B. his "Divine Comedy"? Perhaps it is that he sensed, more acutely than any of his readers, how singular and life-changing an experience his relationship to Basmanova was. There are three key poems supporting this notion: "Elegy" (1982), "Burning," and "Seven Strophes." In "Elegy" the "man who has lost his love" is compared with a "product of evolution," that is, a qualitatively new being, like some sea creature crawling out onto dry land, where it will have to adapt to a different environment and learn how to breathe in a different way. In "Burning," which mimics the imagery of Boris Pasternak's much-anthologized "Winter Night," carnal passion is described in sacramental and sacrificial terms:

> Wail, tremble, shake
> your skinny shoulder
> Let he who is on high
> swallow up your smoke!

"Seven Strophes," the last poem of the three, ends with an identification of earthly love with celestial love:

> . . . Thus they make worlds.
> Thus, having done so, at random
> Wastefully they abandon
> their work to its whirls.
>
> Thus, prey to speeds
> of light, heat, cold or darkness,

> a sphere in space without markers
> spins and spins.

This coda is a paraphrase of the final lines of the *Divine Comedy:* "Love, which moves the stars and suns."

Dmitriy Bobyshev's memoirs depict the love triangle in Dostoevskian terms—a poor man's version of *The Idiot.* Bobyshev assigns himself the role of Myshkin, although after the climactic scene involving all three characters, his fit is hysterical rather than epileptic. Brodsky is cast as Rogozhin, a man in the throes of a dark and overriding passion, brandishing now a knife, now an axe. Basmanova is Nastasya Filippovna, the tormented heroine, who runs first to one man, then to the other, and seems generally inclined to arson. Cute and comic as this bit of literary fluff might seem, it provides us with some psychological insight, especially if we compare it to Brodsky's M.B. poems. What emerges is a stark contrast between Brodsky's rich and complex emotional and intellectual world and the banal one inhabited by his rival. This story is less Dostoevsky than Griboedov, whose lines a younger Brodsky loved to quote: "And you? O God almighty? He's what you've chosen? / You've chosen this?"[39]

The very actions of the heroine in this tale suggest that Marina Basmanova was not just another pretty young woman playing femme fatale on the Leningrad bohemian scene but that she was Brodsky's match in character and depth of emotion. And while their love affair lay at the center of his lyrics, her background and her art may have played no small role in the development of his artistic views and in his creative practice.

Basmanova was the daughter of two talented artists: Pavel Ivanovich Basmanov and Natalya Georgievna Basmanova. Her artistic mentor was Vladimir Sterligov; as young men, Sterligov and Pavel Basmanov had studied with Kazimir Malevich. Brodsky was always skeptical of the avant-garde and its "stunts," and when in 1990 friends suggested that he celebrate his fiftieth birthday at the Guggenheim Museum, he answered: "Sure, as long as they turn the pictures face to the wall." But there were some avant-gardistes of the 1910s and 1920s that he liked (Braque, de Chirico), and there can be no doubt that he absorbed and transposed a great deal from that early avant-garde painting aesthetic into his own poetry. This comes out in his use of color as a symbol (especially his use of white as a "universal color" that he always associates with Malevich, as in "Roman Elegies" and other verses) and in the machines and furniture (Boccioni, de Chirico) that come alive in his "Centaurs" cycle.[40] In "At Carel Willink's Exhibition" he might simply be describing an avant-garde painting on display, or he might be painting a verbal portrait, as he did in a poem addressed to Marina Basmanova on her fortieth birthday:

> You, guitar-shaped affair with tousled squalor
> of chords, who keep looming brown in an empty parlor,
> or snow-white against laundered expanses,
> or dark—at dusk especially—in the corridor
> ("Minefield Revisited")

We can assume that his time with Basmanova, who, like any artist, was constantly sketching, training her hand and eye, had a certain influence on Brodsky's poetic practice. He, too, never parted with the tools of his trade: he, too, filled his notebooks with unfinished sketches, drafts, scribbles, discarded texts—out of which he plucked the best parts to use again.

CHAPTER FOUR

> I have braved, for want of wild beasts, steel cages,
> carved my term and nickname on bunks and rafters.
>
> —"May 24, 1980"

ANNUS MIRABILIS, 1964–1965: IDEOLOGY

THE FALL AND WINTER of 1963 and the first six weeks of 1964 were extremely hard for Brodsky, but not for the political reasons that those writing about him in hindsight assume. His relationship with Marina Basmanova was coming to a disastrous end; he was thinking of nothing else. But as it happened, at this most vulnerable moment, he became a convenient target for three different interest groups: he fell victim to Nikita Khrushchev's ideological policy, to the zeal and ambition of the Leningrad police and reactionaries within the Leningrad Writers' Union, and to the machinations of one Yakov Lerner and his cohorts.

One year before the storm broke over the young poet's head, Khrushchev's "Thaw" was at its warmest. In November 1962, *Novy mir* had published Aleksandr Solzhenitsyn's *One Day in the Life of Ivan Denisovich*. This work went far beyond criticizing "individual flaws within the Soviet system"; it was a parable, an explosive indictment of the anti-human essence of the whole Soviet experiment. Logically, what should have followed was full-scale liberalization.

But that would have to wait for another quarter of a century, for 1963 brought not reform but reaction. The Party bonzes felt their house giving way and sought to repair the damage by manipulating their ever-more-erratic and outrageous Party chairman, Nikita Khrushchev. The latter, stung by the failure of his economic reforms and the humiliating debacle in Cuba, was all too happy to take out his anger on the arts. On November 29, 1962, he swore and stamped his feet at a modern art show at the Manège, Moscow's central exhibition hall. On December 17, at a special event for young writers and artists, he shouted insults at his audience but then, with characteristic inconsistency, immediately raised a toast to Solzhenitsyn, and during a break he democratically waited his turn at the urinal.[1] March 1963 saw another official meeting with the intelligentsia, another dressing down by Party leaders. Efforts to root out sedition continued at an executive session of the USSR Writers' Union in April. The June 1963 plenary session of the Central Committee of the Communist Party signaled a return to stricter policies on art and literature, as Khrushchev addressed the plenum in his usual peripatetic manner, alternating between fits of rage, jocular asides, and irrelevant recollections.

The real policy of the regime was articulated in a speech made by L. F. Ilyichev, the Party secretary for ideology. All his subordinates, top to bottom, would be expected to study it and undertake a set of almost ritual measures. In his speech, Ilyichev fulminated against the "politically immature, overly conceited and vastly overpraised young writers" who had forgotten how to "take joy in the heroic achievements of the [Soviet] people."[2] He also spoke of the need to pay special attention to educating young people in the spirit of Communism, since "amongst our youth we still see do-nothings, moral cripples, whiners" who "to encouraging nods from overseas [are attempting] to dethrone the ruling principles of our art (*ideinost* and *narodnost*), to replace them with the mindless twitter of do-nothings and dropouts."[3] (*Ideinost* and *narodnost* were Soviet propaganda buzzwords; the first meant that art must express an orthodox Marxist outlook, and the second meant that it be rooted in national culture and be understandable to the masses.) At the beginning of his speech Ilyichev chided his audience, saying that "here we are not talking about a choice: 'if I want to work, I will; if I don't, I won't.' Our life and its laws permit no such choice."[4] And indeed, while the Soviet Constitution stipulated nothing more than a very vague *right* to work, the executive order of February 4, 1961, "on combating parasitism" authorized the police to monitor all able-bodied Soviet citizens to make sure they had a regular place of employment.

PERSECUTION IN LENINGRAD

The rules governing Soviet ideological campaigns dictated that whatever happened in Moscow had to happen everywhere else. That is, if young writers and artists in Moscow were given an official whack over the head, young writers in Kiev, Minsk, Tbilisi, and, of course, Leningrad could expect the same. Leningrad security agencies and the Leningrad Writers' Union were ready to provide long lists of the usual suspects. Throughout 1963 and 1964 those suspects were vilified both in the Leningrad press and at specially organized meetings for what in bureaucratese were called the "artistic intelligentsia." Some of the young writers had never published a word; at most, they had given readings in private literary circles or among friends.

In Moscow, the popular and well-established poets Evgeniy Evtushenko and Andrey Voznesensky fell victim to the campaign, and their Leningrad counterparts, Viktor Sosnora and Aleksandr Kushner, equally talented and equally well-known within Russia, might have been expected to bear the brunt of the next attack. But while neither Sosnora nor Kushner had an easy time of it, the chief victim of the inquisition was their younger colleague Iosif Brodsky—whose published work amounted to a handful of translations plus one poem for a children's magazine.

Brodsky had been under surveillance for about three years. Still, he was only one of many rebellious young writers and hardly the most odious among them. Other "unofficial" poets and writers would have fit the role of official scapegoat just as well, perhaps better, because after Khrushchev's tantrum at the Manège the key symptom of ideological rot was officially defined as a tendency toward "formalism" (by which authorities meant any innovation, any deviation from the canons of socialist realism). Brodsky's style was relatively conservative. The majority of young poets—the philologists, for example—were much bolder in their experiments with form.

However, in 1963, the Leningrad KGB and its close ally the Leningrad regional Komsomol committee, noticed that their onetime "person of interest" in the case against Umansky and Shakhmatov was becoming increasingly popular among the city's youth. On January 27, 1963, *Smena* published a speech made by Kim Ivanov, secretary of the Leningrad regional Komsomol committee on industry. This ambitious Komsomolets, who would later become head of the Leningrad KGB, criticized the Writers' Union for failing to properly mentor the coming generation of writers:

"This is precisely why we see so many so-called unrecognized poets like Brodsky floating around the city, reading their decadent and formalist works to young audiences. . . . The Writers' Union distances itself from these young people who consider themselves 'misunderstood geniuses'; it should instead educate them by refuting all that is forced and fanciful in the work of those who are to some degree already famous."[5] It is interesting that Ivanov includes Brodsky in his list of "famous" people. It is also interesting that in the spring of 1963 it was still assumed that Brodsky could be "reeducated."

Later, Leningrad intellectual circles would embrace a sort of sociopsychological explanation for the choice of Brodsky as scapegoat. This version held that however apolitical Brodsky's verse might have been, the "collective unconscious" of the Soviet state sensed danger in the very degree of spiritual freedom that he introduced to his readers. His poems "described a level of spiritual existence unattainable for far too many" of them; his poems satisfied "a longing for the true scope of [human] existence."[6]

There is perhaps a more prosaic explanation, which comes down to chance and circumstance.

The smear campaign against Brodsky began with a virtual nobody named Yakov Lerner.[7] Poorly educated, thwarted in his pursuit of a Party career in the 1940s because he was a Jew, Lerner apparently saw the ideological confusion of the Khrushchev years as an opportunity to advance himself. In 1956 he was working in the modest capacity of head of maintenance at the Leningrad Institute of Technology. That October, a student group that included Rein, Naiman, and Bobyshev posted a news billboard (*stengazeta*) entitled "Kultura," that featured articles on what was new in Western European art and literature. This was not a political act in itself, but it happened to coincide with uprisings in Poland and a revolution in Hungary. In both countries students had spearheaded these protests against the Communist regime, and as the Soviets went about crushing mutinies abroad, they also began clamping down at home. Lerner took it upon himself to warn the authorities about the "hotbed of sedition" at the Institute of Technology and wrote an exposé for the institute's newsletter. An investigation followed, and all those who had worked on "Kultura" were punished. Rein was forced to transfer to a less prestigious school.

Meanwhile community patrols (*druzhiny*) were being established throughout the country to help the police maintain public order. For the most part, this was merely a formal exercise. Small squads of university students and young workers, blue- and white-collar alike, would don red armbands and rove the streets, working off a scheduled number of community-service hours. On occasion they might help the police haul in drunks.

But some *druzhina* squads were more aggressive than others, and in 1963 one of these was headed by Yakov Lerner. By now he was no longer working at the Institute of Technology; he had a new job at Giproshakht, the State Institute of Mining and Engineering, located on Griboedov Canal just off Nevsky Prospekt. Years later, during perestroika, the one-time Dzerzhinsky district prosecutor A. S. Kostakov, the very man who on December 12, 1963, had demanded that Brodsky be turned over to a Writers' Union "community court," told journalists that the mores of the time dictated that the community more or less took precedence over the law. That is, Lerner's patrol and Lerner himself had absolutely free run; they could walk straight into the *raikom* (the district Party offices), into Party secretary Kosareva's office itself. They had all sorts of official authorizations and I.D.'s: "community assistant" to the prosecutor's office, to the detective unit, to whatever.

Members of Lerner's squad were themselves occasionally brought up on criminal charges. Some were nothing more than common thugs. But they had the backing of the raikom, and so Lerner and his team flourished.[8]

The district that Lerner and his "ops unit" patrolled was in the very heart of the city, which gave him a fine platform from which to display both his organizational abilities and his devotion to the Party. The 1963 campaign against the intelligentsia presented him with a new opportunity to draw attention to himself—this time from officials in very high places.

In the Central Committee archives there is a letter from Lerner to Nikita Khrushchev, dated March 11, 1963, written immediately after the publication of the report on Khrushchev's March meeting with writers and artists. The gist of this fawning and not particularly literate missive is what a wonderful leader Khrushchev is. Lerner thanks Khrushchev for ensuring that in the Soviet Union there is no anti-Semitism, nor can there be; he complains of persecution by other Jews because he (Lerner) has a Russian wife, the granddaughter of a Russian Orthodox priest; he writes in great detail about his druzhina unit.[9]

Probably Lerner's primary goal was simply to attract attention. He knew that just dragging bums to the drunk tank and hauling rowdies to the holding cells of the local police station would hardly advance his political career. But exposing an "alien element" within Soviet society and a "corrupt influence" on Soviet youth most certainly would. Brodsky was friendly with Rein, Naiman, and Bobyshev, all of whom Lerner remembered from 1956. Brodsky was a Jew; Lerner was striving to distance himself from his Jewish heritage. Brodsky did not have a full-time job and thus could be accused of "parasitism." (This is an important detail, because by law neither the police nor the druzhina had any jurisdiction over "enemies of the people." However, both the police and the druzhina were fully authorized to deal with "parasites.") Finally, Brodsky was officially registered in the same district where Lerner worked cheek by jowl with the police.

At any rate, Lerner opened his own dossier on Brodsky. This file, which he later showed to the journalist O. G. Chaykovskaya, contains not only Lerner's "surveillance log" but also a copy of a 1956 diary kept by the sixteen-year-old Brodsky, which must have been either stolen outright or obtained through Lerner's contacts in the KGB.[10]

On October 21, 1963, Lerner telephoned Brodsky and, in his capacity as head of the local druzhina, asked the young man to stop in for a chat. As Brodsky understood it, the goal of this fifteen-minute talk was to determine whether or not he had a permanent job.[11] He did not, and Lerner's conclusion was that Brodsky could and should be charged in criminal court as a parasite on society.

On November 29, an article entitled "A Literary Drone" appeared in the newspaper *Evening Leningrad* under Lerner's byline and that of two staff reporters, M. Medvedev and A. Ionin.[12] The piece was written in the same crass style as "The Parasites Crawl Up Parnassus," the article attacking Aleksandr Ginzburg and the contributors to *Sintaksis*.

Lerner and his coauthors repeat their favorite phrase at least four times: Brodsky is "a pygmy, smugly crawling up Parnassus"; "he doesn't care how he crawls up Parnassus"; "he cannot give up the idea of some Parnassus that he aims to climb by any and all dirty means." The authors even impugn him for wanting "to crawl up Parnassus all on his own," as if a group expedition were somehow more acceptable.[13]

Lerner was never very accurate in his denunciations. He didn't bother to check facts, and in this particular article virtually every "fact" about Brodsky is wrong. Lerner adds three years to Brodsky's actual age. He names friends that Brodsky never had. Of the three quotations offered to illustrate the young poet's cynicism, decadence, and general incoherence, only one is actually Brodsky's. The other two are taken from poems by Dmitriy Bobyshev (which Bobyshev himself explained in a statement to the Writers' Union immediately after Lerner's article was published). The one genuine quotation from Brodsky is a mangled version of six lines of "Procession"; Lerner leaves out the first half of each line, making the excerpt indeed incomprehensible.

The article also includes a retelling of the Samarkand "hijack plot" and the encounter with Melvin Belli, whose surname the KGB never quite got straight (Beil? Bialy? Melvin?):

> Beil invited [Brodsky and Shakhmatov] to his hotel room. They talked.
>
> "I've got a manuscript that can't be published here," said Brodsky. "Want to take a look?"
>
> "I'd be happy to," answered Melvin, and after leafing through it, he declared, "Great, we can publish it over there. What name should we use?"
>
> "Anything—just not the author's real one."
>
> "Fine. We'll give him a real American name. John Smith."[14]

Laughable as this idiotic scene might have seemed even to the undemanding readers of contemporary Soviet spy novels, it held an ominous warning. It showed that Lerner had the backing of the Leningrad KGB, because had he not, transcripts and records of the Umansky case would have never appeared in print. Equally threatening was the article's title. In the official jargon of the time, "drone" was a synonym for "parasite." More often than not, the objects of such satirical attacks (other "drones" and "parasites") were expelled from college or kicked out of the Komsomol. Brodsky could not be formally expelled from anything, because he'd never joined.

But he could be charged with "parasitism." The column ended with an accusation: "He persists in leading his parasitic way of life. In the last four years this healthy twenty-six-year-old has made absolutely no contribution to society."[15] A parasite who writes formalist and decadent verse, who grovels to the West—here we have the perfect embodiment of the sort of renegade Ilyichev described in his report to the June plenum of the Central Committee.[16]

Still, why choose this particular charge? Why Brodsky? The historian V. Kozlov explains it this way: "[In] the mid-1960s, both before and after Khrushchev's ouster, the search was on for the most effective means of exerting pressure on dissenters while still observing the official rules of the game that was Soviet law. . . . The Brodsky case was one of a number of experiments by local authorities who might dislike some person or his views, convictions, or ideas, but whom they could not try for those convictions and ideas under Soviet law . . . because [the person] was not disseminating them. . . . Hence, . . . an experiment—charge Brodsky with parasitism."[17]

Meanwhile, Lerner was doing his best to make sure the experiment was a successful one. But even by the letter of Soviet law Brodsky was no parasite. Changing jobs was discouraged but not illegal. The "Decree on Combating Parasitism" was aimed not at job hoppers like Brodsky but at small-time hustlers, prostitutes, beggars, thugs, drunks—people who had no official place of work and no official source of income. So a case had to be made that since Brodsky's return from the Kazakhstan expedition in September 1962, he had not had work of any kind.

But this was the very time he began earning a living from his writing. The November 1962 issue of *Kostyor* (Campfire), a children's magazine, included a long poem entitled "The Ballad of the Little Tugboat," and that fall, the Moscow publishing house Khudozhestvennaya literatura (Art Literature) released an anthology of Cuban poetry with one of his translations. Two more of his translations came out in 1963 as part of a collection of Yugoslav poets, and Brodsky already had contracts for several others.

Lerner made a special trip to the editorial offices of Khudozhestvennaya literatura in Moscow. His tales of Brodsky's anti-Soviet reputation frightened the respectable publisher into canceling all contracts. Brodsky's initial reaction was rather naive—he wrote the newspaper a detailed, point-by-point rebuttal of all the lies and inaccuracies contained in the article.[18] The newspaper did not respond.

The next attempt to seek justice, this time in the company of Boris Vakhtin, a highly respected China scholar and son of the renowned fiction writer Vera Panova, also came to naught. Brodsky and Vakhtin had gone to district Party secretary Nina Kosareva's office to appeal to her directly. Kosareva, who was also responsible for supervising the Writers' Union, plus a number of theaters and other arts institutions, generally liked to play the liberal. But by this time the decision to make an example of Brodsky had already been taken.[19] Never adept at social or ideological mimicry, Brodsky managed to further convince Party secretary Kosareva that he was ideologically rotten to the core. When she asked him why he had not pursued a higher education, he answered bluntly: "I can't attend university because I'd have to take dialectical materialism, and that's not a real subject. I was born to create things; I can't do physical labor. It makes no difference to me whether there is or there is not a Party—for me there's only good or evil."[20] This, taken from Kosareva's brief report on the conversation, is not a verbatim quotation. But it sounds very much like Brodsky.

Because the case had to do with a poet, the Leningrad branch of the Writers' Union had to be involved. At the time, it was headed by Aleksandr Andreevich Prokofyev (1900–1971), a not-untalented poet who had worked for the security services in the 1920s and had been a loyal Party soldier ever since. Fitful and capricious (much like Khrushchev, whom he actually resembled physically), he ruled over his organization with the help of a staff composed of the most pitiful and inept writers to be found in the city—the aged poet Ilya Avramenko, the prose writer Petr Kapitsa, and a coterie of younger hopefuls. But for all Prokofyev's general eagerness to serve the Party, it took a particularly dirty trick to raise his ire against Brodsky. Someone on his staff slipped him a crude epigram (one of many circulating at the time) rhyming the chairman's nickname (*Prokopa*) with a certain part of the human anatomy (*zhopa*). In other words, the chairman was an asshole. Brodsky was accused of writing it, although, according to a close friend, "Iosif never wrote a word about Aleksandr Andreevich; honestly, he never gave the man much thought."[21]

Meanwhile, on December 17, Lerner spoke at a meeting of the secretariat of the Leningrad Writers' Union. He had been directed to present a letter from the district prosecutor; this letter demanded that Brodsky be arraigned before a community court convened by the Writers' Union. Such tribunals had quasi-legal status, and hearings were conducted either at a defendant's workplace or in the city district where he or she was registered. Again, since the defendant was a young writer, it was assumed that the Writers' Union would conduct the hearing—even though Brodsky was not formally a member. Usually such hearings amounted to no more than ritual public humiliation. Occasionally, however, they led to formal charges in a real court. The Leningrad Writers' Union resolved "to express [the Union's] absolute agreement with the opinion of the prosecutor regarding the arraignment of I. Brodsky before a community court [and] to appoint Comrades N. L. Braun, V. V. Toropygin, A. P. Elyashevich, and O. N. Shestinsky to give testimony" and, "in light of anti-Soviet statements by Brodsky and those who share his views, request that the prosecutor file criminal charges against Brodsky and his 'friends.'"[22]

Why such inquisitorial zeal on the part of the Writers' Union?

Simple fear. "The secretariat of the Union had learned their craft during the Stalin years and was still living in that past. The Leningrad organization had suffered enormous casualties in the great purges."[23]

KANATCHIKOV DACHA AND "SONGS OF A HAPPY WINTER"

A community hearing was set for December 25, 1963, but by this time Brodsky had left Leningrad for Moscow, where he would bring in the New Year at Kashchenko Psychiatric Hospital, otherwise known as Kanatchikov Dacha. Friends had arranged an extended psychiatric examination there in hopes that a diagnosis of mental instability might somehow spare him a worse fate.

The plan had been worked out at a council of war attended by Brodsky, Akhmatova, and Akhmatova's good friends the Ardovs, an artistic Moscow family. A sympathetic psychiatrist helped.[24] Brodsky later wrote:

> Here in ward six,
> in this grim billet
> in this white realm of hidden faces
> night flashes white, a key,
> a head doc
>   (Non-poetic)[25]

Exhausted by months of tension and stress, Brodsky began to wonder whether he was indeed losing his mind in this "white realm of hidden faces," and very shortly after his commitment he demanded that his friends get him out of the hospital they had worked so hard to get him into in the first place. They apparently managed to come up with the necessary paperwork and diagnosis, because shortly thereafter, in a letter to the general secretary of the USSR Writers' Union, A. A. Surkov, Akhmatova wrote: "[H]asten to inform you that Iosif Brodsky has been discharged from Kanatchikov Dacha . . . with a diagnosis of schizoid personality disorder, and that the psychiatrist who saw him one month ago says that his health has worsened considerably as a result of the harassment he went through in Leningrad."[26]

Upon his release from the hospital on January 2, Brodsky learned that his lover Marina Basmanova and his onetime friend Dmitriy Bobyshev were having an affair, and he dashed back to Leningrad to confront them.[27] A week later he slit his wrists.[28] For friends and acquaintances, the ongoing campaign against Brodsky and the reprisals sure to follow were fraught with enormous political significance, but for Brodsky himself, the real, the only, tragedy lay in the loss of the woman he considered his wife. For Brodsky, 1964–1965 was the year of the betrayal, not the year of political confrontation. During both his stay at the mental hospital and the next few weeks spent running between Moscow, Leningrad, and Tarusa, dodging arrest, he continued working on a cycle he eventually named "Songs of a Happy Winter." The title was in no way ironic; these poems recalled an earlier winter, that of 1962–1963, a period of love and contentment. Even those dated January 1964 (with their terrifying biographical subtext) are marked by a sort of elegiac detachment:

> These songs of a happy winter
> take as a remembrance,
> so that we recall
> the sounds of silence,
> the place to which you, mouselike,
> scurry on quick feet,
> whatever [that place] might be called,
> however it might fit into rhyme.
>
> . . . .
>
> So now it's spring.
> Blood full in the vein:
> make a small gash,
> a sea roars through the breach.
> (*OVP;* non-poetic)

Considering the actual circumstances under which the "songs of a happy winter" were composed, they are markedly and perhaps even militantly apolitical. At that moment in Brodsky's life, any protest or complaint about fate would have meant surrendering to circumstance, allowing some existential "*absurde*" into his holiest of holies. In his later poetry he would deal directly with whatever life threw his way, but at this point he apparently felt he had to make a choice: he could reflect either on love and nature or on internal passports, writers' unions, and the Lerners of the world. The single exception to this rule was "Letters to the Wall" ("Pisma k stene"), which he never thought worth including in any of his collections. He may have thought that depicting himself as some helpless "baby" afraid of death ("Let me live, let me live, and the hell with anything else") was both ethically wrong and poetically banal. But if nothing else, this work reflects his life in early 1964: jail, hospital, attempted suicide.[29] The other works of that period, including the splendidly rhetorical "Farewell Ode" ("Proshchalnaya oda") give no hint that their author was being hounded or persecuted or felt himself doomed. In light of what we now know about the circumstances under which Brodsky finished "Songs," the slightly ironic but elegiac quality of the poems on love, the meditative quality of the poems on nature, the generally tranquil tone more characteristic of a nineteenth-century Russian or English country squire than of a man on the run from Soviet police, constitute a conscious moral stance, a struggle for inner freedom. He once told me about an episode in mid-January 1964. He was at home working at his desk, taking advantage of the quiet while his parents were out. Suddenly the police burst in and threatened that if he didn't find a job in three days, he would be sorry. "I choked out some sort of response, but in the back of my mind I kept thinking that I had to finish this poem."[30] The poem that he finished once the police had left was about a gardener high in a tree, opening his shears like a bird opening its beak: "Like a thrush, the gardener in his padded coat" (*OVP*).

ARREST AND PRELIMINARY HEARING

On the evening of February 13, just back from his latest trip to Moscow, Brodsky went out to visit a friend, the composer Sergey Slonimsky, and was arrested a few steps away from home. For the next twenty-four hours his parents had no idea where he was. When they asked at the Dzerzhinsky district police precinct office, they were told that their son was not there. In fact he was, and in solitary confinement to boot. On February 14 he had a minor cardiac episode; the ambulance was called, and he was given an injection, but he wasn't moved from his cell. One bit of moral support came from the deputy precinct commander, Anatoly Alekseev, a university classmate of Brodsky's friend and fellow poet Leonid Vinogradov. That evening, after most of the staff had gone home, Alekseev took Brodsky out of the cell, saying, "Unfortunately, this is about all I can do for you," and proceeded to feed him tea and sandwiches in his office. Sometime before this, Alekseev had gotten a call from Izrail Metter, a writer with contacts inside the Leningrad police force. Metter asked for his help. Alekseev replied that there was nothing to be done: "Vasily Sergeevich gave the order; the court will stamp it—game over."[31] The Vasily Sergeevich in question was Vasily Sergeevich Tolstikov, Communist Party secretary for the Leningrad region.

Metter describes his impressions of the February 18 hearing at the Dzerzhinsky district court:

> Never in my life will I forget that insultingly squalid courtroom or that shameful hearing. . . . Courtroom, ha! It was a shabby little place with walls painted the same color as the walls in public toilets, with scuffed wooden-plank floors that hadn't been mopped in years; it barely accommodated the three longish benches for the public and, three meters away, the judge's desk, an ordinary writing desk impossibly scarred and scratched, and a small table, set perpendicular to it like the stem of the letter T, for the defense, the prosecution, and the court recorder. . . . It plunged all of us, the defendant included, into the depths of our utter insignificance.
>
> Those few spectators allowed into the courtroom—Vigdorova, Grudinina, Dolinina, Etkind, and I—managed to fit easily onto the front bench; at the far end of it, closer to the doors, sat Iosif's father and mother. It hurt to look at them. They could not tear their eyes away from the door; it was supposed to open and let in their son. . . .
>
> What struck me was that this young man whom I finally had a chance to see and observe at close range, in circum-

> stances both cruel and unusual for him, radiated a sort of peaceful detachment—Judge Savelyeva couldn't hurt him, couldn't goad him into blowing up; he wasn't frightened by her shrieking at his every other word, . . . from time to time his face expressed dismay, when no one seemed to understand him, or when he in turn could not fathom why this odd woman seemed so unreasonably hostile; he couldn't seem to get across even what in his mind were the simplest of ideas.[32]

Judge Savelyeva's line of questioning was clearly aimed at establishing Brodsky's guilt.

JUDGE: What do you do for a living?
BRODSKY: I write poetry. I translate. I suppose that . . .
JUDGE: No "I suppose's." Stand up properly! No leaning on the wall! Look directly at the court! Answer the court properly! . . . Do you have regular work?
BRODSKY: I thought this was regular work.
JUDGE: Clarify your answer!
BRODSKY: I was writing poetry! I thought it was going to be published. I suppose that . . .
JUDGE: We are not interested in your "I suppose's." Answer [the court]: Why didn't you have a job?
BRODSKY: I did have a job. I was writing poetry.
JUDGE: That doesn't interest us. . . .[33]

The judge asked Brodsky about his temporary factory jobs, his work on geological expeditions, and his literary earnings, but the leitmotif of the examination was the judge's refusal to admit that Brodsky's writing was actually work or that Brodsky himself was a writer.

JUDGE: And what is your profession?
BRODSKY: Poet. Poet and translator.
JUDGE: And who told you you were a poet? Who assigned you that rank?
BRODSKY: No one. (*Nonconfrontational.*) Who assigned me to the human race?
JUDGE: And did you study for this?

BRODSKY: For what?
JUDGE: To become a poet? Did you try to attend a school where they train [poets] . . . where they teach . . .
BRODSKY: I don't think it comes from education.
JUDGE: From what then?
BRODSKY: I think it's . . . (*at a loss*) from God . . .[34]

Even in Soviet times, a trial presupposed an adversarial process; here the silence, the virtual absence of the prosecutor, is bizarre. Judge Savelyeva was essentially doing the work of the prosecution. This put the defense in a difficult position, forcing it to argue not with the prosecutor but with the judge herself. Brodsky was represented by Z. N. Toporova, an experienced, well known, and well respected Leningrad defense attorney. The arguments she could bring to bear against conviction on charges of parasitism were strong ones: her client was not accused of leading an antisocial life, or of being repeatedly drunk and disorderly, or of living on unearned income. Nor could he honestly be charged with refusing to work or earn a living. At the second session of the court, the following exchange took place between Brodsky and the people's prosecutor:

SOROKIN: Is it possible [for someone] to live on the money that you earn?
BRODSKY: Yes. Every day I was in jail, I signed a receipt for the forty kopecks spent on me that day. At the time I was making more than forty kopecks a day.

In fact, if we calculate Brodsky's earnings as he documented them for the court, between his last geological expedition and his arrest he made roughly one ruble a day. In those times, this was at least enough to feed oneself. So it seemed that the court was not accusing him of not working but rather of not earning enough, of living off his parents. This was hardly a crime punishable by law. Still, everyone understood perfectly well that once "Vasily Sergeevich gave the order," the Soviet courts would follow suit. So the defense strategy was to seek a lighter sentence, using the same tactic that Brodsky's Moscow friends had. The aim was to document his mental instability: after all, what can you expect from a crazy man? At the end of the first session, Brodsky's attorney moved that he be referred for a psychiatric evaluation.

PRYAZHKA

In granting the motion, the court outdid itself. The defense had asked that Brodsky be released from custody to undergo evaluation at an out-patient clinic; instead, Brodsky was confined for three weeks in the "violent" ward of the Pryazhka (Psychiatric Hospital No. 2 on the banks of the Pryazhka River). There, his treatment began immediately: he was awakened in the middle of the night, plunged into a coldwater bath, wrapped in wet sheets, and set down next to a radiator. The sheets, contracting as they dried, cut into his flesh. It's not clear why he was subjected to such torture. After all, by all accounts the police and the security agencies were not looking for information, or even for remorse or admission of mistakes (with the exception of the episode with investigator Sh. described in chapter I, but there the detective may have been acting on his own initiative). There are only two possibilities: either the hospital staff truly believed Brodsky to be mentally ill and were "treating" him so that he would be judged competent to stand trial and conviction, or this was simply the sort of sadism the entire world would later learn of from dissidents subjected to Soviet psychiatric terror.[35] This time, there were no psychiatrists sympathetic to Brodsky to be found, and the expert opinion presented to the court, while probably objective, was, in his case, disastrous: Brodsky "manifests certain psychopathic traits but does not suffer from mental illness [as such] and in terms of psychological health is fit to work."[36]

THE TRIAL

The second court session, on March 13, was clearly meant to be a show trial, for which a large hall at the district offices of the Buildings and Construction Bureau (Fontanka 22) had been hired. A placard at the entrance read, "Parasite Brodsky on Trial." When during the proceedings one of the witnesses remarked that this was a violation of the presumption of innocence, the judge had nothing to say.[37] "Relatively few of Iosif's friends or even fellow writers could get in. Two-thirds of the spectators were [construction and factory] workers brought in for a special event, and prepped accordingly."[38] The trial was to consist of three parts: examination of the defendant; witness testimony and cross-examination; and concluding statements by the prosecution and the defense.

The exchanges between Brodsky and Judge Savelyeva were just as absurd in this second session as they had been in the first. She continued to demand that Brodsky answer her question as to why he hadn't worked after leaving school.

JUDGE: Explain to the court why in those intervals [between jobs] you had no work and were in fact a parasite on society.
BRODSKY: I had work. I was doing what I'm doing right now: I was writing poetry.
JUDGE: So, you were writing your so-called poetry? And what was the use of changing jobs so often?
BRODSKY: I started working at fifteen. I was interested in a lot of things. I changed jobs because I wanted to learn as much as I could about life, about people.
JUDGE: So you think that your so-called poetry will be of some use to the people?
BRODSKY: Why do you say "so-called"?
JUDGE: "So-called" because there's no other way to describe it.[39]

This monotonous exchange was repeated throughout the trial: the judge asked why Brodsky had no work; Brodsky answered that he did.

The three witnesses for the defense—Natalya Grudinina, Efim Etkind, and Vladimir Admoni—were all members of the Writers' Union. Grudinina was a poet; Etkind and Admoni were well-known scholars and translators, professors at the Herzen Pedagogical Institute; all three were called as expert witnesses to testify to the fact that writing and translating poetry was not easy, that it was real work, that it required a particular sort of talent and specific professional skills, that Brodsky had done this work in a talented and professional manner. All three also knew Brodsky personally and on the stand spoke of him with warmth and respect.

The prosecution witnesses were a different matter. In a letter later written from exile, Brodsky asked the prosecutor general of the USSR, "How can people who have never even seen me be called 'witnesses'? WHAT did they ever witness?"[40] But Brodsky, a poet, understood the word in its literal, root meaning (*svidetel*, from *videt*, "to see"), while the ritual playing itself out in Judge Savelyeva's court assumed something else, more akin to the Christian evangelical idea of "testifying," but here, affirming one's unquestioning faith not in God Almighty but in the Soviet state and all its lesser forms (the KGB, the police, the Soviet press) and one's righteous hatred of all enemies of the state. This was reflected in the prosecution's rhetoric: the prosecutor Sorokin, one of Lerner's cohorts in the community patrols, declared that "Brodsky's defenders are crooks, parasites, lice, bugs. . . . He himself is a parasite, a lout, a crook, an ideologically corrupt human being."[41]

There were twice as many witnesses for the prosecution as there were for the defense. Only one was a writer—E. V. Voevodin, hastily dispatched by the Writers' Union. The remaining five had no literary expertise whatsoever: there was a certain Smirnov, manager of the Leningrad Officers' Club, a maintenance director from the Hermitage named Logunov, a pipefitter named Denisov, a pensioner named Nikolaev, and a Marxism-Leninism instructor named Romasheva. All six began their testimony by stating that they did not know Brodsky personally.

Strange as it might seem to emphasize *not* knowing the person about whom one was about to give testimony, there was a precedent. Five years earlier, as the campaign for "nationwide condemnation" of Boris Pasternak rolled on, the stock phrase became "I haven't actually read Pasternak's novel, but . . ." Apparently, the logic of Party scriptwriters went as follows: personal acquaintance could lead to personal antipathy, and therefore an objective assessment of the "social face" of the accused could be made only by those representing a cross-section of the Soviet working people. Hence, at Brodsky's trial, the distribution of witnesses by social status, sex, and age: a worker, a soldier, a clerk, a retiree, two "real intellectuals." Men and women, young and old. The symbolism was obvious—the people of the Dzerzhinsky district were united in their outrage. As far as we know, the authorities made no effort to recruit any of Brodsky's personal acquaintances as prosecution witnesses—not, perhaps, because such attempts would have proved fruitless (who knows?) but rather because the trial was an exercise in ritual and ideology rather than law.

Anything these witnesses knew about Brodsky had come straight from Lerner's article, the "letters to the editor" section of the *Evening Leningrad,* and, one has to assume, a preparatory session at the district Party offices. Voevodin had also been prepped by the Writers' Union; pensioner Nikolaev had supposedly seen some of Brodsky's poetry in the hands of his own good-for-nothing son. All their statements, including Voevodin's, were variations on the Lerner-Ionin-Medvedev "exposé." All the witnesses were confident, even smug. When the defense attorney asked Smirnov how he knew that it was Brodsky who had written the "antisocial poems" that had so outraged him (when, as it turned out, they'd been written by someone else), he answered, "I just know. End of question."[42] Not once did the judge challenge prosecution witnesses. Defense witnesses were often rudely interrupted and upbraided.

Defense attorney Toporova tried to shift the argument onto purely legal ground without antagonizing an already hostile judge. She was trying to prove, on the basis of documents and witnesses' testimony, that her client could not be charged under the existing decree on parasites. He might not earn much, but he did work. He was not guilty of "antisocial behavior."

Meanwhile, the prosecution was vilifying him not just because he wrote "so-called poems" instead of holding a regular job but because he had never served in the Soviet Army and because he had known Umansky and Shakhmatov. None of this was relevant to the charge at hand, which Toporova knew perfectly well. She also knew how loosely decrees like this one could be interpreted in Soviet courts, and did her best to parry the attacks, pointing out that the "competent organs," that is, the KGB, had decided against prosecuting Brodsky as an accomplice in the Shakhmatov-Umansky affair and that Brodsky had not dodged military service but had been officially exempted for health reasons.

She later recalled how "Brodsky made a wonderful statement at the end. He said, 'I'm no parasite, I'm a poet, who will bring honor and glory to his country.' The chief judge, the lay judges, and almost everyone else in the courtroom broke out in guffaws."[43]

The session lasted over five hours, ending somewhere past midnight. The verdict stunned even those supporters who had never expected an acquittal. Brodsky was sentenced to the maximum penalty allowed under the decree: "exile from the city of Leningrad for a period of 5 (five) years, to a location yet to be designated; physical labor required as a condition of the sentence."[44]

Over and above the verdict itself, the court issued a separate opinion, quite bizarre from a legal standpoint, censuring Grudinina, Etkind, and Admoni for their statements on the character of the accused and the quality of his work—that is, for the very thing they'd been called into court to provide. These three had "attempted to represent the vulgarity and ideological paucity of his verse as proof of talent and creativity, to assert that Brodsky was some sort of unrecognized genius. Such behavior on the part of Grudinina, Etkind, and Admoni testifies to their lack of ideological awareness and Communist integrity." This opinion, tagged "Report to the court on measures taken," was forwarded to the Writers' Union.[45]

SUPPORT FOR BRODSKY AND INTERNATIONAL FAME

The staunch behavior of Grudinina, Etkind, and Admoni on the witness stand and the Leningrad intelligentsia's overall support and sympathy for the defendant came as a surprise to the orchestrators of the trial. At the end of the first session, on February 18, everyone leaving the courtroom "saw an enormous number of people, young people especially, sitting in the hallways and on the stairs." Judge Savelyeva, too, was surprised: "Such a crowd! I didn't think there would be such a crowd!"[46] The Party functionaries and their KGB advisors who had planned the trial were accustomed to dealing with people who would slavishly—or at least quietly—submit to any action taken by the regime; they did not consider the fact that Stalin had been dead for ten years or the fact that they were dealing with a new generation, one that had never known mass terror. Nor did they realize that this generation might find mentors in the previous one—people who for all their horrific experiences had managed to preserve some sense of dignity and self-respect—and that together the generations would fight for freedom of thought and self-expression. In the rush to injustice, in planning the symbolic trial, the state also forgot that the response to the trial might be equally symbolic. When Judge Savelyeva exclaimed that there was "such a crowd," someone in the crowd shot back, "It's not every day you hang a poet."[47]

As word of the trial spread, twenty-three-year-old Iosif Brodsky, the author of a handful of poems only a handful of people had even read, gradually became a symbol, an archetype—the Poet misunderstood and vilified by an ignorant rabble. It was a classic ripple effect. His early defenders were people who knew and loved him, who were genuinely worried about what might happen to the boy himself (Anna Akhmatova, Mikhail Ardov, Boris Vakhtin, Yakov Gordin, Igor Efimov, Anatoly Naiman, Evgeniy Rein, plus Leningrad writers and scholars who knew him less well but recognized his gift, Grudinina and Etkind chief among them). Next came Moscow and Leningrad intellectuals who leapt to the defense less of Brodsky than of the principles involved—poetry and poets, freedom of speech, justice. A truly popular movement in support of

Brodsky arose to counter the official one against him. It was headed by two truly heroic women: Lidiya Chukovskaya (1907–1996), herself a writer and devoted friend of Anna Akhmatova, and Frida Vigdorova (1915–1965), a journalist and close friend of Chukovskaya. Both wrote letter after letter to Soviet courts and Party offices and sought support from some of the most influential people in the USSR: composer Dmitriy Shostakovich, writers Samuil Marshak, Korney Chukovsky, Konstantin Paustovsky, Aleksandr Tvardovsky, and Yury German. Even the very cautious Konstantin Fedin and Party loyalist Aleksey Surkov were recruited (the latter came to Brodsky's defense out of respect for Akhmatova). They also managed to find a valuable covert ally within the Central Committee in the person of I. S. Chernoutsan (1918–1990), chairman of the subcommittee on literature.[48]

Vigdorova's notes on the trial, recorded in the face of repeated threats by Judge Savelyeva, were to become a document of enormous significance in modern Russian political history and in Brodsky's own life. In the following months, her transcript circulated in samizdat, was published abroad, and was quoted in the Western press. Before 1964 practically no one in the West had ever heard of Brodsky; by the end of the year he was a cause célèbre, especially after complete translations of Vigdorova's transcript were published in France, in *Figaro littéraire,* and in England, in *Encounter.*

Short on detail about the bleak realities of everyday Soviet life or petty local politics, this seemed a romantic story of a young poet harassed and persecuted by malicious, dim-witted bureaucrats, and it captured the imagination of the Western intelligentsia. For those who knew the real face of totalitarianism, Brodsky's trial was simply further proof that freedom of speech was just as impossible under Khrushchev and his successors as it had been under Stalin; for many left-leaning intellectuals the trial represented the final collapse of their faith in the Soviet version of socialism. In October 1964, the French poet Charles Dobzynski (b. 1929) published a long poem entitled "Open Letter to a Soviet Judge" in the Communist journal *Action poétique.* This angry missive ("Tandis que les spoutniks volent vers les planètes / À Leningrad on accuse un poète"—"While Sputniks are flying toward planets / Leningrad prosecutes a poet") ends with

> Et au nom de la poèsie, au nom de la justice,
> Sans quoi le socialisme ne serait que lettre morte,
> Je vous récuse, camarade juge.[49]
>
> (In the name of poetry, in the name of justice,
> Without which socialism is but a dead letter,
> I demand your removal, Comrade Judge!)

An American, John Berryman, expressed the same feelings in better verse:

> . . . seldom has a judge so coarse borne herself coarsely
> and often has a poet worked so hard for so small
> but they was not prosecuted
>
> in this world . . .
>
> . . . like this young man
> who only wanted to walk beside the canals
> talking about poetry and make it.[50]

In England a radio play based on Brodsky's trial was broadcast over the BBC.

It is sometimes said that Brodsky owed his fame to his trial, not to his poetry. This is true in that sudden notoriety in the era of mass media made his story known to a worldwide audience. But other Russian writers both before and after Brodsky have found themselves in the same situation, and with the exception of Solzhenitsyn, Brodsky is the only one whose work measured up to the opportunity presented him.[51] Akhmatova was the first to understand what all these events would mean for her young friend: "What a biography they're writing for our redhead!"[52] (Her joke was based on a popular quotation from a poem by Ilya Selvinsky: "In the far corner they're busy beating someone up, / I went pale: turns out that's how it should be— / They're writing poet Esenin's biography.")

Berryman's image of a young man with his head in the clouds popped up in other literary works as well. Brodsky was the obvious prototype for Gleb Golovanov, the naive poet and eccentric unjustly accused of parasitism in Georgy Berezko's 1967 novel *Unusual Muscovites*. The censors were apparently not expecting any dirty tricks from this respectable Soviet author, and the novel was serialized in *Moskva*, then came out the same year in book form. In London another novel with a plot loosely based on Brodsky's trial was published in 1981—Feliks Roziner's *A Certain Finkelmayer.* Like Metter's trial notes, all these accounts, whether fictional, journalistic, or verbal, paint Brodsky as an idealistic dreamer with no real notion of the real world.

But the hero of this collectively produced myth had little in common with the real Iosif Brodsky, who for all his scant twenty-three years had already seen a good deal of the real world and had few illusions about how it worked.[53] That is, it wasn't that he didn't understand what was happening, but that he understood it all too well: the cruel absurdity of the whole process, the inevitability of conflict with the Soviet state even though he had never written any poetry condemning it—a fact that his supporters pointed out time and time again. The country he lived in was ruled by ideology and was much closer to Plato's totalitarian utopia than it was to Hobbes's pragmatic Leviathan state. There is a famous passage in Book X of Plato's *Republic* about the destabilizing influence of poets (by definition unstable) and the need to expel them from any ideal state because they destroy the "rational part of the soul." In 1977, Brodsky would write "Plato Elaborated," in which a crowd "boiling around me, would bellow / poking me with their work-roughened forefingers, 'Outsider!'" Vigdorova's transcripts include comments by spectators in the courtroom: "Writers! Leeches! Who needs them! Anybody can translate a poem!"[54]

Brodsky was deeply grateful to Frida Vigdorova for her heroic efforts on his behalf. Her photograph hung on the wall over his desk for many years, first in Russia, then in America. She died of cancer a year after his trial, and the untimely death of this remarkable woman who had fought to save the real Brodsky added even more drama to the romantic legend of the young poet.

PRISON

In the courtroom, Brodsky himself was hardly thinking about world fame. Later he said that he was recalling a tenet of Zen Buddhism—if you want to get rid of an unpleasant thought, give it a name, and repeat it over and over again. The word that sounded most often in the courtroom was "brodsky," so he focused on "brodsky," and eventually the word and everything the speakers in the courtroom associated with it ceased to have anything to do with him. However, he also recalled how touched he was by the testimony of defense witnesses "[b]ecause they were saying such positive things about me. And, to tell the truth, I'd never heard anything positive said about me in my whole life."[55] In general, though, Brodsky's recollections of the trial and his emotions during it stand in some contrast to the recollections of many of his defenders and supporters.

At that time, the simple act of walking into a courtroom packed with snitches and members of community patrols was an act of heroism. Taking on the system itself—testifying, circulating petitions calling for the defense of a victim of a kangaroo court—was an even greater one.[56] Brodsky's own reaction to what was happening was one of simple disgust. It was not just the arbitrariness of the proceeding but the lie that was inevitably necessary if he wanted to defend himself. Lerner and his KGB backers had concocted an enormous lie about Brodsky, and the only way for him to protect himself was to be less than honest in return. His lawyer knew perfectly well that the decree of May 4, 1961, was unlawful and unconstitutional even by Soviet standards, but was forced to build a defense based on the notion that this just and excellent law was simply not applicable to her client. Given the choice, his three witnesses, experienced writers, scholars, translators, would probably have simply said that it was wrong to bring these charges against someone who was neither a thief nor a hooligan, who wanted to write poetry instead of working just for a stamp in his passport. Instead, they had to assert that Brodsky's handful of published translations, including ones that were merely ordinary and workmanlike, constituted a major and difficult achievement. And finally Brodsky himself, who had no time for Marxism, who had no illusions about the Soviet system, had to force himself to say, "Building Communism isn't just working a machine or plowing the earth. It also involves the work of the mind, which—" At this point Judge Savelyeva barked at him: "Cut the lofty phrases."[57]

He might even have welcomed the judge's interruption. What for most of his contemporaries was a meaningless convention was for him the worst sort of hypocrisy. By nature intensely sincere and always self-critical, he (or maybe his Zen Buddhist alter ego, brodsky) was caught between the big lie and a few small ones. This is what he had in mind when he later wrote about "learning to flirt with the Law" ("A Speech about Spilt Milk," *KPE*).

But aside from the one broken-off sentence about poetry as a way of building Communism, there is no evidence that Brodsky ever "flirted with the Law." Apparently, for him that one time was enough. He didn't like many of the memoirs of his trial. He objected to newspaper accounts portraying him as a victim of the regime. He wanted to be seen as a poet, not a victim.

As far as we know, Brodsky wrote nothing during his stay at Pryazhka. But between his arrest on February 13 and his transfer there on February 18 he wrote every day. Four short poems under the general title of "Instructions to a Prisoner" are dated February 14, 15, 16, and 17.[58] The one written on the fifteenth was an eight-line poem dedicated to Akhmatova on her name day (which is also Candlemas, *Sretenie,* in the Russian Orthodox calendar); it is a small landscape with allegorical references to the aging poet. The other three are direct reflections of Brodsky's prison experience: the cold in his cell, the blinding light from the single bulb, the lack of sleep, the pacing. At the end of the fourth poem there is a surprising comparison between the dire situation in which Brodsky finds himself and the eleventh labor of Hercules, in which the Greek hero must travel to the ends of the earth to find the golden apples of the Hesperides. The same contrast between the humiliating physical unfreedom of the jailed poet and the infinitely unlimited space of his cultural imagination is even more striking in two six-line stanzas Brodsky wrote on his twenty-fifth birthday, while in Konosha prison. He had been jailed as punishment for being late coming back from a furlough to Leningrad.

Night. Cell. Bulb
screwing straight into my eye.
Guard slurping tea,
me feeling like the garbage urn
where all life dumps its shit,
where shitheads spit.

A lyre of barbed wire
looms just beyond the outhouse.
The swamp sucks in the slope.
The sentry, set against the sky,
looks a lot like Phoebus.
Apollo! How'd you end up here?
(*Uncollected;* non-poetic)

This naturalistic description of the cell and the view of the latrine across a prison yard enclosed by barbed wire includes both obscenity and criminal slang (*blatnaya fenya*); this throws the allusion to Phoebus Apollo into stark relief. The author, with his usual attention to detail, examines his prison cell and himself, the prisoner in it. The speaker is outside the cell, "out" in general—an absolutely free entity. Something important is happening in these unassuming prison sketches; Brodsky's poetic philosophy is being born. Suffering is taken as a term of human existence; the world is taken as is. The proximity of the verb "screws" to the name of the god Phoebus Apollo is not an attempt to shock; these two stylistic poles seem to come together naturally in this text, which neither judges nor complains but simply records. Brodsky's prison poems are remarkable in their emotional restraint, in the lack of the plaintiveness or self-pity common to the Russian prison lyric. This is a matter of principle. Fifteen years later, Brodsky would write a poem summing up this forty years of life on this earth, a recollection of his prison time ("I have braved, for want of wild beasts, steel cages, / carved my term and nickname on bunks and rafters"). He underscores the conscious act of taking suffering upon himself ("I've admitted the sentries' steel eye into my wet and foul / dreams") and the conscious choice to show no inner weakness ("Granted my lungs all sounds except the howl").

In 1995, in an essay entitled "The Writer in Prison" written as a foreword to an anthology of works by writers who had been imprisoned, Brodsky summed up his prison experience. This was the last essay he ever wrote. "In the popular mind, prison is the unknown and thus enjoys a close proximity to death, which is the ultimate in the unknown and in the deprivation of freedom. Initially at least, solitary can be compared to a coffin without much hesitation. Allusions to the nether world in a discourse on prisons are commonplace in any vernacular—unless such discourse is simply taboo. For from the vantage of a standard human reality, prison is indeed an afterlife, structured as intricately and implacably as any ecclesiastical version of the kingdom of death, and by and large rich in gray hues."[59]

After his sentencing, Brodsky disappeared for a month. His friends and relatives had no idea where he was. As it turned out, he was first taken to Kresty, then transported to Arkhangelsk in a prison boxcar—a Stolypin. One encounter during that prisoner transfer would determine

Brodsky's later skepticism about the virtues of the newly born Russian dissident movement.

> This was, you might say, a literal hell on wheels: Fyodor Mikhailovich Dostoevsky, Dante. We're not let out to relieve ourselves, people in the upper bunks piss wherever, and it all runs down. There's no air. Mostly it's hard-timers—people serving out not their first, not their second, not their third, but maybe their sixteenth sentence. And here across from me in the car is an old man—. . . calloused hands, stubbled chin. He'd snatched some paltry bag of grain from his collective-farm barn and gotten six years for it. He was old. And it was absolutely clear that he wouldn't live out his sentence. He would die either in transit or in jail. And not one "intellectual"—Russian or Western—would ever lift a hand to save him. Ever! For the simple fact that no one would ever know he'd existed! This was before Sinyavsky and Daniel. But the human rights movement was in motion—and no one ever said a word in defense of this old man—not the BBC, not the Voice of America. Nobody. . . . All those young [dissidents who were arrested] knew what they were doing, what they were after. Maybe they were really after some sort of social change. Or maybe they just wanted to feel good about themselves. . . . [T]hey always had some audience, some friends, some pals in Moscow. But this old man had no audience. Maybe he had a wife, sons. But neither his wife nor his sons would ever say, "You were right to steal that grain—we had nothing to eat. . . ." And when you see something like that, all those nice words about human rights sound a little different.[60]

And in fact probably none of Brodsky's supporters, East or West, would have taken on his fellow prisoner's case with as much zeal as they did Brodsky's, even had they known the old man's story. One of the slogans of the Soviet dissident movement was "Obey your own laws!" and the theft of a sack of grain was a crime, no matter what the country.

Akhmatova showed profound understanding of Brodsky's attitude toward his exile when she recalled Dostoevsky's *The House of the Dead*. Brodsky's moral intuition went deeper than demands for political rights.

It was not that Brodsky was rejecting democracy or the rule of law; he was not, and he hated the regime that had distorted and corrupted those ideas. But in that Stolypin car there were no human rights activists to meet with an old peasant who had stolen one sack of grain. There was just Iosif Brodsky, who came away with an acute sense of the inequity between his situation and that of the old man, and perhaps with a sense of guilt.

Brodsky's trial has been called Kafkaesque—illogical, absurd, nightmarish. But for Brodsky (and perhaps Akhmatova was the only one who understood this) it was Kafkaesque in a different way. Kafka's *The Trial* not only has to do with someone being accused and convicted without even knowing the charge; it also has to do with the sense of guilt aroused by even being charged in the first place. This general human tendency toward existential guilt, which is not necessarily tied to any Judeo-Christian notion of original sin, was ever present in Brodsky's poetry and in his intellectual life. He liked to call this "his Calvinism," but John Calvin's merciless doctrines of guilt and damnation have little to do with Brodsky's poetry. In Brodsky's verse, guilt and forgiveness are always intertwined. As Akhmatova once wrote, "You do not know just *what* you've been forgiven." For the rest of his life, Brodsky treasured these words like a talisman.[61]

CHAPTER FIVE

> . . . and to my crusted boots cling brown
> stubborn clods of native earth.
>
> —"Autumn in Norenskaya"

ANNUS MIRABILIS, 1964–1965: EXILE TO NORENSKAYA

IN MID-APRIL Brodsky was released from the transit prison in Arkhangelsk to his place of exile in Konosha district, Arkhangelsk region. The transit prison with its abusive guards was a genuine ordeal; life in exile turned out to be less hard. Meanwhile, Western journalists describing Brodsky's lot talked of the "Gulag" and "Arctic labor camps"—which in the minds of readers foggy on Russian geography and the realities of Soviet life called up visions of permanent winter and ragged convicts in shackles.[1]

And so the 2003 Nobel laureate J. M. Coetzee, in his autobiographical novel, *Youth,* describes how a young poet in London, Coetzee's earlier self, reacts to the news. He speaks entirely in the third person.

> There is a talk on the [BBC] "Poets and Poetry" series about a Russian named Joseph Brodsky. Accused of being a social parasite, Joseph Brodsky has been sentenced to five years of hard labour in a camp on the Archangel peninsula in the frozen north. The sentence is still running. Even as he sits in his warm room in London, sipping his coffee, nibbling his dessert of raisins and nuts, there is a man of his own age, a poet like himself, sawing logs all day, nursing frostbitten fingers, patching his boots with rags, living on fish heads and cabbage soup.[2]

> "As dark as the inside of a needle," writes Brodsky in one of his poems. He cannot get the line out of his mind. If he concentrated, truly concentrated, night after night, by sheer attention, the blessing of inspiration might descend upon him, he might be able to come up with something to match it. For he has it in him, he knows, his imagination of the same colour as Brodsky's. But how to get word through to Archangel afterwards? "On the basis of the poems he has heard on the radio and nothing else, he knows Brodsky, knows him through and through. That is what poetry is capable of. Poetry is truth. But of him in London Brodsky can know nothing. How to tell the frozen man he is with him, by his side day by day?"[3]

Exile to a remote village was hardly an idyll. Brodsky was homesick, and at times he felt utterly isolated and abandoned. But later he would say this was "one of the best times of my life. There were some just as good, but maybe none better."[4] Konosha was a local railroad hub, only a day away from Leningrad by train. It lay in the southwestern part of Arkhangelsk region, roughly a hundred kilometers north of Cherepovets, where Iosif had lived as a small child. The climate was more or less the same as Leningrad's.

Exiles were expected to find their own jobs. Brodsky managed to set himself up at the Danilovsky State Farm (*sovkhoz*), where one of his many jobs was to work the fields:

> A. Burov, tractor driver, and I,
> agricultural laborer Brodsky,
> we were planting winter wheat—six hecs.
> I contemplated woodlands
> and a sky with contrails,
> my boot on the lever.
>
> Seeds turned and bristled underneath the harrow,
> the motor's roar filled all the space around.
> Between the clouds the pilot scrawled his signature.
> Face down to the field, back set against the motion,
> I sat atop the seeder like an ornament,
> a Mozart, powdered in fine grit.
> (*Uncollected;* non-poetic)[5]

In other poems he talks of working as a cooper ("The wheelwright died, the cooper," *Uncollected*), a roofer, a cart driver ("Bad Roads," *OVP*); from his personal recollections we know that he also herded cows and split wood. One memoirist mentions that Brodsky also worked as a part-time portrait photographer for the village photo studio.[6]

Exiles were also expected to find their own lodging, and Brodsky found his in the village of Norenskaya: "There were thirty-six, forty cottages there, but only about fourteen had anyone living in them. For the most part it was old people, children—the rest of the village, anyone young enough to have any sort of energy or ability to work—had left the place because it was terribly poor, and utterly hopeless."[7] By the 1960s, these old villagers were the last generation to have lived a traditional way of life; they had grown up before the collectivization of the 1930s and its disastrous aftermath and treated the young Brodsky much the way country people might have treated a Russian writer in exile a hundred years before—with respect and courtesy. They addressed him by his name and patronymic: Iosif Aleksandrovich. Still, day-to-day life was hard: he had to split his own wood, haul water from a well, read and write by candlelight. A. Babyonyshev (Maksudov) writes:

> [I] made my way without any particular trouble or inquiries to a little house on the very edge of the village of Norenskaya. It was square, the sort of notched hut built in Russia time out of mind, logs 3.5 or 4 meters long, which came out to roughly 12–13 square meters of space. A tiny window, the kind that used to be done in isinglass, also typically northern. . . . Here I also learned a new way to fight bedbugs: the walls, the ceiling, and even part of the floor were plastered tight with old newspapers. . . . On one wall there was a pantry in a sort of log alcove, with wide board shelves stacked with canned goods, packets with various labels—a stock of groceries laid up through the efforts of various visitors. . . . There was no furniture, in the city sense of the word. To the left of the window stood a rough desk made of boards, on it a kerosene lamp, a typewriter, and a baroque-style inkwell, which Iosif proudly informed me was a gift from Akhmatova. Over the desk was a bookshelf; on the top shelf stood an open book of Giotto repro-

> ductions. A low bunk with a straw mattress, a wooden stand with a water bucket—this was the extent of the decor. The impression, though, was very nice. Real, private, personal space. For our generation this was an unthinkable luxury. Of course, there was no gas, no plumbing, no electricity, no heated bathroom—none of those wonderful twentieth-century inventions. It lacked even that convenience dreamt up by prudish city folk—an outhouse. But there were four walls, a roof, and a door to close against the world, a place to think, to write and be alone. Brodsky's generation, born and raised in tightly packed communal apartments, knew the longing for a place of one's own. Iosif proudly showed off his domain.[8]

The author of these memoirs had been dispatched to Norenskaya by Vigdorova and Chukovskaya to deliver a typewriter, books, and food. Brodsky's friends and relatives visited him ten times during his eighteen months of exile; Brodsky was given leave to visit Leningrad three times.

BRODSKY AND BASMANOVA

While Brodsky may have remembered his Arkhangelsk exile as one of the happiest times in his life, his real life in Norenskaya was neither tranquil nor carefree. His movements were restricted; he felt trapped, especially because of his separation from Marina Basmanova. She came to Norenskaya to visit him, but her brief stay ended badly; just as she was leaving, Bobyshev arrived, and there was an ugly scene. Basmanova and Bobyshev left together; Brodsky was left alone, abandoned, and jealous.[9] Almost half the poems Brodsky wrote in exile in 1964 (twenty-four altogether, finished and unfinished alike) are dedicated to M.B. or devoted to the theme of parting and separation. Only one of them, "Krylov Elaborated," describes a bucolic scene—two lovers out on a stroll. The following year one-third of his poems would focus on love and loss. In 1965 he wrote "Felix," a poem in which he caricatures his rival, depicting him as an infantile erotomaniac. Brodsky showed the poem to no one; it became known within a very small circle only after Vladimir Maramzin's 1970s samizdat edition of Brodsky's work appeared. Even his release from exile, a triumphal moment long awaited by all those who had fought to free him, paled before this latest chapter in his tangled history with Basmanova. In September

1965, on furlough in Leningrad, he learned that she was in Moscow, and on the 11th he was about to make a desperate attempt to go there to find her. Doing so would have been a serious violation of the conditions of his leave; if caught, he would be rearrested and his term of exile extended. The danger was especially great because the same day Brodsky realized that he was being followed. He and his friend Igor Efimov had to resort to a variety of ruses to shake off the Leningrad KGB tail. And in the end, Efimov, who had assessed the situation far more soberly than had his frantic friend, had to trick Brodsky out of going to Moscow.[10]

ANGLO-AMERICAN POETRY

While Aleksandr Solzhenitsyn was a rather harsh critic of Brodsky, he praised the "life-giving influence of the earth, of all that sprouts and grows, of horses and hard country work" that infuses the Norenskaya poems. "Even through this flood of stunned complaints, the breath of the earth, the Russian village, nature, the seeds of a new understanding begin to sprout: 'In the country God lives everywhere / not just in icon corners, like the scoffers say.'"[11] Solzhenitsyn is only half right. Nature and the cycle of days and seasons that make up country life had been a constant feature in Brodsky's poetry since at least 1962. By 1964–1965 they were encroaching on some of his earlier bookish and city motifs. There were a number of reasons why: he was living outside a city; he was reading Baratynsky's elegies; he was reading Robert Frost for the first time. Judging by certain changes in Brodsky's poetics, Pasternak's late verse may have also been an influence.

One thing, or perhaps the main thing, that Brodsky did during exile was to think through the basics of his art. He laid these out very simply in a letter to Yakov Gordin dated June 13, 1965. He states two basic propositions. The first has to do with the psychology of creativity; the second, which Brodsky calls "practical," has to do with the principles of constructing a poetic text, a poem. Writers must follow their intuition, wherever it might lead them; they must stand independent of rules, norms, established authorities, and hypothetical readers. "Don't look at yourself in comparison to others—stand apart. Stand apart and let yourself do anything and everything. If you're angry, don't hide it, even if it comes out as crude; if you're feeling cheerful—same thing, banal or no. Remember that your life is *your* life. Nobody's rules, however high-minded, are your law. They're not *your* rules. At best they're something *like* yours. Be independent. Independence is the best quality in any language. So what if that leads you to defeat (stupid word)—it's only your own defeat. You keep your own score, because otherwise you have to keep score with lord knows who."[12]

The recipient of this letter, five years older than Brodsky, was wise enough not to be offended by all the imperatives and directives. It was obvious that the younger poet was merely sharing a set of rules he'd worked out for himself. His requirements for poetry were just as categorical:

> Poetry is structure. Not subject, not theme—structure. These are very different things. . . . You have to build a structure. Let's say, for example, you're writing about a tree. You start by describing everything you see, from the ground up, moving up to the top of the tree as you describe. There you have it, the magnitude of the whole thing. You have to get used to seeing the whole picture. . . . There are no parts without a whole. The parts are the last thing you should think about. Rhyme—last. Metaphor—last. Meter's there from the start, like it nor not—thank God for that at least. Or take another structural device—a break. Say you're singing the praises of some girl. You sing, sing, and then in the very same meter you write a few lines about something else. And don't explain, no. . . . But it has to be done subtly, so that you don't switch to another song. So you've got the girl, the girl, the girl, thirty lines for the girl and her outfit, and then five or six about what one of her little ribbons reminds you of. Structure, not theme. For the reader, the theme isn't the girl, it's "what's going on in his [the poet's] heart and soul." . . . Don't connect stanzas by logic; instead, track the movement of the soul—even if no one follows. . . . The main thing—and again here's that same dramatic principle—is structure. I mean, metaphor itself is a composition in miniature. I admit that sometimes I think I'm more an Ostrovsky [nineteenth-century Russian playwright] than a Byron. (Sometimes I think I'm a Shakespeare.) Life doesn't tell us "what." It tells us what happens next. And what came before. That's the first principle. Then, later, the "what" becomes clear.[13]

Lyric as dramaturgy, structure as strategy—this is what underlies the semantic poetics shared by Mandelstam, Akhmatova, and Pasternak.[14] In Brodsky's schematized example, the lines that successively describe root, trunk, and branch embody the implicit theme of the poem—the upward, skyward growth of a living organism. In the other example, the contrast between the description of the girl herself and the associations called up by her ribbon provides a brief snapshot of the speaker's mind ("what's going on in his heart and soul").

Brodsky went into exile one poet and came back two years later a very different one. The change was not instant, but it was certainly quick. Most of the poems from his first year of exile (1964) were written in the same idiom as those of 1962–1963 and so fell naturally into a single book, *New Stanzas to Augusta*. The exceptions were few, but they were notable: the prison cycle discussed above and "Einem alten Architekten in Rom," written at the very end of the year. The name of this last poem echoes Wallace Stevens's "To an Old Philosopher in Rome." Earlier that fall Brodsky had also borrowed a title from Byron, whose "Stanzas to Augusta" became Brodsky's "New Stanzas to Augusta." He would later note that his poem "The woods outside my window, my wooden window" was a variation on Robert Frost's "Tree at My Window."[15]

He had already read a good deal of Anglo-American poetry in translation, but it was not until his time in Norenskaya that he really began to study it. He had a decent English-Russian dictionary and a small hoard of books, including Oscar Williams's *New Pocket Anthology of English Verse*.[16] At night, in his hut on the edge of a village on the banks of a stream, there was nothing to distract him; he plowed through his dictionary for exact equivalents; he spent hours slowly making his way through English texts. One side effect of such close reading was a good passive knowledge of English, but at the time his object was not to learn another language; it was to learn another poetry. Gradually, he began to delve deeper into these poems in English; they didn't resemble Russian ones, nor did they much resemble the translations with which he was familiar.

What lessons did Brodsky take from English-language poetry? At first glance, perhaps those of the metaphysical poets, the English baroque. In Norenskaya he read John Donne (his "Grand Elegy for John Donne" had been written in 1962 with virtually no knowledge of the poet other than the usual quotation about "for whom the bell tolls").[17] He worked on translations of Donne and Andrew Marvell and pored over Shakespeare. Their poetic reflections are more often than not expressed in extended metaphors and similes, also called conceits (from the Italian *concetto,* or "concept"). While such conceits were characteristic of the European baroque in general, Brodsky was for the most part reading either English or Polish originals. Seventeenth-century metaphysical poets usually compare a feeling or an experience to some physical object and its functions, neither of which, on the surface, would seem to have anything to do with the topic at hand. Unlike the emotionally charged, one-time-only similes of romantic poets (for example, Pushkin's "Our youthful pleasures have dissolved / Like dreams, like morning mist") the baroque trope unfolds intellectually and logically, allowing authors to display both their fantasy and their wit. Thus, in "The Definition of Love," Andrew Marvell applies one of Euclid's postulates:

> As lines, so love's oblique, may well
> Themselves in every angle greet:
> But ours, so truly parallel,
> Though infinite, can never meet.[18]

Another often-cited example comprises the stanzas from John Donne's "A Valediction: Forbidding Mourning":

> If they be two, they are two so
> As stiff twin compasses are two;
> Thy soul, the fix'd foot, makes no show
> To move, but doth, if th' other do.
>
> And though it in the centre sit,
> Yet, when the other far doth roam,
> It leans, and hearkens after it,
> And grows erect, as that comes home.
>
> Such wilt thou be to me, who must,
> Like th' other foot, obliquely run;
> Thy firmness makes my circle just,
> And makes me end where I begun.[19]

Brodsky experimented with such metaphors in 1960s poems later included in *The End of a Beautiful Era:* "In Memory of T.B." and "Fountain dedicated to the heroes of Hango" (the latter poem consists of one extended metaphor); an extreme form was in "A Song to No Music," where the controlling geometrical metaphor—estranged lovers' gazes meeting in the sky like the two equal sides of an isosceles triangle—plays out over roughly 120 of 244 lines. He himself once jokingly explained the technique: if, say, you use a grade-school joke ("the earth is shaped like a suitcase") in a poem, then you have to say what's in the case, and which station you're going to, and so on.

Baroque poetics, scorned by neoclassicists and forgotten by romantics, was reborn in modernism, first in the poetry of the French symbolists of the late nineteenth century, later in the literary program outlined by Ezra Pound and T. S. Eliot, whose works and ideas were to exert tremendous influence on twentieth-century English-language poetry. However, the new incarnation of the baroque metaphor was more condensed: no more the complex logical constructions the metaphysical poets used to join seemingly unrelated concepts; the moderns relied instead on the sophistication of the educated reader. The first lines of Eliot's "The Love Song of J. Alfred Prufrock" are a prime example:

> Let us go then, you and I,
> When the evening is spread out against the sky
> Like a patient etherized upon a table.

This sort of metaphoric technique is also characteristic of Russian modernism. Compare, for example, Eliot's simile to Mayakovsky's in "A Cloud in Trousers": "Midnight fell, / like a condemned man's head from the block." Or take Pasternak's in "Out of Superstition": "She walked in with a chair, / took my life down from the shelf, / and blew away the dust." We can imagine a seventeenth-century baroque poet using the same metaphor, but he would no doubt have spent more time explaining that his life was like a book gathering dust in a library, that at some point there came a discerning reader who stepped onto a chair to reach the book, who blew off the dust before opening the book, and like that reader, the poet's beloved . . . and so forth. In fact there are lines quite like this in Donne.[20] For all the difference in individual styles, this sort of condensed metaphor is common with Tsvetaeva and Mandelstam as well, and in all likelihood this is what Brodsky had in mind when he wrote Gordin that metaphor was a "composition in miniature." In the second half of the

1960s he, too, turned primarily to this technique; two good examples are poems written in 1968, both part of *A Halt in the Desert.*

> On Washerwoman Bridge, where you and I
> stood like two arms on a clock face,
> embracing at twelve as if
> parting not just for one day, but forever
> ("Washerwoman Bridge," *OVP;* non-poetic)

> Right now the rainstorm is the only thing
> my ear will let into my drowsing mind,
> as skinflints let poor kin into their kitchens—
> not yet music, but no longer noise.
> ("Almost an Elegy," *OVP;* non-poetic)

We see, however, that when Brodsky was experimenting with baroque devices he was essentially replaying the development of modernist sensibility and its metaphoric means.[21] At times he did so at the expense of emotional expressiveness. We have only to compare his 1965 "A Song to No Music" and his 1977 "Soho" (both dedicated to the same woman) to see how much more emotionally taut and complex the later poem is. Whatever his reasons, Brodsky seemed compelled to relearn the lessons of the seventeenth century and repair some breach in the history of Russian poetry.

It cannot be said, though, that Russian poetry ignored the baroque entirely. Brodsky liked to point to some of Antiokh Kantemir's quite Donnesque lines; he often quoted the very baroque Russian-Ukrainian verse of Grigory Skovoroda and heard echoes of the baroque in Derzhavin and even in Baratynsky. But the natural fusion of intellectual and emotional discourse common to both the baroque and modernism he learned for the most part from close readings of English metaphysical poetry in a candlelit hut in the Russian north, in surroundings reminiscent of the English seventeenth-century countryside.

To say that Norenskaya represented a sudden turning point, a sudden expansion into new genres, would be to simplify the matter. What took place was a radical change in the whole structure and sense of his "poetic I," and this new "I" required new ways to express itself. Just as he learned to distance himself from all that was roiling round him in his

Leningrad trial, Brodsky realized that he might also distance himself from the confessional "I" in his poetry.

> It's the best way
> To salvage strong feelings from a mass
> of weak ones. The Greek notion of the mask
> is back in style.
> ("Farewell, Mademoiselle Véronique," *OVP;* non-poetic)

This new stance came through most clearly in his narrative poems, a genre that in Russian twentieth-century literary circles was perceived as outmoded or, at best, marginal. In the nineteenth century such "stories in verse" had been popular: Pushkin's "Song of the Seer Oleg" and "Upas-Tree," Ryleev's "Meditations," Aleksey Tolstoy's historical ballads, Lermontov's "Dying Gladiator," and Nekrasov's "Vlas" are only a few of many examples. By the twentieth century this genre seemed to have run its course, although narrative poems, short and long alike, were still being written and published and in the Soviet era were praised for being "more accessible" to working folk. The genre served political ends perhaps better than any other.

But Russian high modernism wanted nothing to do with narrative poetry. All of it, from the ecstatic early lyrics of Mayakovsky and Tsvetaeva to the reserved reflections of Akhmatova, the culturological musings of Mandelstam, the lyric verse of Annensky, Blok, Pasternak, and Esenin, was aimed at giving voice to some authentic sense of self. This was purely lyric verse, and its ideal was complete identification of the author with the "I" of the text. Such lyrics were always emotive, and the emotions in the text were always clearly defined: sorrow, despair, contempt, and hatred in Mayakovsky's "Backbone Flute" and "A Cloud in Trousers" and Tsvetaeva's "Poem of the End" and "Poem of the Mountain"; delight in nature and love in Pasternak's *My Sister Life;* the tense solemnity, the emphatic seriousness of thought, in Mandelstam's poems like "Insomnia. Homer," "The stream of golden honey poured," "With the world of empire I was but childishly linked"; and, most often of all, from Annensky to Blok to Esenin, a general world-weariness and self-pity. In terms of the pragmatics of poetic art, lyrics like these establish an intimate and sympathetic link between the author and the reader. The feelings and experiences undergone by the poet are universal and thus infectious, as Leo Tolstoy explains in his tract "What Is Art": "Art is [a form of] human activity in which someone consciously, by means of generally understood external signs, conveys what he feels to others, and these others are then infected by these feelings and also begin to experience them."[22] In a lyric, replacing the "I" with some "other," some imagined character, and moreover one whose circumstances clearly do not correspond to the author's, destroys that intimate link between the poet and the reader. Therefore even the long poems of Russian modernists are intimate and confessional (the above-mentioned poems by Mayakovsky and Tsvetaeva, poems by Pasternak in which lyric confession overwhelms the theme—the Revolution of 1905, the revolt led by Lieutenant Schmidt, the biography of Maria Ilyina). The rare exceptions include some experimental verse (Bryusov's and Selvinsky's, for example), Blok's long poem "The Twelve," popular ballads by Tikhonov, a few pieces by Bagritsky—but for the most part these poets also remained within the mainstream. The only major Russian poet of the twentieth century to break away consistently was Mikhail Kuzmin. From his early "Alexandrian Songs" to his late novella in verse, *The Trout Breaks the Ice,* Kuzmin applied the "Greek notion of the mask" and often wrote poetry like prose—that is, in the form of a story about "another" or "others" that often involved a very complicated plot.

What was the exception in Russian modernist poetry was the norm in English-language poetry of the same period. Thomas Hardy, W. B. Yeats, Edwin Arlington Robinson, Robert Frost, Edgar Lee Masters, T. S. Eliot, and W. H. Auden all wrote in the first person and also in the third—as the "other." They endowed their imaginary characters with nuanced personalities, described scenes from their lives, and often used direct speech. Of course, their young Russian reader would have been interested primarily in how these poets, having rejected direct self-expression, achieved the same effect—infectiousness of emotion, *lyricism.* Speaking in very general terms, we can safely say that long and abundant in detail as these poems might be, what most affects the reader is what is *not* in the text. The carrier of the infection is understatement, a meaningful subtext.[23]

Brodsky always considered Robert Frost a seminal figure in modern Anglo-American poetry, and in one interview he explained what he understood to be the underlying principles of Frost's poetry: "The main force of Frost's narrative comes not so much from description as from dialogue. As a rule, the action takes place within four walls. Two people are talking (and the whole horror lies in what they're not saying to each other!). Frost's dialogues include all the requisite author's remarks and stage directions. He describes the props, he lays out the blocking. It's tragedy in the Greek sense, almost ballet."[24]

Most important here is that Brodsky refers not to classic examples of lyric poetry but to classical Greek tragedy (in the same interview he compared Frost's verse to Pushkin's "Little Tragedies"). The theatricalization of the lyric text (see his letter to Gordin quoted above: "more an Ostrovsky than a Byron"), the use of a "stage" and of actors, allows him to convey the terror and absurdity of everyday life on a universal scale; in traditional forms of lyric monologue, existential drama is all too easily replaced by personal complaint. In one conversation about Frost, Brodsky specifically uses the words "existential dread" and "the absurd": "The woods are a well of death, a synonym for life. This is not mere feeling. This is civilized man looking at nature. Only a highly cultured person could load these props—woods, fence, firewood—with this sort of meaning. . . . There is no existential dread, *none,* in the descriptions of nature found in European literatures. . . . And that dread seeping out of the woods was something Frost sensed like no one else. You can't give a more profound interpretation of the absurd than that. . . . When Frost sees a house standing on a hill, it isn't simply a house, it's a usurpation of space. When he looks at the boards the house is built of, he understands that the tree wasn't exactly planning on this."[25]

Brodsky is talking about lines written in the first quarter of the twentieth century by an American poet, but here we are also justified in seeing "a self-portrait at the Danilovsky sovkhoz." Here the relationships between people and landscape, people and nature, are more complicated than Solzhenitsyn supposed. In another essay on Frost, Brodsky writes that "[n]ature for this poet is neither friend nor foe, nor is it the backdrop for human drama, it is this poet's terrifying self-portrait."[26] And funnily enough, Frost seemed to cede the territory of tragedy to his Russian fellow writer in a wry poem called "New Hampshire":

> I don't know what to say about the people.
> For art's sake one could almost wish them worse
> Rather than better. How are we to write

The Russian novel in America
As long as life goes so unterribly?

Years after Norenskaya, when Brodsky was earning his living by teaching—which meant, for the most part, explicating poetry—he would explain in great detail to students how this or that poem worked. These explications served as the basis for the extended essays he wrote on Tsvetaeva's "New Year's," Mandelstam's "With the world of empire I was but childishly linked," Pasternak's and Tsvetaeva's "Magdalenes," Auden's "September 1, 1939," several poems by Hardy, and two poems by Frost. Going almost literally line by line, Brodsky explains to his readers not *what* the line is suggesting—the poem itself does that—but *how,* how by word choice, by the point and counterpoint of motifs, a poet puts his reader on the right track. Brodsky's essay on Auden was written in 1984, those on Frost and Hardy in 1994–1995 (the last two years of his life), but it seems likely that he had read and grasped the essence of their poetics thirty years earlier, in Norenskaya: the results can be seen in "Anno Domini," "Letter to General Z," "Candlestick," and "Gorbunov and Gorchakov" (1968); in "A Winter Evening in Yalta," "Homage to Yalta," the "School Anthology" cycle and related poems (1969); in "Debut," "Teatime," and "Post Aetatem Nostram" (1970), "Letters to a Roman Friend" (1972), and others. He may have taken his first steps in this direction even earlier, in 1964–1966, when he wrote "Einem alten Arkhitekten in Rom," "On the Death of T. S. Eliot," "Prophecy," "Two Hours in a Container," and "Fountain."

All these are benchmarks in Brodsky's work; very little is stylistically comparable to them in twentieth-century Russian poetry before him. Meanwhile, he continued to work in a more traditional lyric idiom. And finally the traditional and the new (the influence of English-language poetry) converged. He began to move easily between first-person and third-person narration, between irony and pathos (as in "Two Hours in a Container," "Prophecy," "A Winter Evening in Yalta"). By the mid-1970s this eclecticism would lead to a singular strategy for the construction of the lyric "I"—the description of oneself as the "other."

The "absolute nobody," "a man/body in a raincoat," first appears in "Lagoon," after which there comes a series of poems in which the lyric "I" is portrayed within some isolated personal space detached from the world at large—most often a café, a generic hotel room, a bench in a city park; sometimes "I" is even allegorical—a hawk in the stratosphere. The link between this character and the greater world is visual—a gift that in one early poem is called the ability to "remember details" and in a later one is called the "independence of the detail."

EPIPHANY IN NORENSKAYA

In Norenskaya, Brodsky was visited by an epiphany, a sudden moment of illumination. As he describes it,

> [B]y pure chance the book fell open to Auden's "In Memory of W. B. Yeats." . . . They, those eight lines in tetrameter that made this third of the poem sound like a cross between a Salvation Army hymn, a funeral dirge, and a nursery rhyme, went like this:
>
> Time that is intolerant
> Of the brave and innocent
> And indifferent in a week
> To a beautiful physique,
>
> Worships language and forgives
> Every one by whom it lives;
> Pardons cowardice, conceit,
> Lays its honours at their feet.
>
> I remember sitting there in the small wooden shack, peering through the square porthole-size window at the wet, muddy, dirt road with a few stray chickens on it, half believing what I'd just read, half wondering whether my grasp of English wasn't playing tricks on me.[27]

Auden had not counted on such an effect; he, in fact, cut these two quatrains and the one that followed from later versions of the poem. He was merely tossing off an aphorism about Time paying homage to Language (thus staving off complete oblivion for writers and poets) in an attempt to resolve his own doubts. This elegy for Yeats was the first poem Auden wrote after moving to the United States in 1939, when he was in the throes of a profound ideological crisis. He had not yet relinquished his faith in the left, was still a materialist by conviction, and was trying to fathom for himself the greatness not only of the mystic and "reactionary" Yeats but also of two other poets who had influenced him: apologist of empire Rudyard Kipling and conservative Catholic and anti-Semite Paul Claudel.

> Time that with this strange excuse
> Pardoned Kipling and his views,
> And will pardon Paul Claudel,
> Pardons him for writing well.

In conversation, Brodsky often paraphrased the lines that Auden had cut: "and some people God pardons for writing well."

Brodsky had opened the book at random and stumbled onto an oracle. He was wrestling with two spiritual questions at the time, and he saw answers to both of them in Auden's crystalline conclusion. One had to do with existential guilt and the hope for forgiveness, the other with the relationship between language and time. As for the first, he knew himself innocent of the charges on which he had been convicted and exiled. At the same time, he had always been prone to a feeling of existential guilt (his "Calvinist ethic"). And while Heidegger defines existential guilt as an inevitable condition of human existence—of bad choices made in life-and-death situations, of the refusal to make any choice at all—in the day-to-day life of a neurotic this can easily turn into a general sense of guilt: toward parents, toward a lover, toward an old peasant met in a prison boxcar. Again, Akhmatova was perhaps the only person to truly understand the nature of the moral and emotional crisis that Brodsky underwent in exile, as she compared his experience to Dostoevsky's sojourn in the "house of the dead."

Auden's lines also promised mercy for those who fulfilled their calling honestly, who lived by language and served it well. Brodsky's models in this service were always Akhmatova and Auden. He would later write about the two in much the same terms. In a prose tribute to Auden, "To Please a Shadow," he wrote: "But had I not met him at all, there would still be the reality of his work. One should feel grateful to fate for having been exposed to this reality, for the lavishing of these gifts, all the more priceless since they were not designated for anybody in particular. One may call this a generosity of the spirit, except that the spirit needs a man to refract itself through. It's not the man who becomes sacred because of this refraction: it's the spirit that becomes human and comprehensible.

This—*and the fact that men are finite*—is enough to worship this poet" (emphasis added).[28]

He talked of Akhmatova in verse, in a 1989 poem in which he thanks her for finding "words of forgiveness and love":

> ... and also, since we have but one life, they ring
> clearer from dead lips than from some cotton puffs on high.
> ("On Anna Akhmatova's Centennial," *PSN;* non-poetic)

In Auden's eight-line crystal ball Brodsky also spied an answer to his most pressing questions about the nature of time and language. The plain words of the English poet confirmed his belief in the dominance of language over individual consciousness and collective existence. These ideas were in the very air of the times, radiating from the existentialist philosophy of Heidegger, the culturological studies of Edward Sapir, and the rapidly growing influence of semiotic theory, which holds that existence can be reduced to a system of signs and languages—to the transfer and receipt of messages, to a web of connections (as Brodsky writes in "Conversation with a Celestial Being," even faith in God "is nothing more than / one-way mail"). Sapir compared the structure of language to the grooves on a phonograph record; he believed that human thought could move only within these grooves. Heidegger taught that existence is realized through language. Auden added that a language needs poets in order to survive. Of course, he was telling old truths, ones that Brodsky had heard many times. The very word "poetry" derives from the Greek word *poiesis,* "to make," that is, to make by means of language a new sensibility, a new idea. So at a time of great doubt and despair, Auden's words reassured Brodsky that he was on the right track.

This revelation apparently took place in late autumn. In early January Brodsky heard Western radio broadcasts reporting the death of T. S. Eliot. By January 12 he had finished "Verses on the Death of T. S. Eliot," which begins with the line "He died in January, the beginning of the year." Thirty years later some people took this as a prophecy of Brodsky's own death in January 1996.

But in fact the title was another variation on Auden, whose ode to Yeats begins with "He disappeared in the dead of winter." The overall structure of Brodsky's poem, an elegy in three parts, mimics Auden's. The first part compares poetry to time, and time to the ocean. Time is cyclical—days, weeks, years. Poetry, too, is based on regularity, repetition—sounds, rhymes, images, motifs. Time is portrayed as an ocean—waves rising and falling in a certain rhythm, tides that ebb and flow. Ten years later he would return to this complex "metaphysical" simile in "A Part of Speech":

> I was born and grew up in the Baltic marshland
> by zinc-gray breakers that always marched on
> in twos. Hence all rhymes . . .

This ode to Eliot is a series of cinematic takes on a frozen, post-holiday world; it moves from a close-up of "glass shards swept out the door" to a wide shot of the ocean and the continent. The images are specific and concrete, just as Eliot would have required. But the second and third parts do not quite measure up to the model, either in maturity of thought or clarity of expression. When Yeats died in 1939, Auden was considerably older than Brodsky, and certainly a more mature poet. When Eliot died, Brodsky had only just begun to find his way, and this poem dated January 12, 1965, was merely the first stage on this road.

BACK FROM EXILE

In early January 1965, as Brodsky was working his day shift at Danilovsky State Farm and writing about T. S. Eliot at night, an important document was signed in Moscow. Unbeknownst to him, the tireless efforts of Vigdorova, Grudinina, Akhmatova, and other supporters—all the knocking on doors, the writing of letters, the talking with anyone of influence—had begun to have some effect. As we now know from recently published documents, events transpired in the following order.[29] On October 3, 1964, N. Mironov, chief of administration for the Central Committee of the Communist Party, that is, the official ultimately charged with supervision of the courts, the prosecutor's office, the police, and the security agencies, sent a letter each to USSR Prosecutor General Rudenko, KGB Chairman Semichastny, and Chief Justice of the Supreme Court Gorkin directing them to "review and report to the Central Committee on the substance and foundation of the court's decision in the case of I. Brodsky." Had Brodsky's supporters been able to read this classified document at the time, they would have found it encouraging: although one of its four paragraphs simply repeated all the accusations against him, two others summarized statements made in his defense by Marshak, Chukovsky, and other prominent writers, and the concluding paragraph spoke of unrest within the ranks of the intelligentsia—caused by the trial. More important, this high-ranking Party official ended his letter with a statement to the effect that "case materials were insufficiently researched." On the face of it the phrase makes little sense (why would a court decision be subject to further research?), but translated into normal language, this was an order to review Brodsky's case. The bureaucratic machine creaked into motion, as all three agencies—the prosecutor general's office, the KGB, and the Supreme Court—each designated an official (a fairly high-ranking one at that) to review the case and dispatched this troika of investigators to Leningrad. Two months later, on December 7, the investigators sent a detailed report and a set of recommendations to their respective superiors. The Moscow investigators had met with the entire top tier of Leningrad Party officials, as well as with representatives of the courts, the prosecutor's office, and the local KGB. They had also met with Dzerzhinsky district Party secretary Kosareva, who was directly responsible for the prosecution of the case. The investigators' legal conclusions were unequivocal: "Brodsky's apoliticism and exaggeration of his own literary talents cannot serve as cause for application of the May 4, 1961, decree."[30] Their arguments are practically identical to those offered by the defense at Brodsky's trial.

This report makes clear that its authors had gone to Leningrad not only to review the decision of a lower court but also to negotiate with local authorities. The Leningrad Party boss, Tolstikov, and his subordinates were standing their ground on the verdict, but the Muscovites had obviously been instructed to somehow make this whole story of the poet-parasite go away. In the end, they offered a compromise:

> First Secretary of the Leningrad Industrial District Communist Party Committee V. S. Tolstikov, First Secretary of the Leningrad City Party Committee G. I. Popov, Secretary of the Leningrad Industrial District Communist Party Committee Comrade G. A. Bodganov [secretary for ideology], head of administration for the Industrial District Committee of the Communist Party Comrade P. I. Kuznetsov, head of KGB administration Comrade V. T. Shumilov, city prosecutor general Comrade A. G. Karaskov, and Secretary of the Dzerzhinsky

> District Communist Party Committee Comrade N. S. Kosareva believe that Brodsky was found guilty of parasitism with good cause and that the sentence (administrative exile) was appropriate. [As we know from the first part of the document, the Moscow commission did not agree.] They expressed their opposition to the commutation of his sentence, citing lack of grounds for such and the possibility that this might provoke an unfortunate reaction on the part of the public, which has assumed that the court's decision was correct, and might also discredit Leningrad authorities and community organizations [by "the public" and "community organizations" we should understand that Lerner's patrols and Prokofyev's coterie at the Leningrad Writers' Union were meant]. They think it possible to grant Brodsky an early release from administrative exile on condition of good behavior in his place of exile and residence outside the confines of the city of Leningrad upon his release.[31]

In other words, Moscow was putting pressure on Tolstikov and his cronies, and the latter were offering a compromise: they would announce that Brodsky had reformed ("good behavior in his place of exile") and would release him, but only if he didn't go back home. The concluding paragraph of the report states: "According to a communication by the director of the Danilovsky State Farm, Konosha District, Arkhangelsk Region, citizen I. A. Brodsky showed a positive work attitude; no breaches of discipline were noted. In light of this conscientious work ethic he was allowed a ten-day furlough to visit his parents."[32] Indeed, Brodsky had worked hard and gotten along with everyone in the village, and local authorities had treated this friendly, well-spoken, and sober (by local standards anyway) young Leningrader relatively fairly.

And so on January 5 the deputy prosecutor general of the USSR sent an official memorandum to the Leningrad court requesting that Brodsky be granted an early release. But the Leningrad authorities apparently decided to counterattack. The office of the courts declined the request. Brodsky received a notice to that effect in the middle of February, one year after his arrest.[33] There is some gap in the documentation, but on September 4, 1965, the Supreme Court of the USSR reviewed Brodsky's case and reduced his sentence to time served. The court order was mistakenly sent to Leningrad instead of to the Arkhangelsk regional authorities, and Brodsky was not officially freed until September 23.

The stance of the Leningrad authorities is easy enough to understand: they were stubbornly defending their turf and their honor and were unwilling to admit that they had made a mess of things. But the support of high-level Moscow officials for a young man who had been involved in some dubious escapades and who wrote poetry unsuitable for publication in the USSR requires some explanation. On the heels of this decision, Lidiya Chukovskaya wrote in her diary: "Everyone is guessing right now: Who intervened? What prompted the Supreme Court to finally review the case? . . . Frida's notes were the shot heard round the world. Tolstikov can tell us all to go to hell. But he can't tell that to Sartre or the European Union. And they're saying that Sartre wrote Mikoyan to tell him that in October writers from the Union would be coming together in Paris and that they would definitely be talking about Brodsky."[34] The Party leadership, that is, those people on whom Brodsky's fate and, for that matter, the fate of everyone else in the USSR truly depended, could not have cared less about the persecution of the young poet, or the opinions of Chukovsky, Marshak, and Shostakovich, or those of Granin and Dudin (the new heads of the Leningrad Writers' Union), or those of intellectuals in general. The crudely constructed farce in Leningrad began to annoy Moscow only when the farce became international news. At that point it became a matter of politics—better to maintain good relations with the Western leftist intelligentsia than to insist on the infallibility of comrades in Leningrad. So in the following round of bureaucratic confrontations, the foreign affairs division of the Central Committee won out over the Leningrad regional Party committee. Of course, the KGB had a good deal of say in the matter, but by then the agency was less interested in Brodsky himself than in "pursuing those individuals who had aided in the communication of tendentious information about the Brodsky case." However, their chief suspect in this heinous crime was already dead. Frida Vigdorova had succumbed to cancer on August 7, 1965.

On August 17, Jean-Paul Sartre (long considered a great friend of the Soviet Union, especially after he declined the Nobel Prize in 1964) sent Chairman of the Presidium of the Supreme Soviet Anastas Mikoyan a formal letter:

> I take it upon myself to write you this letter only because I have long been a friend and ally of your great country. I have visited it often, met with many of its writers, and understand very well that what Western opponents of peaceful coexistence now call "the Brodsky case" is a puzzling and regrettable aberration. But I must tell you that the anti-Soviet press has taken advantage of this aberration to launch a widespread campaign, has represented this exception as typical of Soviet justice, and has gone so far as to accuse the Soviet government of anti-Semitism and persecution of the intelligentsia. Up until late 1965 we who support international cultural cooperation found it relatively easy to counter this scurrilous propaganda; our Soviet friends assured us that the judiciary was giving the Brodsky incident its full attention and that the verdict would be reviewed. However, since then much time has passed, and nothing has been done. Our enemies, your enemies, are on the attack. For example, I am more and more often asked to speak publicly on this issue. I have so far refused, but it is becoming ever harder to choose—to speak or not to speak.
>
> Mr. President, I must tell you that we are very distressed. We cannot help but know that whatever the social system, rethinking decisions already made is a very difficult thing. However, knowing you to be a great humanitarian and proponent of closer ties between West and East, I appeal to you out of our sincere desire for friendship with socialist nations—our greatest hope—to stand up in defense of this young man who may already be a good poet or who may yet become one.[35]

Sartre's arguments were rather convincing: Why risk censure at an important propaganda event like the upcoming European writers' conference? KGB chairman Semichastny had enough worries as it was: he was about to try Sinyavsky and Daniel; he was already pursuing Solzhenitsyn. These cases were far more important than some overblown story about an obscure boy poet.

In the end, the mess made by a semiliterate hustler was left for the highest-ranking officials in the land to clean up. Brodsky was now a celebrity. How and what he wrote, few people in either Russia or the West really knew. What they did know was that once upon a time in Leningrad there lived a young man who had been thrown into jail and sentenced to forced labor in the far north simply because he wanted to write poetry. Meanwhile, Brodsky himself was glad to be freed, was as obsessed as ever with his tangled relationship with Marina Basmanova, was busy writing poetry, and was trying to think as little as possible about his eighteen-month ordeal. What mainly struck him was the absurdity of the whole business. "The sum of suffering is the absurd," he would conclude some years later ("Letter to General Z," *KPE*). What Jean-Paul Sartre, who had postulated the absurd as a basic condition of human existence, actually thought of Iosif Brodsky we may never know, but his help came just in time for the young poet lost in the far north.

CHAPTER SIX

My song was out of tune, my voice was cracked,
but at least no chorus can ever sing it back.

—"I Sit by the Window"

AFTER EXILE: 1965–1972

IN THE SEVEN YEARS between Brodsky's return from internal exile and his departure from the USSR, his position in Soviet society was a rather odd one. His predicament was much like Bulgakov's or Pasternak's in a more frightening time, the late 1930s; he was free to make a living by writing, but as a poet he did not officially exist.

Overt harassment and persecution by the KGB had ended, but the agency was still keeping an eye on the young man. Meanwhile, his notorious arrest and trial had led to a shake-up in the Leningrad Writers' Union, and a new leadership had been chosen, one that was more or less liberal and sympathetic. Since Brodsky had published virtually nothing, they could not make him an official member, but the union also ran something called a trades group. It consisted of freelance journalists, songwriters, and skit writers for variety shows and the circus. Brodsky was registered in it immediately after his return from exile. This provided him a work stamp in his internal passport, a guarantee against further accusations of parasitism.

So, just as before his arrest, he translated, wrote children's verse (some of it published in popular children's magazines), and tried his hand at other kinds of wordsmithing—dubbing foreign films for the Lenfilm studio, for example. Once in a great while he made some money giving private readings; the organizers would then ask the audience for a contribution.[1] Occasionally he had to patch the holes in his meager budget by selling off some of the beautifully produced art books brought to him by acquaintances from abroad. Their numbers were growing: journalists, university professors, graduate students in Slavic, who had made their way to the USSR and hoped to meet the famous young poet. Some of these became friends for life: Italian journalist Gianni Buttafava, Dutch writer and Slavic scholar Kees Verheul, French art historian Véronique Schiltz. The last three had translated Brodsky's poetry.

The on-again, off-again relationship with Marina Basmanova continued for another two years. They sometimes lived together, they sometimes lived apart. In the fall of 1967 they had a son, whom they named Andrey. But soon after, in early 1968, six years after Brodsky and Basmanova first met, they made a final break.

> So long had life together been that she
> and I, with our joint shadows, had composed
> a double door, a door which, even if we
> were lost in work or sleep, was always closed:
> somehow the halves were split and we went right
> through them into the future, into night.
> ("Six Years Later")

On his way home from Norenskaya, Brodsky stopped off in Moscow. His Moscow friends were hoping to get his verse published in liberal journals like *Novy mir* and *Yunost*. Even for these publishers, however, a certain amount of diplomacy on Brodsky's part was required. This was something he could never quite manage. When Brodsky met Anatoly Rybakov, a well-connected writer who might have been able to help, the young poet annoyed Rybakov so much that thirty years later Rybakov was still fuming about the arrogance of this "jerk" who insisted on reading him his incomprehensible poetry.[2] Brodsky had a different recollection of the meeting: Rybakov's advice was to contact X first in order to pressure Y, and so forth, but it eventually seemed so tangled and Byzantine that Brodsky lost the thread completely and offered to read some poems just as an escape.

But friends were able to arrange an audience with Aleksandr Tvardovsky at *Novy mir*. Tvardovsky had been outraged by Brodsky's arrest, and many memoirists of the time recorded his notorious fight over the Brodsky case with the Leningrad Writers' Union head Prokofyev.[3] But Tvardovsky was a "poet of the people," and Brodsky's work was hardly to his taste. He tactfully told the young man that his poems "did not reflect our [common] experience." He invited Brodsky to come visit him at home. Brodsky replied, "I don't think so."[4] When Vasily Aksyonov took Brodsky to an editorial meeting at *Yunost,* "Iosif, after getting an earful of the Soviet nightmare that the *Yunost* writers were living, practically fainted. . . . He said that it was like attending some witches' Sabbath. But in fact this was as liberal as it got in those days."[5] The "Soviet nightmare" did not mean that Aksyonov and fellow writers like Anatoly Gladilin, Andrey Voznesensky, and Evgeniy Evtushenko, who had established the face of what was for its time a truly liberal journal, had sworn allegiance to the Party and the state. Their general policy, their general behavior, was hardly slavish or conformist; it had more to do with social conventions and with the tactics of publication in Russia. They simply wanted to be read.

In order to be read, they often resorted to "Aesopian language," the use of ironic fable or metaphor ("the censors won't get it, but the readers will"). The young writers of the 1960s were masters of this art. While some among them still believed in "socialism with a human face," and even in the myth of the noble Leninist revolution (which the villain Stalin had later bloodily betrayed), their attitude toward the current Soviet regime was one of covert opposition. At the time, Brodsky was friendly with Evtushenko, Aksyonov, and Akhmadulina, but Aesopian language in either literature or life was never his style.

The creation of a text involves some sort of imaginary addressee, some sort of reader, or, as Stravinsky said and Brodsky liked to repeat, some sort of "hypothetical alter ego." The psychology of Aesopian language is based on allowing a "third person" into the creative process—an imaginary censor standing between the writer and the reader—and the stylistic goal is to get around, to fool, this third person.[6] Brodsky and the rest of the Soviet-era intelligentsia all knew the mechanics of producing a literary trompe l'oeil; seen from one angle, it satisfied all the requirements of official ideology, but seen from another it turned into social satire. But Brodsky insisted on absolute creative autonomy; he could not write poetry while thinking about how a censor might read it. What for another artist might have been a daring and amusing game was for Brodsky the loss of his own inner freedom. The Aesopian strategy (slavish by definition) was morally unacceptable to him. He expressed his utter rejection of it in one scene from "Post Aetatem Nostram":

> In the Epistle to our Rulers slapped
> up everywhere along the streets, a famous
> famous bard, bursting
> with indignation, boldly calls
> (next line) for the Emperor's removal
> from our copper coins.
>
> The crowd gesticulates. Youths,
> gray-haired elders, grown men,
> and those hetaerae who can read
> in unison assert
> "This is a first!"—but
> never quite explaining
> what "this" is:
> courage or servility.
> So that must mean that poetry lies in
> the absence of a clear-cut line.
> (*KPE;* non-poetic)

The poetics of the Aesopian text was indeed built on the lack of any clear line between two ideologically contradictory readings. Brodsky conveys the spirit of the times exactly: every time some especially striking Aesopian work was published in *Novy mir* or in *Yunost,* the intelligentsia would happily exclaim, "This is a first!" Equally apt is his parody of Aesopian methods for making a message ambiguous: "Remove the Emperor," cries a local bard. But what follows is "from our copper coins." Here Brodsky is parodying a famous poem by Andrey Voznesensky in which the latter issues a challenge to "Remove Lenin / from [our] money!" Of course, Brodsky's parody is also a parable. "Post Aetatem Nostram" is also an allegory—but allegory written with no eye to the censors. It was this clash in ethos (rather than personality) that would eventually lead to the breakdown of the friendship between Brodsky and Evtushenko, and Brodsky and Aksyonov.

ATTEMPTS AT PUBLISHING A BOOK

It would be wrong to say that Brodsky did not care whether he was published. Like many genuine poets (as opposed to vain dilettantes), he was of two minds about publication. On the one hand, he dreaded the final separation of text from author. The creation of a poem is always a cathartic act, and the poet wants to prolong it. Unpublished poems are still somehow unfinished, but publishing them means parting with them once and for all. Five years passed between Brodsky's arrival in the United States in 1972 and the release of his first post-emigration collections, *The End of a Beautiful Era* and *A Part of Speech,* although his publisher, Carl Proffer, had been urging him to get a book into print as soon as he set foot in the country. (We have in mind the Russian originals, not the English translations.) Ten years passed between these two 1977 collections and the release of *Urania,* his next book of Russian poems. On the other hand, what Brodsky said in court about his role in society was not mere rhetoric. He was conscious of the need to publish; among his notebooks from the mid-1960s we find a list of poems representing the content of some future book. At the time, he said that publishing them would mean that "justice had triumphed." The tone was mock-bombastic, but he took publication seriously.

One collection had already come out, in New York in 1965, without his knowledge. *Short Poems and Narratives* was pulled together from unauthorized samizdat copies; it consisted of very early poems, most of them written before 1962. Brodsky never acknowledged the book as his.[7] Neither the scattered publications of his verse in hard-to-find émigré journals nor the occasional translations into other languages exactly counted as the "triumph of justice," either.

Brodsky's many well-wishers in Leningrad and Moscow literary circles were hoping that his return from exile would be followed by the publication of a book in Russia itself, and for a time it seemed that collective efforts in this direction were bearing fruit. In late 1965 and early 1966, at the urging of liberal-minded editors, Brodsky submitted a manuscript to the Leningrad branch of Sovetsky Pisatel publishing house. He proposed calling the book "Winter Mail." This collection, unlike the unauthorized New York one, was to consist of poems written between 1962 and 1965. Aleksandr Ghitovich (1909–1966), a talented poet and a friend and neighbor of Akhmatova's, helped him prepare the manuscript; Ghitovich was also to edit it. The routine was the same as with any other submission: the manuscript was discussed by the editorial board, then sent to several internal reviewers, professional writers. The only difference in Brodsky's case was that the process took perhaps a little longer than usual. Brodsky submitted the manuscript at the beginning of the new year, but the editorial board did not discuss it until June 26. The operative word in the editorial discussions seemed to be "small." As though to appease some unseen spirit hovering over the meeting, the editors time and time again emphasized that it would be a short book, a modest book, seven hundred lines at most. The other leitmotif in the discussion was "Brodsky is gifted, but . . ." After the "but" came a list of everything that was unacceptable: biblical themes ("Isaac and Abraham"); direct references to God, angels, seraphim; literary allusions. The participants in the discussion seemed to be explaining to their invisible but ever-present bosses that this book (this *little* book) should be published because it would put an end to all sorts of talk, would "do away with the legends that have sprouted up around his name."

Internal reviews by the poet Vsevolod Rozhdestvensky and the critic Vladimir Alfonosov are dated October and November, respectively. Both reviewers solidly supported publication. If this was only to be expected from Alfonosov, a critic roughly Brodsky's own age and close to young Leningrad intellectual circles, the response from Rozhdestvensky (1895–1977) is surprising; even "Isaac and Abraham" he deemed "interesting in terms of its idea, substantive and bright in terms of its shading" (in Soviet critical jargon "bright" meant optimistic despite the tragic theme).[8] A minor poet of the Acmeist school, Rozhdestvensky had never been anything but cautious and self-serving. Apparently he was confident that support for Brodsky, and even for Brodsky's notorious religious themes, was a safe enough course of action. Not until December 12, 1964, roughly one year after the manuscript was submitted, did editor in chief Smirnov send Brodsky a reply.[9] Although the editorial board and both reviewers were favorably disposed toward publishing the book (with certain cuts), Smirnov apparently took his cue from the local Party leadership and returned the manuscript. In the accompanying letter he demanded, in essence, that half of the book consist of poems that "clearly expressed civic motifs" and "the author's artistic ideology, his attitude toward the most crucial and pressing issues of contemporary life." If we translate this out of Soviet officialese into normal language, Smirnov was telling Brodsky to come up with ten or so ideologically correct poems. If Brodsky did so, then the other half of the book could be made up of "nature poems about the [Far] North."[10] Brodsky never did write the prescribed poems focusing on "civic motifs," but the fight to publish the book went on. The editorial archives contain a second round of internal reviews, these dating from June and July 1967. Four Leningrad writers—Vera Panova, Leonid Rakhmanov, Vadim Shefner, and Semyon Botvinnik—were all in favor of publication. Shefner spoke his mind firmly: "It seems to me that this little book, 'Winter Mail,' doesn't really need yet another reviewer's opinion (however favorable it might be) as much as it needs the reader's. Because, to my mind, Brodsky has already reached the stage of artistic maturity at which a poet needs reassuring comments and encouraging pats on the back much less than he needs his work to be subjected to the impartial judgment of his reader. I'm for the publication of this book."[11]

In contrast to these four positive reviews stood one extremely negative one, written by the poet Ilya Avramenko, a mid-level functionary in the Writers' Union. "Brodsky's poems have no roots in the life of the people," he wrote; they lie "outside the traditions of Russian poetry." On the poem "The People," which even the editor in chief of Sovetsky Pisatel publishing house found acceptable, Avramenko wrote that "it is hard to imagine what people he is talking about." The manuscript "does not merit consideration in general, because in most of the poems there is more muddle than sense."[12] Avramenko's opinion eventually prevailed. The publishing house strung Brodsky along for another year, at which point he simply took back the manuscript. Roughly two years later he was summoned to Leningrad KGB headquarters, where he was offered a deal: if he would provide information on the foreigners he met, the KGB would use its influence to help him publish his book. After this meeting, Brodsky gave up once and for all on publishing his works in his homeland.[13]

A HALT IN THE DESERT

His first "real" book, *A Halt in the Desert,* came out in 1970, in New York.[14] It was not "small" at all: it included seventy short poems, two long ones ("Isaac and Abraham" and "Gorbunov and Gorchakov"), and four translations from John Donne. Some of the content overlaps with that of *Short Poems and Narratives* ("Isaac and Abraham" and twenty-two early pieces), but more than two-thirds is new work. He discarded everything he considered imitative or immature, even such popular pieces as "Stanzas" and "A Jewish Cemetery"; he laid out the sections and the order of poems himself. Most of this manuscript he had given to Professor George Kline, his American translator, in June 1968. Getting the manuscript out of the country was a risky proposition for the American smuggler, but even more so for Brodsky himself. After the trial of Sinyavsky and Daniel, "transmission of documents to the West" was equated with espionage or treason. Although nothing in Brodsky's verse resembled the sort of political satire those two had written, there were passages in "Letter in a Bottle," "A Halt in the Desert" and "Gorbunov and Gorchakov" that the security agencies could easily have taken to be anti-Soviet. In the 1950s and 1960s people had been jailed for merely reading and sharing Pasternak's *Doctor Zhivago*.

As George Kline tells it:

> When Brodsky, on returning from exile in November 1965, first saw *Poems*, he had mixed feelings. On the one hand, it was flattering for this twenty-five-year-old poet who had never published anything in his homeland to see his work published abroad. But between 1957 and 1965 he had grown as a poet, and it was disappointing to see how much juvenilia there was in the book. He was also annoyed by numerous typographical errors and certain mistakes, although he undoubtedly understood that it would have been impossible to publish a decent edition without any contact with the author, using only unauthorized samizdat copies. He quickly typed out a list of twenty-six poems written between 1957 and 1961 that he did not want to include in the new collection. Twenty-two of these twenty-six had found their way into *Poems*.[15]

Kline was worried that the publication of yet another book in the West—this one authorized—would cause even more trouble for its author. But Brodsky insisted.

And so they found a publisher. Chekhov Publishers in New York had produced a great number of books in the 1950s, but in the 1960s it had practically ceased to exist—until a businessman and human-rights activist named Edward Kline (no relation to George Kline) resurrected it. Professor Max Hayward was chosen to be editor in chief, and the first book in line for publication was *A Halt in the Desert.* The book, as George Kline recalls,

> could have come out in 1969, but we were waiting to receive Brodsky's remarkable . . . narrative poem "Gorbunov and Gorchakov." He had finished it in late 1968, but we didn't get it until mid-1969. Carl Proffer had managed to send the manuscript from Moscow via a diplomatic pouch. In the book, Max Hayward was listed as editor, but in fact it was edited by me. Hayward, Ed Kline, and I had decided that it would be better not to mention me by name, because after 1968, largely owing to my contacts with Brodsky, I was on the KGB watch list. . . . I myself considered Brodsky the real editor, since he was the one who chose what to include and decided on the order of the poems and the names of the six sections. Amanda Haight met with Brodsky and Naiman in Moscow in September 1970 and wrote me that "on the whole, they very much approved of the book" and that the author was "definitely thrilled." But Brodsky immediately began correcting typos and minor mistakes in the copy that Amanda had brought. . . . Later he sent me a list of his changes.[16]

The émigré press was quick to respond. In the July 7, 1967, edition of New York's *Novoe russkoe slovo,* M. K. Eisenstadt ("Argus") hailed the book as proof of the younger intelligentsia's opposition to the Soviet regime—that is, he barely noticed the poetry itself. Eloquently but not very coherently, and certainly without much understanding of the symbolism of Brodsky's metaphysical world, he wrote that "Brodsky has been forced, on his own road to immortality, to make several halts in the desert, the scorching desert that is Soviet literature." In *Novy zhurnal,* the poet and scholar Yury Ivask singled out "Gorbunov and Gorchakov" as proof of Brodsky's maturity as a poet: "In many of the poem's monologues we no longer hear the prattle of a promising novice but the speech of a grown man, a serene and powerful master freely and seemingly effortlessly turning out iambic pentameter within the narrow confines of a monumental decima."[17] Vyacheslav Zavalishin, on the other hand, declared that Brodsky's first book had been more interesting, had shown greater poetic invention: "But reading *A Halt in the Desert* leaves somewhat of a bitter taste in the mouth: Brodsky's gift has somehow faded, gone dull here, as compared to his earlier verse.... The tragedy of Brodsky and those like him is that they, lacking any real mentor, have lost their way. Left to himself, his own devices, Brodsky has not taken another step forward; instead he has gone backward." Writers who contributed to *Novoe russkoe slovo* were outraged by the book's foreword, signed "N.N." (Anatoly Naiman); Zavalishin complained that "much of it is incomprehensible, and what is even half readable is often either unfair or shameless."[18] The critics were outraged by Naiman's "groundless" comparisons of Brodsky's work to Russian classics and also by his wholesale condemnation of several contemporary poets: "Publishing Brodsky's book with a foreword like this is no favor to Brodsky himself. It's a provocation."[19] In a letter to the editor, Edward Kline tried to justify himself: "The notes that served as the basis for the introduction were written in haste, and the author had hoped to rewrite them. Unfortunately, the editors never received the reworked text."[20]

The book is arranged around the two long poems, with "Isaac and Abraham" near the beginning and "Gorbunov and Gorchakov" near the end. In Brodsky's spiritual evolution these two works correspond to the two stages in which he learned the Old and New Testaments. In his evolution as a poet they mark the development and establishment of his style: his compositional technique, imagery (symbolic lexicon), and innovative versification.

LONG POEMS (1): "ISAAC AND ABRAHAM"

"Isaac and Abraham" is Brodsky's first poem on a biblical theme and the only one based on an episode from the Old Testament. The story told in Genesis 22 has often been retold in Western art, and Brodsky could not help but know it, if only through Rembrandt's painting in the Hermitage. His work on the poem, however, also coincided with his first reading of the Bible: "I wrote 'Isaac and Abraham' literally just a few days after I read Genesis."[21] Meanwhile, Brodsky was also reading Kierkegaard's *Fear and Trembling*. This is where, as he meditates on Abraham's sacrifice, Kierkegaard comes to his famous conclusion on the irrationality of religious sentiment and the need for a "leap of faith." At the same time, Brodsky was reading Lev Shestov's *Kierkegaard and Existentialist Philosophy*. But "Isaac and Abraham" is not simply a verse illustration of Kierkegaard's and

Shestov's thought. In this poem, all the spiritual questions of the young Brodsky converge. According to his longtime friend Georgy Ginzburg-Voskov, at the time Brodsky was intrigued by teachings and systems with complex symbolic patterns, everything from the Kabbalah to the tarot. As he worked on "Isaac and Abraham" he was not so much borrowing particular symbols from these systems as the notion of a symbolic pattern in a text.

Natalya Gorbanevskaya recalls Brodsky's account of his work on the poem during that May of 1963: "[H]e told me—in great detail, you might even say *brick by brick,* about his poem 'Isaac and Abraham,' which was still in the works. For example, what each letter in the word BUSH meant. Exactly as it was in the poem later—except that here he was *telling* it. I was struck: I didn't know—and to this day don't really understand it—that poetry can be written this way too, that a poet might know everything, plan everything ahead of time. (But we might also remember how Pushkin planned.)"[22]

Andrey Sergeev gives a clue to what else might have suggested this particular plan: "[H]e said that as he was trying to figure out Robinson's 'Isaac and Archibald,' he turned the protagonists into Isaac and Abraham."[23] Edwin Arlington Robinson's 1902 poem was almost a pastorale: Russian readers might be reminded of Chekhov's "Steppe" as they read Robinson's description of a twelve-year-old boy walking with old man Isaac to visit old man Archibald. The subtext to Robinson's poem is the contrast between life's end and its beginning, a child's first thoughts on death. Although the content of these two poems might seem to have little in common, we should consider the following remark by Brodsky: "I remember that Akhmatova and I were once talking about the possibility of a verse adaptation of the Bible. Here, in America, no poet would even attempt such a thing. Edwin Arlington Robinson was the last one who could have taken on something like that."[24]

Some scholars consider "Isaac and Abraham" one of the few poems that Brodsky ever wrote on Jewish themes. The most elaborate such interpretation is that of the Russian-Israeli critic Zeev Bar-Sella, who sees it as a verse exegesis of the Torah. The poet decodes the story of Isaac and Abraham in the spirit of the Kabbalah; he seeks to decipher the fate of the Jewish people and simultaneously, by this creative act, resolve for himself the question posed by Theodor Adorno: Is poetry possible after the Holocaust? Bar-Sella comes to the conclusion that "Brodsky does not establish a new covenant with God; he tears up the old one. Once he had studied [through "Isaac and Abraham"] the fate of his people, Brodsky came to an understanding of his own—God had not made a pact with the Jews; he had pronounced sentence on them. And Brodsky walked the same path as his people, to his very death. . . . After ["Isaac and Abraham"] Brodsky was left with two paths: stop living or stop being a poet. He found a third way: he stopped being a Jewish poet."[25] As we already know, Brodsky always made a distinction between himself as poet and himself as Jew ("I'm a Russian poet and a Jew"). While Bar-Sella seems to be stretching the point, hints of the Diaspora and Holocaust to come are nonetheless subtly present in the poem.

If the Israeli critic contends that here, through Kierkegaard, Brodsky is addressing the metaphysical side of Jewish history, Valentina Polukhina sees the poet as a writer more Christian than Kierkegaard himself: "In his poem, as he strives to unlock the meaning of the story of Abraham, Brodsky switches perspective. The son, not the father, stands at the center of the narrative. Just as Abraham puts his trust in God, Isaac puts his trust in his father. After reading the poem, we begin to come to the conclusion that the answer to this grim riddle set by God was always right in front of us. In the final analysis, God asked no more of Abraham than He asked of himself: the sacrifice of his own son to a belief."[26]

In any case, in terms of Brodsky's future life and works, the main significance of "Isaac and Abraham" lies in the assimilation of Kierkegaard's theology, or at least its basic principles: despair as a condition of human existence; ontological sin/guilt; humankind in the direct presence of God. One phrase in a personal letter dated May 14, 1965, speaks to the singular place of "Isaac and Abraham" in his spiritual development. He writes disparagingly of his other work: "The only real thing is 'Isaac and Abraham.'"[27] For the author this poem was the tool by which he forged his own version of an existential philosophy according to which he was not a member of a particular faith, a particular ethnic group, or a social class, but simply a human being, and as such doomed to a never-ending and tortuous spiritual search.

"Isaac and Abraham" also marks an important stage in the development of Brodsky's semantics. Desert, sand, bush, woods, leaves, candle, fire—these images, central to the text, become truly understandable only when considered within the context of Brodsky's work as a whole. This is where the "independent detail" becomes his main means of creating a symbol; one such detail is the description of the board—detail truly independent because the author gives no explanation of what sort of board this is or how it came to be in the tents of the Israelites. He describes a nomad encampment and peers into one of its tents as if putting his eye to a crack in a board—and then come thirty-two lines of description beginning with "Nobody knows cracks like a board does." This description is striking in that this close-up is overlaid by pictures on an entirely different scale. The author examines the cracks made by a knife thrust into the board; in equally detailed fashion he notes "sap turned to dust inside dark pores." Later he compares these tiny voids to windows. A house emerges, its walls lashed by blizzard winds. A biblical scene in a Palestinian valley converges with a scene in another place and another time.

Various critics have speculated that the board in the poem represents (1) the boards on which Russian icons were painted, (2) the boards from which coffins were made, (3) Jewish resistance, in that the cracks made by the knife represent the attempt to wipe out the Jewish people, or (4) the Torah, since in Hebrew *luakh,* or "board," also means a sacred scroll, and that the knife thrust represents (5) Kierkegaard's leap of faith. Each of these different readings has its own logic and its own merits, but the sheer variety of interpretations testifies to Brodsky's success in creating an image/symbol with a multiplicity of potential meanings. At the same time, "Isaac and Abraham" is often overelaborate; the author's command of language cannot quite control the flood of imagery washing over him. It would take two or three more years for him to fully master his craft.

LONG POEMS (2): "GORBUNOV AND GORCHAKOV"

As time went on, Brodsky grew more skeptical of the worth of much of his early work, but twenty years after writing "Gorbunov and Gorchakov," he still considered it an "especially solid piece."[28] The years that produced this poem were perhaps the most dramatic in all his life: police persecution, arrest, trial, exile, return; reconciliation with the love of his life, the birth of a son, a final break. The enormous stress of all this and the resultant psychological changes in the poet himself form the substratum to the poem; moreover, work on "Gorbunov and Gorchakov" truly became part of the poet's work on himself: the next-to-last line of the third canto contains a prayer in which the author's alter ego asks God-in-Heaven to grant him "victory over silence and suffocation."

The real-life circumstances that served as material for "Gorbunov and Gorchakov" were Brodsky's stints at Kanatchikov Dacha and Pryazhka, and the poem includes all the squalid details that made Soviet psychiatric hospitals so like Soviet prisons: crowding, cold, and stench; bad food and bad company (and odd camaraderie); the antediluvian "cures" meant to force patients to "admit to" their delusions. When asked by a journalist and friend in 1987 what part of his life in the USSR was worst, Brodsky unhesitatingly answered, "The prison psychiatric hospital in Leningrad. They would shoot me up with tranquilizers. They would wake me in the middle of the night, dump me into a bathtub of cold water, wrap me up in wet sheets, and set me next to the radiator. The sheets would dry out from the heat and cut into me."[29]

Brodsky underwent these "cures" because his friends, his relatives, and his lawyer all hoped that a sympathetic diagnosis would save him from arrest, or a trial, or a prison term. Psychiatric prison wards as a form of punishment for dissidents did not become common until several years later. So this young poet, who indeed in these years was painfully emotional and sensitive, had none of the moral support that would later help dissidents bear the horrors of punitive psychiatry, and he could indeed at times doubt his own sanity. He undoubtedly applied Akhmatova's description of a split personality to himself:

> Already madness spreads a wing
> That covers half my soul.
> It plies me with a fiery wine
> And beckons toward the black vale.
> And I have understood that I
> Must cede it victory,
> As I listen to my ravings
> As if they were not mine.
> (Akhmatova, "Requiem"; non-poetic)

Writing "Gorbunov and Gorchakov" proved therapeutic: it staved off a plunge into the "black vale." Brodsky took the most horrific experience in his life and turned it into a text, a script: he took the voices he heard there and turned them into characters in that script. The cold, foul-smelling hospital ward is sometimes a background, sometimes a foreground, but the real setting is the poet's mind, his brain. And in Brodsky's poetry the word "brain" stands in for earlier poets' "heart." This is clearly reflected in the concordances: in the concordance to Pushkin's works the word "heart" occupies three and a half pages of small print, Mandelstam uses it 50 times, Brodsky 102, but both Pushkin and Mandelstam use the word "brain" just 6 times each, while in Brodsky's poetry it occurs 73 times.[30] Brodsky's thoughts just before his first open-heart surgery reflect this: "I said to myself, all right, yes, it's the heart. . . . But at least it's not the brain! . . . And at that thought I calmed down."[31]

"I said to myself" is probably the key to the poem. Contrary to what some critics have claimed, the doubling of the lyric voice is not a representation of a split personality, nor of hallucinatory "voices in my head."[32] It is the personification of the two hemispheres of the human brain. "In all the most profound forms of creative activity, whether mathematics or music, the greatest achievements of all are linked primarily with right-brain intuitive imagery, but their embodiment (usually verbal or written, or at least involving a collection of discrete units, as in the words that make up a natural language) requires the use of the left (speech) hemisphere."[33] These are the very characteristics assigned to Gorbunov and Gorchakov at the beginning of the poem: Gorbunov, with his "prosaic" surname, is inclined to complex logical constructions like the concept of duality, as in canto III ("Gorbunov at Night"), where his dreams are encoded in a series of discrete symbols (chanterelles, islands, bobbers); Gorchakov, whose name many readers may associate with Pushkin, dreams in pictures and images—street scenes, memories of childhood, and most important, music ("Concerts, a forest of bows"). His late-night monologue in canto VII ("Gorchakov at Night"), which is symmetrical to Gorbunov's monologue in canto III, is an almost incoherent series of agitated declarations bristling with exclamation points (something quite rare for Brodsky—here there are twenty-nine of them, while in canto III there is only one). Gorbunov's verbal and thus cognitive function in the poem is repeatedly emphasized: "How odd that Gorchakov should speak / in Gorbunov's mad words!" This is why, as a rule, Gorchakov asks the questions, and Gorbunov gives the answers and explications. And since in Brodsky's hierarchy of anthropological values, language occupies the very top rung, at the end of canto X we read: "How do we tell these late night gabbers apart / though there's no point in it at all / If it's higher, then it's Gorbunov / if it's lower, that's the voice of Gorchakov."

There is only one place in the poem that might make readers doubt that Gorbunov and Gorchakov are really two incarnations of a single person. In canto VII, Gorbunov says, "I was born in May, a Gemini"—as was the author of the poem. Gorchakov, on the other hand, explains that he was born in March, under the sign of Aries. The context is a comic exchange of astrological explanations for their differences in character, but the differences might have more to do with embryology than astrology. The human brain begins to develop three months before birth.

This symmetry and asymmetry—the connection and conflict between this pair who, like the left and right hemispheres of the brain, cannot function without each other—is graphically reflected in the structure of the poem, in the parallel content and contrast of symmetrically placed cantos. The author underscores this structure by the titles he gives his cantos: these titles taken together form something like a sonnet (*aabbcaabbcaadd*):

(I) Gorbunov and Gorchakov [Gorbunov i Gorchakov]
(II) Gorbunov and Gorchakov [Gorbunov i Gorchakov]
    (III) Gorbunov at night [Gorbunov v nochi]
    (IV) Gorchakov and the doctors [Gorchakov i vrachi]
        (V) Song in the third person [Pesnya v tretem litse]
(VI) Gorbunov and Gorchakov [Gorbunov i Gorchakov]
(VII) Gorbunov and Gorchakov [Gorbunov i Gorchakov]
    (VIII) Gorchakov at night [Gorchakov v nochi]
    (IX) Gorbunov and the doctors [Gorbunov i vrachi]
        (X) Conversation on the porch [Razgovor na kryltse]
(XI) Gorbunov and Gorchakov [Gorbunov i Gorchakov]
(XII) Gorbunov and Gorchakov [Gorbunov i Gorchakov]
    (XIII) Conversation about the sea [Razgovory o more]
    (XIV) Conversation about conversation [Razgovor v razgovore]

The formal symmetry is striking. All fourteen cantos are practically equal in length, one hundred lines apiece, with the exception of cantos I and XI, which have ninety-nine. (The entire poem consists of 1,398 lines.) All of the "dialogue" cantos are broken into ten-line stanzas, five rhyming pairs (which is yet another way to underscore the dialogue within the monologue). Cantos V and X are the only exception; these have longer stanzas, and the rhymes do not repeat.[34]

Throughout the poem Brodsky takes ironic jabs at the pansexual doctrines of Freud. Like Akhmatova and Nabokov (but unlike Auden), Brodsky had little patience with psychoanalysis: "Freud was a remarkable gentleman in his own right; he broadened our notion of our selves [of the self]. But [at the time] none of this really made much of an impression on me. . . . One simple example of this gentlemen's silliness is his claim that the nature of creativity all comes down to sublimation [of sexual urges]. This is total nonsense, because the creative process and erotic . . . how best to say this? . . . behavior are two different things—it's not that one is a sublimation of the other, it's that both are sublimations of a general urge to create."[35]

Even before "Gorbunov and Gorchakov" Brodsky was experimenting with dialogue, both in "Isaac and Abraham" and in shorter poems. We recall that this is what most impressed him in Frost. Frost had created an atmosphere of existential fear and dread through dialogue. Interestingly enough, in Brodsky's dialogue poems, there are no indications of who is speaking. Nor are there any stage directions in his dramatic works *Democracy!* and *Wood* (1964–1965?).

In "Gorbunov and Gorchakov" Brodsky even uses the rather extravagant device of putting all "he said's" in canto V ("Song in the Third Person") and then, in canto X ("Conversation on the Porch"), which mirrors canto V, putting quotation marks around phrases that are not direct speech but fragments of a monologue by the author ("Isn't this a conversation too / since everything's described in words?"). This intensifies the impression that this is an interior dialogue; it blurs the boundary between the characters' dialogue and the author's monologue.

In a certain way "Gorbunov and Gorchakov" serves to illustrate Mikhail Bakhtin's theory of polyphony—that is, that any work of art is composed of multiple voices, and there can never be one "neutral, single voice."[36] Brodsky was writing this poem just as Bakhtin was being resurrected and "rehabilitated." Once, when I asked Brodsky if he'd read Bakhtin, he said, "I skimmed through his book on Dostoevsky; I liked the quotes." Still, while we cannot speak of direct influence, Bakhtin's theory that it is impossible to be oneself without being in direct communication with others is reflected in the poem in lines like Gorbunov's from canto VIII: "I don't feel quite like I'm real / unless there's someone to talk to!"[37]

I cannot agree with Carl Proffer's assertion that "[h]ere we are given to understand that what is presented in 'Gorbunov and Gorchakov' is a kind of Platonic ideal of dialogue. It is dialogue in its essence, in a kind of pre-existential purity."[38] If Plato's own dialogues correspond to the "Platonic ideal of dialogue," then "Gorbunov and Gorchakov" has very little in common with them. Plato's dialogues are closely scripted, consisting for the most part of monologues by Socrates, and the remarks of the other participations are there, for the most part, merely to give Socrates a chance to elaborate his reasoning. (There are certain exceptions, such as the myth of the origin of Eros told by Aristophanes in "The Symposium," but these are rare.)

Finally, in reading the poem, we cannot help but notice that its chronotope is tied to the Christian calendar: we have scenes in a madhouse during Lent, and both joking and serious allusions to Lent and Easter occur throughout the poem. The subject of "Gorbunov and Gorchakov" also incorporates the religious significance of Lent as a "spiritual journey, the goal of which is to lead us from one spiritual state into another."[39] The seven pairs of cantos correspond to the seven weeks of Lent (see the analogical composition of "To a Chair," the Easter poem by Brodsky included in *Urania*). The familiar words from the Lenten prayer of Saint Ephraim Sirin (made famous by Pushkin's adaptation)—"Give unto me [the gift] to see my own transgression and to refrain from condemnation of my brother"—are the key to the entire text. The heightened opposition between the flesh that betrays and the spirit that is betrayed by it is also indicated by analogies from the Gospels: Gorbunov is compared to Christ doomed to suffer on the cross; Gorchakov to Judas. In this sense Brodsky's dialogue poem also resembles a medieval mystery play. Judas-Gorchakov's concluding lines in canto VIII read, "[I] love and give you over into torment." In this scenario, the betrayer and the betrayed are inextricably linked. "How strange that Gorbunov upon the cross / should count on Gorchakov beneath [it]," remark the doctors-torturers (canto IX, line 8). At the end of the next stanza, the comparison with Golgotha becomes even starker. In a parody of the biblical passage in which Christ is offered a sponge soaked in vinegar, the doctors say, "Hey, Gorbunov, you want some coffee?" and Gorbunov answers, "Oh why have you forsaken me?"

Yet another allusion to Christ can be found in the titles of cantos IV and IX—"Gorchakov and the Doctors" and "Gorbunov and the Doctors."

"Christ among the Doctors" is a common theme in Eastern Orthodox icons and in European religious paintings. The source is Luke 2:46, 47: "And it came to pass, that after three days they found him in the temple, sitting in the midst of the doctors, both hearing them, and asking them questions. And all that heard him were astonished at his understanding and answers." The psychiatrists interrogating Gorbunov-Gorchakov are reminiscent of the sinister and grotesque "learned doctors" interrogating Christ in Dürer's famed *Christ among the Doctors*.[40]

Brodsky wrote "Gorbunov and Gorchakov" to make some sense of his horrific experience in the psychiatric hospital.[41] In that experience he had found a religious paradigm. There were no "Napoleons" or "vegetables" in the madhouse where Gorbunov-Gorchakov was lodged. In this mournful place, madness was not pathology but the misfortune of human existence: the betrayal of friends and family; cruelty; one's own biological vulnerability. The real madness lay in surrendering to this misfortune, in losing one's identity, one's self. The loneliness of those who resist such misfortune is like that of Christ on Golgotha. There is a moment of vision in the poem with parallels to the Old Testament:

> But wait! A man . . . a well . . . and sands like Tartar
> hordes a-whirling round . . . He hasn't got
> a drop to drink; he's thin; it's hotter, hotter . . .
> Sun is at . . . what do you call it . . . at
> the zenith. Hostile ground. It's getting harder
> now to see. Then, boom, a well . . .
> (Canto IV, stanza 5)

This is written in two languages: in Russian and in Brodsky's own symbolic system, in which "sand" and "Tartar" and "hot" go far beyond their dictionary definitions. Such symbolic images are to be found in "Isaac and Abraham," in the poem that gave the book its name, and in a number of other texts.

The biblical Joseph managed to find a way out of the pit into which his brothers had cast him, and find fame and honor in a foreign land.

LEAVING THE USSR

On May 12, 1972, Brodsky was summoned to his local visa and registration office (OVIR).[42]

> I knew that OVIR didn't call people in for no reason; I even wondered if maybe I had some distant foreign relative who'd left me an inheritance. I told them I'd be there fairly late, around seven in the evening, and they said fine, come at seven, we'll be expecting you.
>
> I'm met by a colonel who politely asks what's up with me. I tell him things are fine. He says: you've received an official invitation to Israel. Yes, I say, to Israel, and to Italy and England and Czechoslovakia.
>
> And why not accept that invitation to Israel? asks the colonel. Maybe you thought we wouldn't let you go? Well, I did think that, I answer, but that's not the point. So what is? asks the colonel. I don't know what I'd do there, I say.
>
> At that point the whole conversation changes. He switches from the polite *vy* to the informal *ty*. Listen, Brodsky. You're going to fill out this form and write a statement, and we'll make a decision. I ask him, what if I refuse? and colonel says in that case, you're in big trouble.
>
> I'd been in prison three times. Two times were in the loony bin . . . and everything that anyone else might have learned in college, I'd learned there. Fine, I say, so where are the forms? . . . This was on a Friday evening. On Monday I got another call: please come in to surrender your [internal] passport. Then came the negotiations about departure dates; I didn't want to leave so soon. But, they said, you have no passport.[43]

Usually it took three or four months to do all the paperwork involved in getting permission to leave. Brodsky was on a plane to Vienna within about four weeks of his first phone call from OVIR. It was not that Brodsky was considered especially dangerous; this treatment was part of an overall strategy aimed at purging the country of dissidents.

By the late 1960s the hermetic seal around the USSR had begun to show a few cracks. A certain number of Soviet citizens were being allowed to leave the country on the grounds of "family reunification." Between 1968 and 1970 roughly a thousand Soviet Jews per year emigrated to Israel. In 1971 the number jumped to thirty thousand; in 1972, to thirty-two thousand. The Soviet Union was undergoing the beginnings of economic crisis that eventually led to its downfall two decades later. In the early 1970s, Brezhnev was left with no choice other than to slow down the arms race and improve relations with the West. Both Soviet missiles and Soviet citizens wishing to emigrate were pawns in the great geopolitical game being played out. The spike in the number of Jews emigrating from the USSR, which took place in the spring of 1972, can be explained very simply: President Richard Nixon was coming to Moscow on a state visit.[44] The United States and its powerful Jewish lobby had always pushed for easing restrictions on emigration from the USSR, and the Soviet powers that be were giving Nixon an advance on grain deliveries and détente.

Brodsky already had his *vyzov*—his official invitation, certified by the government of Israel. Many Soviets, Jewish or part Jewish, found foreigners willing to provide a generic version "just in case." Some people received these invitations without ever asking for them. Apparently this was the case with Brodsky. At any rate, he was not planning to act on it. At the time he was still assuming that his situation might change and that he might eventually get a chance to travel outside the USSR—a privilege sometimes accorded even to not-so-official writers like the avant-garde poets Viktor Sosnora and Gennady Aigi. But even legally sanctioned emigration from the USSR meant a complete break with the past, with no chance to return even for a family visit. Official propaganda equated emigration with treason. Brodsky was too attached—to his parents, his son, his friends, his native city, his language—to want to leave any of them forever.

The Leningrad KGB, however, had its own designs. This was a convenient way to get rid of an unpredictable character once and for all. Brodsky had hardly any time to pack or even say his good-byes. On June 4, 1972, ten days after his thirty-second birthday, armed with a briefcase full of manuscripts and a manual typewriter, he was put on a plane to Vienna.

CHAPTER SEVEN

> A loyal subject of these second-rate years,
> I proudly admit that my finest ideas
> are second-rate, and may the future take them
> as trophies of my struggle against suffocation.
>
> —"I Sit by the Window"

THE WORLD ACCORDING TO BRODSKY

THE POEMS COLLECTED in *A Halt in the Desert* and *The End of a Beautiful Era* present a world created by an already mature poet. That is, whatever the next quarter-century might bring, from this point on, Brodsky himself would not change. He would simply become more accomplished in his own idiom; the language in which he spoke of his own universe would become increasingly more precise and sophisticated. This maturity manifested itself in the clarity with which he spoke of the world, of faith, of people, of society. This was true even of his seemingly contradictory views on Christianity and culture, Russia and the West, ethics and aesthetics; the contradictions themselves were expressed both precisely and vividly.

Brodsky was antidoctrinarian on principle; he rejected all systems, philosophical, religious, or political.[1] When a journalist once asked him to describe his philosophy of life he answered: "I don't have a philosophy of life: I have a number of convictions. If [I were] to call it a philosophy, I would call it a philosophy of endurance—of the possibility of endurance. It's very simple. When you have some bad situation, there are two ways to deal with it—just to give up or to try to stand it. Well, in some sense, I prefer to stand it as far as I can. So this is my philosophy—that's all, nothing special."[2] Still, certain attitudes prevail in his poetry, and in his remarks on religion, philosophy, and politics.[3] But first of all, while we acknowledge the formalists' rule forbidding the reader to a priori identify the author of a text with its "lyric hero" (its "I"), both Brodsky's extra-literary statements and his general behavior through his life testify that the motto of the Russian romantic poet Batyushkov—"Live as you write, write as you live"—is just as applicable to this twentieth-century poet. Between Brodsky in life and Brodsky in verse there is very little difference.

POETRY AND POLITICS

Brodsky liked to say that the only thing poetry and politics had in common were their first two letters. Compared with Evgeniy Evtushenko and other masters of Aesopian language, or with poets of the previous generation—Boris Slutsky or Naum Korzhavin—he was indeed apolitical. His apoliticism lay not in an avoidance of political issues but in his refusal to see them in any other way than sub specie aeternitatis. For Brodsky, social manifestations of good and evil were simply examples of the Manichaean split in human nature itself. A prime illustration is his rethinking of a classic representation of evil that he found in Auden's "Shield of Achilles":

> A ragged urchin, aimless and alone,
> Loitered about that vacancy; a bird
> Flew up to safety from his well-aimed stone;
> That girls are raped, that two boys knife a third,
> Were axioms to him, who'd never heard
> Of any world where promises were kept
> Or one could weep because another wept.

Brodsky recalls these lines in his own poem "Sitting in the Shade" (*Urania*):

> I watch the children
> running in the park.
>
> Their fierce and frantic games,
> their inconsolable wail,
> would trouble all the world to come
> had it the eyes to see.

And eleven stanzas later he says:

> A wiry hellion,
> a street cherub
> sucking on hard candy,
> slingshot aimed at a sparrow in the park,
> isn't thinking "I can hit [it]"—
> he's convinced "I can kill [it]."

Auden's urchin commits a senseless crime because he has been born and raised in squalor and the cruelty it begets. Brodsky's hellion does the very same thing for fun.

Brodsky once said that this stanza by Auden "should be carved on the gates of every existing state, indeed on the gates of our whole world," but it is clear that the younger poet has reinterpreted Auden according to his own lights.[4] For Brodsky, the common cruelty of children has more to do with anthropology than with either sociology or economics.

Equally famous is Auden's line from "September 1, 1939": "We must love one another or die."[5] Brodsky had often copied this poem's rhythmic patterns, overall composition, and style of self-description. He did this not only in "Sitting in the Shade" but in other poems as well. The Christian invocation to practice universal love and charity as the only alternative to universal self-destruction was something that Brodsky accepted unconditionally. At times he affirmed it in colloquial and even rough terms: "we didn't give [blacks] birth / not for us to give them death" ("A Speech about Spilt Milk"); at times he found strikingly new words to express eternal truths, as in "No matter what was around, no matter," in which he says that the star of Bethlehem stands out from other stars in its "capacity for confusing brothers with others."

Brodsky's disagreements with his favorite poet were not over Christian ethics or dogma, but rather over the roots of xenophobia, war, genocide. In the 1930s, Auden's views on war and revolution were more or less Marxist: "Hunger allows no choice." Brodsky thought otherwise. He thought that these issues could be resolved.

> Mainly, you should get the masses food and jobs.
> (This is something you can read in Hobbes.)
> ("A Speech about Spilt Milk"; non-poetic)

According to Hobbes, a good part of the human race had already constructed various forms of a unified state, and these Leviathans had more or less done away with wars that pitted "every man against every man" by creating systems aimed at ensuring the welfare of the society. However, in a police state even a full stomach hardly guarantees a happy life. The inevitable tragedy lies in humans' biological capacity for endless reproduction. As Brodsky almost presciently writes in January 1967, well-fed masses also are subject to mass suffering. The suffering simply takes on a different form:

> The euphoria, the high,
> will dictate its own rules.
> ("A Speech about Spilt Milk"; non-poetic)

Brodsky had a grim Malthusian vision of the coming apocalypse.

> The work of so many hands
> won't perish by the sword,
> but by cheap pants
> stripped off in heat
>
> The future's black, but
> [black] with people, not
> because it
> seems so black to me.
> ("Sitting in the Shade"; non-poetic)

There are too many people in the world, and there are more of them each day. The crowd, the army, the chorus, are always hostile to the private person, the individual. Twenty years later Brodsky would begin his Nobel lecture with the following words: "For someone rather private, for someone who all his life has preferred his private condition to any role of social significance, and who went in this preference rather far—far from his motherland, to say the least, for it is better to be a total failure in democracy than a martyr, or *la crème de la crème* in tyranny—for such a person to find himself all of a sudden on this rostrum is a somewhat uncomfortable and trying experience."[6] In a true democracy, society is grounded in a contract agreed upon by private individuals; but in an ochlocracy (rule of the mob), which is inseparable from tyranny, the private individual is at best marginalized and at worst persecuted as an apostate and criminal (see "Plato Elaborated"). That is how it has always been, and that is how it always will be:

> In the future, population,
> beyond a doubt, will keep on growing. Peons
> will rhythmically ply the hoe
> beneath the scorching sun. A man in specs
> will sadly leaf through Marx in coffee bars.
> ("An Encyclopedia Entry")

The dream of the private person (the political hypostasis of Brodsky's lyric hero) is to settle down with his lover in a place "walled off from the continent / by a very high dam" ("Prophecy," *OVP*), or "[i]f one's fated to be born in Caesar's Empire / let him live aloof, provincial, by the seashore" ("Letters to a Roman Friend"). But in fact he is doomed to live among the crowd, and all he can do when the tyrant appears is "hiss through clenched teeth, 'You creep'" ("Plato Elaborated"). This dream, and the pariah motif too, often take the shape of some life in an imagined country, city, or era, none of these so much fantastic as ideal—ideal in the sense that they describe some Platonic ideal reality. The USSR was in essence an empire. The Soviet metropolis was in essence Plato's ideal city. A private life in a collectivist empire required walling oneself off from the world "by a very high dam."

Brodsky favored the term "tyranny" for this most hateful form of government, and in 1979 he laid out his thoughts on the subject in an essay entitled just that: "On Tyranny." In Brodsky's definition, tyranny combines the three worst forms of government described by Aristotle: tyranny, oligarchy, and ochlocracy. By the twentieth century these three had become indistinguishable; oligarchy had simply become single-party rule. This single party sets a tyrant atop the pyramid of state, which is made possible and perhaps inevitable by the "stampede of the masses."[7] There are too many people in the world. "The idea of one's existential uniqueness gets replaced by that of one's anonymity."[8] The collective political will of the masses is reduced to the lowest common denominator: strength and stability. A rigid pyramid of power with one party and a tyrant at its apex is in the common mind the most reliable and convenient form of organization, because tyranny "structures your life for you. It does this as meticulously as possible, certainly far better than a democracy does.

Also, it does it for your own sake, for any display of individualism in a crowd may be harmful: first of all for the person who displays it; but one should care about those next to him as well. This is what the party-run state, with its security services, mental institutions, police, and citizens' sense of loyalty, is for. Still, all these devices are not enough: the dream is to make every man his own bureaucrat."[9]

For all their differences in personality, the three Soviet leaders under whom Brodsky lived came to power and ruled precisely in the way his essay describes. Brodsky saw Stalin as the most "monstrous." But it was under Khrushchev that Brodsky was jailed, and it was Khrushchev who, when briefed on his case, said that "the trial itself was stupid and ugly, but Brodsky should be glad that the charge was parasitism and not politics, because those poems could have gotten him a good ten years."[10] It was under Brezhnev that Brodsky returned from internal exile and was, seven years later, rather humanely (by Soviet standards) forced to emigrate to the West. However, much of the detail in Brodsky's description of a tyrant suggests Brezhnev rather than Stalin or Khrushchev. For Brodsky it was Brezhnev's sheer ordinariness, his purely bureaucratic climb to power, that made him a typical tyrant. There was nothing unusual about Brezhnev: unlike Lenin, he was not obsessed with an idea; unlike Stalin, he was not especially Machiavellian or cruel; unlike Khrushchev, he never played the capricious paterfamilias.

In Brodsky's poetry the tyrant always has an aura of banality about him. In "Anno Domini" (*OVP*) the ruler suffers liver problems; in "To a Tyrant" he snacks on a croissant in a cheap café; in "Post Aetatem Nostram" (*KPE*) he grunts and strains on the toilet; in "The Residence" he dons a lavender sweatshirt and dozes off over columns of numbers.[11] He is a slow-witted, aging, ailing man. The most human thing about him is that he is mortal.

In a letter to Brezhnev dated June 4, 1972, the day Brodsky left the Soviet Union, the poet writes: "From evil, anger, hate—even if justified—we none of us profit. We all face the same sentence. Death. I who write these lines will die; you who read them will, too. It's hard enough to exist in this world—there's no need to make it any harder."[12]

Brezhnev, of course, did not reply to this letter in a bottle. He probably never even saw it; his assistants would hardly have troubled the general secretary with something so trivial and impertinent. And even if he had seen it, he probably would not have understood anything other than "you too will die." Poetry and philosophy were irrelevant to the life of a dyed-in-the-wool bureaucrat; any dialogue between the Party leader and the populace had always taken a certain ritual form: the leader stood at a microphone and read a prepared speech (Brezhnev did this with some difficulty), after which the audience expressed its unanimous approval with thunderous applause or a "forest of hands" raised by the Party rank-and-file in their vote for the "petty but predatory demon."[13]

The word "petty" (*melkii*) is the key to Brodsky's problematics of evil. The "banality of evil" was a phrase first coined by Hannah Arendt in her book *Eichmann in Jerusalem* (1961). What she meant was not that evil itself is banal but that those who do evil often are. This anti-romantic view has its roots in the Russian literature of the nineteenth century. Tolstoy depicts Napoleon as a thoroughly ordinary man; Dostoevsky's devil in *The Brothers Karamazov* is equally unremarkable. The twentieth century has shown time and time again that great evil, be it Stalin's mass collectivization and purges, the Nazi obliteration of the Jews, Mao's Cultural Revolution, or terror and genocide in Cambodia and Rwanda, is most often done not by demonic supermen but by ordinary people. The average person may have psychotic tendencies or may not, but in either case he is perfectly capable of committing unthinkable crimes on a very grand scale. Brodsky was all too well acquainted with this notion. His persecutors and tormenters—the Lerners-Tolstikovs-Savelyevas-Voevodins of the world—were nondescript, vulgar people driven by primitive wants and fears; their speech was either clumsy or clichéd; their ideological training had left them unable to think for themselves. In essence, these people were no different from those at the top of the pyramid in that their evil sprang from a common intellectual and moral void. The banality of evil reveals what Judeo-Christian ethics has traditionally called the "insubstantiality of evil": evil fills a void; evil requires emptiness, it requires hollow people, in order to exist.

This is the theme of Brodsky's very first essay published in the West, as well as of a commencement address he later gave at Williams College.[14] In his message to the graduating class of 1984, he states that "the surest defense against Evil is extreme individualism, originality of thinking, whimsicality, even—if you will—eccentricity."[15] A less provocative term for this might be "critical thinking" or "self-examination." However, in

Brodsky's essays and poems one motif flies in the face of his pronouncements on individualism and eccentricity. When speaking of the villains of Russian history, this poet, whose main claim to fame is that "My song was out of tune, my voice was cracked, / but at least no chorus can ever sing it back" ("I Sit by the Window"), always uses the pronoun "we."

MOTHERLAND: US AND THEM

Whenever an interlocutor used the common Russian turn of phrase *u nas,* meaning roughly "where we come from" or "our way of doing things," Brodsky never missed an opportunity to interrupt with a sarcastic *u vas* (*your* way). The sarcasm was usually joking, playful, but this almost automatic response suggests a basic stance: no concessions, no quarter given to collectivist ideology. So the first readers of "A Halt in the Desert" (*OVP*) were all the more struck by his unusual use of "we":

> There are so few Greeks now left in Leningrad
> that we have torn down the Greek church,
> to make an open space
> to build a concert hall.
> (Non-poetic)

Once a center for the Saint Petersburg Greek Orthodox community, the "Greek church" was razed in 1967, and in its place the city authorities built a concert hall to commemorate the fiftieth anniversary of the Russian Revolution. The first stanza speaks of the ugliness of the new building. But the original church was no architectural gem either, and while many regretted the passing of a city landmark, the intelligentsia more or less ignored the event. Five years earlier, the razing of the Church of the Assumption had caused a burst of futile protest. Brodsky's poem is not a meditation on cultural or architectural preservation as such; rather, it is a meditation on the symbolic significance of what has just happened: Russia has broken with its Christian and Hellenistic cultural heritage, and here at the end of its history a "flat and ugly line has been drawn." The use of the first-person plural "we" at the beginning of the poem might seem strange, because the decision to tear down an old building and raise a new one was made by the very same Leningrad bureaucrats who were hounding Brodsky. But the further we ourselves read, the better we understand that Brodsky is not speaking of yet another crime against culture committed by the Soviet regime but of the collective guilt of a nation that produced this regime, that refused to accept the historical alternative, the heritage of Greece and Greek democracy. "A Halt in the Desert" ends with a coda of questions addressed to the future; these questions are not asked by an "I" sitting on the "ruins of the apse" in the Greek church. They are asked by a "we."

> This night I'm looking out the window
> and thinking, Where have we gone?
> Which are we further from—
> the Church or Hellenism?
> What are we close to? What lies ahead?
> Perhaps a different era?
> And if so, what's our common duty, then?
> And what will we have to bring in sacrifice?
> (Non-poetic)

This motif of Russian historical responsibility manifests itself even more forcefully as a sense of personal shame and disgrace. When asked if he ever wanted to leave Russia, Brodsky answered: "Yes, when Soviet troops entered Czechoslovakia in 1968. I remember that I wanted to leave, go somewhere, anywhere. Mostly out of shame. Out of knowing that I belonged to a nation that does things like this. Because for better or for worse, some part of the responsibility for that falls on the citizen of that nation."[16] His satiric poem "Letter to General Z" (*KPE*) is a response to the occupation: the speaker, an old soldier of the empire, refuses to fight: "General! I've got the shakes. / Can't quite get why—out of shame? out of fear?" In "Lines on the Winter Campaign, 1980" he expresses his feeling about the Soviet government's latest escapade even more directly:

> Glory to those who, their glances lowered,
> marched in the sixties to abortion tables,
> sparing the homeland its present stigma.

In "Anno Domini," written two years after "A Halt in the Desert," Brodsky says directly where the guilt lies. It lies in every one of "us." It is in the conformist urge to be "like everyone else," in the refusal to be an individual.[17] Collectivism is a denial of divine predetermination of life itself:

> The grave will render all alike.
> So, if only in our lifetime, let us be various!

If we ("we") chose anonymity and apathy, we have chosen the comfort of entropy over the uncomfortable right to think and judge:

> we cannot judge our homeland. The sword of justice
> will stick fast in our personal disgrace:
> the heirs, the power, are in stronger hands . . .
> How good that vessels are not sailing!
> How good that the sea is freezing!

In Brodsky's poems of the 1960s and 1970s, the motif of the motherland is always couched in terms of immobility, lifelessness, entropy. (The word "stagnation," *zastoy,* would not enter political discourse for another twenty years.) In earlier Russian poetry on civic themes, rhetoric had been the rule: in Brodsky's poetry historical or political themes are presented in visual images, detailed and elaborate, but still essentially metaphor. In "A Speech about Spilt Milk" (*KPE*), "The Funeral of Bobo" (*KPE*), and other pieces with the real Leningrad as a backdrop, the metaphor is the freezing cold that brings the city to a standstill. In "Letter to General Z" (*KPE*) it is an impassable tropical swamp in a mythical landscape: "Our cannon are stuck nose down in mud." In the bold combination of two allegories in the "Emperor" chapter of "Post Aetatem Nostram" (*KPE*) it is the lack of movement in both the emperor's bowels and in the historical process.

> These days we're barely scraping by.
> The empire's like a trireme
> up a canal too narrow for a trireme.
> The rowers bash their oars against dry land
> and rocks score the hull.
> (Non-poetic)

We refer to Brodsky's historical and political verse as lyric because even in those poems with a primarily political subject the author and his mental state occupy center stage. This subjective lyrical approach to politics is characteristic of a whole number of very different twentieth-century poets: Mandelstam, Pasternak, Tsvetaeva, Akhmatova, Auden. The opening lines of Auden's "September 1, 1939" are so piercing precisely because they are spoken not from on high ("cotton puffs on high") but from "one of the dives / On Fifty-Second Street" in a private voice "Uncertain and afraid."[18]

Russian nineteenth-century practice divided poetry into lyric verse and civic rhetoric. This is one reason why Brodsky was of two minds about Tyutchev: "Tyutchev is, of course, an important figure, but for all the talk about the metaphysical qualities of his verse, people seem to miss the fact that Russian literature never gave birth to a more slavish patriot. . . . As for me, I can't read the second volume of Tyutchev's collected verse without—I won't say disgust—without amazement. On the one hand, we've got the chariot of the firmament and the stars of the heavens making their appointed rounds; on the other, as Vyazemsky put it, 'odes in uniform.'"[19]

BRODSKY'S ASIA

On the surface, "A Halt in the Desert" is a simple enough text. It begins with a scene from the poet's own life: one night he watched the first stages in the razing of the Greek church from the apartment of friends, two sisters from a Tatar family. His historical reflections on the destruction of the church are written in iambic pentameter, but although the content could be told just as well in prose, the verse monologue has a certain dramatic tension (which Brodsky himself would have called lyricism). It develops gradually as the poet alternates between meditations on history and everyday chitchat. A word that might have a narrow and specific meaning in everyday life hints at larger meanings.

> It all started with those Tatar conversations;
> and then some sounds broke in;
> at first they blended with the talk
> but soon they drowned it out.
> An excavator drove into the churchyard,
> an iron wrecking ball dangling from its crane.
> And then, gently, all the walls gave way.
> (Non-poetic)

This at first looks like a simple description of the facts. The only thing slightly odd is the adjective "Tatar." It is hardly likely that his hosts were speaking among themselves in a language that he wouldn't have known; more likely, this is another example of Brodsky's joking use of deliberately naive language (as in "No humanity at the crossroads / or rather, no humans," or "an old lady surrounded by a shepherd— / that is, the dog was running circles round her" from the cycle "February through April," *KPE*). The only thing that "Tatar" means in this text is that Brodsky's friends are Tatars by heritage. But the subtext has its own dynamic. "It all started with those Tatar conversations"—all what? The destruction of the Greek church? If so, the wrecking ball (*girei* in the grammatical case used here) is a hint at the name of the famous Crimean Tatar dynasty founded by Haji Girei after the disintegration of the Golden Horde. Such a pun made obvious would sound too comic in an elegy, but Brodsky does not make it obvious; he leaves it as a subtext. Nonetheless, the subject of Russian historical consciousness has been introduced: Are we Europe or are we Asia?

For Brodsky, Europe and its Hellenistic wellsprings signified harmony (structure), movement, and life. Asia signified chaos (lack of structure), immobility, death.

> . . . death in its speckledness
> looks like the vague outlines of Asia.
> ("1972")

(The association of Asia with death was not new to Brodsky; he had encountered it several times before in reading Vladimir Solovyov).[20]

Geographic (or geopolitical) themes are always presented in a strict paradigm of opposites: East/West, Islam/Christianity, forest/sea, cold/heat, and again, long before "stagnation" became part of the current political lexicon, stagnation/movement.[21] When Brodsky wrote at the end of 1970, "And now I'm gripped by heat! I've got to get out of here!" ("On the 22nd of December 1970, for Yakov Gordin from Iosif Brodsky"), even in this light verse, heat and movement ("out of here") are set against the image of a frozen empire (frozen in both senses of the word: cold and immobile): "The climate too's immobile, in that country" (from "Grand Elegy for John Donne," *OVP*).[22]

We might relate this set system of images embodying the East-West theme to that of the neo-Eurasian school of political philosophy—for example, the question of how a cold climate figures into the self-image of Russians. As one neo-Eurasian scholar said, "January's negative isotherm is the [real] border between Russia and the West."[23] The same paradigm includes the contrast between Islam and Christianity.

Any mention of Islam in Brodsky's early poetry can be puzzling, as in "A Speech about Spilt Milk" (*KPE*). The main thrust of this long monologue (forty 8-line stanzas) is directed at exposing attempts to control the march of history, to "organize" universal happiness. The poet expands the intellectual framework of the poem as he goes, equating all teachings that prefer the collective to the individual and that promise their recruits such things as a life without suffering, earthly bliss, and euphoria (hence the sudden shifts from anticommunist to anti-Tolstoy statements, and the comparison of both to drug addiction). The impetus for this characterization of all ideologies that pretend to an exhaustive explanation of the world and all things in it as "Islamic" probably came from Lev Shestov's *Potestas Clavium*. In an essay on the philosophy of Vyacheslav Ivanov, Shestov speaks ironically about "Muhammedan gnoseology," the most extreme form of which is Marxism.[24] In "A Speech about Spilt Milk" this theme announces itself in the very first few lines, as a rather odd metaphor:

> I arrived at Christmas with empty pockets.
> The publisher's dragging his feet with my novel.
> *Moscow's calendar is infected by the Quran.*
> (Non-poetic; emphasis added)

Mentioning a calendar at Christmas is natural enough, but how and why has the calendar been infected by the Quran? The simplest explanation has to do with tear-off calendars on which the phases of the moon decorate each leaf: the poet notices this and cleverly reminds us of the Islamic symbol of the crescent moon. But the proximity of "Moscow" and "Quran" inevitably calls up some famous twentieth-century lines associating Moscow with Asia. There are Esenin's:

> I love this elmwood city,
> For all its bloat and sag,
> Golden, drowsy Asia
> Sleeps atop its domes.
> (Non-poetic)[25]

And Mandelstam's:

> Midnight in Moscow. Lush Buddhist summer.
> Streets part to the tap-tap of iron boots,

> The boulevard rings, round as pockmarks, rest in bliss.
> (Non-poetic)[26]

In Mandelstam's poem, Moscow's "Buddhism" is linked with plague ("smallpox") and euphoria ("bliss"). In Brodsky's poem, "Moscow's calendar is infected by the Quran"; later Brodsky will bring in the motif of narcotic euphoria. In another poem, phallic minarets are part of the night skyline, and later:

> . . . the crescent moon floats in the dusty window glass,
> high over Moscow's crosses, like a smashing win for Islam.
> ("The season—winter. All quiet on the borders," *KPE;*
> non-poetic)

The second reference in "A Speech about Spilt Milk" comes in the middle of a satirical attack on Marxist political economy, where *Islam* rhymes with *popolam* (equal distribution):

> Knock on wood, we weren't brought up in Islam,
> cut the yakking about equal distribution.
> (Non-poetic)

Brodsky's more direct criticism of Marxist political economy is couched in terse, categorical statements: "Labor is no commodity—that's an insult to the workers"; "Labor is the goal of existence and its form." The source of these ideas can be found in *Phenomenology of Spirit,* in which Hegel maintains that the true essence of labor is in the production of goods, not in their use; Father Sergius Bulgakov developed these ideas in his *Philosophy of Economy*. The joke about Islam/*popolam* also recalls another Bulgakov. In Mikhail Bulgakov's satirical novel *The Heart of a Dog,* a former dog, now a Marxist, explains his economic program as "Take it all, divide it up." But more likely than not, Brodsky was thinking of S. L. Frank's article in *Signposts* (*Vekhi*), where the author wrote: "The moral pathos of socialism is focused on the idea of distributive justice and is exhausted by it. This morality also has its roots in the mechanistic-rationalistic theory of happiness, in the conviction that it is not necessary, generally speaking, to *construct* the conditions for happiness, they can simply be taken or seized from those who have appropriated them illegally for their own self-interest."[27]

While the invectives against the Marxist theory of surplus value, the ironic asides on Eastern religions, and the contemptuous remarks on drug addiction might seem hopelessly jumbled, there is method to Brodsky's madness. Indeed, if work is not what we do but what we sell, a commodity rather than an occupation, then the perfect deal comes down to no work and all pay—idleness in exchange for endless pleasure. This is a spiritual dead-end, and Brodsky sees it in drug highs, Buddhist nirvana, and Muslim paradise alike—in any and all utopian dreams of universal happiness.

We should not forget that this poem was written in an ironic key and that Brodsky's metaphors have to do with the societies dominated by these religions rather than with the religions themselves. These societies are by and large despotic societies where human rights are generally ignored. For Brodsky the words "Asia," "Islam," and "Tatar" are symbols not only of a collective way of life but of a collective way of thought. His essay "Flight from Byzantium" (1985) would focus on the same issue; it is a protest against a society that denies the "I" in favor of the "we," in which there is no difference between a mass of people and a massive dust storm.

What was Brodsky's attitude toward the real, nonmetaphorical Asia?

In 1990 he made some remarks that on September 11, 2001, would seem prophetic:

> Our world is turning quite pagan. And I wonder whether this paganism might not lead to a clash—and I'm very afraid of this—to an extremely brutal religious clash . . . between the Islamic world and a world that has only a vague recollection of Christianity. The Christian world will be helpless to defend itself; the Islamic world will pressure it relentlessly. All this comes down to population ratios, to demographics. And I see this clash as something very real. . . . [I see] a future rent by a conflict between the spirit of tolerance and the spirit of intolerance. . . . The pragmatists say that the difference between these two worlds is not so great. I don't believe that for a second. And I think that we should be done with the Islamic view of the world. After all, our world is six hundred years older than Islam's. So I think we have some right to determine what's right and what's wrong.[28]

"Admonition," a poem written in 1987, is devoted entirely to the theme of Asia as a dangerous place where travelers meet treachery at every step, where human life is cheap. This poem also holds another key to Brodsky's ambivalence toward Asia. On close reading, we find a collision between Asian (more accurately, Central Asian) realia—high and wide cheekbones, dark-brown eyes, silt-filled rivers, tall mountains, bare plains, the smell of dried-dung campfires—and the Russian language itself. If in the first line the reader is sent to Asia ("Trekking in Asia, spending nights in strange dwellings"), in the second line Brodsky lists these dwellings in strictly Russian terms. This stylistic nuance is lost in translation: "in log cabins [*izba*], bathhouses [*banya*], storage sheds [*labaz*] and even wooden palaces [*terem*]." All four have associations with old, rural, folk-tale Russia. This strategy of mixing "Asian" and "Russian" continues throughout the poem. The second stanza begins with the caution to "be wary of broad cheekbones," but in the third we are back to the "*izba*" with the "*muzhik* [Russian peasant] and his wife." In other words, we are dealing with a frightful image of a Russia-Asia, with Eurasia, with Solovyov's "Russia of Xerxes," if you will.[29]

Brodsky's thought here is not to tell us yet again what so many nineteenth-century writers already have: "Scratch a Russian and you'll find a Tartar." It is that Asia is not a geopolitical construct so much as a mental one. In his 1985 polemic "Why Milan Kundera Is Wrong about Dostoevsky" he treats this theme frankly.[30] As long as Central Europe continues to live under despotic regimes and collectivist ideology, it might as well be called "Western Asia." To some degree, Brodsky's Asia mythologem encompasses both Solovyov (Asia is our eternal and dangerous enemy) and Blok (Asia is us / we are Asia): the difference from either traditional myth lies in Brodsky's moral stance. Unlike Solovyov, Brodsky does not challenge his readers to take up arms in some apocalyptic battle between civilizations; unlike Blok in his (in)famous 1918 poem "Scythians," he does not herald the coming of "Asia." For Brodsky, these myths are two sides of the same coin: both manifest a collective sense of national righteousness and pride. Solovyov takes pride in the fact that *we* are no "herd of slaves"; Blok takes pride in the fact that *we*, unlike the decadent West, have not lost our collective élan vital. Brodsky is willing to share in the collective national guilt over the destruction of the church, but for him, any sense of achievement can only be a private one—individual freedom and personal autonomy.

In Brodsky's world there was another "East," one that had nothing to do with Islam. This was the Far East. He was drawn to this part of the world all his life, beginning with his father's tales of wartime China. He pays tribute to classical Japanese and Chinese literature in his "Letters from the Ming Dynasty," where the poet fantastically intertwines events from his own life with images and motifs borrowed from Sei Shōnagon, Ryūnosuke Akutagawa, and classical Chinese verse. In the 1980s this poem became part of his standard repertoire for public readings. His interest was strong enough that toward the end of his life he even began studying Chinese.[31]

Brodsky was roundly criticized for his interpretation of the East-West dichotomy, and especially for his 1985 essay "Flight from Byzantium." Solzhenitsyn saw it as yet another attempt to slander Russia, Russian history, and the Russian Orthodox Church.[32] Sanna Turoma, examining Brodsky's essays in the light of the postcolonialist theoretician and essayist Edward Said's *Orientalism,* came up with a different diagnosis. Brodsky was suffering from nostalgia for imperialism and stereotypical "orientalist" perceptions.[33] These criticisms come from opposite poles of the political spectrum, but they have one thing in common: both read Brodsky's texts as ideological statements.

But Brodsky was not writing ideology; he was writing lyric prose. He never offers his reader a finished conceptual system; he is giving us impressions: shepherds' huts on the slopes of the Tian Shan; the hot, dusty streets of Istanbul. Any ideology here is imposed by the reader: by the true believer and Russian patriot Solzhenitsyn, by the postmodernist Western scholar—and, no doubt, by the writer of these lines, who has his own bias.

QUESTIONS OF FAITH

In "A Speech about Spilt Milk," Brodsky's stylistically motley, fevered credo reads, "Usually he who spits on God / spits on people first." This boy raised in an atheistic society and a secular family was interested in philosophical issues from the start; he became acquainted with the tenets of Hinduism and Buddhism before he ever learned anything about Judaism or Christianity. He did not read the Bible until he was twenty-three.

Was he a believer? If so, in what? Was he a Christian, a Jew, a Buddhist—or someone who belonged to no religious confession but has his own relationship with the Almighty?

It wouldn't be appropriate for this author to speculate about Brodsky's faith—or lack of it. The only straight answer Brodsky himself ever gave to such a question was that he "would rather not resort to any formal religious rite or service."[34] In "The Fifth Anniversary" he is sharper: "I never liked crassness, and never kissed an icon" (*Urania*). The line prompted an outraged response from an anonymous group calling itself Russian Orthodox Christians from the USSR, who shot off a letter to the editors of *Kontinent*—it was entitled snappily but rather inaccurately "Judases."[35] Brodsky responded in kind. Two years later, in his panoramic "A Show," he caricatures a set of born-again monsters who have replaced faith with ritual, jingoism, and xenophobia.

> Some true believer walks in, says "Now *I'm* in charge;
> my soul is full of Firebirds, nostalgia for the tsar.
> Prince Igor will return, enjoy his Yaroslavna.
> If you don't let me cross myself, I'll smack you in the face.
> The plague out of the West is worse than leprosy or mange.
> Sing out my squeezebox, drown out the saxophone,
> that spawn of jazz."
> Then in tears they kiss the icons,
> victims of the circumsci——
> (*Urania;* non-poetic)

The unfinished last word is deliberately ambiguous: it could be either "victims of [the] circumcision"—meaning Jewish intellectuals who flirted with Russian Orthodoxy—or "victims of the circumcised," meaning garden-variety Russian anti-Semites.

Brodsky's skepticism toward Orthodoxy and its rituals does not mean that he was any less skeptical of Protestantism and its various evangelical offshoots. Still, whenever he addresses God-on-High in his verse, he invariably speaks informally, in the evangelical manner.

> Lean over, I'll whisper something to you: I am
> grateful for everything
> ("Roman Elegies")

> . . . in God's whorled ear,
> closed to the clash of day's discord,
> whisper four syllables, soft and clear:

Forgive me, Lord.
("Lithuanian Divertissement")

Brodsky's faith manifests itself not in prayers for salvation from torment but in gratitude and forgiveness, in what is in essence happiness.[36] "Yet until brown clay has been crammed down my larynx, / only gratitude will be gushing from it" ("May 24, 1980"). His comment on Akhmatova's line "You don't know just what you've been forgiven" was that it was the "soul's response to existence"—"because the one who forgives is always greater than the hurt, or the one who causes it."[37]

In interviews, Brodsky might talk about his Calvinism, but this was a figure of speech, a trope. The only thing Calvinist about his metaphysics was the belief in original sin (or, in Brodsky's case, original guilt) that cannot be prayed or worked away. "According to Calvinist doctrine, people answer to themselves, for everything. That is, to a certain extent, we are our own Last Judgment."[38] In "Letter to the President" (1993) he writes: "Don't we all harbor a certain measure of guilt, totally unrelated to the state, of course, but no less palpable? So whenever the arm of the state touches us, we regard it vaguely as our comeuppance, as a touch of the blunt but nevertheless expected tool of Providence."[39] Here Brodsky is not talking about sin in the traditional Christian sense of the word but about existential guilt, the failure to be true to oneself, about Heideggerian inauthenticity. Or, as the name of his essay "Less Than One" makes clear, the fault lies in being less than oneself. This real self, which each moment lives to its full capacity, is an authentic being, never a member of a herd. The moral vector of life is the striving to become equal to oneself—something that only happens when one creates.

Brodsky's statements about the Judaic notion of an inexplicably arbitrary God are also to be taken with a grain of salt. As I noted above, such declarations have little to do with the Jewish faith itself or with Talmudic or Hasidic tradition. The God that Brodsky speaks of has nothing to do with organized religion. This is the God of Kierkegaard and Shestov. Brodsky's "Isaac and Abraham" was a direct reaction to Kierkegaard's *Fear and Trembling* and probably to Shestov's reflections on Kierkegaard.[40] It would not be an exaggeration to say that Brodsky's stance for the rest of his life was also a reaction to these texts.

In 1992, at the suggestion of Petr Vail, Brodsky published a small book of Christmas poems. When Brodsky autographed this book for his friends, he would sign it "from a correspondence-course Christian." For him, loving Christ was natural; worshipping him was not. On one hand, we have his Christmas poems, and others, too, all of which share an element of *imitatio Christi* ("Gorbunov and Gorchakov," "Nature Morte," "To a Chair"). On the other, we have sincere regret over the metaphysical insufficiency of Christianity. It seems as if Brodsky is the only serious modern writer to truly regret the death of polytheism. Of Julian the Apostate he says: "Risking the charge of idealization, one is tempted to call Julian a great soul obsessed with the recognition that neither paganism nor Christianity is sufficient by itself and that, taken separately, neither can exercise man's spiritual capacity to the fullest. There are always tormenting leftovers, always the sense of a certain partial vacuum, causing at best, a sense of sin. The fact is that man's spiritual restlessness is not satisfied by either font, and there is no doctrine which, without incurring condemnation, one may speak of as combining both, except, perhaps stoicism or existentialism (which might be viewed as a form of stoicism, sponsored by Christianity)."[41] We should note also his choice of words; he terms the person who incorporates the best of human qualities "a great soul" (*anima magna*). We should remember that this is also how he defines Akhmatova in a lapidary poem written in 1989 on the centenary of her birth. In Auden, too, he finds a "generosity of spirit."

However "religious" Brodsky's poetry may or may not be, one thing is clear. This is the poet who brought metaphysics back into Russian poetic discourse. He sometimes prided himself on restoring the word "soul" to the Russian poetic lexicon, and, indeed, "soul" is one of the words he uses most often: 204 times.[42] But what he has in mind is not the word itself. (How often, even in official Soviet poetry, have we heard about the "Russian soul"?) Vladimir Maramzin once wrote that modern man uses this word "only in its poetic sense, but meanwhile he's been taught not to believe in either poetry or sense."[43] But for Brodsky, the word "soul" means exactly what it means in Vladimir Dahl's standard dictionary of the Russian language: "an immortal spiritual entity possessing both mind and will." This is not to say that Brodsky was the only Russian poet exploring this theme in the 1960s. But the most popular poets of his generation—Evtushenko, Voznesensky, Akhmadulina—for all their political boldness and flair, were relatively indifferent to questions of faith and belief. If they ever touched on the subject, the touch was little different from that of the regime—as in Akhmadulina's starkly atheistic 1962 poem "God." Bulat Okudzhava sometimes used religious imagery in his poems of the 1950s and 1960s, but only and always as a metaphor for some generic human nobility (as in "Please lower the dark blue blinds" or "I have to pray to someone" or "Prayer").

Meanwhile, Akhmatova was still alive (if not well), and many of the "underground" poets close to Brodsky were also exploring spiritual themes.[44] What distinguishes his work from theirs is that while they were discussing God in some abstract modernist framework, Brodsky was addressing the Almighty in highly familiar—and archaic—terms, as if he felt some need to go back to an earlier tradition before setting off on his own. This is as true for his simple but very popular "Stanzas" (*Uncollected*)—"And tirelessly the soul / rushing into the dark / will flicker under bridges in the smoke of Petrograd" (non-poetic)—as it is for the monumental "Grand Elegy for John Donne" (*OVP*). In the "Grand Elegy" Brodsky, without stylization, turns directly to an archaic genre: the conversation between the soul and the body. But even in "Stanzas" and the "Grand Elegy," and other poems written at age twenty ("The losses of the spirit, the cries of the soul" and "Now more often I feel tired"), the soul is not a metaphor for the conscience or other moral attributes, but an "immortal spiritual entity."[45]

Young Brodsky, who belonged to no religion and who had not even the rudiments of a religious upbringing, was somehow operating within a framework of "soul" and "God," accepting a religious worldview apophatically, so to speak, because for him atheism was inseparable from the Soviet regime. His poetic imagination was working at full strength, but his religious thematics were not yet fully thought through. He even wrote his "Grand Elegy" without having read either John Donne's poetry or the celebrated sermons. At the time, everyone was reading Hemingway, and those who hadn't read *For Whom the Bell Tolls* (not yet published in the USSR) at least knew the famous epigraph: "No man is an island . . . and therefore send not to know for whom the bell tolls, it tolls for thee." As Brodsky recalled afterward, he thought at the time that these were lines from a poem, and eighteen months later, when Lidiya Chukovskaya sent a collection of Donne's poetry to Norenskaya, he tried to find the poem.[46] More sophisticated, contradictory, and dramatic is the interpretation of faith in his post-1964 poems, written, that is, after Brodsky acquainted himself with the Bible, began reading works by religious thinkers, and, most important, came face to face with serious personal trials.

The two poems in which this flickering religiosity, sometimes faith, sometimes agnosticism, is most fully expressed are "Conversation with a Celestial Being" (1970) and "Nature Morte" (1971), both of which were published in *The End of a Beautiful Era*. Brodsky always said that the part of the Bible that made the greatest impression on him was the book of Job. The tragic and desperate tone of "Conversation with a Deity" is the same as in Job's complaint. But Job knows for certain just whom he's addressing, and Job gets an answer. Brodsky's speaker is more like the characters in Beckett's *Waiting for Godot;* he is not sure of the celestial status or even the existence of his addressee. Sometimes it's an angel, sometimes it seems to be the Supreme Being himself (since the speaker's gift is returning to him), sometimes it's one of the "puppets crisscrossing the dome of the sky," all of which leads in turn to conclusions that are either agnostic ("speech has no addressee") or quasi-religious and existentialist ("all faith is nothing more than one-way mail"). Moral support, the "courage to be" in the face of suffering and death, is to be sought not in God but in oneself.

"Conversation" predates "Nature Morte" by not much more than a year, but the latter poem provides a more decisive, though hardly simple, answer to the unanswerable questions of the former. When "Nature Morte" was written, doctors suspected that Brodsky might have cancer; later, the diagnosis would turn out to be less frightening. The poem contains lines mentioning the symptoms of anemia that accompany the disease:

> My blood is very cold,
> its cold is more withering
> than iced-to-the-bottom streams

and

> These two
> thighs are like blocks of ice.
> Branched veins show blue against
> skin that is marble white.

There is no "soul," but there is an "absurd," which migrated into Brodsky's vocabulary straight from Camus's "Myth of Sisyphus." Brodsky cites Camus's thoughts on the absurdity of human existence in other poems from *The End of a Beautiful Era:* "Letter to General Z" ("the sum of suffering equals the absurd") and "Homage to Yalta" ("But this is the apologia of the absurd! The apotheosis of senselessness!"). Camus's attitude toward the absurd is ambivalent. Given the inevitability of death, human existence itself is absurd: "That idea that 'I am,' my way of acting as if everything has a meaning . . . all that is given the lie in vertiginous fashion by the absurdity of a possible death."[47] But the discovery of the absurd brings man a tragic freedom and even happiness, says Camus, and "[i]t drives out of this world a god who had come into it with dissatisfaction and a preference for futile suffering."[48] But Brodsky does not always share Camus's heroic atheism. In "Nature Morte" he answers the challenge of the absurd with an affirmation of faith, and does so with remarkable poetic inventiveness.

As always in Brodsky, composition is one element of meaning. But with the possible exception of "Gorbunov and Gorchakov," nowhere else does symmetry-asymmetry play such a crucial role as in "Nature Morte." The poem consists of ten numbered sections, each with three quatrains. The first nine are a monologue like that in "A Speech about Spilt Milk," but here focused on the theme of death. As mentioned above, this theme is presented as an opposition—human being versus thing. Like Gaev in *The Cherry Orchard,* who tearfully praises the constancy of the "esteemed wardrobe," Brodsky ironically sets up a contrast between a sideboard, as solid and unshakeable as Notre Dame, and humans, with their pitiful fear of death. Parts 1–3 and 6 are about a human, himself, an "I": "I sit on a bench" (1), "I'm ready to start" (2), "I don't like people" (3), "I sleep in the daytime" (6). In this nine-stanza structure, parts 4 and 7–9 are symmetrical with 1–3 and 6. They deal with things: a tree, a stone, dust, things and objects in general. The "I" is utterly absent. In the middle stands part 5—"Cabinet." Here we find an observation on a specific thing, but the observer is not removed from the text; there is an "I," although it appears as an indirect object: "The old cabinet . . . reminds me . . ." The predominance of the inanimate over the personal in the second half of the poem suggests a deadening, suggests that which becomes a still(ed) life, the literally "dead nature" of a nature-morte. In the ninth stanza, which brings this theme to its close, the author speaks directly of death's coming to what is already in essence a lifeless body, which can now, like an object, a mirror, do nothing more than reflect the face of death.

Here the author's direct monologue ends. But "Nature Morte" does not. Outside the strictly symmetrical structure, as a sort of non sequitur, there is a tenth part, a quasi-Gospel dialogue between the crucified Christ and Mary.[49] It has to do with the mystery of resurrection, the victory over death.

> Mary now speaks to Christ:
> Are you my son?—or God?
> You are nailed to the cross.
> Where lies my homeward road?
>
> "Can I pass through my gate
> not having understood:
> Are you dead?—or alive?
> Are you my son?—or God?"
>
> Christ speaks to her in turn:
> "Whether dead or alive,
> woman, it's all the same—
> son or God, I am thine."

No difference between death and life? It sounds like Kierkegaard's "leap of faith." But Brodsky's lapidary lines provide a poetic justification of this response to the tragic dichotomy. There is no difference because "I am thine." The standard practice in modern Russian is to leave out present-tense forms of the verb "to be," so Russian readers tend to forget that the full grammatical construction presupposes it (*esm'*—now considered archaic). When bound to others by love, people *are*. Without these bonds, *homo homini res est* (man is a thing to man).[50] However the courageous isolation of Camus's "l'homme absurd" might have appealed to Brodsky, in "Nature Morte" his answers to humankind's "accursed questions" are always couched in traditionally Christian terms. And not just in "Nature Morte." Love as salvation is a theme that runs throughout his later work. And in spite of one provocative line claiming that "People are not my thing," he would later say that many "—essentially everyone!—in this world at least / is worthy of love" (*Urania*).

THE WORLD ACCORDING TO BRODSKY (CONCLUSION)

In summary, here are the essentials of Brodsky's worldview.

In it we can find echoes of many philosophers and philosophical schools.[51] But his political philosophy is quite orderly and internally consistent. He interprets Russian history in the spirit of "Westernizers" from Chaadaev to Fedotov. As a matter of principle, he is opposed to Communism. He is a liberal, if we define liberalism as the assertion that personal freedom is an absolute value (compare Solzhenitsyn in chapter 9 of *The First Circle,* where "Liberalism is love of freedom"). He assessed capitalism in the same liberal spirit. In 1980 he said that Polish freedom had been crushed by "Soviet tanks and Western banks" (in that the West, more interested in trade and economic relations with the USSR than in Polish Solidarity, stood by and did nothing). But his basic tendency was to focus on individual psychology and aesthetics rather than on politics: "Man's greatest enemy is not Communism, not Socialism, not Capitalism, but rather the vulgarity of the human heart, of human imagination. The primitive imagination of Marx, for example. The vulgar imagination of his Russian followers."[52]

There is no consistency to Brodsky's approach to morality and ethics, no perfect match with any philosophical system. In his stubborn preference for "thoughts about things" over things themselves, to time over space, we see the influence of Platonic and Neoplatonic classical tradition.[53] But his verse also contains poisonous barbs aimed at this tradition ("Elaborating Plato"). Many of his most important poetic texts are permeated with a Christian morality, a Christian spirit of universal love and forgiveness, yet in his Nobel lecture and in many of his other declarations he asserts, like Nietzsche, the primacy of aesthetics over ethics. On Brodsky's philosophical system—or lack thereof—A. M. Ranchin writes, "The coexistence of mutually contradictory statements in Brodsky's writings is a consequence—perhaps an unconscious one—of a belief in a certain ideal Text that encompasses all possible statements and thoughts, including incompatible ones: this Text absorbs them and thus transcends their incompatibility."[54] We might say this in a different way. Brodsky is deeply philosophical but anti-ideological. He does not espouse any consistent ideology or worldview. To paraphrase Paul Ricoeur, ideology is the symbolic prison in which reality sits and rots; "freedom" and "system" are antonyms.[55] Brodsky's poem "A Talk in the Sorbonne" deals with the meaninglessness of any philosophy outside individual life experience. For Brodsky as for Kierkegaard, Dostoevsky, Nietzsche, and Camus, reality, life as such, supersedes all logic, and it demands, requires, a passionate and poetic approach.

EXISTENTIALISM

Brodsky and existentialism is far too broad a topic for this small book.[56] Let us restate the obvious. Existentialism was not a doctrine but a disorganized philosophical movement. Nonetheless, it defined much of twentieth-century thought and without doubt defined the way Brodsky came to think. He admired Kierkegaard, Dostoevsky, Shestov, Kafka, and Camus; he was less taken with Nietzsche and Sartre, despite the latter's role in his own life. We know nothing of his thoughts on Karl Jaspers or Martin Heidegger. Perhaps more—or most—important is that Brodsky absorbed existentialist aesthetics, which took shape in works of art rather than in formal treatises: in the novels of Dostoevsky, Kafka, Camus; in the plays of Beckett; in the essentially poetic texts of Kierkegaard and Nietzsche. Brodsky read all of Shestov from cover to cover.[57]

It is hard to evaluate Brodsky's lyric hero—the anonymous loner who has consciously chosen loneliness and anonymity—outside the context of twentieth-century literature and film. With the exception of some nostalgic recollections of childhood and a brief and happy love, he always speaks as an outsider: he has no home, no family; he sits at a table in a café or on a bench in a park; he is in a foreign city, a foreign country. A classic example is "Lagoon," where the guest at the Venetian hotel L'Accademia is a "nobody in his raincoat." This is a crystallization of a whole range of literary and film characters, from Camus's Jean-Baptiste Clamence (*La Chute*) to the lone-wolf detectives of Hollywood's film noir.

Even in such a brief discussion of Brodsky and philosophy, or Brodsky and existentialism, we have to ask whether the question should be posed at all. When Brodsky wrote,

> I'm no philosopher. No, I won't lie.
> I'm old, but no philosopher,
> though I can't just wave away
> some of these mad questions,
> (*Uncollected;* non-poetic)

he was warning his reader against reading concepts, let alone whole ideological systems, into his poems.

> Making beginnings and endings meet
> is more the job of the acrobat.
> I'm either in between or all outside.
> (*Uncollected;* non-poetic)[58]

Being "in between or all outside" all systems means living in a constant state of imbalance, instability, emotional tension, and angst. Shestov, who asserted that true thinkers never quite make their "ends meet" in an elegant system, wrote that "[t]o create is to go from one failure to another. The general state of someone who creates is ambiguity, ignominy, uncertainty for the future, undone nerves."[59] However, in poetry—in Brodsky's poetry, at least—this spiritual discomfort, this clash of incompatible ideas, makes for both dramatic tension and a *style.* Earlier we noted that Brodsky called existentialism a contemporary version of Stoicism. In strictly textbook terms, this is completely wrong. The Stoics preached impassivity; Kierkegaard and Nietzsche taught that life must be lived passionately ("dangerously," said Nietzsche). So how do we live dangerously and impassively at the same time?

When we talked of the influence of film on Brodsky's existentialist style, we did not mean films that pretended to be on the cutting edge of philosophy. Those, Brodsky could not stand. One such film was *Deviation,* which was awarded the Gold Prize at the Moscow Film Festival of 1967. He wrote an epigram about it:

> A gray lock in his hair,
> no features to his face,
> he stalks a whore
> along a palace wall.
> (Non-poetic)[60]

He loved Hollywood westerns and war movies. One of his favorite actors was Steve McQueen, especially in the 1960 film *The Magnificent Seven.* On the surface, McQueen's characters are terse and unflappable; underneath the macho mask, they are sentimental and self-sacrificing. In essence, they are the existentialist and the stoic combined. They are as impassive as Marcus Aurelius, as "dangerous" as Nietzsche demanded. In a word, they are "cool." These characters are interesting because they are dramatic, and the drama derives from the conflict between inner turmoil and outer calm, inner emotion and outer lack of it—in facial expression, in gesture. If we knew what was going on inside the taciturn and impassive McQueen character from the plot alone, we would know very little. The image would make little impression. But McQueen is not photographed in this pose or at that angle—he *plays* his characters. His acting is all movement, catlike grace as precise and fluid as ballet.

The lyric energy of Brodsky's mature verse is underwritten by the same conflict between an impassive narrator (who carries on a monotonous, neutral monologue reflected in the very rhythm of the lines) and a passionate life full of love, betrayal, evil, and injustice, as well as by the poet's insatiable hunger for the real—his five senses are always sharply attuned to the world around him.

The random, the spontaneous, the purely associative, has no place in Brodsky's poetry. He is a poet, and his answer to the "ultimate questions of life" lies not in religious revelation or the arguments of reason but in the creation of a perfect text. But since creating an ideally perfect poem is impossible, every time the poet writes, the poet starts again: Sisyphus and his stone, Brodsky and his poetry. Sisyphean, à la Camus acceptance of the absurd as the principal condition of human existence is Brodsky's stance in both life and poetry.

Brodsky grew up in the heyday of existentialism, but neither Kierkegaard nor Dostoevsky nor Shestov nor Camus "taught" him to be an "existentialist." These writers simply helped him articulate what he already knew by intuition: the sense of isolation and abandonment, the absurdity of being in the face of nonbeing, a passionate individualism, a sense of guilt and responsibility, an urge to identify with those in pain and need. In the highly publicized rift between Sartre (more a philosopher than a writer) and Camus (more a writer than a philosopher), Brodsky came down solidly on the side of Camus.[61] When and if he philosophized, he kept himself in check. The moral and ethical core of a personality was ontological for him—that is, not subject to rationalization or discussion. One simply cannot make others suffer.

A rather ordinary episode might serve as an illustration. Nina Nikolaevna Berberova, a writer and the widow of the poet Vladislav Khodasevich, was someone Brodsky knew and respected both as a strong and independent woman and as a "remnant of a huge fire."[62] In 1989, after nearly seventy years away from the USSR as an emigrant, Berberova traveled to Russia. In spite of a warm welcome, and her history of left-leaning views, she didn't like what she saw. Soon after returning, she and Brodsky met at a party, and she began to relate her rather grim impressions, saying that she "looked at that crowd" and thought, "Bring in the machine guns!" Brodsky, who had been listening with a certain amount of sympathy, objected: "Nina Nikolaevna, you can't do that!" "Why not?" frowned Berberova. "You just can't, it's not Christian." "I don't understand this kind of talk," snapped Berberova, turning her back. Brodsky himself could make brutal jokes (he once said that the best view of Moscow was from the belly of a bomber).[63] He could be irritable, he could be sharp. But he never hated anyone.

CHAPTER EIGHT

> And as for where in space and time one's toe end touches,
> well, earth is hard all over; try the States.
>
> —"The classical ballet, let's say, is beauty's keep"

ARRIVAL IN THE WEST: AUDEN

IN THE 1970S, leaving the Soviet Union was always tinged with tragedy for both those leaving and those left behind. Both sides assumed that they were saying good-bye forever, and farewell gatherings felt like wakes. Those leaving, especially those who had never set foot outside the USSR, had a painful sense that they were about to step past some point of no return; their native land policed them ferociously as they approached that point. Customs agents at Pulkovo Airport, in search of who knows what, mercilessly combed through Brodsky's meager baggage and even took apart his little manual typewriter.

His flight from socialist Leningrad to capitalist Vienna was a short one, but the landing was rough: this otherworld was bright, sharp, and loud. The colors were different. The speech was different. The air smelled different. Soviet streets seemed poor and drab in comparison with the streets here, given the sheer number of cars in the streets and goods in shop windows. It was a shock. Two weeks after arriving, Brodsky wrote: "My head is permanently turned to one side [as I look at shop windows]. Abundance is just as hard to take as poverty, maybe harder. The latter's preferable, because the soul is engaged. I personally can't take anything in—everything seems to bounce around, I've got spots before my eyes."[1] However, this first shock and all the vague but overwhelming impressions would recede when Brodsky came face to face with the one person he esteemed above all others: W. H. Auden. This almost chance encounter would have an enormous effect on the rest of Brodsky's life.

Brodsky met Auden just one day after leaving Leningrad. On June 6, 1972, he and his American friend Carl Proffer rented a car and set out in search of the village of Kirchstetten, where Auden had summered since 1958. It took them some time to find it, and by chance they pulled up to Auden's cottage just as the man himself was walking back from the train station after a trip to Vienna. Here Brodsky caught his first glimpse of the poet whose words about language and time he had read eight years before in a hut in the Russian north, words that had turned his life upside down.

In "To Please a Shadow," Brodsky talks about a photograph of Auden taken around 1968 or 1969: "The features were regular, even plain. There was nothing specifically poetic about this face, nothing Byronic, demonic, ironic, hawkish, aquiline, wounded, etc. Rather, it was the face of a physician who is interested in your story though he knows you are ill. A face well prepared for everything, a sum total of a face. . . . It was the stare of a man who knew that he wouldn't be able to weed those threats out, yet who was bent on describing for you the symptoms as well as the malaise itself."[2] The Auden that Brodsky saw at the gate to the house in Kirchstetten was considerably older than the one in the photograph. Auden had aged badly. His face was so wrinkled that his friend Stravinsky joked that "soon we shall have to smooth him out to see who it is."

As Brodsky tells it in "To Please a Shadow," when Proffer explained to Auden just who was coming to dinner, Auden exclaimed, "Impossible!" and invited them in.[3] Auden certainly knew the name, knew about the ludicrous trial, but only recently had he learned about Brodsky's return from exile.

Two years before the appearance of his unexpected guest, he had written a short foreword to George Kline's translations of Brodsky. It is a cautious piece, which Auden begins by acknowledging that not knowing the language makes it hard to judge either the translation or the poet. But the overall tone is positive, and some of his comments are remarkably perspicacious. Brodsky was flattered and happy that the great Auden had written a preface to his verse, but there was a fly in the ointment: Auden had been equally enthusiastic about Andrey Voznesensky and had even done a brilliant translation of Voznesensky's "Parabolic Ballad." In other words, the greatest living English poet was so distant from Russian poetry that he could not tell the difference between these two absolutely dissimilar writers.

Auden's writing a foreword to Brodsky's book had nothing unusual about it. Auden was a working writer; he made his living by the word.[4] By the time Brodsky met him, he had a long-standing routine: he would sit down and write from morning till evening, with a break in the middle for lunch. Part of the routine involved plying himself with alcohol throughout. Both the routine and the alcohol made a great impression on Brodsky during the days he spent with Auden:

> W. H. Auden drinks his first dry martini around 7:30 a.m., after which he sorts through his mail and reads his newspaper, sipping sherry and scotch. Then he has breakfast, not clear what it is—something pink and white with something dry on the side. Then he sits down to work, and since he writes with a ballpoint pen, the bottle on his desk holds Guinness rather than ink. Lunch is at one o'clock. Depending on the menu, it might end with a cocktail. After lunch, a nap, which I think is the only sober hour in his day. On waking up, he takes a second dry martini to change the taste in his mouth, then sits down to work (introductions, essays, poems, letters, and so on), all the while sipping a scotch on the rocks out of a sweating glass. Or brandy. By suppertime, which comes around 7 or 8, he's pretty well crocked. Before bedtime he sips some aged Chateau d'whatever. By nine o'clock he's in bed and sound asleep.
>
> In the four weeks we spent together he never once changed this routine: even on the flight from Vienna to London he was sucking down vodkas and tonic and working on a crossword in German from *Die Presse,* which edition also featured yours truly's Jewish mug.[5]

When Brodsky met him, Auden was hardly in good health. He was old and alone, he was drinking more and more, and his old friends were alarmed at the changes in his behavior, for the ever-kind Auden was becoming ever more rude. He had stopped talking with people and started talking at them, launching into monologues that until six in the evening were as brilliant as they'd ever been, but which became less coherent the more alcohol he downed.[6]

Still, Brodsky's recollections of Auden in Austria and London paint a different picture. Although the communication may have been one-sided, given Brodsky's lack of conversational English and Auden's complete lack of Russian, the elder poet clearly took very good care of his unexpected guest. Charles Osborne, who organized a yearly poetry festival in London at which Auden was more or less the main feature, wrote that "Wystan fussed about him like a mother hen . . . an unusually kindly and understanding mother hen."[7]

We have to give Auden's intuition its due: he sensed something in this young poet who wrote in a language he could not understand; Auden liked him and tried to help him through his first days in a strange place. But this was hardly a meeting of equals. Auden had no idea what lay behind Brodsky's verse; Brodsky did not know enough English to explain. Brodsky's arrival in the West was a media event, and Auden was too old and too wise to take much of that seriously. At the time, he himself was a celebrity who often had to fight off reporters and cameramen.

Brodsky was only one of many young poets in need of moral and material support—both of which Auden gave freely. But Brodsky's recollections suggest that the English poet was also intrigued by the Russian connection—Dostoevsky, Tolstoy, Chekhov.[8] His sympathy for Brodsky went hand in hand with his antipathy to the Soviet regime, especially after its incursion into Czechoslovakia in 1968. Still, for the aging Auden, this encounter was nothing particularly extraordinary. For Brodsky it was the very hand of providence. "One may call this generosity of the spirit if it weren't that the spirit requires a body to refract itself through. It's not the man who becomes sacred through this refraction: it's the spirit that becomes human and comprehensible. This—and the fact that men are finite—is enough for me to worship this poet."[9]

Brodsky's poem commemorating the centenary of Akhmatova's birth is almost a paraphrase of the same thought: a great poet has found words to express both forgiveness and love:

> . . . since we have but one life, they [these words]
> sound clearer from mortal lips than from cotton puffs on high.

But there is no real symmetry in Brodsky's relationships with these two poets. Brodsky knew Akhmatova for years; he spent hours and hours talking with her. He spent only a few weeks with Auden, mostly in one-sided conversations. In remembering Akhmatova, Brodsky emphasized her moral example; as poets, they had little in common. Auden was a different story. Whether through direct influence, conscious study, or common temperament (or all of the above), practically everything in Brodsky, from turns of phrase to an understanding of poetic genres and poetry in general, finds a parallel in Auden.[10] Their personalities were fundamentally alike in some ways and wildly different in others, but the point is that this young Russian poet, born in 1940, was writing verse strikingly like that of an Anglo-American poet twice his age. This encounter with Auden may have helped Brodsky appreciate the full depth of this rare "elective affinity," and to the end of Brodsky's days, Auden would be his benchmark and model.

BRODSKY IN AMERICA

Brodsky flew from London to Detroit on July 9, 1972.[11] He hit the ground running. On July 21 he flew to Massachusetts to meet with his translator George Kline.[12] There he spent much of his time writing in a tree: he was much taken by a little tree-house built into the branches of an old oak in Kline's yard.[13] Newspaper and television reports had heralded the arrival of the exiled poet, and Brodsky was showered with invitations to speak and read. Kline recalls that between the summer of 1972 and the spring of 1973 he and Brodsky gave roughly thirty readings at American colleges and universities. Brodsky was touched by all the letters he received, by the offers of hospitality from all sorts of people both famous and obscure. But he already had a place to live (aside from the tree).

To the Immigration and Naturalization Service, Brodsky was only one among tens of thousands of Soviet Jews applying for entry into the United States in the 1970s. He, however, and a handful of other artists, prominent scientists, scholars, and dissidents were already assured a future in the new country. His name was already known in academic, journalistic, and government circles, and thanks to Carl Proffer, he had already been offered a position at the University of Michigan, with a yearly salary of $12,000, a decent sum in those days, especially for a single person with no family to support.

Finding a job and making a living are only one aspect of the cares that beset the immigrant. All new Americans experience culture shock as they try to adapt to a society built on principles entirely different from those on which they themselves were reared. The basic concepts of American civilization were dizzyingly different from the Russian concepts. Success and failure, wealth and poverty, people and government, and even such concrete notions as a house, a town, a car, a dinner, visiting friends, meant something different. Personal freedom, complete responsibility for one's own existence (spiritual or material), was a trial for those unaccustomed to it. Brodsky turned out to be more prepared than most for this uncozy and alien world. He had had a wealth of experience with alienation in his native land: a schoolboy in a factory shop, a sane man in a crazy house, an intellectual on a kolkhoz, a stranger in a strange land—there wasn't much difference. He always seemed to be leery of feeling too comfortable in any society, of falling into some sort of mental entropy; years before, he had had no desire to fit in with the would-be frondeurs who sang Bulat Okudzhava's "Join hands, friends, so we don't go down alone!" as if it were their anthem. He had dashed out of his own house on his own birthday when the celebration became too emotional.

And besides, the United States was not so unfamiliar. Brodsky belonged to a small group of intellectuals who arrived fairly well schooled in American culture. Hollywood, jazz, and American literature had provided a colossal amount of cultural information. Brodsky was not joking when he began his lectures on freethinking in Soviet Russia with recollections of Hollywood Tarzans and swashbucklers and cowboys.[14] Johnny Weissmuller and Errol Flynn, swinging through the jungle or swinging a sword, may have given this impressionable child his first lessons in individual freedom as an absolute value; cowboys and sheriffs were examples of what he called "instantaneous justice." As the child grew up and, like many of his generation, was drawn to jazz, he detected in this music the same basic principle of personal independence, a lonely sort of freedom. In Melville's *Moby-Dick,* in the poetry of Edwin Arlington Robinson, Robert Frost, and Edgar Lee Masters, he would discover some of the darker sides of individualism. But the basic ethic, Paul Tillich's "courage to be," the individual taking a stand against the chaos and terror of the world, was far more attractive to him than either amoral Marxist determinism—"freedom is necessity recognized"—or the cynical relativism of one of Evtushenko's speakers: "There's no real freedom, not among us, not among you."[15] Earlier in this book I quoted Auden's famous stanza about the feral boy who does evil because he does not know a world where any "promises are kept." In essence, Auden is echoing what is perhaps the most famous (or at least the most anthologized) poem of twentieth-century American literature: Frost's "Stopping by Woods on a Snowy Evening," which ends with:

> These woods are lovely dark, and deep,
> But I have promises to keep,
> And miles to go before I sleep,
> And miles to go before I sleep.

This is merely one example of how a close reading of American poetry gave Brodsky some understanding of a society in which personal responsibility is axiomatic.

Brodsky often said that the only thing that made living in another country possible was "loving some one thing about it."

> What I like is being left alone to do what I can do. And for this I am grateful to both circumstance and the country itself. What I've always been drawn to here is this sense of personal responsibility, this principle of personal initiative. Here you're always hearing, "Let me try and see what happens." In general, in order to live in another country, you have to love some one thing about it especially deeply: the spirit of the laws; the chance to do business; the literature; the history. I personally love two things: American poetry and the spirit of [American] law. My generation, the people to whom I was so close when I was twenty, were all individualists. And our ideal was the U.S. because of this spirit of individualism. So some of us, coming here, had the sense that we were coming home; we were more American than the Americans.[16]

CARL PROFFER AND ARDIS

Still, in the three hectic weeks between his summons to OVIR and his plane to Vienna, Brodsky wasn't really thinking about where he might eventually land. As it happened, the American professor Carl Proffer was in the USSR at the time, and once Proffer heard the news, he set up an appointment for Brodsky at the University of Michigan, then met the poet in Vienna, the transit point for most emigrants leaving the USSR.[17] From there, emigrants would fly on to either Israel or other destinations.

In 1972, Proffer was a rising star in American academe. At thirty-four, when most Ph.D.'s in the humanities were still slogging away as humble assistant professors struggling to write their first scholarly book, Proffer had already written two and had been appointed full professor at the prestigious University of Michigan. The son of a factory foreman, the first child in his family to attend college, he chose literature over basketball. In 1957, when the launch of Sputnik set off a flurry of interest in Soviet political and cultural affairs, Carl was in his second year of college. He decided to major in Russian language and literature. Proffer had a multitude of talents: he was fluent in Russian and, unlike many of his colleagues, was also well versed in more than one period of Russian literary history. His first book was on Gogol, his second on Nabokov.[18] For an academic, Proffer was an unusually good writer. He was a talented translator of Russian poetry and prose. Above all, he was exceptionally hardworking.

Annoyed at the slowness and conservatism of American publishers and publications in the field of Russian art and literature, tired of the lack of publishers in general, Carl and his wife, Ellendea, decided to start their own publishing house. They called it Ardis, the name of the house in Nabokov's *Ada*. Nabokov himself, who was very particular about his editors, publishers, and interviewers, had come to trust Proffer and had given him the copyright for all his Russian works. Ardis published these and many other hard-to-find early twentieth-century authors in facsimile editions: poetry collections by Akhmatova, Gumilyov, Zabolotsky, Mandelstam, Pasternak, Khodasevich, Tsvetaeva, and a host of other Silver Age poets; prose by Sologub, Kuzmin, and Bely. It also put out a substantial literary journal called *Russian Literature Triquarterly* and published works by a number of contemporary Russian writers who had no chance of being published at home: Ardis was the first to publish Vasily Aksyonov's *Island of Crimea* and *Burn,* Yuz Alezhkovsky's *Nikolay Nikolaevich* and *Masquerade,* Andrey Bitov's *Pushkin House,* Vladimir Voinovich's *Ivankiada,* Sergey Dovlatov's *Invisible Book,* Fazil Iskander's *Sandro from Chegem,* Vladimir Maramzin's *Two-Toned Blonde,* and Sasha Sokolov's *School for Fools.* It also published memoirs by Lev Kopelev and collections of verse by Yury Kublanovsky, Eduard Limonov, Semyon Lipkin, Vladimir Uflyand, and Aleksey Tsvetkov. When in 1979 a group of Moscow writers (including Aksyonov, Akhmadulina, Voznesensky, Vysotsky, Gorenshtein, Viktor Erofeev, Kublanovsky, and Rein) put together an uncensored almanac, which they dubbed *Metropol,* one copy was smuggled out of the USSR and published by Ardis, first as a facsimile, later typeset. Relatively few Ardis publications were actually brought into the Soviet Union as contraband, but the very existence of a free Western publishing house, printing free Russian literature, was a fresh wind blowing through Andropov's airless Russia. As one of Dostoevsky's characters puts it, "Every man must have somewhere to go." For Russian writers in the 1970s, that "somewhere" was Ardis. Brodsky, in his eulogy for Proffer, said: "In terms of Russian literature, Carl Proffer might be compared to Gutenberg. That is, he invented a printing press. By publishing Russian originals and English translations that might have otherwise never seen the light of day, he saved many Russian writers and poets from obscurity and distortion, from neurosis and despair. Moreover, he changed the very climate of Russian literature. Writers whose works had been rejected or banned now felt themselves freer because they knew that for better or for worse, they could send a piece to Ardis."[19]

Ardis was a tiny firm working out of the basement floor of a former golf club where the Proffers also made their home; it operated on borrowed and reborrowed money. In the best of times it had only three or four full-time paid employees. Carl and Ellendea Proffer spent nights on end editing manuscripts, setting type, packing books, and sending them off. For the Russian intelligentsia, this real Ardis would take on the same mythical stature as Nabokov's imaginary estate.[20]

Brodsky considered Proffer much more than just a friend. Carl was almost family. Brodsky arrived in the United States just as the press was taking its first steps, and he did what he could to help. He edited; he read manuscripts. He plucked Sasha Sokolov's *School for Fools* out of the slush pile; he put together Yury Kublanovsky's first collection of verse.[21] On his recommendation Ardis published Eduard Limonov's first book of poems, *Russkoe.* As for Brodsky's own work in Russian, Ardis would become his publisher once and forever, beginning with *The End of a Beautiful Era* and *A Part of Speech* in 1977, continuing with *New Stanzas to Augusta* in

1983, *Urania* in 1987, and *Landscape with Flood* in 1996. Brodsky did not live to see the last one in print.

THE END OF A BEAUTIFUL ERA AND *A PART OF SPEECH*: A PHILOSOPHY OF PROSODY

To the casual observer of Brodsky's life, the most important events of 1964 were the kangaroo court and exile to Arkhangelsk. To Brodsky, the main event was reading an anthology of English poetry. So it was in 1972: after culture shock and the trauma of the move had passed, he heard a new sort of music, which in turn became a new sort of diction. "Music of verse" may be a metaphoric expression, but that music—phonetics and rhythm—is also the only element of poetry that can be quantified. In *A Halt in the Desert,* 55 percent of the poems, long and short alike, are written in the unhurried iambic pentameter characteristic of narrative and meditative Russian verse. The rest are written in other classical meters (five in iambic tetrameter, five in anapest, etc.). Twelve of the sixty-nine poems in the book (roughly 18 percent) are in *dolnik* meter, a more complex, singular, and unpredictable meter than the five classics. ("There are so few Greeks now in Leningrad" is in iambic pentameter; "If I end my days beneath a dove's wing" is a dolnik.) By 1970 the ratio had begun to change, and in *The End of a Beautiful Era,* which comprises poems written between 1964 and 1971, dolniks already amount to 29 percent. A great quantitative and qualitative leap took place between these two books. In *A Part of Speech,* only 36 percent of the poems are written in classical meters; the rest are in dolniks.

Only someone unversed in poetry would consider this reorientation a purely technical matter. Prosody, the organization of the text by sound and meter, is the very genesis of Russian verse. Consider the moment when intimate recollections of a former love ("Stood like some Jacob in a foyer / watching for a beauty / running down the stairs") and the immediate impressions of a thunderstorm breaking outside ("Far off thunder stops my ears") come together into a single lyric text in "Almost an Elegy":

> Right now the rainstorm is the only thing
> my ear will let into my drowsing mind
> as skinflints let poor kin into their kitchens—
> not yet music, but no longer noise.
> ("Almost an Elegy," *OVP;* non-poetic)

This is the creative act itself—the transformation of meaningless "noise" (random memories, items plucked from the stream of consciousness, discrete observations, and impressions) into the meaningful music of verse.

Brodsky's choices in prosody were no less important than his verbal choices and, in fact, preceded them. After all, in purely physical, auditory terms, what is rhythm? It is the alternation of words in a particular order determined by the intervals between accented syllables. These intervals may last seconds, or tenths of seconds, but in any case, they occur in a temporal framework, in time. Prosody is the manipulation of speech within time. "[M]eters are simply different forms of distributing time. They're seeds of time in the poem. Every song, even the bird's, is a form of restructuring time."[22] Thus, for Brodsky, the choice of rhythmic structure is a philosophical one. No matter what the subject of the poem, the contrast between the metrical model and the rhythm introduced by the poet reminds the reader of the two contexts in which that subject is elaborated: one is the monotonous, indifferent beat of time marching on (meter), and the other is an attempt by an individual (the author, the lyric hero) to break that monotony—to slow time, to speed it up, to turn it back (rhythm). The dolniks that begin to dominate Brodsky's verse in the 1970s allowed him far more leeway to work out his individual concept of time than classical meters could have. Granted, rhythmic nuance is possible within classical Russian metrics, too, but these dolniks were created by Brodsky for Brodsky to suit his personal relations with time. Other writers have tried to employ them, with little success. (A whole number of poems imitating Brodsky's rhythmic patterns were to appear in print in the 1980s, but as Brodsky once said on another topic: "Every line bears the stamp: 'Stolen,' 'Stolen,' 'Stolen.'")

Brodsky's dolniks are unique. We encounter three-ictus and even two-ictus lines among them (an ictus is a metrically strong syllable in the line). One very early example is "Hills" (1962; *OVP*): "Together they loved / to sit on the slope of a hill." The subject of the poem suggests that the source of its rhythmic structure was the Spanish *romancero* (Machado, Lorca) in Russian translation. Much later, Brodsky would indicate as much in his stylized poem "Mexican Romancero," part of his "Mexican Divertimento" cycle (1975). There is also no doubt that Brodsky, in Russian, attempted to find a metrical equivalent for Auden's verse. "Nature Morte" (1971) does not merely mimic the plot of Auden's "September 1, 1939" (exposition:

"I'm sitting in a public place, I'm watching people, and I don't like them"; development: philosophical reflections on this subject; conclusion: the absolute need for Christian charity and love) but also uses Auden-like three- and two-ictus dolniks with masculine endings throughout.

But another direction was to prove more productive—dolniks written in longer lines. Of all that he wrote between 1972 and 1977, Brodsky was most fond of the cycle "A Part of Speech." Fifteen of the twenty short poems that make it up begin with what seems to be an anapest: "From Nowhere with Love," "The North buckles metal," "I recognize this wind," and others. In Russian poetry, the anapest has a certain sentimental semantic aura to it, perhaps arising from its waltz-like three-beat rhythm. It is rarely found in Blok's lyric verse, while for Mandelstam it was the rhythm of cheap, vulgar romance. So, for example, "Nadson" was the ironic name that Mandelstam gave his own "For the resounding valor of ages to come," an allusion to the meter favored by Semyon Nadson, K.R. (Konstantin Romanov), and other popular writers of sentimental verse in the late eighteenth and early nineteenth centuries. Interestingly, Vladimir Nabokov, that scourge of vulgarity, somehow never sensed this undertone. Several of his most intimate lyrics ("L'inconnue de la Seine," "You and I so believed," and "To Russia") are written in anapest, and in his programmatic (also anapestic) poem "Glory" he interrupts the flow of seductively false dreams of a return to his homeland with the lines:

> And then I will laugh, and straight from my pen
> flies my beloved anapest,
> like a rocket at night, so swift
> the *cursive* turns to gold.
> (Non-poetic)[23]

Brodsky chose a different way to make the anapest the prosodic foundation of some of his most important texts, those on love and nostalgia. The lines in "A Part of Speech" are very long for anapests (five or six feet, as a rule), and in most of them the anapest is actually transformed into a dolnik by a minimal but decisive break in the meter: immediately before the last stress in the line, one unaccented syllable goes missing. Heretofore, such anapest-like dolnik lines were quite rare in Russian poetry. Perhaps only in Bryusov's experimental verse do we find them, in a reproduction of Ausonius's hexameters: "All that is fragile in this world is born, and led, and crushed by Fate."[24] The prolific versifier Konstantin Balmont also has several poems written in anapestic pentameter (and one in hexameter).[25]

When young, in 1961 and 1962, Brodsky wrote perhaps half a dozen poems using a long, purely anapestic line.[26]

If the younger Brodsky was stretching his poetic line in an attempt to create the poetic equivalent of a jazz improvisation (he speaks of this directly in "From the outskirts to the center," where "[t]he jazz of the outskirts says welcome"), the author of "A Part of Speech" is listening only to the rhythm of time as it emerges from under the "hum of words." ("The change of Empires is intimately tied to the hum of words," he asserts in "Lullaby of Cape Cod.")

> These words were dictated to me not by
> love or the Muse but by a searching, dull
> voice
>
> ("The Thames at Chelsea")

In addition to his new meters, from the early 1970s on, Brodsky was using enjambment more often, and his enjambments were becoming more radical, as in the Russian original of the above "Thames at Chelsea" when he chops the line between the negative particle *ne* and the nouns that follow. As Efim Etkind writes: "This is a philosophical poet, whose powerful thought, retaining its independence, expresses itself in the syntactical drive of his speech: a calmly prosaic, almost scholarly complex phrase moves forward no matter what the metrical or strophic hurdles in its path, as if it were taking no part in the 'poetry game' at all. But that isn't true—it is not only taking part in the game, it is the very fabric of the poetry that forms it; the relationship between the two is paradoxical or, more accurately, ironic."[27]

Etkind considers this conflict between meter and syntax, the result of which is enjambment, to be a fundamentally philosophical element in both Brodsky and Tsvetaeva. The content of this philosophical conflict underlying all of Brodsky's mature verse is the same content that dictates his choice of rhythm: man against the metronome; individual, finite, mortal life against the even flow of time that has no beginning and no end. Small wonder that in both his early poem "From the outskirts to the center" and his last finished poem, "August," we find an allusion to

Pushkin's "young, unfamiliar tribe," a motif significantly more tragic than the usual interpretations of it suggest. We might also say that the conflict between prosody and utterance that underlies Brodsky's poetics is derived from a Pushkin image: "playful life" and "indifferent [*ravnodushnaya*] nature." We should remember, however, that Pushkin was using the adjective not in the worn-out everyday sense of "uncaring" or "apathetic." In its direct sense, the Russian *ravnodushnaya* is a calque of the Latin *aequanimis*. What we have here is the evenhandedness, the egalitarianism, of nature, which does not recognize the individual, does not distinguish between good and evil, does not prefer life to death. Brodsky constantly reminds us of this in his metrics. We can even find direct statements more or less in the spirit of Buddhism on the need to accept wholeheartedly the conditions of our existence, "to merge with God as if merging with a landscape" ("Conversation with a Celestial Being"). To Evgeniy Rein's remark that Brodsky's later verse was "more relaxed" in tone, Brodsky replied, "Not more relaxed—more monotonous," and recited from memory a work by the ancient Greek poet Leonidas of Tarent: "Throughout your life try to imitate time, do not raise your voice, do not rage. If, however, you do not succeed in following this prescription, do not grieve, for when you lie under the earth and fall silent, you yourself will resemble time."[28]

In *The End of a Beautiful Era* and *A Part of Speech,* Brodsky sometimes succeeds in imitating the monotony of time (in his rhythms), but sometimes he does not: he raises his voice, he rages, he lives passionately. And so what emerges in these books is what the ancient Greeks called *agon*—the battle between two elemental forces, without which drama does not exist.

THE END OF A BEAUTIFUL ERA AND *A PART OF SPEECH*: PUBLICATION

Carl Proffer intended to publish a collection of new poems written after *A Halt in the Desert,* or at least a volume of selected works, very shortly after Brodsky arrived in the United States. But Brodsky was in no hurry. The main reason for the delay was creative; his "old" pieces, that is, those written before 1970, no longer interested him, and there were not enough newer ones to make up a book, or so he thought in 1973 and 1974. The short verse cycle "A Part of Speech," which he wrote over 1975 and 1976, had enormous significance for him; his fears that his creative powers would wither outside his native linguistic environment had proved false, and now he could think about a book. The book was to be named for the cycle. Brodsky and his publisher-friend were at odds over the content: what the poet really wanted was to publish his new (post-1971) work, but that would mean that some fine poems written after *A Halt in the Desert* would be left out of the collection. Proffer insisted on a larger book.

Meanwhile, I had emigrated to the United States in the summer of 1976 and on Brodsky's recommendation had been offered a job at Ardis; my first major editorial project was Brodsky's book.[29] At one point it occurred to me that we might apply the wisdom of Solomon: split the one book into two and publish them simultaneously. The first would consist of poems written before leaving Russia, the second of poems written in the West. Both the poet and the publisher agreed. This split also turned out to be profitable, since the combined price for the two sold separately could be set higher than the price of a single volume of the same size, and the number of potential buyers would be the same. I also suggested using the title of one of the poems, "The End of a Beautiful Era," as the title of the first volume; it gave this collection of Brodsky's last Russian poems an ironic ring. Brodsky, of course, made some major amendments to this plan. He was adamantly opposed to leading off the second volume with "1972," which would draw a strict borderline between poems written in his homeland and poems written outside it. Just as he refused to regard his trial and internal exile as remarkable or fateful events, he refused to see his exile from Russia and move to America as anything other than a "continuation of space." He felt that whatever qualitative change had taken place in his life and his art, it had taken place at the turning of the year, 1971–1972—not five months later, when he boarded a plane. Later he would say that "1972 represented some sort of borderline—if nothing else, the state border of the Soviet Union. . . . But in no way was it a psychological border, for all that I moved from one empire to another that year."[30] "To a Tyrant," "The Funeral of Bobo," "Sketch," "Letters to a Roman Friend," "The Song of Innocence Being Also the Song of Experience," "Nunc Dimittis," and "Odysseus to Telemachus" were all written in Russia over the winter of 1972. "Butterfly," "1972," and "The classical ballet, let's say, is beauty's keep" were also begun there.

As both books were being prepared for publication, Brodsky was clearly more interested in working on *A Part of Speech* than on *The End of a Beautiful Era*. He was proud of the title and of the cycle itself. The notion that what is made by man, his "part of speech," is greater than man as a biological or social entity was very dear to him. Thirteen years later he was to choose the same name for the first representative collection of his poetry to appear in his homeland.

Like all of Brodsky's collections (with the exception of *New Stanzas to Augusta*), *A Part of Speech* opens with a Christmas poem—"December 24, 1971." Its concluding poem, "December in Florence," was added at the last minute, just as the book was ready to go to press. There is an obvious thematic resonance between the two Decembers. The "human assault-wave" crashing into store counters in the Leningrad poem finds an echo in the poem dedicated to Florence, where we find "the streetcar's multitudes, jostling" at a corner.

A Part of Speech differs from Brodsky's other collections in that its sixteen single poems are in the minority. The bulk of the book is made up of four cycles ("Letters to a Roman Friend," "Twenty Sonnets to Mary Queen of Scots," "Mexican Divertimento," and "A Part of Speech"—fifty-six poems in toto) plus longer poems similar in structure to the cycles: "The Funeral of Bobo" (four parts); a diptych, "The Song of Innocence Being Also the Song of Experience" (two parts, three poems each); and, finally, "Lullaby of Cape Cod." Strictly speaking, any genre divisions between the lyric "Lullaby" and the cycles are fairly blurred, but that does not change the overall picture. Between 1972 and 1977, the poet tended to create series of stylistically similar and more or less thematically linked lyric texts.

At the author's request, the almost identical cover designs for the two books depicted winged lions: the image on the first book was from Bank Bridge in Leningrad; the lion on the second, from Saint Mark's in Venice. Ardis could not afford a professional artist, and the result—smudged blue silhouettes against a gray-blue background—was less than attractive.

In his homeland Brodsky, like many of the best writers of his day, was totally excluded from public culture. Abroad, the Russian audience was relatively small, and literary criticism in the émigré press was by now practically nonexistent. In a normal universe a poet writing in his own language would have been reviewed and discussed by critics and other poets; instead, Brodsky had become the property of scholars. He was the subject of dissertations and articles, of conference presentations, but only after *A Halt in the Desert* was published did the émigré press begin to engage in any lively critical discussion.

The Parisian *Russkaya mysl* was the only émigré newspaper to print a review of the two new books. Aleksandr Bakhrakh, a poet and critic whom Tsvetaeva thought talented, now one of the last exemplars of the so-called Paris school, gave Brodsky's new work high marks: "In these new collections we see the face of the poet in clearer, higher relief, we see his distinctive 'handwriting,' his originality. Was it not himself he was thinking of in these two lines: 'All people are different, / but he was more different than most'? . . . Brodsky is drawn toward large-scale forms that he has not quite mastered yet, so some of his longer poems seem to drag. . . . Dispensing with comfortable clichés, Brodsky hopes to arrive at a new harmony. But even so, Brodsky is no nihilist who, in the name of revolt, wants a complete break with the past."[31]

The remaining responses came from English and American Slavists, all of whom compared *A Part of Speech* to *The End of a Beautiful Era*. Byron Lindsey wrote: "[*A Part of Speech*] is by comparison brighter, more mobile and more difficult. Brodsky seems to explore with simultaneous pleasure and trepidation the real sites of his ongoing imagination. . . . In American exile Brodsky seems still more distant, more elusive, philosophically perhaps more courageous."[32] Henry Gifford did a detailed analysis of both books but focused on the second. Noting that the motif of exile in *A Part of Speech* is represented as exile from the native language, Gifford writes: "Whatever Brodsky may fear, he is still marvelously at home in the language. At the same time he is putting exile to good use, by seeking out affinities and extensions." And he concludes: "Meanwhile, by an irony characteristic of our time, it could be that the best poetry from America in recent years is the work of this Russian."[33]

BRODSKY THE PROFESSOR

Unlike pop songwriters, genuine poets—even famous ones—cannot live by words alone. And even if they could, there's another problem. "Work as a poet?" asked one American poet, amazed. "And do what for the remaining twenty-three and-a-half hours a day?" If "labor is the goal and form of existence" and "something beyond subsistence," as Brodsky asserts in "A Speech about Spilt Milk," and poems come sporadically, appear unpredictably, a choice has to be made between regular, predictable work and a parasitic, bohemian existence. In the Soviet Union, however, all forms of art were ultimately seen as ideological statements, and therefore poetry was an officially recognized profession that could guarantee an officially recognized poet a regular income. This was a socialist economy; the size of the edition or the size of the honorarium had nothing to do with actual demand. The state was funding the "education of the masses." As for officially *un*recognized poets, well, their profile was much the same as Brodsky's at the time of his trial. Writers unconnected with the system often worked as laborers at low-paying and literally low-level jobs, such as monitoring boilers in the basements of massive apartment buildings.[34]

In America there were no professional poets at all. People who wrote poetry held other jobs, ones often far removed from literature: two well-known examples are classics of American modernism, William Carlos Williams and Wallace Stevens. The first was a practicing pediatrician; the second worked in insurance. Poets might live on a grant or a stipend from a foundation for a short time, but most often they were attached to one of America's three thousand or so universities and colleges. And so Brodsky found himself appointed poet-in-residence at the University of Michigan, only the second in the history of that university. Robert Frost had been the first (1921–1923). Auden had taught there in 1940 and 1941, but simply as a regular instructor with no special appointment.

Neither in Europe nor in Soviet Russia was there anything resembling the world in which Brodsky now found himself. The European pattern of a cultural oasis surrounded by provincial desert did not apply to the United States. London, Paris, Rome, Milan, Madrid, Barcelona, Moscow, Petersburg, three or four German cities, a handful of big cities in small countries—this was where the cultural life of the old continent was concentrated, this was where both the native and the foreign intelligentsia gathered. But in the United States the intelligentsia has always been scattered and always mobile. Yes, there was New York, home to some of the world's best presses, theaters, museums, orchestras. And yes, there was Chicago; there was Boston, San Francisco, Washington. But the pattern was entirely different.

In America he lived in Ann Arbor, Michigan; New York City; and South Hadley, Massachusetts. Ann Arbor was his first home, and after Leningrad, Vienna, and London, his impression was that he had landed in the sticks. That feeling is reflected in his first poems written in America, where Ann Arbor is "a modest little town proud of being on a map." But Ann Arbor was not so small and, at thirty miles from Detroit, was hardly the sticks. In the 1970s it had a population of 130,000. Aside from the university and its 30,000 students, the town boasted a number of high-tech companies and scientific laboratories both large and small. South Hadley, where Brodsky lived and taught part-time from 1981 on, was indeed just a dot on the map, a few blocks bordering Mount Holyoke College. But South Hadley had the advantage over Ann Arbor; it was a mere two-hour drive from New York City (ninety minutes if the state police weren't looking). Brodsky liked being able to escape from New York to South Hadley, and vice versa.

Brodsky sometimes enjoyed teaching, sometimes found it a burden, but always approached it conscientiously (just as in Leningrad he had never treated writing children's verse or dubbing films as throwaway hackwork). He might have complained, sometimes in fun, sometimes in earnest, about having to teach, write articles, crank out reviews, but it was obvious that he liked being busy. Here, as ever, his model was the indefatigable Auden, who lived up to the maxim "No day without a line," who wrote radio and stage plays, librettos, travel notes, and countless reviews, and who had also taught at both secondary schools and universities.

But there was a crucial difference between the Oxford-educated Auden and the self-taught Brodsky. Brodsky knew nothing about teaching methodology in general and less than nothing about Anglo-American teaching methods. So what he proposed to his American students was what he knew he could do: read works by his favorite poets, then talk about them. However his courses might have been listed in university catalogues—"Twentieth-Century Russian Poetry" or "Comparative Poetry" or "Roman Poets"—the routine in class was always the same. Poems were read aloud and discussed in detail.[35] A few of Brodsky's former students have written memoirs, and Sven Birkerts, now a well-known literary critic, recalls that

> Brodsky was at one and the same time the worst and the most vital and compelling teacher I've ever had. Worst because he did nothing, *absolutely nothing,* to make our confrontation with a difficult body of poetry pleasant or conventionally instructive. This was owing in part to the fact that his English was still

very much a work in progress. But mainly it was an expression of who he was and what he believed about poetry. Poetry was not something to be "gotten," mastered, and regurgitated in paraphrase. It was not something notched on the belt of attainments. It was, rather, a struggle waged in fear and trembling, an encounter with the very stuff of language that might put our core assumptions about existence into jeopardy. Brodsky would bring his students—us—into the arena, but he would not fight our battles for us. It could feel at times almost sadistic. All of us, at times, felt utterly exposed, not only in our ignorance or the blandness of our assumptions about poetry, but in our way of reading the world.

"What do you think of this one?" he might begin, pointing to some poem we were to have read. The poem would be by Mandelstam or Akhmatova, or Montale. Brodsky's tone on these occasions carried—I don't think I imagined it—a slightly bored contemptuous edge, but also, to quote Auden (his favorite) quoting Sergey Diaghilev, a sense of "astonish me." He made each of us want to say the brilliant thing, to earn that rarest of accolades: "Terrific." But the anxiety was usually more powerful. The question would be posed and the room would grow silent—a deep sedimentary silence.

Somehow we all pushed on, even managed to form a certain prison cell camaraderie—one that, oddly, included Brodsky himself. Which is not to say that he relaxed one whit his vigilance, his insistence on adequate response to what we were reading. But he somehow—bored sighs notwithstanding—made himself a part of our collective grappling inadequacy. How did he manage it?

Class after class, Brodsky would arrive in the room late. After we had all begun to fidget. He would be fingering an unlit cigarette, conveying thereby that he would much rather be alone somewhere, smoking it, than in our midst. Then, almost invariably, he would heave up from his depths a shuddering, groaning sigh. But there was humor in it. For a moment later his beaked, tragic-mask expression would loosen. He would look slowly around the room and, taking us all in, smile, as

> though to communicate that at some level he knew what it must be like for us, as though to forgive us for our blandness. But then it would begin again, the relentless kneading of the language. A line from Mandelstam, a question, silence. Only when the silence became unendurable would he lead us into the thickets of sound and association, with asides on the logic of poetic images, abbreviated lessons on the ethics of utterance, on the metaphysics of nouns, of rhymes.[36]

If some students like Sven Birkerts appreciated their unconventional professor, some did not. The average student who expected to be taught how to "get poetry" in order to turn in a good paper and make a passing grade was both annoyed and disappointed by Brodsky.

> Brodsky seminar. XX century poetry. University of Michigan. Graduate school. Long and boring analysis of Akhmatova's "From the Armenian." We're working on two stanzas, it takes ninety minutes going line by line. What she had, what she wanted, why she didn't say whatever. Didn't learn a thing from Brodsky himself about XX century literature (or his interpretations of it, about poetry). Disappointed. Next class. Long and boring analysis of another work by Akhmatova, then of Tsvetaeva's "Attempt at Jealousy."[37]

Brodsky's first American poem, "In the Lake District," mirrors his student's complaint:

> . . . [I] was living at a college near the most
> renowned of the fresh-water lakes; the function
> to which I'd been appointed was to wear out
> the patience of ingenuous local youth.

In some ways his task (that is, teaching students poetry, not trying students' patience) might have seemed hopeless. Poetry is the art of the word. Usually the highest praise for a poet, his "patent of nobility," is to cite his freshness, originality, and "a voice like no other." But words sound new only in comparison to words already said. Poetry is a referential art; it has its being in culture and context. The point is not obscure cultural references or parodies or literary allusions but the language itself, passed from generation to generation and yet always spoken in an entirely new way. By "language" I mean not simply vocabulary and grammar but also poetics, with all its phonetic, rhythmic, intonational, compositional, figurative, and genre features. Inevitably, the reader must have at least approximately the same cultural baggage as the poet. Otherwise, both Akhmatova's poem and Brodsky's commentary on it will indeed seem "long and boring." By the time Brodsky ended up in the United States, the educational system there had, thanks largely to the theories of John Dewey, shifted its focus from the acquisition of knowledge to the development of independent thinking, "the ability to think," "the ability to *use* knowledge." As often happens with reformist theories applied en masse, good intentions went awry, and many young Americans were finishing high school and entering college with relatively good critical-thinking skills but with little concrete knowledge of anything. Put simply—none of them had read very much. It was not just a question of Dewey's pedagogy, of course, but also of television's assault on book culture and of postmodernism's aggressive rejection of a literary canon made up of "dead white males." Brodsky paid absolutely no attention to academic orthodoxies and during his first class would hand out his own "canon." This was not a list of required readings but something more like a map of culture and poetry. One of Brodsky's former students recalls: "On the first day of class, handing out a list of readings, he said, 'Here's how you need to spend your life for the next two years.'"[38] That list began with the Bhagavad Gita, the *Gilgamesh Epic,* the Old Testament, continued with roughly thirty works by ancient Greek and Roman writers, then moved on to Saint Augustine, Saint Francis, Thomas Aquinas, Luther, Calvin, Dante, Petrarch, Boccaccio, Rabelais, Shakespeare, Cervantes, Benvenuto Cellini, Descartes, Spinoza, Hobbes, Pascal, Locke, Hume, Leibnitz, Schopenhauer, Kierkegaard (but neither Kant nor Hegel!), Tocqueville, Custine, Ortega y Gasset, Henry Adams, Hannah Arendt, Dostoevsky's *The Possessed,* Robert Musil's *The Man without Qualities, Young Torless,* and *Five Women,* Italo Calvino's *Invisible Cities,* Joseph Roth's *Radetzky March,* and finally wound up with a list of forty-four poets starting with Tsvetaeva, Akhmatova, Mandelstam, Pasternak, Khlebnikov, and Zabolotsky.

Brodsky's papers include several different such lists; evidently he enjoyed making them. They are interesting as a clue to Brodsky's own reading, which corresponds roughly with Soviet university programs in philology, philosophy, and the literature of the twentieth century. That is, he read approximately what his university-educated peers had—and more. Strange as it might seem, some American students had mastered, if not everything on the list itself, something similar in spirit and scope. Brodsky was not always dealing with ignorant hicks.

I can't help but wonder what effect teaching had on Brodsky himself—whether it might not have occasionally helped him rethink and refine what he had known only intuitively before. After all, he wasn't simply giving lectures; he had to assign homework and check it and grade it. One of his assignments starts like this: "I would like you to assess this work by Akhmatova—how well does her description of fire really work?"[39] Of course, pity the poor student who is given such vague directions by an obviously inexperienced teacher—but what are we talking about here? The memoirs do not tell us exactly which text Brodsky wants to discuss, but in all likelihood it is from the "Sweetbriar" cycle (*From a Burned Notebook*), which had always affected him greatly. Here Akhmatova's mastery of her craft shines through in the constant but never forced variations on the motif of fire: a burning notebook filled with poems, the flaming expanse of space, the bright flame of victory, the funeral pyre of Dido, and so on. In explaining such things to students, perhaps the poet learned some lessons himself.

BRODSKY IN NEW YORK

In April 1977, Brodsky rented an apartment in Greenwich Village, on a quiet side street that stretches between Eighth Avenue and the Hudson River. His lodgings at 44 Morton were fairly typical for the West Village: a flat in a narrow, three-story brick townhouse, which was owned by a New York University professor, Andrew Blaine, a specialist in the history of the Russian Orthodox Church. Blaine himself lived in a little annex off the back courtyard and rented out the rest of the apartments to friends and acquaintances. Brodsky soon got to know the rest of the tenants, and later these neighbors would become almost like an extended family. Closest of all, rather like an older sister, was Masha Vorobyova, who lived one floor above. She had been born in Vilnius, the daughter of a professor of architectural history, and had come to the United States as a young girl in the great wave of post–World War II emigration. When Brodsky met her, she was teaching Russian language and literature at Vassar College, just up the Hudson from the city. The small apartment across the terrace was occupied on and off by Margo Picken, a longtime friend from Brodsky's Leningrad days who had spent her life working for international relief organizations. But all who came and went over the years tended to be people he knew—editors, writers, university instructors—and they looked after him, never letting him sink into a sad and hapless bachelor life.

From the street side Brodsky's apartment looked like a half-basement, but in the back it was a ground-floor flat opening onto a shaded, paved terrace, with a small table onto which, from early spring to late fall, Brodsky would plop his Colibri manual typewriter and work in the fresh air. For a Russian, New York seemed something like the Crimea, someplace just short of the tropics. The breeze blowing through the little courtyard was almost Mediterranean, ocean-salty with the occasional whiff of freshly brewed espresso: just down the street were Greenwich Village's famed coffeehouses, the Reggio and the Borgia. Little Italy was just around the corner.

Morton Street dead-ends at the Hudson River, at an old wooden pier where in Brodsky's day a decommissioned warship housed a culinary school. When the weather was good, there were fishermen and lovers all around, hooking fish and sucking lips, respectively. Brodsky loved walking to the pier. The sea wind, the plash of the waves, the old ship, and the brick warehouses reminded him of the docks off the Malaya Neva and the Nevka.

His apartment had only two proper rooms. There was a bedroom that faced the street, a room opening onto the courtyard, and a kitchen-hallway connecting the two. The courtyard room served as both living room and office. It had a fireplace, a leather sofa and chairs, and, for a long time, a homemade desk—an unfinished door propped on file cabinets, just like the one he'd improvised for himself in Ann Arbor. Later Mikhail Baryshnikov would give Brodsky an enormous pigeonhole desk.

During perestroika, when Brodsky finally began hosting guests from Russia, some of them were surprised at how modestly he lived. After all, he'd won the Nobel Prize. Two small rooms in a ground-floor flat were hardly the dream of the ambitious Soviet writer, or the anti-Soviet one either.

TRAVELS

The pace set in Brodsky's first days in the West never slowed. He was always on the road, and probably no Russian writer ever traveled more. His contemporaries Evtushenko and Voznesensky might have visited more cities and countries. But traveling under both official police watch and unofficial pressure ("buy me something that I can't get at home") was entirely different from traveling as a private citizen with some command of English and money of one's own. Brodsky gave readings from Canada to Rio. He lived for extended periods in London, Paris, Amsterdam, Stockholm, Venice, and Rome, everywhere making real friends. He did not want to be a tourist, did not want to do the usual rounds and see the usual sights. He was very adept at making his way around a new town, finding local cafés, reading local newspapers, tuning in to local gossip. His *Watermark,* which Russian and American readers might see as a purely poetic text, "a crystal whose facets reflect an entire life, with exile and ill health glinting at the edges of planes whose direct glare is sheer beauty," was taken otherwise in Venice, where some readers saw the book as an attack on their leftist mayor and local wheeler-dealers.[40] In it they also found unflattering portraits of some local characters.[41]

Herein lies the difference between Brodsky's travelogues (whether in poetry or prose) and those written by most of his Russian counterparts. The lyric hero of "In the Lake District," "An autumn evening in the modest square," "A Part of Speech," "Lullaby of Cape Cod," "The Thames at Chelsea," "Roman Elegies," "San Pietro," "Piazza Mattei," "On Via Julia," and "On Via Funari" is not simply a tourist passing through these places. He is living in them.[42] He is a displaced person and, given the range of his travels, a true citizen of the world.

More typical of standard travel accounts are his Mexican and Lithuanian "divertissements"; his first Venetian poem, "Lagoon"; his "December in Florence." In these and a handful of others, the poetic landscape might look old and familiar (America in "August," Italy in "San Pietro" and "On Via Funari") or new and exotic ("Mexican Divertimento"), but however lived-in the place might feel, this traveler keeps a certain distance.

As I said earlier, he seems to cherish this alienation; he seems to seek a certain existential discomfort. Brodsky's lyric "I" is constantly at odds; his prose "I" is much more responsive to new sights and sounds.

Bożena Shallcross in her very interesting book on two Poles and a Russian, Zagajewski, Herbert, and Brodsky, notes that all of them describe some epiphany, some turning point, when, in a strange and alien place, they suddenly come upon something mysterious and beautiful.[43] For Zagajewski this was Vermeer's *Music Lesson* at the Frick Museum; for Herbert it was Torrentius's *Still Life with Bridle* in Amsterdam; for Brodsky it was Venice as a whole. His moment arrives at the end of *Watermark,* when he peers through the window of a late-night café to see his best-loved poets, most of them long dead, talking and laughing around a table.

We should also note what is *not* on Brodsky's map of the world. Moscow and the Russian countryside are there, as are Lithuania and the rest of the Baltic states, Ukraine, the Crimea, Central Asia, and practically every other country the poet visited, whether physically (Central America and Europe) or mentally (China, Afghanistan, Oceania). But in only four of his mature poems does Leningrad figure; New York, his home for the latter half of his life, is the setting for only one.[44]

When asked to explain why he had never written much about New York, Brodsky alluded to his home city. Why write explicitly about a place when the place is implicit in everything you write?

> Seriously speaking, the Petersburg landscape is classic in the sense that it becomes the equivalent of a mental state, of a psychological reaction. At least the author may think his reactions are its equivalent. It's a sort of rhythm, a quite conscious one. Even perhaps a natural, biological rhythm.

Petersburg's colors, its light and shadow, its architectural rhythms, all folded into the poet's psyche and inevitably made up the very fabric of his verse. He went on to say that

> what happens here [in New York] seems to happen in a different dimension. And assimilating that psychologically, that is, turning it into your own internal rhythm is, I think, simply impossible. At least it's impossible for me.

Earlier in the same interview, in comparing New York to Petersburg, he said, "Just try and find yourself a colonnade here."[45]

FRIENDS AND FOES

The wildly diverse megalopolis that is New York may not figure in Brodsky's lyrics, but New York was a place where he truly found a niche and felt at home. In some way the everyday Brodsky was very much like the everyday New Yorker, or at least like the standard image of one—energetic, impatient, and mouthy. A note in the *New York Times* from December 13, 1987, describes a meeting between Brodsky and then-mayor Edward Koch. Koch had invited the new Nobel laureate to the city hall for official congratulations, but within a few minutes, as reporters watched, the polite conversation turned into a verbal duel of wits. At the end of their talk Koch asked Brodsky whether he had ever suffered from anti-Semitism in the USSR. Brodsky answered that he had sometimes been teased because he couldn't pronounce L's and R's correctly. Koch was surprised. "'Is that a Jewish trait, not being able to say R and L?' the Mayor asked. 'Yes,' said Mr. Brodsky. 'It is? I can say R and L,' said Mr. Koch. He paused a beat and then with great exaggeration roared an R and yelled an L. Mr. Brodsky had an answer. 'Maybe,' he said, smiling, 'you're not a perfect Jew.'"[46] And when in the 1990s the city began plastering subways with short quotations from the work of city poets, Brodsky's poster featured an impromptu couplet that might serve as a New York motto:

> Sir, you are tough, and I am tough.
> But who will write whose epitaph?[47]

Like many European artists and intellectuals before him, he fit easily into New York intellectual circles. He wrote many of his articles (essays on Cavafy, Montale, and Nadezhda Mandelstam) and his first short memoir ("A Room and a Half") for the *New York Review of Books,* a periodical widely read by American highbrows regardless of profession. But he also published in the more widely read *New Yorker,* in the book section of the *New York Times,* and even in *Vogue,* where his essays on Virgil and Petersburg were framed by fashion ads. He wasn't snobbish about where he was published; he just as willingly sent work to small magazines as to big presses.

His chief English-language publisher was Farrar, Straus and Giroux, which put out three of his English poetry collections (*A Part of Speech* in 1980, *To Urania* in 1988, and *So Forth* in 1996) and two volumes of his prose (*Less Than One* in 1986 and *On Grief and Reason* in 1995). By modern standards, Farrar, Straus and Giroux was a small house. Founded by the three enlightened publishers whose names make up its own, it specialized in contemporary prose and poetry, English-language and translated alike. Roger Straus (1917–2004), who was also chief editor, enjoyed a reputation as the last of the gentleman-publishers in an industry increasingly dominated by faceless international conglomerates.[48] "Other publishing houses could be compared to factories, but FS&G isn't a publishing house; it's an extension of my home," said Brodsky in a *Time* magazine interview in 1988.[49]

Straus's friends used to joke that he had a standing hotel reservation in Stockholm and that every December he would complain "Oh God, not Stockholm again!" And in fact he and his colleagues especially prided themselves on the fact that many of the writers they published went on to win the Nobel Prize in Literature: before Brodsky, there were Aleksandr Solzhenitsyn, Czesław Miłosz, Elias Canetti, William Golding, and Wole Soyinka; after him came Camilo José Cela, Nadine Gordimer, Derek Walcott, and Seamus Heaney.

Straus himself was the product of two very wealthy and influential New York families, the Strauses and the Guggenheims. Both are known for their philanthropy, especially in support of the arts—hence the Guggenheim Foundation, the Guggenheim Museums in New York, Venice, Berlin, Bilbao, and Las Vegas (this last a joint project with the Hermitage).[50] But from its very start, Farrar, Straus and Giroux was run as a business. While its profits may have been modest in comparison to those of popular presses, it was still a commercial operation and did not rely on family money. Its reputation was such that writers would sometimes turn down more lucrative contracts in order to publish with it. One economical in-house tradition was the practice of asking its own authors to review manuscripts, and Brodsky occasionally did so, especially if the manuscript was a translation from the Russian. One such review led to bad blood between Brodsky and Vasily Aksyonov; Brodsky gave a blunt assessment of Aksyonov's novel *The Burn,* and Aksyonov's next novel, *Say Cheese!,* featured a cheap opportunist named Alik Konsky, who sets himself up as a victim of totalitarianism in order to make a name for himself in the West.

Brodsky's circle of friends in the 1970s was made up primarily of those writers who published with the *New York Review of Books* and Farrar, Straus and Giroux and included such celebrities as the essayist

Susan Sontag and the poet Derek Walcott. But before them came the Liebermans.

Alex Lieberman (1912–1999) left Russia as a child, soon after the Revolution. He was an unusually gifted man. He came to New York shortly after World War II, started with nothing, but soon became the managing editor at Condé Nast (publisher of *Vogue,* which explains Brodsky's connection with the fashion magazine). Lieberman was also a talented artist, sculptor, and photographer, one of the leading representatives of the New York school; his works hung in New York's Metropolitan and Guggenheim Museums and in the Tate Gallery in London. One tribute to his friendship with Brodsky is *Campidoglio,* a marvelous book in which Lieberman's photographs of Rome are set to Brodsky's text.[51]

Tatyana Lieberman, née Yakovleva (1906–1991), is best known to Russian literature as "Mayakovsky's last love." A famed Russian beauty in 1920s Paris, she was well acquainted with the hardships of émigré life. She and her husband eagerly took in new arrivals at both their New York house and their Connecticut estate, but they came to love and admire Brodsky in particular. In an interview with Viktor Erofeev, she said that in all her life she had known only two geniuses: "Picasso and . . ." Her interviewer was waiting for "Mayakovsky," but instead she said, "Brodsky." And while this might reflect nothing more than Tatyana Lieberman's private scale of values, it explains much about how Brodsky was received not only in the Liebermans' home but also in New York's intellectual circles.[52]

Among Brodsky's close friends in and around New York were other recent émigrés: the writer Yuz Aleshkovsky, the dancer Mikhail Baryshnikov, the translator and art historian Gennady Shmakov, and the Lithuanian poet Tomas Venclova. But Brodsky was never really part of the rapidly growing émigré community of the late 1970s and early 1980s. He was always willing to read his own poetry or introduce other poets to a Russian-speaking audience, but he had no circle of his own and tried to stay clear of the tangled and often petty politics of the émigré ghetto. Although his longtime friend and admirer Sergey Dovlatov constantly praised Brodsky on the pages of his newspaper, the *New American,* other émigré publications launched blistering attacks. So when Brodsky wrote that "they accused me of everything but the weather," he may have been talking less about his troubles in the Soviet Union than about the attitude of his fellow émigrés.

In Israel, where he published in the Russian-language journal *22*, he had his loyal readers, but also his critics, who found him suspect for choosing to settle in the United States. Still, the nastiest attacks came from his fellow "new Americans." These were not the critiques of his work by Yury Karabchievsky, Yury Kolker, Naum Korzhavin, and, later, Aleksandr Solzhenitsyn, but rather attacks ad hominem.[53] At the very beginning of his American life, he was reproached for his first major article in the *New York Times Magazine*, in which he reflected on his literary life.[54] For one thing, he wrote that he bore no grudge against his native country. In his mind, Russia and the Soviet regime were two separate things. Some émigrés saw this as nothing more than political maneuvering. "Your article is pure politics, and it stinks. . . . It's written for the Liteiny-Lubyanka crowd [i.e., the KGB in Leningrad and Moscow, respectively], in the hopes that they'll read it and realize what a good boy you are. You say nothing terrible or critical, you 'don't tar the gates of our Soviet home.' . . . These people, once they appreciate the godlike apoliticalness you've so carefully cultivated, will in time let you 'come home,' and then if you behave yourself, you'll be a 'free Soviet citizen' just like Evtushenko and Voznesensky, with the right to trot back and forth."[55] The journalist Lev Navrozov, under the aegis of an ultra-conservative publishing house called the Rockford Papers, published a brochure in English that purported to expose Brodsky as the "architect of the Brodsky sensation, which is calculated to culminate in a Nobel Prize." Navrozov goes on to condemn not only Brodsky but also his "mafia and minions."[56] Among the mafiosi and the minions were Yuz Aleshkovsky, Sergey Dovlatov, and Eduard Limonov. ("Minion" Limonov would soon have something to say about his erstwhile patron.) These were writers that Brodsky had indeed helped, as he helped many others: he set up contacts with publishers, wrote introductions, wrote recommendations for teaching posts. (In fact, Brodsky wrote so many recommendations that Slavic departments began to take them with a grain of salt.)

Limonov, at the time, considered himself part of the Russian avant-garde, and his comments on Brodsky came out in a short-lived avant-garde Parisian journal called *Muleta-A*. The article was entitled "The Poet as Accountant" and began with a position statement. "To the innocent and inexperienced reader, the writer is something sacred. To his fellow writers he's more or less just another charlatan with his own methods of duping the public. We can either learn his tricks, or despise him for his lack of imagination and outmoded technique." And Brodsky is just another charlatan, he has his own tricks, but we have nothing to learn from him. Brodsky lacks imagination; he is out of date: "His verse has become more or less a catalogue. . . . He names a thing—compares it to something else, names a thing—compares it. A few pages of comparison and there you have your poem. . . . A bureaucrat. An accountant, counting up and costing all the posts, the beams, the pilasters, the columns, and the nails of the world. The feathers on a hawk."[57] In a way, this is an accurate description of Brodsky's poetics. What might strike some readers as the ability to create a detailed picture of the world of things through keenly observed detail and unexpected metaphor strikes the avant-garde poet not at all. There's no trick in it, no way to fool the public.

Brodsky, for his part, had expressed his views on the infantilism of avant-garde poetry (and in part on its childish erotic fixations) as early as 1965, in "Feliks":

> Yes, kids are only kids. Let their ardor
> be whipped up by March approaching.
> However, avant-garde is avant-garde,
> And we too were once the avant-garde.[58]
> (Non-poetic)

What irritates Limonov more than Brodsky the poet is Brodsky the man. That is, by Russian émigré standards Brodsky the man is making too good a living.

> Exile for Brodsky is impressive, luxurious, decadent. An exile for people of means. It is Venice, Rome, London; it is museums, churches, the boulevards of European capitals. It is a fine hotel with a view looking out not on some peeling wall in New Jersey but on a Venetian lagoon. Hundreds of Russian poets have emigrated to the West. Brodsky alone manages to maintain a standard of living that allows him to think, to travel, and, if he has to rage, to rage against the universe.[59] . . . Brodsky's poetry is written for conformists defending doctoral dissertations in Slavic departments at American universities. The author of such poetry will no doubt be elected to all sorts of

> academies, is being elected, but I am sure that with the aid of the New York Jewish intellectual elite, which was so delighted to have a Russian-speaking poet in its midst, Iosif Aleksandrovich Brodsky will soon get the prize named after the inventor of dynamite.[60]

Later Limonov would admit that at one time he was simply envious of Brodsky's "wealth," and he even names a sum—$34,000 a year for five years. He was talking about the MacArthur Fellowship awarded to Brodsky in 1981. Still, Limonov's numbers were slightly off. The first year Brodsky received all of $40,000.[61] For a time this "genius award" combined with his earned income guaranteed Brodsky a secure but hardly luxurious existence. He was already in ill health, and the MacArthur at least freed him from some of his onerous teaching duties. But both before it and after it he always had to earn his own keep, and any "wealth" was only in the mind of nonconformists who could neither write, nor publish, nor teach in English.

Émigrés' badmouthing of Brodsky generally took one of two forms: Navrozov-style carping that the poet had orchestrated his own "sensation" and exile in order to make a name for himself in the West, or Limonov-style insinuation that Brodsky owed his reputation to an influential circle of New York Jews. Neither one is worth refuting, but what is interesting is that the pathetic Navrozov and the envious Limonov both see a Nobel Prize in Brodsky's future. As early as 1980 there were rumors that Brodsky had been nominated, but these were just rumors. The nomination process was a well-kept secret.

And besides, a Nobel nomination does not mean a Nobel Prize. The first round of nominations generally includes 6,000 or more names. The last round includes almost 150. What is interesting is that even Brodsky's foes acknowledged that he was now a key figure in the Russian diaspora and far beyond it.

NONMEETINGS: BRODSKY AND NABOKOV

Two other Russian writers living abroad were at least as well known as Brodsky: Aleksandr Solzhenitsyn and Vladimir Nabokov, one and two generations away, respectively. Both were hermits after their own fashion, and when they pontificated *urbi et orbi,* it was not in a language that the city and the world easily understood. The European Enlightenment's vision of the world as a "grove of nations," a philosophy that permeates Solzhenitsyn's work, was embraced neither by the Western intelligentsia nor by a good part of the Russian intelligentsia, who alike tended to put a higher value on personal freedom, individualism, and cosmopolitanism. Nabokov, for his part, did not have the temperament for social debate; he was too much of an elitist to want to play any significant part in it.[62]

But the "nonmeeting" (as Tsvetaeva might have put it) between Brodsky and Nabokov merits a short digression. As we know, Brodsky read Nabokov earlier than did many of his contemporaries. In a May 1990 interview with David Bethea, who was writing a book on Brodsky's poetics, Bethea remarked that Nabokov had gone into prose but that Brodsky had gone into poetry. He asked what they had in common, which of Nabokov's works Brodsky knew: which he had liked, which he hadn't. Brodsky replied:

> I adore *Invitation to a Beheading,* I adore *Gift.* I adore parts of *Pale Fire.* I've read, I think, everything: *The Luzhin Defense, Pnin.* . . . Actually the first book that I read was *Camera Obscura,* which I liked right off. I liked it not so much for the story itself but for that transition from straight narrative to stream of consciousness. . . . To answer your question: Nabokov, to his own mind, was first and foremost a poet. And he wanted to prove that to himself and everyone else. He did not understand that although he was a poet, he was not a great one. In a sense, his meeting Khodasevich was tragic perhaps for him, but this was [his] only tragedy. He recognized the distinction between a true poet and himself. . . . Take all his novels (save *Camera Obscura*); all of them are about one and the same thing—about a double, about another existence, about a twin, about a mirror image. . . . So in the final analysis . . . what it's all about is the principle of rhyme. It is the rhyme principle going king size.[63]

In 1969, Carl Proffer sent a copy of "Gorbunov and Gorchakov" to Nabokov in Montreux. Vera Nabokova replied: "Thank you for your letter, the two books, and Brodsky's poem. 'It contains many attractive metaphors and eloquent rhymes,' says VN, 'but it is flawed by incorrectly accented words, lack of verbal discipline and an overabundance of words in general. However, esthetic criticism would be unfair in view of the ghastly surroundings and suffering implied in every line of the poem.'"[64]

We may never know whether this great master of allusion was alluding to a remark by Emperor Franz Josef II, who, after a performance of Mozart's *Abduction from the Seraglio,* supposedly said to the young composer, "Too many notes, my dear Mozart, too many notes!"

After relaying her husband's response to the poem, Vera Nabokov continues: "I am particularly grateful [to you] for sending those dungarees. Please tell me how much I owe you."[65] On Nabokov's behalf, Proffer had taken Brodsky a pair of jeans (at that time both expensive and hard to get in the USSR). This was the only direct contact between the two writers.[66]

BRODSKY AND SOLZHENITSYN SPEAK TO AMERICA

Brodsky, for all his proclaimed contempt for politics, for all the complexity of his poetic thought (and the stunning paradoxes it produced in his essays and public appearances), had willy-nilly become a spokesman for thinking Russia. Whether he admitted it or not, he did have the temperament for social debate and frequently found himself taking part in discussions on current political events. In 1974, with the aid of the German publishing magnate and humanitarian Axel Springer, Vladimir Maksimov founded *Kontinent,* which would become the most influential journal of the Russian diaspora for the next two decades. Brodsky had known Maksimov's co-editor, Natalya Gorbanevskaya, for many years. The first issue of the new journal opened with greetings from Aleksandr Solzhenitsyn, Eugene Ionesco, Andrey Sakharov—and poems by Brodsky. Leading off the selection was "On the Death of Zhukov," which expressed the political stance of both the author and the journal as a whole: pride in Russia's heroic history and high culture; disgust with the cruelty of Russian totalitarianism. Throughout the journal's existence, Brodsky regularly sent new poems to *Kontinent* and supported it in all its endeavors. Living in the United States, he was relatively detached from the rivalry and conflict between Maksimov's *Kontinent* and the newspaper *Russkaya mysl,* on the one hand, and Sinyavsky and Rozanova's *Sintaksis* and Efim Etkind, on the other—quarrels that divided the Paris émigré community for years on end. But Brodsky always admired Maksimov's uncompromising and often ferocious anti-Communism; he compared Maksimov to a soldier leading a desperate charge, shooting "round after round from the hip." He was as leery of the "socialism with a human face" promoted by Etkind and *Sintaksis* as he was of Limonov and the homegrown avant-garde.

Why did public appeals by Solzhenitsyn—whose *One Day in the Life of Ivan Denisovich* and *Gulag Archipelago* had truly shaken the world—make so little impression on the Western intelligentsia, and even drive away a certain part of it, while Brodsky's opinions, literary and political alike, were recorded in countless interviews, generally respected, and seen as representative of freethinking in Russia? The explanation apparently lies more in style than in content. One particular image of Solzhenitsyn made the rounds of the Western press: reports on his commencement address to Harvard's class of 1978 were accompanied by a photograph of a tall man sporting an Old Testament beard and a custom-made quasi-military tunic, shaking his finger at his audience. Solzhenitsyn was accusing the West of lack of faith, lack of strength, of moral degeneration and political cowardice. He spoke as one who knows the truth, the whole truth, the only truth, incontrovertible and unchallengeable. Now imagine the average American intellectual in that audience on that spring day. He or she is probably stunned by the impassioned authoritarian tone and the angry outpouring of accusation and prophecy. The American audience tries to fit the speaker into its own system of cultural coordinates, and the closest analogy it can find is a fire-and-brimstone evangelical preacher threatening his flock with the flames of hell. Brodsky, on the other hand, looks and acts more like a New York type à la Woody Allen; he isn't preaching; rather, he is thinking out loud, constantly emphasizing that whatever he says is his personal opinion, that he is not in possession of absolute truth. The antitotalitarian message is almost the same as Solzhenitsyn's, but to the Western audience it is more convincing—and certainly more palatable.

AFGHANISTAN AND POLAND

An especially telling example of Brodsky's influence on American intellectual culture is the case of Susan Sontag. One of the most formidable figures of the American intelligentsia, a liberal and a leftist, a feminist, a fierce critic of conformist consumer culture, she had always maintained that the American political system was in thrall to corporate interests. During the war in Vietnam, she and some likeminded friends traveled to Hanoi to express their solidarity with the Viet Cong. So it was a major scandal when in 1982, at a grand gathering of unions and radical activists in support of Poland's Solidarity movement, Sontag, to growing noise and heckling from the crowd, declared that someone who had read nothing other than *Reader's Digest* for the past thirty years knew a great deal more about Communism than did readers of the *Nation*.

Events in Poland—the outbreak of public protest against the Communist regime, General Jaruzelski's declaration of martial law and the repressions that followed, the threat of Soviet intervention—presented a problem for American socialists and quasi-socialists. Here we had a socialist government mercilessly quashing a genuine working-class revolt. The organizers of the meeting in support of Solidarity had a twofold goal: first, to distance themselves from the USSR and its puppets in Poland, because neither represented "genuine socialism"; second, to persuade the audience that the plight of U.S. workers was no different from that of Polish workers in Gdansk, that Ronald Reagan's imperialist policy in Latin America was no different from Brezhnev's in Central Europe. So said the first speakers at the meeting—Gore Vidal, Kurt Vonnegut, Pete Seeger, and many others. It was expected that Sontag would say the same. And while she agreed that police repression in Poland and police repression in El Salvador and other Latin American countries had much in common, she couched it in these words: "Communism is Fascism with a human face." The difference, she asserted, was that Communism was simply a more successful form of Fascism. For this insight she thanked her Eastern European friends, including Czesław Miłosz and Joseph Brodsky, and quoted the latter's remark about crushing the Poles with "Soviet tanks and Western banks."[67]

Brodsky also spoke at the meeting, and announced that as a symbolic gesture, he was closing his account at New York's Chemical Bank, which underwrote the Polish ruling government. In answer to those orators who kept comparing Communist repression in Poland to U.S. intervention in Latin America, where "people have at least a minimum of freedom,"[68] he said: "Not only is drawing a parallel from PATCO to Polish workers an outright obscenity, it distracts people from the real issues and leaves Poland out in the cold, where it is already. You liberals should try to solve one problem instead of diffusing your energy all over the world!"[69]

He was booed and hissed: "You cynical bastard!"[70]

Brodsky took what was happening in Poland very close to heart. Natalya Gorbanevskaya recalls that "[i]n December 1980, when the threat of Soviet intervention in Poland seemed inevitable, Joseph, Tomas Venclova, and another Lithuanian and I sat down and seriously discussed a plan to organize an international brigade for the defense of Poland. And all four of us were planning to be part of the first wave."[71]

Brodsky was especially fond of Poland; he was less fond of Islamic states. Still, he reacted to the Soviet incursion into Afghanistan in much the same way. When an interviewer asked whether his political views were reflected in his writing, he answered: "I don't believe in writing it—I believe in action. I think it's time to create some sort of International Brigade. It was done in 1936, why not now? Except that in 1936 the International Brigade was financed by the GPU—that is, Soviet State Security. I just wonder if there's anybody with the money . . . somebody in Texas who could financially back the thing."[72] The interviewer asked just what such an international brigade might do.

BRODSKY: Well, the International Brigade can do essentially what it did in 1936 in Spain, that is, fight back, help the locals. Or at least give some sort of medical assistance—food, shelter. If there is a noble cause, it is this—not some Amnesty International . . . I wouldn't mind driving a Red Cross jeep. . . .

INTERVIEWER: It's hard to identify clear moral sides sometimes. . . .

BRODSKY: I don't really know what kind of moral sides you are looking for, especially in a place like Afghanistan. It is quite obvious. They've been invaded; they've been subjugated. They may be just backward tribesmen but slavery isn't my idea of revolution either.[73]

Ten years later he would say the same about the war in Chechnya.

The two poems that Brodsky wrote about the Soviet war in Afghanistan—"Lines on the Winter Campaign, 1980" (*Urania*) and "On the Negotiations in Kabul" (*PSN*)—are an unsentimental but not cynical look at this long and bloody conflict. The emotional content of both texts comes down to sheer repulsion. The first poem is a reaction to the aggression of an evil empire, to a stupid, unnatural, mechanical force. The aggressors are not human beings but things—bullets, airplanes, fake elephants (tanks)—that nightmarishly mimic the actions of living beings: "[a]rmour, wetting its metal sheets with oil slick." Powerful images replace pacifist clichés: instead of "cannon fodder," we have "dank and freezing . . . human pig meat"; instead of "better they [the young soldiers] should never have been born," we have "[g]lory to those who, their glances lowered, / marched in the sixties to abortion tables, / sparing the homeland its present stigma!" In the latter poem he is repulsed by "stiff-necked mountain tribes" who may live by cruel archaic law but are all too eager to trade in their ancient civilization for the dubious benefits of Western consumer culture (this, according to Brodsky, is the real gist of the negotiations in Kabul).[74]

These two poems might be considered a sort of "Afghan diptych," but in terms of Brodsky's political philosophy, what is most important here is that he does not equate the three sides: tribal-Islamist, Soviet, Western. None bears the absolute truth, all are carriers of evil, but in Brodsky's dark but perhaps realistic political universe, there are degrees of evil, much as in Dante's *Inferno*. In "To Evgeny" from "Mexican Divertimento," Brodsky says that as horrible as the disease and genocide brought by the Spaniards were, "better syphilis than . . . sacrifice like this." All in all, better foreign rule than the prevailing local despotism and the human sacrifice it entailed. The West might be stupid and vulgar, but it's still "better than where the ruler is a cone / and the only thing to stroke is a rifle butt." Totalitarian Communism lies close to the bottommost circle of Dante's hell, where the worst sinners of all are frozen in ice: "slavery's ice age is coming, / oozing over the atlas."

In his first essay published in the West, in 1972, Brodsky wrote: "Life—the way it really is—is a battle not between Bad and Good, but between Bad and Worse. And today humanity's choice lies not between Good and Evil, but rather between Evil and Worse. Today's humanity's task comes down to remaining good in the Kingdom of Evil, and not becoming an agent of Evil."[75] In poems written that year this attitude is reflected more concretely: "I, for one, prefer a vulture to a vampire" ("Letters to a Roman Friend")—words that twenty-five years later, in post-Soviet Russia, would be taken as prophetic. In his Afghan verse, in his English-language poems on the genocide in Kosovo, in his 1980 essay "Playing Games," written in support of the boycott of the Moscow Olympics, and in many of his public appearances Brodsky chides the West on the intellectual and moral bankruptcy of the "mental bourgeois enjoying the ultimate comfort: that of his convictions."[76] As the Solidarity rally demonstrated, the comfort of those convictions suggested that all things were equal, that the uglier sides of Western democracy were the moral equivalent of the mass crimes committed by totalitarian regimes. Brodsky's message got through to at least some in the West; Solzhenitsyn's message, couched in prophecy and religious-utopian rhetoric on moral purification, often did not.

BRODSKY AND SOLZHENITSYN

We should emphasize once again that the chief difference between Brodsky and Solzhenitsyn is stylistic. Brodsky's verse might sound ironic and cynical at times, but its content was dictated neither by cynicism nor by pragmatism. Brodsky's discourse with the West, like Solzhenitsyn's, had a spiritual subtext. If in a 1972 article his sermon on the good has an abstract ring, in his 1984 commencement address he quotes Christ's Sermon on the Mount directly. But nowhere in Brodsky does the good attain such metaphoric intensity as in his 1980 Christmas poem, "Snow is falling, leaving the whole world outmanned."

> So much light packed into this shard of star
> at nightfall! Like refugees into a boat.
> (Non-poetic)

If the light from the star of the Nativity is the energy of Good in its purest form, the quantum of that light is the boat in which the most unfortunate and deprived people of the world seek refuge from the Evil that pursues them. In the late 1970s and early 1980s television and print news constantly featured boat people—Cubans, Vietnamese—setting out in frail, often homemade craft, fleeing from their Communist rulers.[77]

Brodsky and Solzhenitsyn never met in person, although South Hadley, Massachusetts, where Brodsky lived and worked for so long, was only an hour and a half drive from Solzhenitsyn's compound in the town of Cavendish in southern Vermont. If Brodsky was ever asked about Solzhenitsyn as a writer, he would invariably repeat what he'd once heard Akhmatova say: "The point is that the book [*One Day in the Life of Ivan Denisovich*] ought to be read by all 300 million people living in the Soviet Union." Or: "I really think that in him the Soviet rule got its Homer; what he managed to reveal, the way he kind of pulled the world a little bit around."[78] However, his remarks on Solzhenitsyn's political views could be pointed. In 1995, when one journalist remarked that in Solzhenitsyn's opinion, "Russia is the keeper of certain values that the West has betrayed," an obviously annoyed Brodsky answered, "What Solzhenitsyn says is monstrous nonsense. It's the usual demagoguery, except with a plus sign rather than a minus. As a politician he is a total zero."[79] Brodsky went on to explain his complaint in a calmer tone: Solzhenitsyn, like Blok, like Pasternak, like Mandelstam in part (but unlike Akhmatova and Tsvetaeva), was hampered by the "provincial Russian tendency to see the hand of Providence in everything that happens, in every odd experience. . . . Solzhenitsyn did not and does not understand one very simple thing. He thought he was dealing with Communism, with a political doctrine. He didn't understand that he was dealing with human beings."[80] The teleology, the religious and romantic construct of history from which the Slavophiles, Dostoevsky, Leontyev, Berdyaev, and other predecessors of Solzhenitsyn derived the "Russian idea," as well as Solzhenitsyn's notion of key moments when the full force of human evil came crashing down on Russia, interested Brodsky not at all. For him there was no human history outside individual human lives; the central object of a writer's interest had to be the person whom history had made suffer most. Any speculation on the meaning of history deflected attention from the human tragedy. "For all my regard for Aleksandr Isayevich, this was something that bothered me even in *One Day in the Life of Ivan Denisovich*. What can you say? It's a remarkable book. But then there's Ivan Denisovich himself. He survives; he's a wonderful person. But what about those who don't survive? When they aren't quite so wonderful?"[81]

Brodsky spoke out on Solzhenitsyn in other venues as well. In 1977 he published an admiring review of the English edition of *The Gulag Archipelago;* in his 1984 essay "Catastrophes in the Air" he recalled the powerful impression made by *Cancer Ward*.[82]

For Solzhenitsyn's part, his opinion of Brodsky's poetry changed considerably over the years. In May 1977 he wrote to Brodsky: "I never miss any of your publications in Russian journals, I never cease to admire your brilliant mastery [of your craft]. Sometimes I fear that you're about to demolish the line, but even that you do with incomparable talent."[83] In a long article in *Novy mir* published after the poet's death, he was much more critical. While he notes a few especially well-turned phrases or particular poems, he takes apart Brodsky's poetics, aesthetics, and philosophy. Even the poet's public demeanor seems suspect to Solzhenitsyn: "While in the USSR he never once made a single serious political statement. . . . The Jewish question, so pressing in those years, might have been a platform for him, but no. . . . 'Roadshow' ['Predstavlenie'; *PSN*] is a cheap trick, a breakdown into Soviet slang and obscenity, a caricature more of Russia than of Sovietness, a caricature of the disgustingly beastly and simple Russian folk, and of Russian Orthodoxy, too. . . . Brodsky is essentially alienated from the Russian literary tradition . . . philosophically, spiritually, and intellectually—from both Tolstoy's legacy and Dostoevsky's."[84] Solzhenitsyn is a mystic, that is, a man whose faith rests on revelation, on religious experience, who cannot fathom the agnostic whose metaphysical doubts arise out of the very inability to know God as some transcendental Absolute and Other who exists outside time, space, and logic. In casting about for new and newer poetic means to express these metaphysical riddles, Brodsky is continuing the line of *both* Tolstoy and Dostoevsky, especially the latter, who projected his own unease with any theodicy, with any attempt to find God in a logical, time-and-space-bound world, onto his protagonists. Agnosticism, as these great examples demonstrate, is torment for the person; it is a source of drama and power for the writer.

Solzhenitsyn and Brodsky were the most famous Russian writers of their time—both Nobel laureates, both longtime residents of the United States. Their differences had nothing to do with their international status or with émigré squabbles; it had everything to do with Russian culture, with the old quarrel between Slavophiles and Westernizers. We should recall that a Slavophile was not someone who loved the Slavs above all else, but someone whose romantic philosophy of history placed national destiny and the collective spirit of the nation above all else. Nor did the Westernizers, who were equally Russian, merely ape the West: their goal was to establish Russia as a Western nation, to build a civil society on their own terms. Brodsky "the Westernizer" was just as eager as Solzhenitsyn "the Slavophile" to leap to the defense of Russia and Russians, especially when the latter were accused of being aggressors by nature, or slaves by nature, or some sadomasochistic combination of both.

In 1985, when the Czech writer Milan Kundera, then living in France, published a rather frivolous essay on the relative merits of Dostoevsky and Diderot, his unassuming little piece provoked a vitriolic reaction from Brodsky. The point of Kundera's essay was that in 1968, when Soviet tanks rolled into Prague, he was asked to do a stage adaptation of Dostoevsky's *The Idiot*. He couldn't stand Dostoevsky; he was trying to figure out why. He decided that it wasn't a matter of hating all Russian writers, since he still liked Chekhov. Meanwhile, after a short conversation with a Soviet officer, he suddenly saw the light: Russians are impossibly sentimental—that is, their every feeling becomes an absolute value and an absolute truth. Dostoevsky embodied this attitude toward life and the world better than anyone else. But "a world in which everything comes down to feeling" is fraught with breakdown, hysteria, aggression. And Kundera felt a certain nostalgia for the world of the French Enlightenment, in which, as in Diderot's *Jacques le fataliste*, emotion is balanced and controlled by reason. Brodsky objected that "[e]ven if one were to reduce Dostoevsky's novels to the level Mr. Kundera offers, it is clear that they are not about feelings per se, but about a hierarchy of feelings. What's more, those feelings are reactions to expressed thoughts, and most of those are highly rational thoughts picked up, in fact, in the West."[85] Brodsky may be shooting down sparrows with a cannon here, but Kundera gave him a chance to speak his mind on one very sore point: "The atrocities that were and are committed in that realm, were and are committed not in the name of love but of necessity—and a historical one at that. The concept of historical necessity is the product of rational thought and arrived in Russia by the Western route. . . . It may be a tribute to Western rationalism that 'the specter of Communism,' after wandering about in Europe, had to settle in the East. But it should also be noted that nowhere else has that specter encountered stronger resistance, starting with Dostoyevsky's 'Possessed' and continuing through the blood bath of the Civil War and the Great Terror; and the resistance is far from over even now."[86] Solzhenitsyn could have signed off on every word.

CHAPTER NINE

> dined with the-devil-knows-whom, in tails, on truffles.
>
> —"May 24, 1980"

FAME AND FORTUNE

BRODSKY'S LIFE in Russia could hardly be called easy. At eighteen months of age he was evacuated from Leningrad under enemy fire. When he was fifteen, he left school. At eighteen he was already becoming notorious; at twenty-one he was arrested and indicted. By twenty-three he had spent time in jail and in a mental hospital and was soon to become both victim and hero of a show trial heard round the world. At thirty-two he was shipped into exile.

The short version of Brodsky's life in the West looks very different; it seems to be one success after another. It began with well-paid work at well-respected universities (Michigan, New York University, and Columbia). By 1980 he was teaching regularly at the "five colleges" consortium: Amherst, Smith, Hampshire, Mount Holyoke, and the University of Massachusetts at Amherst. He was garnering virtually every prize a writer could: a genius award from the MacArthur Foundation in 1981, a Nobel Prize in Literature in 1987, the post of American poet laureate in 1991. He was awarded honorary doctorates from Yale, Dartmouth, Oxford, and other institutions, given France's Légion d'honneur, and made an honorary citizen of Saint Petersburg.

But to Brodsky's mind, any contrast between these two parts of his life was purely superficial. In answer to the standard (albeit natural) interview question about how exile to the West had affected him, Brodsky would patiently (or sometimes not so patiently) reply that the move was simply a "continuation of space." In part 4 of "Lullaby of Cape Cod" he lists the changes:

> The change of Empires is intimately tied
> to the hum of words, the soft, fricative spray
> of spittle in the act of speech, the whole
> sum of Lobachevsky's angles, the strange way
> that parallels unwittingly collide
> by casual chance someday
> as longitudes contrive to meet at the pole.

It is hard living in those unfamiliar angles, in someone else's corner of the world, speaking someone else's language, doing unfamiliar things like splitting wood for a Massachusetts stove. But in the end

> the giddy pen
> points out resemblances, for after all
>
> the device in your hand is the same old pen and ink
> as before, the woodland plants exhibit no change.

In a way, both everyday successes and everyday failures were troubling, because both distracted him from the "main thing"—which was writing. In 1964, when the police burst into his apartment, he was bothered because he could not finish a poem. He was upset by the incessant fuss over his trial. But he was also troubled by the fact that when he received one of his first bank statements in the United States and saw that he had over $3,000 in his account, he suddenly thought, "But five thousand would be better"—when back in Leningrad he'd been lucky if he had two rubles in his pocket for taxi fare. The very idea of having money scared him because it meant that he would actually have to spend time thinking about savings, expenses, bank accounts, and other such things. Likewise, he was agitated and nervous when he returned to the United States after the Nobel Prize ceremonies in 1987. What if all the fame and hubbub got in the way of his writing? What if suddenly he couldn't write at all? But then December 24 rolled around, and so did his Christmas poem "Star of the Nativity." "So I figured everything was fine," Brodsky recalled.

Once in the West, Brodsky was never poor. But neither was he rich. He managed to receive the Nobel Prize the very year that the monetary award connected with the prize was at a record low ($340,000), and because of new legislation, subsequently repealed, he had to pay hefty U.S. taxes on the money he received. He may have been the only Nobel laureate who had to do so. What remained of the prize was roughly equal to the yearly salary of his New York dentist or cardiologist. This was all he had in the last years of his life, even as he started a family and needed a bigger apartment. In the early 1990s a decent apartment in New York could cost half a million dollars or more. And while readings and publications provided some income over and above his university salary, he had never been good at saving money. That one brief mercenary urge had scared him off once and for all. After that, whenever he received a check, he would tack it onto his bulletin board and let it hang there for weeks on end, amid a collage of notes, postcards, and photographs.

THE POLITICS AND MORALS OF THE AMERICAN CAMPUS

Brodsky arrived in the United States in the early 1970s, a time of turmoil and dissent. The war in Vietnam was coming to an inglorious end; an oil crisis had shaken the American economy. In 1973 the country was also shaken and shamed by Watergate, which led to Richard Nixon's resignation the following year. The anemic Jimmy Carter administration rounded off the second half of the decade.

Brodsky's American contemporaries—the young university professors, writers, editors, and students whom he encountered in his classes—were products of the 1960s. Not all of them had been outright hippies or antiwar activists, but one thing they shared was an ingrained skepticism toward American democratic institutions and a rather feckless brand of pacifism. While they were very good at exposing the evil designs of the American military-industrial complex, they were naively enthusiastic about "peaceful initiatives" by the Brezhnev administration and stridently opposed to any arms programs proposed by their own government—deployment of mid-range American missiles at bases in Europe, for example, or development of tactical weapons such as the neutron bomb. In the previous chapter we noted Brodsky's contempt for the dishonest or perhaps simply dimwitted parallels drawn between the problems of a democratic society and the nightmares of a totalitarian regime. "The

West! He loves the West," fulminates Solzhenitsyn in the conclusion to an article on Brodsky as he claims that such Westernism derives from Brodsky's belief that only in the West does some Moral Absolute exist.[1] But while Solzhenitsyn apparently read all of Brodsky's verse, and certainly the essay "Flight from Byzantium," he must have missed a number of other essays and speeches. In his criticism of totalitarian regimes, Brodsky was following in the footsteps of his idols George Orwell, W. H. Auden, and Czesław Miłosz; he was consciously "standing on the shoulders of giants." But unlike them, he was not born and raised in a capitalist society; unlike them, he never flirted with socialism. But *like* them, for all his hatred of totalitarianism, he never looked at the West through rose-colored glasses. He was hardly an Ayn Rand.

On the 1970s American political scene, he behaved more like a liberal than a conservative, although he generally kept his distance from both camps. The notion of "difference"—black rather than white, homosexual rather than heterosexual, woman rather than man—was taking on political overtones, becoming a question of political and economic equality. For some it was also a question of ethics and faith. On the everyday level this struggle for equality expressed itself in a taboo against the very mention of any difference in sex, race, or sexual orientation. Brodsky was of one mind about equality, but he refused to take part in the hypocritical word games played around it. On affirmative action, he expressed himself rather crudely but succinctly: "Better they should sit in class than be hanging out on street corners."

Political correctness is at best an attempt at politeness, respect, and tact; at worst it is a crude form of cultural relativism, a denial of any cultural or aesthetic absolutes. As Brodsky said on a different topic: "But bad politics make for bad morals / And who should know better than us!" At any rate, he wrote about the writers he most admired without giving much thought to political correctness. If he thought that Cavafy's homosexuality influenced that poet's approach to the world at large, he said so.[2] If he thought that Auden's homosexuality and Walcott's mixed-race background were not reflected in their poetry, he barely mentioned the fact.

The America to which Brodsky came in the early 1970s was also a land in which the sexual revolution seemed to have been won. But the new norms hardly bore out the fears of traditional moralists, and the sexual practices of the younger generation were hardly reminiscent of the libertinage of the eighteenth century, the orgies of Rome, or the vices of Sodom and Gomorrah. This victory was more in the spirit of the early socialist Clara Zetkin's notion that having sex should be as natural as drinking a glass of water, that "comradely attitudes toward women" should be the norm. In the Russia that Brodsky left, the sexual revolution that Zetkin and a handful of other Bolsheviks thought so necessary never came to pass. In fact, in the poet's youth, the opposite was the rule. The USSR of the 1940s and 1950s was a hypocritically puritanical state in which the dark side of officially propagated morality expressed itself in all manner of neuroses and complexes, in sordid office affairs, quickie sex in the bushes at vacation resorts, and "special services" provided for the elite at government hunting lodges and saunas. Both official ideology and unofficial practice tended to reinforce age-old stereotypes of male and female behavior. Within the family, relationships were patriarchal; outside it they were predatory—there were Don Juans and their conquests. But on American campuses in the last third of the twentieth century Don Juan had lost much of his allure. The new ideal was a free and equal partnership. Cohabitation and one-night stands were no longer considered deviant or immoral. Pharmacology had provided reliable contraceptives; feminism had provided ideological defense. When Brodsky, in response to a reporter's question about how he felt about teaching at a women's college, answered, "Like the fox in the chicken barn," the newsletter received indignant letters from *men*. "Any teacher who views his students with such a sexist and predatory mind-set should not be in the profession," wrote a George Klawitter from La Crosse, Wisconsin.[3]

While Brodsky may have meant to provoke, the outrage against him was misdirected. When translated directly into political discourse, his lyric poems suggest an almost radical feminism. The central tenet of feminism holds that a woman exists in and of herself; she is not automatically some man's lover, some man's wife or the mother of his children. She is a free and equal partner in any relationship, official or no. And in the poem "I was but that," which concludes *New Stanzas to Augusta*, the male speaker finds himself dependent on the woman for his very face and form, for his ability to create.[4] While it might be naive to equate poetic discourse with political rhetoric, the author of these lines can hardly be accused of male chauvinism.

Still, it was often charged that his attitudes toward women, and those of his speakers as well, were old-fashioned at best. Even Michael Ignatieff, a British scholar and writer who obviously liked Brodsky, noted that when he heard "Altra Ego" (first read as a presentation to the British Academy) he was embarrassed by the "sort of slightly cheap way in which he [Brodsky] talked about women."[5] But Brodsky, as a lyric poet, could not help but clash with the sexual revolution. As Allan Bloom wrote in his best-selling book on American culture and thought, *The Closing of the American Mind,*

> The eroticism of our students is lame. It is not the divine madness Socrates praised; or the enticing awareness of incompleteness and the quest to overcome it; or nature's grace, which permits a partial being to recover its wholeness in the embrace of another, or a temporal being to long for eternity in the perpetuity of his seed; or the hope that all men will remember his deeds; or his contemplation of perfection. Eroticism is a discomfort, but one that in itself promises relief and affirms the goodness of things. It is the proof, subjective but incontrovertible, of man's relatedness, imperfect though it may be, to others and to the whole of nature. Wonder, the source both of poetry and philosophy, is its characteristic expression. Eros demands daring from its votaries and provides good reason for it. The longing for completeness is the longing for education, and the study of it is education. . . . The sex lives of our students and their reflection on them disarm such longing and make it incomprehensible to them. Reduction has robbed Eros of its divinatory powers.[6]

BRODSKY AND THE EROTIC

Brodsky's attitude toward the erotic was determined by his own sad and perhaps even tragic love story. In 1967, when that story was coming to an end, he wrote a small poem entitled "Postscript" (*OVP*). It begins: "What a pity that for you / my being never came to be / what yours became to me." This is precisely how Brodsky understands love: as one being, one existence, focused entirely on another. In 1983 he collected all the poems dedicated to M.B. in *New Stanzas to Augusta*. Brodsky's poetic corpus, however, cannot be divided into love lyrics versus everything else. His work is erotic through and through, as he explains in "Altra Ego":

"A poem about love can have for its subject practically anything: the girl's features, ribbons in her hair, the landscape behind her house, the passage of clouds, starry skies, some inanimate object. It may have nothing to do with the girl: it can describe an exchange between two or more mythic characters, a wilted bouquet, snow on the railroad platform. The readers, though, will know that they are reading a poem informed by love, thanks to the intensity of attention toward that detail of the universe. For love is an attitude toward reality—usually of someone finite toward something infinite. Hence the intensity caused by the sense of the provisional nature of one's possessions. Hence that intensity's need for articulation. Hence its quest for a voice less provisional than one's own."[7]

In chapter III we noted that, in the tradition of Dante, Brodsky makes Eros a universal and cosmic force in the ending of "Seven Strophes." While Brodsky's assertions in "Altra Ego" might be considered merely an author's subjective opinion on his own texts, a formal and objective analysis of Brodsky's lyrics shows that very few of his love poems limit themselves solely to the relationship between the poet and his lover. The title poem of *New Stanzas to Augusta* springs from the notion that nature is indifferent to individual human existence. In "Prophecy" (*OVP*), a lover's idyll is colored by hints of an apocalyptic future—a sinister reference to a Geiger counter in the midst of pastoral bliss. His "A Part of Speech" cycle opens with a poem about lovers parting, but two other love poems in the cycle—"I recognize this wind" and "You've forgotten the village"—are ambivalent. The controlling metaphor in the former is quite elaborate and, as usual with Brodsky, quite concretely realized: it involves an epic clash with the Tatar horde, an association provoked by his lover's Tatar name. In the second poem there are direct references to Norenskaya:

> Old Nastasya is dead, I take it, and Pesterev, too, for sure,
> and if not, he's sitting drunk in the cellar or
> is making something out of the headboard of our bed:
> a wicket gate, or some kind of shed.

In "Altra Ego" Brodsky writes: "Pasternak's famous exclamation 'Great god of love, great god of details!' is poignant precisely because of the utter insignificance of the sum of these details. A ratio could no doubt be established between the smallness of the detail and the intensity of attention paid to it, as well as between the latter and one's spiritual accomplishment, because a poem—any poem, regardless of its subject—is in itself an act of love, not so much of an author for his subject as of language for a piece of reality."[8]

In a paradoxical way, because Brodsky sees Eros as a cosmic, harmonizing force, his poetry does not emphasize the "erotic" in the everyday sense of the word. To put it another way, in Brodsky's poetry sex without love is never erotic, and his stylistics reflect this. As we have already noted, Brodsky frames the erotic in terms of lovers *and* the world: a woman's hand touches a man at night, and the planet "spins and spins" ("Seven Strophes"); their bedstead becomes a gate onto the world at large ("You've forgotten that village"). The act itself never takes front stage, for "love as an act lacks a verb" ("I Sit by the Window"). When he talks about sex without love, his diction turns slangy and obscene. In "Lagoon," the bed is a grimy workbench; in "The Residence" a crows' nest in far trees reminds the tyrant of his former mistress's "beaver"; in "To a Friend: In Memoriam," bohemian Moscow is "a moist universe / of mean blabbering squinchers and whispering innocent beavers."

By the 1930s, in English-language verse (Auden's included), obscenity had lost much of its shock value. But in those years perhaps the only major Russian poet who felt free to use "unprintable" language, and then only rarely, was Mayakovsky (see "At the Top of My Voice"). Pasternak was far more circumspect: "I might not have shunned / unprintable words" ("To Elena"). This was less conformity or decorum than it was the assumption among Russian poets that a reader's entire perception of the text might hang on a single word. (As Jules Renard once wrote in his diary, "If a phrase contains the word 'ass,' the audience, no matter how sophisticated, will hear nothing but that word.") The authors of the exposé in *Evening Leningrad* in 1964 had accused Brodsky of writing filth: He "writes his little ditties, flip-flopping between gibberish, whining, pessimism and pornography." But in fact Brodsky's early love lyrics are rather chaste. What Lerner and his coauthors interpreted as pornography may have been the occasional obscenity used by characters in "Parade," or perhaps even words like "sperm" and "condom."

Still, Eduard Limonov writes the following about Brodsky's mature verse: "Brodsky does not know how to behave in moments of intimacy—trying to be frank and manly, he suddenly spouts filth. On the lips of the refined intellectual that Brodsky would like to be (and which he is, at least

75 percent so), this obscenity, these attempts to introduce substandard expressions like 'screwing doggy-style,' come off as cheap and vulgar. The God whom Brodsky so often invokes did not give him a gift for the love lyric; when Brodsky tries to be intimate, he is merely coarse."[9] Like Brodsky's persecutors of twenty years before, Limonov is shocked less by the subject itself than by the vulgar way it is treated. These accusations, old and new alike, deserve to be taken at face value in spite of the motives underlying them—police harassment in the case of the first, aesthetic disagreements in the case of the second. Prerevolutionary Russian middle-class linguistic etiquette imposed a strict taboo on oaths or foul language of any sort, and indeed on any mention of sex. Behind such taboos lay a desire to emphasize one's gentility, to separate oneself from the lower classes. The Soviet middle class in the Stalin era was equally "genteel," and profoundly hypocritical: it was all right to swear, but "not in front of the ladies"; it was all right to tell dirty jokes and boast of one's sexual exploits in the crudest of terms, but not in "polite company"—which meant that in academic discourse, journalism, literature, and art, sexual themes were taboo. And as Limonov's tirade shows, the ban on words has been far stronger than the ban on subject matter. Limonov himself gained literary fame as a writer who depicted sexual encounters in frank detail, yet he was outraged by Brodsky's use of crude expressions. These expressions, though hardly central to or determinate of Brodsky's poetics as a whole, are nonetheless determinate of the reader's ability to read a poetic text in which the word functions differently from the way it does in everyday speech. The publishers of Brodsky's first (and unauthorized) collection of verse understood this very well: in a letter to his coeditor, Gleb Struve, Filippov wrote: "No, I don't think we should worry about all those words in 'Procession' ('shit,' 'dickhead,' and the like). Someone's always going to bitch, and besides, those crude words DO NOT LOOK AT ALL CRUDE IN THE CONTEXT OF THE POEM: in fact, the contrast underscores the lofty pathos of the poem."[10]

Yury Tynyanov's notebooks contain a passage on bourgeois sex that is remarkable in and of itself, all the more so because it predates one of the central issues of late-twentieth-century feminism by several decades: treating a woman as a sexual object, a thing.[11] "Love of limited space, . . . enjoying a part of a woman rather than the woman herself," writes Tynyanov.[12] Here we find an encapsulation of the two basic motifs in Brodsky's treatment of the theme. In purely sexual encounters the woman as a whole is hardly there; she is a thing, a function of her parts. In "Lithuanian Divertissement" we read: "Sleeplessness. Part of a woman . . . Something lipsticked." (The Russian original is more explicit: "The lipsticked part of a woman.") In "I Sit by the Window" we have: "Who needs the whole girl if you've got her knee?" In "Letters to a Roman Friend" we have: "To a certain point a girl can satisfy you— / if you don't go farther than her knees or elbows." And in "Mexican Divertimento" (*ChR*) we see a window that "frames a beauty's thigh."[13] All this comes back to the motif of sex as an annihilation of space, most vividly expressed in "The End of a Beautiful Era":

> To exist in the Era of Deeds and to stay elevated, alert
> ain't so easy, alas. Having raised a long skirt,
> you will find not new wonders but what you expected.
> It's not that they play Lobachevsky's ideas by ear,
> but the widened horizons should narrow somewhere, and here—
> here's the end of perspective.

The "widened horizons" are literally bodied forth in the spread of a woman's legs; the gap shrinks to nothing; perspective ends in "some part of a woman." We should note the skillful use of enjambment here, the rhythmic repetition of "here-here" at the end of the line and the beginning of the next, suggesting the mechanical rhythm of coitus. The dead end of carnality and the limitless space of Eros is a theme that runs clearly through all of Brodsky's lyric verse.[14]

URANIA

Ten years would pass between *The End of a Beautiful Era* and *A Part of Speech* and Brodsky's next collection, *Urania*. In Greek mythology Urania was the Muse of astronomy, but there was also an Aphrodite Urania (celestial) as opposed to Aphrodite Pandemos (Aphrodite of all the people), "the vulgar Aphrodite." *To Urania,* the English version of the book, published in 1988, corresponds for the most part to the Russian, but the change in title clarifies Brodsky's intentions somewhat. The autograph on the title page of the copy he gave us reads, "To Nina and Leo—My inner bio."

The name of the collection also alludes to Baratynsky's "The Last Poet," which is addressed to "cold Urania's admirers." But as usual with Brodsky, the allusion is polemical. Unlike Baratynsky's poet, who sings of the "bliss of passion," Brodsky sings of the "cold muse" of astronomy and geography, the muse of objective, independent creativity. *Urania* is a cold book in the literal sense of the word. Of the seventy-three poems in it, twenty-four speak of cold, of winter, of fall: only ten mention spring or summer. While *Urania* includes some quite joyous pieces, like "Piazza Mattei," "Roman Elegies," and "Burning," the book's overriding theme is resignation; its tone strives to be aloof and impartial. This change is particularly striking in the light of Brodsky's earlier works. The political pathos of poems like "Letter to General Z" here gives way to the grim sarcasm of "Lines on the Winter Campaign, 1980" and "The Fifth Anniversary." The passionate search for God ("Conversation with a Celestial Being" and "Nature Morte") turns to irony and agnosticism in "To a Chair." His 1968 poem "Strophes" ("Not a sound on goodbye") ends its account of lovers parting with "torments of the afterlife / burn also in this"; but in a 1978 poem with the same title, he writes:

> True, the more the white's covered
> with the scatter of black,
> the less the species cares
> for its past, for its blank
> future.

And in the following stanza:

> You won't receive an answer
> if "Where to?" swells your voice,
> since all parts of the word are
> joined up in the kingdom of ice.

Two long poems, odes, stand in stark contrast; both deal with existence on the cusp of life and death. The first is "Butterfly" (*ChR*); the second is "The Fly" (*Urania*). The butterfly is a traditional symbol of the soul, of life reborn. In "The Fly," however, Brodsky sings the praises of an impossibly listless, shabby, half-dead insect. And he does praise it, rather than paint it in the sordid and contemptuous terms common to Western poetry after Baudelaire. In a humble fly crawling "under a half-lit bulb" in "colorless dust" this poet finds a symbol of metamorphosis, death, and rebirth.

In *Urania,* Brodsky has created something quite unprecedented: a lyric of *taedium vitae*—the monotone of everyday life.

BRODSKY IN ENGLISH

When people talk about Brodsky the American writer, they usually compare him to two other Russian-born writers: Joseph Conrad and Vladimir Nabokov.[15] But such a comparison is superficial and unfair. Conrad left his native Poland at age seventeen and spent the rest of his life among English speakers. Nabokov was only a little older when he first went to England; moreover, he had been raised by English tutors and governesses. Conrad wrote exclusively in English from the start; Nabokov, after 1940, wrote all his novels in English. Unlike either of them, Brodsky was a grown man when he left Russia, and although he could read English at the time, he was not fluent in it. He never thought of himself as an English or American writer; rather, he often called himself a Russian poet and an American citizen. His reputation in the English-language world is based primarily on a few dozen essays, articles, and speeches. Some of these he wrote himself; some of these he edited after they had been translated for him. These forty or so essays make up the content of three books: *Less Than One* (1986), *Watermark* (1992), and *On Grief and Reason* (1995). He wrote a number of poems in English; he also painstakingly translated his Russian poems into that language.

But while his essays by and large received critical praise in the English-speaking world, his poetry met a mixed reaction. His own attitude was complicated as well. On the one hand, he more than once emphasized that the poetry he wrote in English was nothing serious, a sort of verbal game. When once asked, as he was often, whether he considered himself an English poet, he answered: "That's never been my ambition, though I can write some quite decent poetry in English. But when I write poems in English, it's more a game, more like chess or building blocks. . . . But as for becoming a Nabokov or a Conrad—I've got no such ambition."[16]

On the other hand, as years passed, he ever more stubbornly continued to compose in English—not just light verse but lyrics, philosophical poems, and reflections on the tragedies of the modern century. He less and less often entrusted the translation of his Russian poems to English-language poets and translators. In the five-hundred-page *Collected Poems in English* that came out four years after his death, none of the translations was done single-handedly by his translators; all were done either in collaboration with the author or by the author himself. On exactly what "with the author" meant in this context, the poet and Nobel laureate Derek

Walcott, Brodsky's friend, says: "What is true for all Joseph's translations is that he does an awful lot of the work himself, even metrically, even with rhyme. It isn't as if he's floundering, as if he needs any help. Very often he's on a level with his translators, so that if you're working along with him and some metaphor comes along he's quite prepared to change a metaphor for a rhyme in English."[17]

How good was Brodsky's English? We know that in school he received Ds in the subject, then studied the language on his own, and finally began studying it seriously while in Norenskaya, poring over difficult poetic texts and dictionary entries. When he arrived in the West, he could read quite well, but he could barely speak, as his meeting with Auden demonstrated. Carl Proffer thrust Brodsky into a University of Michigan classroom just the way parents once tossed their children into swimming pools—here's the water, sink or swim. The bold experiment worked. Brodsky's extensive passive vocabulary, his thorough knowledge of the English and American poetry he was expected to teach, his persistence, his habitual readiness to overcome obstacles, all had their effect, and he quickly learned to use the language professionally.

After several years in America, Brodsky could speak fluently on any topic in both professional and everyday situations.[18] "It only took him three months to start picking up American slang," recalled a Michigan colleague.[19] Nonetheless, he never became completely bilingual: he spoke with a noticeable accent, his usage and diction sometimes seemed slightly off, and his English-speaking friends regularly corrected his use of articles and verb forms in his written pieces. The deficiencies in his English pronunciation were aggravated by his inability to pronounce rolled *r*'s and hard *l*'s and by the nasal quality of his speech in general.[20] This caused no particular problem in small groups but occasionally made itself felt at large-scale public performances. Sir Isaiah Berlin, who later also became a friend, spoke of the lecture that Brodsky gave at the British Academy on October 11, 1990: "No one understood a thing . . . nor did I. He was speaking English quickly, swallowing his words. And I couldn't catch it, couldn't quite understand what he was saying. Listening to him was enjoyable, because he was animated, but I didn't understand until afterwards, when I read [the text]."[21]

Brodsky often remarked that his initial decision to write exclusively in English for American journals was a purely practical one; there would be no need to spend time and effort on translation. Gradually, thinking in two languages became a habit. Following in the footsteps of the linguist Edward Sapir, Brodsky believed that the grammatical structures of one's native language predetermine one's perception of the world to a great degree. In Russian and Slavic morphology, suffixes play an enormous role. *Starukha, starushka,* and *starushonka* are three variations of "old lady," but no strict declension governs their use. The difference lies in nuance, in the attitude of the speaker toward the person or object spoken of. Moreover, the use and understanding of these suffixes is quite subjective and resists easy definition. In English, morphology plays practically no part in the organization of meaning. For this there are separate and independent lexemes that combine to produce a concept: if *starukha* is simply "old lady," *starushka* is "little old lady," and *starushonka* is "miserable old woman"—or simply "hag" or "crone." Russian and English syntax are even more at odds. Russian is an inflected language, in which word agreement in a sentence is accomplished by way of endings (flexions) that indicate gender, number, and case. For that reason words can occur in almost any order in a sentence. A native speaker with a fine-tuned ear will sense different shades of meaning in "The old woman came home" versus "home came the old woman," but again, these are nuances determined subjectively for the most part. Contemporary English is an analytic language. It has almost no case endings, no grammatical gender, and changing word order, if possible at all, usually changes the meaning of the sentence. When Brodsky, as a young man, first realized how strictly statements in English were structured, he often said that "in English it's impossible to say anything stupid." (As years passed he came to understand that this was a rather hasty conclusion.)

At any rate, what was once a practical necessity became an enormous advantage, as he counted it, an opportunity to expand the mind beyond national boundaries: "When you have those two languages—an analytic one like English and a synthetic, very sensual thing like Russian . . . you get an almost psychotic sense of humanity that permeates nearly everything. It can help you understand, and it can discourage you, because you see how little can be done. Certain evils are the result of bad grammar, and the analytic approach leads of a kind of superficiality, insensitivity."[22] This pronouncement is inarguable in terms of his own experience, and perhaps the assertion that a person who has mastered two (or more) languages has a deeper, more sophisticated view of the world than a person who only speaks one is quite fair. But the question of what a *poet* gains from being a polyglot is far more complicated.

Obviously, a good acquaintance with the particular genres and rhetoric of poetry in another language can enrich a poet's work in his own. This is nothing new. We spoke in chapter V of the influence of Anglo-American poetry on Brodsky's lyric "I" and on his construction of metaphor, among other things. But the deeper strata of the poetic text—prosody, the poetic use of grammar, the semantics of the collision between style and register—are entirely dependent on the peculiarities of the poet's native language and thus resist translation.[23] One vivid example of this resistance is rhyme, which by its nature is phonetic. For example, the triple rhyme (*aaa*), which is rare in Russian but common enough in English (in Auden, for one), was used by Brodsky to great effect in "The Fifth Anniversary" and "Fin de siècle," in his prologue to a translation of Euripides' *Medea,* and in "The Theatrical" (*PSN*). So it might seem that there would be no problem in translating what was taken from English back into English. Yet, as Derek Walcott notes: "In English triple rhyming becomes ironic like Byron or it becomes comic. It's very hard to defend such endings in English; they have a comic or ironic edge to them. But, obviously, in the Russian language you can do that and . . . it rhymes and . . . you have all the complexities of design that [go] with the sound of Brodsky. But I think that to try to attempt it in English, it can lead to all kinds of structural disasters."[24]

Critics, whether well disposed or not, commented on his frequent use of feminine rhyme (in which the accent falls on the next-to-last syllable of the line). In Russian poetry feminine rhyme is just as common as masculine (last-syllable) rhyme and is stylistically neutral. In English, feminine rhyme tends to be used in light verse or comic opera; when applied to serious subjects, it sounds like parody. So it is practically impossible to reproduce the rhythmic structure of a Russian poem in an English translation. Most Russian words are polysyllabic; the most frequently occurring English words are monosyllabic. At the same time, polysyllabic Russian words have a single accent; polysyllabic English words have more than one. So when a rhythmic pattern natural to Russian is imitated in English, what the English speaker hears is a jingle, a tin-tin beat. Nonetheless, Brodsky always insisted that his translators try to reproduce both the rhyme and the rhythm of his poems. He always rejected the attempts to anglicize this part of his work as "too smooth."[25]

In the opinion of even well-inclined critics, Brodsky's use of English-language idioms was at times problematic. In a conscious imitation of Auden's poetics, Brodsky filled his English texts with conversational turns of phrase—and here is where his American and British readers felt something was not quite right. Anyone who has had to speak a foreign language on a daily basis knows that colloquialisms and slang must be used with caution. Unlike standard lexicon and phraseology, they require an especially intimate sense of the speech context into which they can fit without sounding awkward to listener or reader.

Five books of poems by Brodsky in English were published during his lifetime.[26] The first—*Elegy to John Donne,* which came out in England in 1967 in a rather weak translation by Nicholas Bethell—he disavowed.[27] Like the Russian selection of his verse published in the West in 1964, *Elegy to John Donne* was compiled without his knowledge or participation. The first English book on which Brodsky actually worked was his *Selected Poems,* with translations by George Kline and a foreword by W. H. Auden. This collection consisted of roughly one-third of the poems in *A Halt in the Desert,* with translations of newer works added at the end: "Post Aetatem Nostram," "Nature Morte," "Nunc Dimittis," and "Odysseus to Telemachus."[28]

While Brodsky's reputation as an eminently successful English essayist and *the* leading Russian poet of his time holds firm, his verse legacy in English is much more vulnerable to criticism. His most receptive readers have been either Slavists who saw the English Brodsky through the prism of Russian poetry or else fellow poets, personal friends—Stephen Spender, Derek Walcott, and Seamus Heaney, among others.[29] The poet-friends spent hours discussing poetry in general with him, plus had the advantage of hearing his detailed commentaries on his own poems. This no doubt played a major role in their attitude. But perhaps, in the final analysis, Isaiah Berlin was right: "How could anyone who had not read him in Russian understand him by his English poems? It's utterly incomprehensible. Because there is no sense that they were written by a great poet. But in Russian . . . From the very beginning, as soon as it starts, you are in the presence of genius. And that is a unique sort of feeling—being in the presence of genius. . . . A poet can write only in his native language, in the language of his childhood. There is no French poetry not written by a Frenchman. So Oscar Wilde wrote Salome in French, but it goes nowhere, nowhere does it reflect his genius. A poet speaks only his native language."[30]

Brodsky would read quite a few sour or even vitriolic reviews of his English-language editions. Sometimes the attacks came from lesser poets clearly envious of this foreign upstart, but withering criticism occasionally sounded from the literary heights as well.[31] The British poet Christopher Reid, who had inherited T. S. Eliot's post of poetry editor at prestigious Faber and Faber, entitled his review of the English *To Urania* "Great American Disaster." In it, Reid finds Brodsky's poetics pompous and pretentious, enumerates the poet's sins against the English language, and claims that Brodsky's reputation is greatly inflated.[32] Just a few months after Brodsky's death, Craig Raine, a well-known poet and Oxford professor who occupied the same highly influential editor's chair in the years between Eliot and Reid, published an article excoriating Brodsky's last English publication and the author himself; it was if some long-simmering resentment within the small English poetry establishment had finally spilled over.[33] Raine's tone goes far beyond the bounds of literary civility and civility in general. Brodsky's writing in English is "awkward and skewed"; as a thinker he is "fatuous and banal," he is "a nervous, world-class mediocrity."[34]

Brodsky was discouraged less by spiteful attacks and sheer invective (some of it ad hominem) than he was by the more balanced reviews whose authors had made an effort to read his English verse impartially but still found it lacking. Reviewing a posthumously published selection of Brodsky's poems in English, Adam Kirsch summed up the attitude of English-speaking readers in this way: "Certain poets, whose energies are primarily metaphorical, might not suffer as Brodsky often does in translation. Wisława Szymborska comes across extremely clearly in English, since she is a genuinely Metaphysical poet. . . . But Brodsky, though lucid and brilliant in his imagery, seems often to be more interested in rhythm, sound, and rhetoric than in idea and argument; and so there is more to be lost. . . . These poems are intelligent, rich in imagery and movement, but too often do not cohere musically or even semantically."[35] Kirsch quotes the American poet and translator Robert Haas on Brodsky's English verse: reading it is "like wandering through the ruins of a noble building."[36] The most colorful description of the impression made by

Brodsky's verse in English was penned by the Anglo-Irish Nobel Prize–winner Seamus Heaney: "So, in spite of his manifest love for English verse, which amounts almost to a possessiveness, the dynamo of Russian supplies the energy, the metrics of the original will not be gainsaid and the English ear comes up against a phonetic element that is both animated and skewed. Sometimes it instinctively rebels at having its expectations denied in terms of both syntax and the velleities of stress. Or it panics and wonders if it is being taken for a ride when it had expected a rhythm. At other times, however, it yields with that unbounded assent that only the most triumphant art can conjure and allow."[37]

ESSAYS

In America and, to a considerable extent, in the West overall, Brodsky's reputation as a writer was ultimately solidified by his essays. In nineteenth-century Russian literature this genre flourished. We have only to recall names like Chaadaev, Gogol, Belinsky, Herzen, Dostoevsky ("Diary of a Writer"), and Konstantin Leontyev. But in the Soviet era it began to fade away. If Brodsky has any direct ancestors among Russian essayists, they are surely Tsvetaeva, the early Shklovsky, and their predecessor Rozanov.[38] Among only this handful of writers do we find the same combination: reflections on a particular theme, which is required by the genre, and lyric elements—impressionistic observations and confessional or self-analytical passages. Interestingly enough, Brodsky was indifferent to Rozanov and Shklovsky alike. In his foreword to a collection of Tsvetaeva's prose he reluctantly acknowledges Rozanov's influence on her but hastily notes (quite rightly) that nothing could have been more diametrically opposed to Rozanov's perception of the world than the harsh and at times almost Calvinistic spirit of personal responsibility that informs Tsvetaeva's mature work.[39] So the similarity could hardly have arisen out of apprenticeship or influence; some isomorphic creative processes were apparently taking place.

The passionate, philosophical essays of Lev Shestov that Brodsky found so engaging are stylistically worlds away from what Brodsky himself did in this genre. The subject and the emotion of Shestov's work always stays within the boundaries of his intellectual theme, while for Brodsky the life of the mind was inseparable from life in general—everyday life, history, the physical and spiritual life of the author. This lyricism manifests itself most fully in memoirs like "Less Than One," "In a Room-and-a-Half," "Trophies," "To Please a Shadow," and "The Keening Muse," and in travelogues like "After a Journey, or Homage to Vertebrae," "Flight from Byzantium," and "Watermark," but the very style of his literary-critical essays, too, is lyrical, that is, subjective, colored by emotion. It takes Brodsky seventy-three pages to say everything he wants to say about Tsvetaeva's "New Year's Greetings" and forty-four pages to deal with Frost's "Home Burial," and the content of these pages hardly resembles the standard lit-crit explication; what we read is, rather, a soliloquy spoken by a poet immersing himself in another poet's world.

Of the sixty essays included in Brodsky's collected works in Russian (*SIB-2*, vols. 5–7), only seventeen essays, articles, and notes were written originally in that language.[40] These include his two essays on Tsvetaeva, "After a Journey," "Flight from Byzantium," his Nobel lecture ("Uncommon Visage"), the text of a lecture on Mandelstam's "With the world of empire I was but childishly linked," and "A Note on a Commentary," which was a brief piece on the poetic correspondence between Pasternak, Tsvetaeva, and Rilke. But basically Brodsky was an essayist and a literary and political polemicist in the English rather than the Russian tradition, and while he might occasionally complain about having to write yet another English essay to meet yet another deadline ("Better to write a poem!"), he rarely turned down an offer if the subject happened to intrigue him. In fact, he sometimes threw himself into heated polemics in print. For example, it was in response to a rather frivolous essay by Milan Kundera that he wrote "Why Milan Kundera Is Wrong about Dostoevsky" (1985). His answer to Václav Havel's speech "The Post-Communist Nightmare" was "Letter to the President" (1993). Although sixty prose texts were included in his collected works, an almost equal number written in English were left out: articles, talks, notes, forewords, letters to the editor. Apparently, the diligent and prolific Auden was once again a model—but so was the equally prolific George Orwell.

Orwell's influence can be felt especially in memoirs and sketches devoted to history and politics, in the straightforward reporting of the facts, the bold simplicity of the reasoning, the spareness of the language.[41] Brodsky, as a poet, detected yet another feature in Orwell that makes his prose so powerful: its rhythmicality, whether expressed in the rhythm of a phrase, a sentence, or an entire text: "Rhythm, beat, linking all the 'little words,' avoiding any sort of 'rounding off' (that is, amorphousness)—all this we can interpret as an introduction of the principles of poetic speech into prose, and therefore as a synthesis of the poet's prose."[42] The closest analogy in Russian is again not Tsvetaeva but Shklovsky (early Shklovsky), but without the latter's somewhat forced paradoxicality and fragmentedness. In Brodsky as in Orwell, paradox and irony do not advertise themselves; they are muted, a subtext.

In conversations with me, Brodsky often mentioned lessons gleaned from Orwell. It is interesting that Brodsky's British and American readers propose other parallels that may seem convincing within a particular review but contradict each other when reviews are compared. David Bethea begins his review of *Less Than One* with Tsvetaeva's phrase "shower of light" (her description of Pasternak's verse), but, shifting from the language of a poet to the language of a critic, he writes: "[I]t can be compared only with the autobiographical and critical prose of Vladimir Nabokov, although the charm of his lavishly recalled detail and mnemonic embalming process is accompanied in Mr. Brodsky's work by a fierce metaphysical and ethical probing only hinted at (or scorned) in Nabokov's 'Speak Memory' or his lectures on literature."[43] John le Carré, himself an elegant stylist, had this to say about Brodsky and his prose: "I never was able to make a bridge between the Brodsky I knew, whom I regarded as inarticulate in English, and the Brodsky writing, apparently in English, on a page. . . . I suspect that an intricate process of translation must have gone on. He writes with a finesse and with a foreign accent syntactically and grammatically beautiful, which is only comparable with Joseph Conrad. If you have German, which I think for Conrad was the most influential language, you really can read it with a German accent and it is still beautiful. And Conrad comes closer than anybody to the great, big, multiple-storey paragraphs of Thomas Mann. This is what you felt, I think, with Joseph when you read his English essays."[44] John Bayley, in an unusually perceptive article entitled "Mastering Speech," writes that Brodsky as a poet and an essayist has only one equal—and that is Auden: "Brodsky and Auden are the only really civilized great poets of their respective generations."[45] And it seems that Bayley alone among critics understood that what Brodsky said about his conversion to English prose was not a mere figure of speech. In "To Please a Shadow" Brodsky writes that his "sole purpose . . . was to find myself in closer proximity to the man whom

I considered the greatest mind of the twentieth century: Wystan Hugh Auden." In his memoir "A Room and a Half" he says of his parents, "I write this in English because I want to grant them a margin of freedom."[46]

Again, Brodsky's conversations with Auden were one-sided. Neither to Auden nor to that part of the human race that spoke Auden's language could he say what he could say to his Russian reader. It is hard to resist the notion that a more genuine and true *translation* of Brodsky's poetic universe into English was in his prose rather than his poetry. The scattered range of comparisons—Nabokov, Conrad, Mann, Auden—testifies to the confusion of even the most qualified of readers. They found themselves confronted by something absolutely new. While good essayists may be praised for their style, they are judged first and foremost on the ideas they "essay" to discuss. But it was the beauty, the expressiveness, and the emotional impact of Brodsky's essays that provoked an almost universal admiration. As John Updike wrote of *Watermark:* "We read *Watermark* enraptured by its gallant attempt to distill a precious meaning from life's experience—to make a spot on a globe a peephole into universal circumstance, and to fashion of one's personal chronic tourism a crystal whose facets reflect an entire life, with exile and ill health glinting at the edges of planes whose direct glare is sheer beauty."[47]

Brodsky's English prose is of one cloth with his Russian poetry. Further proof may be found in the motifs, images, and tropes that they share. As Valentina Polukhina's detailed study of Brodsky's Russian and English prose demonstrates, Brodsky constructs a prose text (be it an essay, an article, a lecture, a letter to an editor, or even a remark) using primarily poetic devices—the same devices so often encountered in his poems. (We should note that in conversations about prose, Brodsky always talked about the rhythmic structure—or lack of it—in any specific piece.) While meter is usually understood as a certain simple regularity in the alternation of accented and unaccented sounds, rhythm occurs on all levels of a text. On the phonetic level, Brodsky's prose abounds in alliteration, assonance, internal rhyme, and half rhyme, and Polukhina cites many examples: "an attempt at *dom*estication—or *dem*onizing—the *di*vine"; "*gl*ittering, *gl*owing, *gl*inting, the element has been casting itself"; "has more to do with *Claude* than the *creed*"; "they don't so much *help* you as *kelp* you." On the rhetorical level, rhythm is sustained by the repetition of a word throughout the text, at the beginning of a phrase (anaphora), at the end (epiphora), or in both places (epanalepsis).[48] He constructed his essays as if they were poems.

In his longest prose piece, "Watermark," he reproduces the mirror-like structure of "Venetian Stanzas," a poetic diptych written originally in Russian.[49] In other words, in "Watermark" Brodsky develops the lyric rather than the narrative. In his travelogue poems he does not offer a blow-by-blow account of his adventures in Venice, Istanbul, or Leningrad; nor does he, in his essay about Kim Philby, tell the story of the spy; nor does he, in his essay on Tsvetaeva's "New Year's Greetings," give a beginning-to-end explication of the poem. All these essays are essentially internal monologues, emotionally colored reflections—often impressionistic, absolutely subjective—transformed into an organized text by the same poetic means that Brodsky so brilliantly used in his Russian verse.

The West understood Brodsky's essays much better than it understood his poetry; and the Nobel Prize was awarded to him in 1987 as much for the former as for the latter.

THE NOBEL PRIZE

Once upon a time in Leningrad, amid the doodles of lions and naked ladies that Brodsky left behind after an evening at our apartment, we found a couplet in the few words of French that Brodsky knew at the time:

> Prix Nobel?
> Oui, ma belle.

While he clearly realized the element of chance involved in winning the prize, Brodsky apparently always assumed that he had as good a chance as anyone. He had a competitive streak; his early reaction to other people's poetry was "I can top that."[50] He was pragmatic about the awards with which he was showered from 1973 on; though grateful for the extra income, he tended to take them all with a grain of salt. But the Nobel Prize was different. In a Russia isolated from the outside world, this award had always retained an aura of myth—not just for Brodsky but for Russians in general. If in the West the average more-or-less educated person might not know or care who had just won the latest Nobel Prize in Literature, the average Russian did, thanks in part to the monstrous idiocy of the propaganda campaigns against the recognition of Pasternak in 1958 and Solzhenitsyn in 1970 and also to the official outpourings of joy for Mikhail Sholokhov in 1965. Early that year, in Brodsky's circle of friends, there was constant talk of a *nobelevka* for Akhmatova; as Brodsky was returning from exile in the fall of 1965, many of Akhmatova's friends speculated that she had been a finalist but that Sholokhov had won because the Swedes wanted to placate the Soviets after the scandal over Pasternak. Chukovskaya writes that when she heard that the prize had been awarded to Sholokhov, "it was as if I'd been slapped in the face with a dirty towel."[51] As it turns out, Akhmatova's name had in fact been discussed by the Nobel committee in 1965, but she, like Auden, had only moderate support among committee members. Sholokhov's only real Russian rival was Konstantin Paustovsky.[52]

The Nobel committee deliberates in secret, but rumors about a nomination for Brodsky were circulating as early as 1980, when the prize eventually went to Czesław Miłosz. As is customary, once on the short list, a name remains there for some time, and in 1987 the choice fell on Brodsky. Journalists' versions of the 1987 short list vary, but most of them include Octavio Paz, Seamus Heaney, V. S. Naipaul, and Camilo José Cela as well. All would become laureates in the years to follow.

When the prize is announced, the Nobel committee gives a brief summary of the chief merits of the laureate. Brodsky's certificate read, "[F]or all-embracing authorship imbued with clarity of thought and poetic intensity." In presenting the new laureate, Permanent Secretary Sture Allen began with these words: "A characteristic feature of the Nobel prizewinner Joseph Brodsky is a magnificent joy of discovery. He sees connections, words them pithily, sees new connections. Not seldom they are contradictory and ambiguous, often caught in a flash like this: 'Memory, I think, is a substitute for the tail we lost for good in the happy process of evolution. It directs our movements.'"[53]

Allen's short speech reflected the nascent changes in Eastern Europe. When awarding prizes to Soviet writers in the past, the Swedish academicians had taken naive care to underscore the apolitical nature of their decisions. Hence Pasternak was awarded his prize for "his important achievement in contemporary lyrical poetry and in the field of the great Russian epic tradition," and then Secretary Anders Österling emphasized that *Doctor Zhivago* rose "above all party-political boundaries and [was], rather, antipolitical in its overall humane outlook."[54] Sholokhov was praised in 1965 for the "artistic power and integrity with which, in his epic of the Don, he has given expression to a historic phase in the life of the Russian people." In 1970, Solzhenitsyn was honored for the "ethical force with which he has pursued the indispensable traditions of Russian literature."

By 1987, *perestroika* and *glasnost* were the words of the day in the USSR, and the Swedes chimed in. Sture Allen openly mentioned Brodsky's collisions with the Soviet regime ("Through all hardships—trial, internal banishment, exile—he has retained his integrity and his faith in literature and language") and was so bold as to characterize the Soviet regime as "totalitarian."[55]

Public reaction to the announcement of a Nobel Prize in Literature is often a mix of dissatisfaction, puzzlement, and disappointment. Unlike sports, literature has no stopwatches, no scores, no quantifiable indicators, and the Nobel committee charged with judging literary merit faces a difficult task. The criteria established in Alfred Nobel's will are fairly broad; the award is to be given to "the person who shall have produced in the field of literature the most outstanding work of an idealistic tendency." In the early twentieth century, "idealistic tendency" meant a religious or philosophical one. So the lack of an idealistic tendency was the justification for the academy's scandalous refusal to award a prize to Tolstoy, Ibsen, or Strindberg: Tolstoy was looked upon as an eccentric, a social dropout who tried to rewrite the Gospels; Ibsen was either too preoccupied with social issues or too obscure; Strindberg was too decadent. Later, "idealistic" came to mean simply aesthetically accomplished and humane.

Yet in the eighty-odd years that the Nobel Prize has been awarded, the list of brilliant writers who have *not* won it may well eclipse the list of writers who have. Aside from the three mentioned above, the list of losers includes such pillars of modernism as Conrad, Proust, Joyce, Kafka, Musil, Brecht, Nabokov, and Borges and nationally recognized writers like Claudel, Rilke, Frost, Auden, and Akhmatova, not to mention those names that simply never made it to Stockholm in time: Chekhov, Blok, Tsvetaeva, Mandelstam, Čapek, Federico García Lorca, Celan.

In October 1987, Brodsky was staying in London, a guest of the pianist Alfred Brendel. He learned of his award while at lunch in a little Chinese restaurant in Hampstead, where he'd been invited by the spy novelist John le Carré. As Le Carré recalls, they were "eating, drinking, chatting (silly Joseph-talk, sort of girls, life)."[56] Renée Brendel, the pianist's wife, tracked them down to tell them that the house was under siege by the media. Brodsky had been awarded the Nobel Prize. As Le Carré describes it: "He looked miserable. So, I said, 'Joseph, if not now, when? We've got to be able to celebrate our life at some point.' 'Yeah, yeah,' he murmured. Then we went outside and he gave me a big Russian hug and produced a great line: 'Now for a year of being glib,' he said, which was beautiful."[57] Flip as the remark might seem, Brodsky was truly distressed at the thought of spending all his time in the upcoming months giving interviews, talking to journalists, and dealing with all the rest of the hoopla.

But he wrote his Nobel lecture with the utmost seriousness and strove to set out his artistic credo in the most concise of terms. Unlike most of his essays, impressionistic mosaics that force the reader's imagination to make the same leaps as the author's does, his Nobel lecture is limited to two themes, both of which are clearly and logically developed (even as he warns his audience that what they are about to hear is merely "a number of remarks . . . disjointed, perhaps stumbling, perhaps even perplexing in their randomness").[58] These themes are familiar ones, but here he lays them out with particular force: first, he speaks of the anthropological significance of art; second, on the primacy of language in the art of poetry.

There is nothing new in the idea that art (the highest form of which is poetry, says Brodsky) is in itself a sentimental education, a moral education, that art makes each one of us better, stronger in the face of faceless historical forces that would crush the individual self. Brodsky notes Plato's triad of Beauty, Good, and Reason, and Dostoevsky's oracular "beauty [that] will save the world"; he names other names as well. This reasoning leads to the conclusion that literature is not merely a matter of culture or civilization but also a matter of anthropology. That is, literature can alter the very nature of the species. According to Brodsky, only *Homo legens*, "reading man," is capable of individualism and altruism. The greater part of the human herd is not.

Here Brodsky seems to be proposing his own version of human evolution. Unlike the "new man" of some socialist utopia, Brodsky's better man is an individualist. But unlike Nietzsche's *Übermensch*, he is a humanist. Two circumstances—one explicit, one implicit—give these remarks poignancy. Brodsky proceeds from the tragic reality of his own century when he speaks of the need to read great literature. This was a century in which populations exploded, in which genocide and mass brutality were practiced on an unprecedented scale: the Nazi Holocaust; Stalinist collectivization and terror; China's Cultural Revolution. Brodsky calls Russian Stalinism the greatest manifestation of evil in the twentieth century ("the number of people who perished in Stalin's camps far surpasses the number of German prison camp victims").[59] Brodsky credits his own generation with restoring Russian culture to itself, with stopping Stalinism from completely sucking the soul out of the Russian people.[60] The conclusion is obvious: "[F]or someone who has read a lot of Dickens, to shoot his like in the name of some idea is more problematic than for someone who has read no Dickens."[61] Therefore, "aesthetics is the mother of ethics."[62]

The lecture also contains an implied criticism of the fads and fashions of Western intellectuals. While Brodsky never once glosses over the shortcomings of Western or American society, he states unequivocally that the greatest evil perpetrated in modern times consisted of the socialist experiments conducted on a mass scale—first and foremost, in his own country—and he states this at a time when Western intellectual circles tended to see the two social systems, capitalism and communism, as equally flawed and therefore providing checks and balances on each other. Any frontal attack on socialism/communism, let alone any definition of political systems in terms of good versus evil, was perceived as reactionary. Equally reactionary (or at least outmoded and naive) seemed the notion that literature might be an instrument of moral progress. Such a notion assumes a certain content underlying a single text by a single author—by Dante, Balzac, Dostoevsky, or Dickens (only a few of the more than twenty writers and philosophers whom Brodsky named in this short lecture). The reigning intellectual mode of the day had proclaimed "le mort d'auteur," and one of postmodernism's chief postulates was that any given text had an infinite multiplicity of meanings. What Brodsky said in the modest lecture hall of the Swedish Academy raised some intellectual hackles, which the skeptical tone of the questions and comments that followed made quite clear.[63]

But in general the choice of Brodsky was far less controversial than some of the Nobel committee's earlier decisions. By 1987 he was well known and for the most part well regarded in European and American intellectual circles. And whether he liked it or not, the dramatic circumstances around his trial and eventual exile contributed to his reputation.

Western readers had found his prose memoirs both poignant and astute. They respected and sometimes admired his poetry in translation; they acknowledged his fame in Russia. According to longtime Nobel watchers, when the awards were announced, Brodsky's name evoked especially long and loud applause.

In his first interview after the unfinished Chinese lunch, he said: "It is Russian literature that got it. And it's an American citizen that got it."[64]

The news of the prize reached Russia on the brink of great change. The foundations of the Soviet regime had begun to crack under the weight of a prolonged economic crisis; the ideological elite, though shaken by Gorbachev's perestroika, were still holding on for dear life. In years past, when the prize had been awarded to Solzhenitsyn, Pasternak, and, before them, Ivan Bunin, the Soviet press had responded with hysterical outcries accusing the Nobel committee of pandering to capitalism, imperialism, et cetera, et cetera. When the prize was awarded to Brodsky, the silence was deafening. It took two weeks for the Soviet press to even report the decision. Foreign audiences were treated to a statement by a mid-level official from the Ministry of the Interior, perhaps because U.S. Secretary of State George Shultz arrived in Moscow the very day of the announcement. At a press conference, the press corps accompanying Schultz asked Gennady Gerasimov, head of the ministry's information section, to comment on the selection. Gerasimov replied that the choice was "strange," that there was a "political tinge" to the prize, but that "there's no arguing over taste," and that he himself would have voted for V. S. Naipaul.[65] The first mention in the Soviet press came on November 8, a full two and a half weeks after the prize was announced, and even this was in *Moscow News,* a paper aimed mainly at foreign audiences. The correspondent asked the Kyrgyz writer Chingiz Aitmatov, "What do you think of the decision to award the Nobel Prize to Brodsky?" Aitmatov answered: "I'll speak only for myself. Unfortunately, I never knew him personally. But I would say that he belongs to the cohort of leading Soviet poets: Evtushenko, Voznesensky, Akhmadulina. Perhaps (and I'm just guessing) his poetry will be published here. It's one thing if a poet is acknowledged by one small circle. If he's known to a mass audience, that's entirely another."[66]

Anyone who depended on *Literaturnaya gazeta* for their news of the outside world had to wait until November 18 to see the announcement in print. Buried in the international news on page 9 was a note to the effect that the Nobel Peace Prize had been awarded to Costa Rican president Óscar Arias Sánchez. The first paragraph of the article listed other Nobel laureates for the year, and at the end of the list was "Joseph Brodsky (USA)."[67] A week later, in a note on a Paris forum entitled "Literature and Government," it was mentioned that "Nobel laureates Czesław Miłosz and Joseph Brodsky did not attend."[68] Given past hysterics on the part of *Literaturnaya gazeta,* the average reader might have taken this nonjudgmental mention of Brodsky as a positive sign. The paper was, after all, still headed by A. B. Chakovsky, who in 1964 had told American reporters that "Brodsky is what we call scum, just plain scum."[69]

Elsewhere, representatives of the failing regime were putting out feelers to their famous exile. According to one Swedish diplomat, the Soviet embassy had offered to send an official representative to the awards ceremony as long as the poet promised to abstain from any attacks on the USSR, Lenin, or Communism. Brodsky made no such promise, and the Soviet ambassador, B. D. Pankin (a literary critic in a past life), did not attend.

But in Moscow and Leningrad the winds had already shifted. On October 25, Feliks Medvedev, a journalist, had stepped onstage at the Moscow Writers' House and announced the award to a wild ovation. The actor Mikhail Kazakov then read a few of Brodsky's poems.[70]

Meanwhile, Oleg Chukhontsev, head of the poetry division of *Novy mir,* had managed to get official permission to publish a small selection of Brodsky's work in the journal's December issue. He had met with Brodsky in April 1987 on a trip to America. Appropriately but perhaps unintentionally, most of what went into that selection were Brodsky's "letters": "Letters to a Roman Friend," "Letters from the Ming Dynasty," "Odysseus to Telemachus," and "From Nowhere with Love."[71] The choice recalled lines written twenty years before:

> the wind,
> like a prodigal son, returned to its father's house,
> and suddenly got all its mail.
> (*KPE;* non-poetic)

CHAPTER TEN

> On the whole, bear in mind that I'll be around.
>
> —"To My Daughter"

CHANGES AT HOME

WHEN BRODSKY LEFT RUSSIA in 1972, he had no idea whether he would ever see his homeland again. At that time, emigration from the USSR was a one-way street, and whatever the United Nations might proclaim about the right to freedom of movement, the Soviet Union was having none of it. On rare occasions emigrants who could not adjust to life in the West might be granted a permit to come back home, but only if they publicly repented of their decision to leave, humbly acknowledged their mistakes, and agreed to tell the press how awful life was in capitalist hell. There was no returning to visit family or friends, nor could family or friends get out.

On the one hand, the government simply feared any economic comparisons between life in the USSR and life in the West. On the other, ideological bias came into play. Only a traitor and enemy of the people would voluntarily leave a socialist society, and therefore even legal emigration was a betrayal. This was especially true if the exile was a writer, a journalist, a political activist—anyone who in Soviet terms automatically belonged to the realm of ideology—for ideology required that one be either all friend or all foe, with us or against us.

Those exiled were not the only ones to suffer. Their families did too. Twelve times Brodsky's parents applied to visit him (either separately or together), and twelve times their applications were denied. One particularly idiotic justification given by the government was that such a visit had "no apparent purpose." Marya Moiseevna and Aleksandr Ivanovich had a very clear purpose. They wanted to see their only son. Still another answer, according to the elder Brodskys' documents, was that their son had emigrated to Israel (or, as one bureaucrat put it, "we *referred* him to Israel"), "so why are you asking for a visa to the U.S.?" Brodsky knocked on the door of anyone and everyone who might have some influence with the Kremlin. He found help at the U.S. State Department and support from senators and bishops, but the Soviets would not yield. His parents died without ever seeing their son again—Marya Moiseevna on March 17, 1983, Aleksandr Ivanovich just over a year later.

With Gorbachev's rise to power, the hermetic seal around the USSR began to crack. Journalists began asking Brodsky when he would be going home for a visit. Initially, he said that he would go back if and when his books were published there.[1]

Soviet newspapers and magazines began publishing his works in 1987–1989, and the first books appeared in 1990.[2] As more and more books and more and more articles about him came out, as the flow became an avalanche, Brodsky began to have doubts.[3] His attachment to his country, and, above all, to his native city, was a personal and complicated matter. Any visit under the current circumstances would entail official meetings and greetings, television and the press, hordes of strangers. Gradually he began to shrug off questions about returning and joked that one should never return to an old lover or the scene of a crime. He spoke to one interviewer in more detail:

> In the first place: you can't step into the same river twice. Second: now that I've got this halo, I'm afraid I might become the object of . . . various hopes and positive feelings. And being the object of positive feelings is much harder than being an object of hatred. Third: I wouldn't like to end up being in better circumstances than the majority of people. I can't stand the thought of a situation—although it's perfectly possible—in which someone asking you for spare change turns out to be your classmate. There are some people who aren't scared at the prospect, who find it appealing, but that's a matter of tempera-

> ment. I'm of a different temperament, and the prospect of riding into Jerusalem on a white stallion doesn't appeal to me. Once upon a time I made plans to slip into Russia incognito, but either there was no good time to do it, or my health was bad, or something came up.[4]

DEMOCRACY!

Brodsky was skeptical of Gorbachev's efforts to liberalize the Soviet regime. He keenly understood, as many of his friends and acquaintances did not, that this was not a democratic revolution but rather a mutation of Russia's usual form of rule: the bureaucratic-imperial leviathan was simply adapting to a changing world. In the late 1980s, Brodsky had begun work on a one-act play called *Democracy!,* which he finished in 1990.[5] In 1992, after the 1991 coup attempt and the collapse of the USSR, he wrote a second act. The play was his first and last attempt at straightforward political satire. Even "Letter to General Z," a monologue by a tired and despairing old imperial soldier, a direct response to the suppression of reforms in Czechoslovakia, was a satire tempered with lyricism.

Democracy! is untempered by anything—it is pure satire, pure caricature. Just as in Brodsky's other political allegories ("Anno Domini," "Post Aetatem Nostram"), the action is set in some province of some empire. The difference lies in the fact that in the poems, the empire is generic and conventional. In the play it is not. Here the empire is clearly the USSR, and the province is a composite Baltic republic.[6]

Theater was hardly Brodsky's passion. While in Sweden for the prize ceremonies he was invited to meet with the troupe of the famed Stockholm Royal Dramatic Theater, and the first thing he confided to that assembled group of actors and directors was, "I mean, plays are much more interesting to read than to watch, no?"[7] Like his philosophical play *Marbles* (1984) and his unpublished "Tree" (1965?), *Democracy!* was meant to be read rather than performed.[8] There is no dramatic action, no plot to speak of. There are some farcical contretemps, but basically, the quartet of provincial bosses (who in the second act are now rulers of an independent country) gather round a table to do the one thing that makes the struggle to represent the starving masses worth the effort—eat well. They are also drinking hard and smoking Cuban cigars, and the men in the group are ogling Matilda, their sexy secretary. As they talk, they cast apprehensive glances at a stuffed trophy bear, the only character that has no lines. In the first act the bear turns out to be a surveillance device relaying information to the capital; in the second act it is also a robotic CNN feed. The message of the satire is simple enough: no matter what reforms or "trickle-down revolution" the government might foster, nothing ever changes: the bureaucrats above enjoy the good life by keeping the populace below in a perpetual state of obedience and fear.

But this satire also includes two motifs that reflect Brodsky's own singular and skeptical political philosophy. For him, neither democracy nor national independence is an absolute value. Roughly around the time he was writing the first act, he said to an interviewer: "Let's imagine that a democratic system comes to power [in Russia]. But ultimately, a democratic system leads to some degree of social inequity. That is, no society can ever be perfectly happy no matter what the weather. It will always have too many different individuals in it. But it's not really a matter of individuals, or of natural resources, et cetera. I don't think that there is any such thing as a happy economy."[9]

In short, no amount of social reform can make human existence more tolerable. Only a "revolution in the brain" can accomplish this, and for lack of positive characters in the play, the squabbling ministers themselves give voice to this idea: "History is being made here. In the brain!" (Granted, this thought, which is obviously the author's, has already been travestied in the line "We are the brain of the state.")[10]

Without a "revolution in the brain," the modicum of freedom allowed the masses does nothing but turn them into brute beasts. In the second act, Matilda—the play's sole representative of the masses—literally becomes a wild animal, a she-leopard: "When history ends, zoology begins. We've already got democracy, yet I'm still young. Therefore, my future is nature. More exactly, the jungle. In the jungle it is either the strongest who survives or the one with the best mimicry. The leopard is an ideal fusion of the former and the latter."[11]

Brodsky was equally skeptical about the notion of identifying the welfare of the nation with national independence and sovereignty. As Bazil Modestovich, head of government in the play, says: "Then again, it's always better if an oppressor . . . is a foreigner. Better to curse a foreigner than your own countryman. That's what makes empires tick. Remember the Caesars or, worse comes to worst, Stalin. It's a kind of psychotherapy.

It is healthier to hate a stranger than your own."[12] Brodsky thought it perfectly fine that Lithuania (where he had many friends), Latvia, Estonia, and other former Soviet republics had become independent nations. In *Democracy!* he was simply warning that independence itself might not make everyone—or anyone—happy. Homegrown tyranny might be even less palatable than the imperial version.

Still, Brodsky was not entirely unmoved by the collapse of the Soviet empire. Even people who knew him well were surprised at how saddened he was by the secession of Ukraine. It became obvious that in his mind the Baltics, Central Asia, and the Caucasus were separate countries and nations—but the space that stretched from the White Sea to the Black, from the Volga to the Bug, was a single land, and it was his native one. He was not alone in thinking so: "An imperial . . . mentality was as characteristic of inhabitants of Poltava and Zhitomir, Nezhin, Chernigov, Gomel and Polotsk as it was for those of Tver or Vyatka. That is, from the earliest days of empire, from the days of Peter the Great, this mentality has counted Kiev and Belarus part of the metropolis. And how could it be otherwise for people who had learned from first grade that 'Kiev is the Mother of Russian cities'?"[13] I will not go into the rather convincing historical, linguistic, anthropological, and ethnographic arguments in favor of regarding Russians, Ukrainians, and Belarusans as three separate and distinct peoples. They indeed are, but that does not make the collapse of a cultural and historical union any less dramatic or keenly felt. The only time in his life that Brodsky exercised self-censorship had to do with Ukraine.

On February 28, 1994, he gave a reading at Queens College, where, early on in his American life, he had taught for a short time. The audience was for the most part English-speaking, and he read mainly in English. The audiotape of the event records only four poems read in Russian, and as he shuffles through his manuscripts, Brodsky says, "Now let me find one poem that I like," and adds, as if to himself, "I'll risk it." This risk was "On Ukrainian Independence" (1992; *Uncollected*). And on first reading, it can indeed seem somewhat shocking. The poem is an invective against Ukrainians; it is rife with crude language and ethnic slurs. Brodsky's characteristic heterogeneity of style is heightened here, as he throws in every stock Ukrainianism he can find, interspersing them with words and phrases from criminal argot. The effective meaning is that separating Russia and Ukraine is nothing less than a crime.

We'll tell them, marking all our pauses by a ringing motherfuh:
Good riddance, ukies, take a hike.
Go trot off in your *zhupans,* not to mention uniforms,
to a place with just four letters, the four corners . . .
. . . .
So long, ukes! We spent some time together—nice while it lasted.
Hock a loogie in the Dnieper? Who knows, it might speed back
so proud, so sick of us, an express train packed
with swag and age-old grievance.
(Non-poetic)

The poem begins with an address to King Charles of Sweden: "Dear Charles the Twelfth, the battle of Poltava, / thank God, is lost." While Sweden's defeat at Poltava on June 27, 1709, had enormous consequences for Russia and Europe in general, Brodsky's first lines are ambiguous; only as we read further does it become obvious that three hundred years later, Russia is the loser. As Voltaire put it: "What is most important about this battle is that of all of the battles that have stained the earth crimson with blood, this was the only one that, instead of producing destruction alone, served human happiness, since it gave the tsar an opportunity to enlighten such a large part of the world."[14] Pushkin, in *Poltava,* proceeds from the same ideological assumption. And so Brodsky's poem ends with a cautionary note to those who decide to break away from the "enlightened world"—the cultural continent founded by Peter and maintained by Russian-speaking (but not necessarily Russian) writers, including Pushkin, Gogol, Leskov, Babel, Paustovsky, and Bagritsky.

Adios, brave Cossacks, hetmans, screws.
But when your time comes, lunkheads,
when you're clawing at your mattress, you'll be
wheezing Aleksandr's lines—not Taras's bull.
(Non-poetic)

(A zhupan is a traditional Ukrainian coat with long skirts. In the Cossack hierarchy, a hetman was the rough equivalent of a general. "Aleksandr" is Aleksandr Pushkin; "Taras" is Taras Shevchenko [1814–1861], the revered Ukrainian nationalist poet and artist.)

"On Ukrainian Independence" was the only poem Brodsky ever decided against publishing because of its political content rather than its poetic quality. He did not want it to be taken as an expression of Russian imperialism or chauvinism.[15] He realized that Ukrainians might take offense or that, even worse, some Russians might take malicious glee in reading such an indictment, and that neither side would pay any attention to what had prompted him to write the poem in the first place. What had prompted him was sorrow: "sadness at the split," as he said after the reading. He speaks of that sorrow directly in the text; the emotional range of the poem includes not only anger and hurt, but profound grief as well:

> We'll get along somehow. And as for tears,
> there's no edict that they wait until next time.
> (Non-poetic)

However important Leningrad/Petersburg may have been to him, Galicia —and, more generally, Ukraine—was his ancestral home (see chapter II).

The third text (after *Democracy!* and "On Ukrainian Independence") written in response to events in the former USSR was "Imitation of Horace" (*PSN*). It might better have been called "In Spite of Horace." Horace's "To the Republic" warns the ship of state of the terrible dangers ahead and calls for caution. Brodsky takes the diametrically opposite tack and calls for a dash into the unknown: "Fly, little boat!" is his leitmotif here. "Fear not!" is repeated twice. This is a cheerful poem. Horace's classic metaphor might have been developed in a variety of ways; Brodsky chose a bold and audacious one. The poem comes off as merry and fearless; it is packed with extravagant and playful devices. In half of the stanzas the rhymes depend on assonance—*korablik-rublik, rebrakh-rybakh-khrabrykh,* for example. The shortened fourth line of each stanza drives the poem forward. The author seems in a hurry; he has no time to find the right word; he plugs in anything that rhymes; he has no time to think about how little sense the paranomastic pairing of *gorizont* and *gore* ("horizon" and "sorrow") makes, or to question whether punning on "Hyperboreus" and "Borya" (the short form of Boris, an allusion to Yeltsin) is really in good taste.

If Brodsky is imitating anything in Horace, it is the vivid elaboration of the ship-of-state metaphor, ancient even in Horace's time.[16] The strength of Brodsky's poem lies in its immediacy: for all its brevity and dash, for all its repeated assonances, the content goes beyond a call to daring and adventure; the short and energetic lines themselves put the reader in the midst of the action. In a mere twenty words Brodsky makes us see it all:

> The sheathing splits along the seams and ribs.
> The pilot babbles about predatory fish.
> Even all the bravest of the brave puke up
> their food.
> (Non-poetic)

The ship can barely keep up with the poet's imagination. In seven lines bridging the fifth and sixth stanzas, Brodsky outlines a story within a story:

> So, they find an island
> where later, sailors' crosses will stand white,
> and a century from now
>
> letters tied with ribbons will be
> offered up for sale by charming
> children, native offspring,
> with startling blue eyes.
> (Non-poetic)

The squealing republics at the beginning of "Imitation" recall both *Democracy!* and "On Ukrainian Independence," but the enthusiasm of "Imitation" stands in contrast to the bitterness of the former and the cold sarcasm of the latter. Finding a single common denominator in these three pieces is difficult, but that does not make Brodsky's attitude toward historical changes in his homeland inconsistent or incoherent. To put it simply: he believed in freedom and rejected nationalism.

Brodsky took contemporary history to heart; he never shut himself off from it. Current events concerned and engaged him. He could talk about politics for hours; he hated to miss the evening news. He was happy to hear that Leningrad had once again become Petersburg; he was outraged by Russian actions in Chechnya. In 1993, after the bloody confrontation between the Yeltsin government and a rebellious Duma (parliament), he sent me a postcard from Italy with a rhymed couplet:

So—we've lived to see
Tanks flirting with TV.

BUSY YEARS: 1990–1995

Brodsky was neither for nor against either Gorbachev or Yeltsin. For Brodsky, Yeltsin was in equal part "brave Captain Borya" and a pragmatic politico who exploited a bloody war in Chechnya. Gorbachev he first thought a babbler, a talker who had no idea of the forces he himself had unleashed. But when Brodsky saw the man in person, he was unexpectedly moved: "It's a huge hall, or rather a room, twenty people sitting in it asking him questions about why he did this or that, and he says nothing. Either he won't answer, or he can't. Probably he can't. And at some point it seemed to me that Clio had just walked into the room—all we can see are her feet and the hem of her robe. And somewhere on the level of her soles are all these people. Me included."[17]

The last five years of Brodsky's life coincided with enormous changes in Russia and the world at large. He was truly engaged in all that was happening, spoke about it, wrote about it both in English and in Russian, in verse and in prose. In these five years he was perhaps busier than he had ever been: he continued to teach; he took part in all sorts of public forums. He crisscrossed the United States and several oceans as well. As poet laureate he launched a campaign to promote the reading of poetry; he launched another to establish an academy of Russian poetry in Rome.

In September 1990 he married Maria Sozzani, a young Italian woman with Russian roots. He found himself surprisingly happy in his newfound family life. In 1993 they had a daughter, Anna.

These last few years were prolific: he wrote roughly a hundred poems, a dozen essays, and a play. But all the while his health was declining precipitously, and he knew that he didn't have long to live.

ILLNESS

Brodsky's heart began to fail quite early, even while everyone around thought him a perfectly sound and healthy young man—and he certainly behaved like one. The young doctors who first treated him in exile in Norenskaya found "symptoms of . . . heart disease—pain, blood in the sputum."[18] His predisposition to heart and vascular disease was probably inherited: his father suffered several heart attacks, although they did not keep Aleksandr Ivanovich from living to the venerable age of eighty. "Twenty-six years shaken up / and shaken down, dragged through trials" may have taken their toll: the link between stress and strokes is well proven, although it is hard to say which causes which. The backbreaking work and bad food in Norenskaya did their part to undermine his health; so did his solitary, unsettled life abroad. In his first months in Ann Arbor, Brodsky bought a bicycle and swam at the university pool—but this took time away from writing, and he soon abandoned both. Brodsky drank quite moderately by Russian standards but was all too fond of strong coffee and strong cigarettes. When I asked Brodsky's New York cardiologist about the basic cause of death, the doctor said simply, "Smoking."

So when Solzhenitsyn ended a 1977 letter to Brodsky with wishes for "good health and good spirits," this was not just some epistolary cliché. Five months before, on December 13, 1976, Brodsky had suffered a massive heart attack. Although he would live for another nineteen years, his health declined steadily from that point on. In December 1978, he had a bypass; seven years later, after suffering two more heart attacks, he had a second bypass in December 1985. Over the last ten years of his life he was often hospitalized. His doctors discussed a third operation and toward the end talked of a transplant. They were frank about the risks involved. Brodsky was aging rapidly; he looked much older than his years. Eventually any sort of physical effort became almost unbearable. "It's hard to walk the length of a building," he wrote Andrey Sergeev in December 1995.[19]

Heart disease is peculiar in that angina episodes come and go unexpectedly. Some are more painful, others less, but all evoke a sense of imminent danger. Angina pectoris (or, as Brodsky liked to joke, "angina dentata") leaves the sufferer with the sense that death is ever present. He might die at any moment, he might be spared for another day. A heart patient who keeps a busy work schedule is not unlike a wounded frontline soldier in the midst of a battle: neither has much time to focus on health.

All of Brodsky's mature poetry was written in the presence of death. He was never a hypochondriac; he had a gift for living life fully and even joyously, especially when the illness abated for a time. In 1979, the year following his first bypass, he published nothing, perhaps because of postoperative depression, perhaps for personal reasons, perhaps out of a desire to write differently than he had before.[20] In fact the poetics of *Urania* and his last book do contain some quite new elements. But even newer is the author's sense of the world. It seems that once Brodsky realized how short his span of days might be, he abandoned the grim resignation of pre-1979 poems like "The Thames at Chelsea" (1974; *ChR*), "Quintet" (1977; *Urania*), "Stanzas" ("Like a glass" [1978]; *Urania*). Instead, he began writing pieces that cannot be called anything other than sunny and joyous: "Piazza Mattei" (1981), "Roman Elegies" (1981), "Venetian Stanzas" (1982), all of which went into *Urania*. And later, among the poems of his very fruitful last seven years that made up the content of *Landscape with Flood,* we find not only elegiac or ironic pieces but also compositions in an undeniably major key: "Spanish Dancer," "Cloud," "Imitation of Horace," "Ritratto di donna." There is a greater dose of humor in this last book than in any of his previous ones. Humor dominates "Centaurs," "Landwehrkanal, Berlin," "You can't tell a mosquito," "The Theatrical," "The Temple of Melpomene," and the almost clownish and farcical "Roadshow." But it is also present in other, more serious pieces. "To Cornelius Dolabella," written in autumn 1995, ends with a solemn and tragic line: "And marble narrows my aorta." Here, hardening of the arteries is reimagined as a hardening of flesh to stone; those worthy of immortality turn into statues. But the poem begins by comparing a marble Roman statue to a man jumping out of the shower and wrapping himself in a towel.

"Prophets are not meant to be healthy," wrote Brodsky in his "Farewell, Mademoiselle Véronique" (1967). He regarded his ill health not as some anomaly but as the normal course of events for a poet, or a human in general. The notion that a sense of impending death gives meaning to life is hardly new. Shakespeare expressed it succinctly in the final couplet of Sonnet 146:

> So shalt thou feed on Death, that feeds on men,
> And Death once dead, there's no more dying then.

Even more stark was Wallace Stevens's line in "Sunday Morning": "Death is the mother of beauty." Brodsky's own Leningrad friend and fellow writer Aleksandr Kushner writes about the same notion in an early poem as he compares the ever-present thought of death to a poisonous seed:

> But without this seed, the taste
> is off, the wine does not go down.
> (Non-poetic)

The ending of a short poem in part 1 of *Urania* clarifies Brodsky's attitude toward ill health.

> Those who do not die live on
> to sixty or to seventy;
> they bugger on, pen memoirs,
> stumble round.
> I peer into their features,
> like Miklukho-Maklay
> at the tattoos
> of approaching savages.
> (Non-poetic)

(Miklukho-Maklay was a nineteenth-century Russian anthropologist who studied primitive societies in New Guinea.)

What does living to sixty or seventy have to do with savages? For all Brodsky's dislike of Thomas Mann, the best answer is Naphta's monologue from *The Magic Mountain:*

> Illness is supremely human . . . because to be human was to be ill. Indeed man was ill by nature, his illness was what made him human, and whoever sought to make him healthy and attempted to get him to make peace with nature, to "return to nature" (whereas he had never been natural, that whole pack of Rousseauian prophets—regenerators, vegetarians, fresh-air freaks, sunbath apostles, and so forth—wanted nothing more than to dehumanize man and turn him into an animal.[21] Humanity? Nobility? The Spirit was what distinguished man—a creature set very much apart from nature, with feelings very much contrary to nature—from the rest of organic life. Therefore, the dignity and nobility of man was based in the Spirit, in illness. In a word, the more ill a man was the more highly human he was, and the genius of illness was more human than that of health.[22]

"BEING-TOWARD-DEATH"

Brodsky defied superstition when he began his "Fin de siècle" (1989) with a prediction: "The century will end soon, but I'll end sooner" (non-poetic). Even in the generally sunny "Roman Elegies," death is always on his mind. But here the thought of early death is mitigated by gratitude and joy. Here we find the only direct address to God—we may call it a prayer—in all of the poet's six books:

> Lean over. I'll whisper something to you: I am
> grateful for everything: for the chicken cartilage
> and for the chirr of scissors already cutting
> out the void for me—for it is your hem.
> Doesn't matter if it's pitch-black, doesn't matter if
> it holds nothing: no ovals, no limbs to count.
> The more invisible something is,
> the more certain it's been around,
> and the more obviously it's everywhere. You
> were the first to whom all this happened, were you?
> For a nail holding something one would divide by two—
> were it not for remainders—there is no gentler quarry.
> I was in Rome. I was flooded by light. The way
> a splinter can only dream about.
> Golden coins on the retina are to stay—
> enough to last the whole blackout.

Even in the dashing lines of "Piazza Mattei" the same motif slips in: "what's left of flesh," "*as the curtain was coming down,* I gulped at some freedom" (emphasis added). Here we have Pushkin's thrill at standing "on the edge of the grim deep"—but Brodsky never took the leap of faith over that existential chasm. Instead, his joyous late verse throws down the gauntlet to fate and death. (See "To Cornelius Dolabella" and "Aere Perennius.") Most of his Christmas poems, too, were written in the last decade of his life, but Solzhenitsyn said it well when he remarked that Brodsky's "Christmas theme seems framed separately, like a warmly lit square."[23] Among the things that Brodsky loved—oceans, rivers, and city streets, feminine beauty, and some poets—was the story of the Holy Family: the birth in the stable, the cosmic link between the star and the child, the halt in the desert on the flight into Egypt.

Yet his love for the Gospel story had nothing to do with any belief in personal salvation. As we can judge from some of his other poems, the only form of afterlife Brodsky ever acknowledged was writing, the "part of speech," the Horatian monument. The poet's pen is truer than the trappings of the pious: "Its furrow through the centuries is longer / than your eternal life and incense burning" ("Aere Perennius," *PSN*).

Aside from "Exegi Monumentum," there are other meditations on death. One involves remembrance: "Those who have left leave a part of themselves, for us to keep, and we need to live on in order that they do too. And this, in the end, is what life comes down to, whether we recognize it or not."[24] Or another example, more laconic: "We are them."[25] We find variations on this motif in his many poems with titles that include the words "in memory of" or "on the death of." In *Landscape with Flood* alone there are six: "On the Centenary of Anna Akhmatova," "In Memory of My Father: Australia," "In Memory of Gennady Shmakov," "Vertumnus" (in memory of Gianni Buttafava), "In Memory of N.N." and "In Memory of Clifford Brown."[26]

Another constant theme is the continuation of organic life after the author's death. This, too, was one of Pushkin's ("tribe young and unbeknown to me"), and in Brodsky this theme appears in "From the Outskirts to the Center" (*OVP*), "1972" (*ChR*), "Fin de siècle" (*PSN*), and "August" (*PSN*), the last poem he completed. There are other poems in which the picture is more brutal, when life after death comes down to desiccation and decay: "carrion is freedom—from cells, freedom from / it all; the apotheosis of the particle" ("Only ash knows what it means to burn to nothing"; *PSN*). For all its naturalism, this verse speaks of more than mere organic life. The carrion that some archaeologist will one day discover is also "passion buried in the earth." This posthumous dualism, the dualism of disintegration in which the spiritual, as well as the material, form of existence disintegrates—but rather than disappearing, is transformed—was probably gleaned from Marcus Aurelius: "There, [on earth], after a short respite, change and decay make way for other dead bodies. Similarly, souls transferred to the air exist for a while before undergoing a change and a diffusion, and are then transmuted into fire and taken back into the creative principle of the universe; and thus room is made for the reception of others."[27]

But Brodsky has his own variation on this theme. This variation is the one most broadly represented in his poetry, especially at the end of his life, although it emerged as early as 1972, in "Letters to a Roman Friend." It might be called "the world without me."

The "Roman Friend" to whom the letters are addressed is named Postumus. As in several of his other poems (cf. Fortunatus in "Plato Elaborated"), the name of the addressee is significant: Postumus, "he who comes after," was a name commonly bestowed on a male child born after the death of his father. Horace played with this meaning in his ode "To Postumus": "O Postumus, Postumus! How swiftly / The years slip by" (*Odes,* 2.14). Brodsky's "Letters" and Horace's famous ode are linked not only by the theme of transience but also by the their endings, a depiction of a life that goes on after their lyric heroes have been subtracted from its sum. Like Horace, Brodsky mentions the cypress at the end of his poem, the tree that traditionally graced Roman cemeteries.

In a preliminary draft this "posthumous" motif was absent.

> Beyond the pines' black fence the sea is sparkling
> a boat fights wind around the cape.
> I'm sitting in a rocker, Pliny the Elder in my lap
> A thrush sings in the hairdo of a cypress.
> (Non-poetic)[28]

The complete final version of the final "letter" goes as follows:

> Dark green laurels on the verge of trembling.
> Doors ajar. The windowpane is dusty.
> Idle chairs and the abandoned sofa.
> Linen blinded by the sun of noonday.
>
> Pontus drones past a black fence of pine trees.
> Someone's boat braves gusts out by the promontory.
> On the garden bench a book of Pliny rustles.
> Thrushes chirp within the hairdo of the cypress.

There is an important difference between the two drafts. In the final draft there is no "I." The physical world, though "idle" and "abandoned" (no accident that these words collide in a single line), does not change; it is as dynamic as ever, offering itself up to live sensation and perception: the leaves of the laurel tremble, cloth turns warm in the sun, the sea roars in the distance, a sailboat fights the wind, a thrush sings. But no one is there to squint at the bright light, to bask in the sun, to listen to the sounds of the sea and the birds, follow the boat's progress, finish a book. And the unread book, by the way, is an attempt at a complete description of that physical world; it is Pliny the Elder's *Naturalis Historia.*

Brodsky's imagination is particularly prolific when it ventures toward absence. For him, a place is always characterized by those who once lived in it: "Along with the heating, in every house / there's another system—a system of absence" (*PSN*); "the emptiness where once we loved" ("You've forgotten the village lost in the rows and rows"). In *Urania,* describing four rooms from a nightmare, he says:

> In the third, the dust lay thick like fat
> like emptiness; no one had ever lived there.
> I liked that more than my father's house
> because that's how things will be everywhere, ever after.
> ("The room smelled of rags and tap water"; non-poetic)

Mikhail Lotman made the following observation on this poem: "And so for Brodsky an empty space, if not transcendental, is at least otherworldly; it is codified in images almost sacred ('I believe in emptiness'). This emptiness, this void, is the foundation of the world of things, it is the stuff of things, it is their essence, or, rather, their absolute remainder. It is precisely because there is a void that the thing is not finite."[29] Lotman's remarks are surely true but altogether too cautious. At times Brodsky consciously sacralizes "the void":

> Emptiness. But the mere thought of that
> brings forth lights as if out of nowhere.
> ("December 24, 1971")

He had always been interested in religious teachings in which emptiness/nothingness was the essence of being, the essence of the divine: Buddhism, the Kabbalah, the mysticism of Jakob Böhme.

An earlier article by Yury and Mikhail Lotman treats the theme of nothingness as central to Brodsky's "anti-Acmeist" poetics and Neoplatonic philosophy. The authors dub Brodsky's poetics anti-Acmeist because the Acmeism described by Osip Mandelstam in his 1919 manifesto puts "space over time (it is founded on three dimensions!) and imagines reality as space won away from nothingness and filled with matter."[30] In Brodsky, beginning with *Urania,* say the Lotmans, the thing "is always in conflict with space." The authors quote "To a Chair": "the thing placed in space as if in Aitch-two-O . . . / yearns to crowd space out." They write:

> The matter of which things are made is finite and time-bound; the form of things is infinite and absolute; cf. the concluding formula of "To a Chair": "matter is finite. But a thing is not." . . . Given this primacy of form over matter, it follows that the chief mark of a thing is its limits: the reality of a thing is the hole that it leaves behind in space. Therefore the transition from material object to a pure construct that can fill up all the emptiness of space, this Platonic ascent to an abstract form, to an idea, does not weaken reality but strengthens it, is not impoverishment but enrichment:
>
> The more invisible something is,
> The more certain it's been around,
> and the more obviously it's everywhere
> ("Roman Elegies XII")[31]

Critics apparently took up the phrase "a hole in space" on reading "The Fifth Anniversary," although this poem talks only of the author's absence from his home city rather than from the physical world ("Some moss combined with lichen, / encountering the whole I've made, will quickly stitch it"). Thus, in 1989, in "Fin de siècle" (*PSN*) the "chamber version of black holes" is a pun on removing superfluous people from the cultural landscape—not by killing them but by putting them in jail (in Russian, a *kamera* can be a chamber as in "chamber orchestra," and also a jail cell)—a dystopic theme earlier explored in "Post Aetatem Nostram" and later in *Marbles*. It is interesting, however, that at the end of "Taps" (1994), this image stands forth precisely as interpreted by the Lotmans, that is, as a passage from a physical space to an ideal, metaphysical one. This was the poem that Brodsky chose to end his last book. It was by no means his last poem, but it was the one he wanted as his valediction:

> . . . non-being's blue armor plate,
> prizing attempts at making a sifter of it,
> might use my pinhole, at any rate.

In this farewell poem the hole in space merges with a star—another sacred constant in Brodsky's poetry, harking back to the Old Testament and Ovid.[32] In "To the Next Century," another poem written in 1994, the poet also talks of stars: "since for them the speed of light is a disaster, / their presence is their absence, their being the result of their nonbeing." Brodsky applies the same metaphor that Mayakovsky gives us, albeit in the negative, in his poem "At the Top of My Voice": "My verse will reach you . . . not like light from dead stars."[33] The fundamental difference is that for Brodsky, physical absence—nonbeing—is the ideal form of being.

At the beginning of an article, "The Poet and Death," Mikhail Lotman writes that in Brodsky "the intrusion of the word into the realm of silence, emptiness, death, has particular meaning: he is taking the battle to the enemy."[34] The "struggle against suffocation" ("I Sit by the Window"), death's defeat by "a part of speech," is a pivotal theme inherited not only from Pushkin and Horace but also from ancient Indo-European poetic tradition.[35] Taken in the context of all of "The Funeral of Bobo," the line quoted by Lotman ("I believe in emptiness") is merely a statement of a thesis within the antithetical conclusion of the poem:

> Now Thursday. I believe in emptiness.
> There, it's like hell, but shittier, I've heard.
> And the new Dante, pregnant with his message,
> bends to an empty space and writes a word.

The antithesis is that the empty space is filled in by the word, the white by the black, nothing is made nothing.

We should not forget, of course, that Brodsky's fascination with the theme of emptiness and absence is first and foremost artistic rather than dogmatic or philosophical.

> Ultimately, one's unbound
> curiosity about these empty zones,
> about their objectless vistas, is what art seems to be all about.
> ("New Life")

While Brodsky may abstract the creative process by reducing it to the writing of some generic word on a piece of paper, or even to filling up white space with black (he always preferred fountain pens to ballpoints and used only black ink), the reader is not dealing simply with "something black on something white" ("Letter to General Z," *KPE*); he is dealing with a poet's imagination captured in a letter of the alphabet. The ideal expression of his belief in emptiness might be the blank page often found in avant-garde experiments.[36] But such jokes were not for Brodsky; his imagination truly could not abide empty space. For him, neither an apocalypse nor one's own death would bring about the end of the world. In Czesław Miłosz's "Song at the End of the World," Judgment Day comes and goes, but the rhythm of life never changes: "There will be no other end of the world." This is very much like what transpires in both "Post Aetatem Nostram" and in *Marbles*.[37]

In a number of poems Brodsky limits himself to a single futuristic detail or aside: the dam in "Prophecy" (*OVP*); the warheads camouflaged as colonnades in "The Residence"; the introductory clarification ("even here, / in the future that came") in "A Footnote to Weather Forecasts." For Brodsky, history is not the one-way street laid out by monotheistic religions, Hegel, or Marx. Nor is it entirely cyclical. Rather, it is a set of mirrors, the past reflected in the future. All of "Noon in a Room" (*Urania*) is devoted to this notion: "in the future, i.e., in the amalgam, i.e., / in a reflected yesterday." And further:

> We will not die when that time comes!
> But some child's fingernail
>
> will scratch us off
> the amalgam in the mirror!

This is why the future is both so tangible and so varied. Now we see features of classical antiquity, now of the modern age ("New Life"), now of primitive communal life ("Robinsonade"). Solipsism is the last thing Brodsky is inclined to: in yet another poem from *Landscape*, "Porta San Pancrazio," he wryly notes, "Life without us is, darling, thinkable." The coffee bar in this poem is Gianicolo, an ordinary little place atop the hill of the same name, not far from the American Academy, where Brodsky spent the winter of 1980–1981. He loved sitting there over a cup of coffee, observing the young regulars. Returning for a residency at the American Academy in 1989, he found the café itself unchanged, but found himself watching a different generation. After the short nativity poem that opens his last collection, there are three long poems, in all of which "life without us" unfolds in a wealth of both surrealistic and realistic detail.

His diptych "Venetian Stanzas" is also a "landscape that can do / without me." What does that landscape consist of? Here, in the first stanza of part 1, is sunrise in Venice:

> A sleep-crumpled cloud unfurls meal mizzens,
> slapped by the baker, matte cheeks acquire
> a glow. And in pawnbrokers' windows
> jewelry catches fire.
> Flat garbage barges sail. Like lengthy, supple
> sticks run by hot-footed schoolboys along iron grates,
> the morning rays strum colonnades, red-brick chimneys, sample
> curled seaweed, invade arcades.

In the middle of the stanza we have the very prosaic sign of an ordinary morning in Venice: "Flat garbage barges sail." Everything else relates to the trope. The actual description of the sunrise is presented entirely as metaphor and simile: a cloud is a sail, the glow on the cheek is the pinkish-brown crust on a freshly baked loaf of bread (in Russian, it is a natural comparison; the same word, *rumyanets,* applies); the morning rays of the sun play across buildings and canals like the sticks that schoolboys bang along fences as they run to class. The rosy cheek of dawn is a traditional metaphor, a cliché. It becomes fresh again in that the terms of the comparison do not take us out of the awakening city but return us to it, enriching the cityscape with concrete, solid detail: bread baked fresh in the early morning, the juicy smack of hand against dough. The same with the mischievous schoolboys: this comparison brings movement and dynamism to the overall picture of a Venice morning. Equally real, concrete, and characteristic of Venice are the jewelry in the shop windows, the seaweed, the arcades. When the Lotmans assert that Brodsky's poetry is a "refutation of Akhmatova and Mandelstam's Acmeism, couched in the very language of their Acmeism," they have in mind this very thing—that Brodsky's texts aspire to the material, the concrete, even if the content of the text is a landscape that can live without an observer, even when the observer has been removed from it.

The world without the author is emphatically material and decidedly unexotic. In "After Us" the grotesque political system of the future is based on climate and the change of seasons; the climate, however, is temperate, and the middle section of the poem consists of a list:

the god of commerce
only revels in the rising demand for tweeds,
English umbrellas, worsted topcoats. His most dreaded enemies
are darned stockings and patched-up trousers.

Removed from the landscape, the author loses connection to ordered space and time—hence, "From Nowhere with Love" or "Yesterday tomorrow began, at three o'clock in the afternoon. / Today's already 'never' or the future" (*PSN*).[38]

In Brodsky's personal canon, one poem that held pride of place was Gavrila Derzhavin's "On the Death of Prince Meshchersky." Its tone is not at all elegiac; rather, the poem's main theme is dread at time passing, the awfulness of death itself. "O time's language, metal peal! / Your fearsome voice undoes me . . . / Death, all the world atremble, fear!" Another place was held by Samuel Beckett's novel-as-monologue *Malone Dies*. These two pieces, plus a few works by Donne, Kafka, and Faulkner were the only ones that Brodsky acknowledged as adequate literary expressions of the primal instinct that makes humans fear death. And despite his long-standing dislike of Leo Tolstoy, he nonetheless, in an early poem called "Hills" (1962, *OVP*), describes the horror of death by way of an extravagant device that, if not borrowed from Tolstoy, is at least identical to one that Tolstoy used. The opening lines of the poem are deceptively like a traditional crime ballad, but the author is not interested in who killed whom and why; he writes only about this horror of death, this trembling of nature, that penetrates everything. The theme reaches its culmination in the fifteenth stanza. In public appearances, at this point Brodsky's rapt reading would reach an almost ecstatic plane:

Death is in a vain chase
(like someone tracking thieves).
From now on, red will be
the milk from these cows.
In a red, red boxcar,
Off the red, red rails,
in a red, red milk can,
to feed red tots.
(Non-poetic)[39]

This cinematic device à la Paradzhanov (*ante factum*), when everything around the horrified observer turns blood red, can be found in Tolstoy. This is what historians of Russian literature call Tolstoy's "Arzamas horror," an acute attack of fear and anguish that Tolstoy actually suffered in September 1869 and later described in his unfinished "Notes of a Madman."[40] The narrator calls this horror "red, white, square," and these absurd epithets emerge out of the description, one page earlier, of the provincial hotel room in which the fit occurred: "A pristinely whitewashed square little room. . . . There was one window, with a red curtain." Another echo of Tolstoy, probably involuntary, can be heard in a much more tranquil and even reasoned poem from 1968, "In Memory of T.B." (*KPE*), in the aphoristic line that states: "Death is what happens to others." This is exactly how Ivan Ilyich's colleagues react to the news of his death in *The Death of Ivan Ilyich:* "Every one of them either thought or felt, 'What do you know, he died. But I didn't.'" Later in Tolstoy's tale the same attitude to death is reflected in Ivan Ilyich's indelicate attempt to revise the syllogism "Caius is a man, all men are mortal, therefore Caius is mortal. There was a man Caius, a common everyday man, and this was perfectly fine; but he wasn't Caius, and he wasn't a common everyday man, he had always been a being wholly, wholly distinct from all others." Tolstoy is ironic on the cowardice and self-love of Ivan Ilyich and his colleagues; Brodsky rethinks this in philosophical terms. Brodsky's thought here is true, in that unlike everything else that happens to us, our own death cannot be a personal experience.[41] After 1965 the fear of death disappears from Brodsky's poetry. If, for his beloved Stoics, philosophy was an exercise in dying, for Brodsky, poetry was that exercise. The horror of death receded, replaced by an intense and even humorous attention to the richness and variety of fleeting human life; imaginary excursions into the "world without us," meditations on the themes of empty space (absence-presence), and Stoicism sometimes manifested in outrageous and even rude form. I have in mind "Portrait of Tragedy" from *Landscape with Flood.*

This poem has an odd history. As Brodsky explained to his editor after *Landscape* had been sent to the printer, he had simply forgotten to include it. When the book was reissued in 2000, after Brodsky's death, the poem was restored. "Portrait," dated 1991, is the first of what might be called a "theater cycle," consisting of four parts. After "Portrait" come poems for a production of Euripides's *Medea,* "The Theatrical," and "The Temple of Melpomene." It is tempting to speculate on how Brodsky managed to block out the memory of this by no means small and by all means significant poem. Perhaps he managed because he was happy and content in his personal life? Perhaps because he was finished with the theme once and for all? I have no idea.

"Portrait of Tragedy" is a summing up, like "Aere perennius" and "Taps." In it we find a recapitulation of motifs present in Brodsky's poetry for at least thirty years. For example, there is the star (absent in his English version):

> To press against the cheek of tragedy! To the black curls of the
> Gorgon,
> to the rough board on the backside of the icon,
> with a star rolling down the cheekbone like a boxcar heading East
> (Non-poetic)

In Brodsky's verse, a star might be many things: a celestial meeting place for parted lovers ("A Song to No Music"); the fatherly eye of God ("Star of the Nativity"); a tear of desperation ("In the Lake District"); a boat packed with hapless refugees ("Snow is falling, leaving the whole world outmanned"; *Urania*). But the star was always the point at which human suffering and divine love were joined. In "Portrait of Tragedy" the star is first a tear running down a cheek; the second half of the comparison likens it to a boxcar rolling east—that is, one of the boxcars that hauled Osip Mandelstam and hundreds of thousands of others away to pain and death in the Gulag.

The rhyme in this passage (*Gorgony-ikony*) is one that we have seen before. In "The Fifth Anniversary" Brodsky writes:

> I never liked fat cats, and never kissed an icon.
> And on a certain bridge, a black cast-iron Gorgon
> seemed in those parts to me the truth's most honest version.

As it turns out, this rhyme is truly significant—something only hinted at in "The Fifth Anniversary." The reverse side of the icon (the rough board) is Perseus's shield. The front of the icon gazes down at the believer from Heaven; its reverse is a monster from the depths of the earth and sea, the incarnation of chaos. Its gaze is death.

The shield of Perseus is a mirror. At the beginning of the poem, when Brodsky invites the reader to look into the face of tragedy, the poet first of all sees himself:

> Let's look into the face of tragedy. We'll see its creases,
> its aquiline profile, its masculine jawbone.

Then, as the poem progresses, come the ever more repulsive minutiae of illness and decay: "her flabby rubble," "her stench of armpits and feces." Once upon a time tragedy was "a beauty." In the world of Sophocles and Racine, tragedy is the revolt of man against divine predestination, against the forces of fate. In the world of Beckett and Brodsky, tragedy lies in the human body itself, in the inevitable road to death and decay. In *Poetics,* Aristotle defines tragedy as the most noble of genres. It must be reasoned (chapter 6); it must avoid vulgar expressions (chapter 22). "Portrait," with its gerontophilic—or even necrophilic—arabesques, is beyond vulgar:

> Let's tumble into her arms with a lecher's ardor!
> Let's drown in her flabby rubble; yes, let's go under.
> Let's burrow through her and make mattress fodder.

In Brodsky, tragedy moans and wails and swears:

> Go ahead, tragedy! Among our vowels,
> pick out the *yi,* born in the Mongol bowels,
> and turn it, ripping our gushing ovals,
>
> into a noun, a verb, an adjective! *yi,* our common gargle!
> *yi,* we barf out as our gains and our losses ogle
> us, or as we storm the exit. But there, an ogre,
> you're looming large with your oblong cudgel and bulging goggle!

This foul coupling with the grunt-like sound *yi* is reminiscent of Longinov's obscene "Hussar Alphabet": "*Yi*'s never letter number one. / *Yi*'s what whores yell when they're done."[42] This is what (or whom) Brodsky is comparing tragedy to, and the entire poem is a challenge to chaos and the dissolution of matter. It is an extended metaphor for what might be called, in its shortest version, a "fuck you" in the face of death.

DEATH

It seemed quite probable that illness would eventually turn Brodsky into an invalid and that he would die either in a hospital or on an operating table. But as Derzhavin wrote, "[D]eath comes to him like a thief in the night / And steals life sudden away." On the evening of January 27, 1996, a Saturday, Brodsky packed his briefcase with manuscripts and books to take to South Hadley. Spring semester was to start the following Monday. He said good night to his wife, told her he had some work to do, and went upstairs to his study. That is where she found him the next morning, on the floor—fully dressed. On his desk there lay a blank sheet of paper, a cigarette, and an open book: a volume from Loeb's *Greek Anthology*. According to the doctors, his heart simply stopped. Death was quick.

The first plan was to bury him in South Hadley. He himself had assumed that that was where he would lie. But other people had other plans. The Russian Duma deputy Galina Starovoitova sent a telegram proposing that the poet be buried on Vasilievsky Island in Petersburg, but this meant that someone would have to decide the question of "return" for him. It would also have meant a hardship for his family. Moreover, Brodsky didn't even like the youthful lines that apparently prompted this offer ("I'll come back to die / on Vasilievsky"). In the end, his friends in Europe managed to reach an agreement with the city of Venice. Brodsky would be buried in the old cemetery of San Michele.[43]

Since he was neither Catholic nor Eastern Orthodox, his grave lies in the Protestant section of the cemetery. Surrounded by a brick wall, the small Protestant section resembles a country churchyard, but beyond the walls one can hear the lapping of waves on the lagoon. Brodsky's modest marble headstone is inscribed with a line from Propertius: *Letum non omnia finit*, "Death is not the end."[44]

Susan Sontag remarked that Venice was the ideal place to bury Brodsky, since it was essentially nowhere. That is precisely the return address that Brodsky gives at the beginning of one of his loveliest lyrics, "From Nowhere with Love."

NOTES

For a list of abbreviations used in citing sources and for full citations of sources given here only in brief, see the selected bibliography.

PREFACE

1. In the course of the past two centuries more than one attempt has been made to describe the phenomenon of genius in scientific terms. Some researchers (Cesare Lombroso, Max Nordauer) considered it an anomaly; others (Koltsov et al.) attributed it to a rare combination of genes. See also Ernst Kretschmer, *The Psychology of Men of Genius* (New York: Harcourt, 1931); Penelope Murray, ed., *Genius: The History of an Idea* (New York: Blackwell, 1989); Irina Sirotkina, *Diagnosing Literary Genius: A Cultural History of Psychiatry in Russia, 1880–1930* (Baltimore, MD: Johns Hopkins University Press, 2002); Karl Leonhard, *Akzentuierte Persönlichkeiten* (Berlin: VEB Verlag Volk und Gesundheit, 1976). While some authors have offered interesting psychological insights, there is yet no sound theory that explains the exceptional creative power possessed by certain artists. It can be argued that such a theory is impossible in principle, since the aesthetic judgment necessary to distinguish a great work from the effusions of a graphomaniac is not quantifiable.
2. Marina Tsvetaeva, *Ob iskusstve* (Moscow: Iskusstvo, 1991), 74. Very similar ideas are to be found in Nicolas Berdyaev's *The Meaning of the Creative Act* (Moscow: G. A. Lemon and S. I. Sakharov, 1916): "Genius is always a human quality, not merely an artistic, scientific, philosophical, or political one. To be a genius means to possess a special intensity of spirit rather than to possess a special talent."
3. A. S. Pushkin, *Pisma* (Moscow: GIZ, 1926), vol. 1, 160.

4. "A Cat's Meow," in Brodsky, *On Grief and Reason,* 300.
5. To be published in Russian in the Biblioteka Poeta series.

CHAPTER ONE

1. Brodsky writes of this in an unpublished memoir: "I asked my mother and father several times about that day, but they didn't say much of anything. All I know is that I was born somewhere on the Vyborg Side, in 'Professor Tur's clinic.' My mother said that the professor himself attended her. This 'Professor Tur' and his favorable assessment of me have stayed with me my entire life" (NLR, file 63, folio 181). A. F. Tur (1894–1974) was a famous Russian pediatrician.
2. This was 2/6 Ryleev Street, apartment 10, on the third floor (the numbering of the apartments later changed; ibid., folio 184). Elsewhere, Brodsky says that the family moved to the Muruzi (Liteiny 24/27, apartment 28; the building is on the corner of Pestel [Saint Panteleimon]) in 1952 (Brodsky, *Bolshaya kniga intervyu,* 413). In an article by Dmitriy Novikov, "Ob ekonomii mramora. K literaturnoy istorii Doma Muruzi" (*Avrora,* no. 6 [1989]), the date is given as 1955. The later dates are apparently the correct ones, since in 1954 and 1955 Iosif was attending schools in the Kirov district because his father's residency permit was for a building on the corner of Prospekt Gaza and Obvodny Kanal; that is, this was probably before his father and mother exchanged their separate single rooms for the two-room flat in the Muruzi.
3. From a brochure by A. Kobak and L. Lurye, *Dom Muruzi* (Leningrad: Svecha, 1990).
4. NLR, file 63, folio 190.
5. Brodsky mistakenly assumed that these were trophies taken in the Crimean War (see "A Room and a Half," chapter 34).
6. Brodsky, *Less Than One,* 491–492.
7. Mirrors are a constant image in Brodsky's work. The chief feature of oceans and rivers is their mirrorlike quality: they reflect time (*Watermark*). Petersburg is not a "window on Europe" but its mirror ("Guide to a Renamed City"); the city is also Narcissus, mesmerized by his/its own reflection (also in "Noon in a Room," *Urania*). A mirror is a border between life and death: "at the road's end, / a mirror by which to enter" ("Torso"). The mirror is the poet himself: "the body viewing the ocean. It is selfless, flat / as a mirror as it stands in the darkness there" ("Lullaby of Cape Cod"), "playing your double like / an insanity-stricken mirror" ("From Nowhere with Love"), "We will not die, when the hour comes! / But with a fingernail / some child will scrape us off / the silvering on the mirror" ("Noon in a Room," *Urania*). There are other variations on this motif.
8. From Benedikt Livshits's poem "Days of Creation" (1914).
9. Brodsky, *Less Than One,* 458.
10. Information on the history of the Muruzi is available in a booklet by E. Z.

Kufershtein, K. M. Borisov, and O. E. Rubinchik, *Ulitsa Pestelya (Panteleimonovskaya)* (Leningrad: Svecha, 1991).

11. Brodsky, *Less Than One,* 452.
12. "A Petersburg Romance," chapter 27 (Brodsky, *SIB-2,* vol. 1, 65).
13. Ibid.
14. Shults, "Iosif Brodsky v 1961–1964 godakh," 77.
15. In Nikolay Gumilyov, *Sobranie sochinenii* (Washington, DC: Izdatelstvo knizhnogo magazina Victor Kamkin, 1962–1968), vol. 4, xxxv–xxxvi. Aleksandr Blok died of "nervous exhaustion"; Nikolay Gumilyov was executed and buried in an unmarked grave.
16. Brodsky, *Less Than One,* 450.
17. NLR, file 67, folio 52.
18. Brodsky, *Less Than One,* 488.
19. We do not know how well she spoke German. In "A Room and a Half," Brodsky recalls his mother "clasping her hands exclaiming 'Ach! oh wunderbar!' in German, the language of her Latvian childhood and her present occupation as an interpreter in a camp for German POWs" (Brodsky, *Less Than One,* 464). From this we might conclude that German was his mother's family's first language. On the other hand, in an early verse memoir of childhood, written in 1962 ("I thank the great Creator"), i.e., before the memory of his parents became the stuff of nostalgia, Brodsky remarked on his mother's German with a certain light irony: "For her knowledge of three hundred German words / I thank my very own mother: / she could understand the POWs— / while I was in the cottage yelling 'wa-ah,' / a prison camp provided her 'emploi'" (NLR, file 59). It is possible, too, that this was his source for the half-Yiddish, half-German gobbledygook he used in "Two Hours in a Container" (*OVP*).
20. Brodsky, *Less Than One,* 482.
21. NLR, file 63, folio 192.
22. NLR, file 63, folio 188.
23. Nadezhda Mandelstam, *Vtoraya kniga* (Moscow: Moskovskii rabochii, 1990), 90.
24. NLR, file 63, folio 187.
25. NLR, file 63, folios 188–189. See also Brodsky, *Less Than One,* 18.
26. Brodsky, *Bolshaya kniga intervyu,* 179.
27. Ibid., 180, also 163: "[My father] always thought I was a do-nothing, a lunkhead. He was rather strict, the way a father should be. A remarkable guy."
28. Ryūnosuke Akutagawa's original lines were "I don't have a conscience. I've just got nerves."
29. Brodsky, *On Grief and Reason,* 4.
30. From an unfinished poem (1961?); NLR, file 59, folio 75.
31. An exhibit of captured German weapons was opened in Solyony Gorodok in 1943; in 1946 the building became a museum. In 1953 purges of Leningrad Party higher-ups and the concurrent efforts to destroy Leningrad's

traditional image as the northern capital led to the museum's closing. It was reopened in 1989.

32. Brodsky, *Less Than One,* 466.
33. Ibid., 5.
34. E.g.: "in Russian literature before this Jew there had never been a genuine imperialist!" (Bar-Sella, *Tolkovaniya na . . . ,* 231).
35. Brodsky, *Less Than One,* 467.
36. Brodsky's 1968 poem "Pismo generalu Z" ("Letter to General Z," *KPE*), a satirical allegory of the Soviet invasion of Czechoslovakia, echoes Saint-Exupéry's pacifist essay "Letter to General X," written in North Africa in 1943, two months before his death. Several samizdat translations of it, including one by Brodsky's friend the young writer Rid Grachev, were circulated in Leningrad in the 1960s. The poem begins and ends with a same trope—gambling. It is very likely that gambling, too, was associated with Saint-Exupéry and originated in a story often told by Ekaterina Bulgakova, Grachev's widow, about meeting Saint-Exupéry at a party at the American embassy in Moscow on May 1, 1935: "The Frenchman, who turned out to be a pilot [in addition to being a journalist], was spinning tales about his dangerous flights and showing off card tricks" (Marietta Chudakova, *Zhizneopisanie Mikhaila Bulgakova* [Moscow: Kniga, 1988], 567).
37. The extensive literature on the cultural semiotics of Leningrad often talks of theatricality of the city. Consider: "In 1920 Mandelstam saw Petersburg as half-Venice, half-theater" (Anna Akhmatova, *Sochinenia v dvukh tomakh* [Moscow: Khudozhestvennaya literatura, 1986], vol. 2, 206) and "Petersburg is theatrical. The city is a stage: the center, Nevsky Prospekt, the embankments, the tip of Vasilievsky Island, the fortress of Saint Peter and Saint Paul, and the Rostral Columns—which are just prop lighthouses that were never lit. The fortress never defended anyone from anybody" (G. Tulchinsky, "Gorod—ispytaniy?" *Peterburgskie chtenia po teorii, istorii I filosofii kultury—chteniya I. Metafizika Peterburga* [Saint Petersburg: Eidos, 1993], 105).
38. Cf. the following about Mikhail Kuzmin's "Alexandrian Songs" (1908): "Antiquity in Russian Symbolism and, more broadly, Modernism, was extraordinarily widely used not only as a means to point to analogies in contemporary life . . . but also as a way of imagining modern times as an actual continuation of the mythology that the ancients had created and that had, as it passed through the centuries, been transformed into contemporary myth" (N. A. Bogomolov and John E. Malmstad, *Mikhail Kuzmin: Iskusstvo, zhizn, epokha* [Moscow: Novoe literaturnoe obozrenie, 1996], 105).
39. For a more detailed examination of Petersburg eschatology, see V. N. Toporov, "Petersburg and 'the Petersburg Text of Russian Literature' (Introduction to a Theme)," in Toporov, *Mif. Ritual. Simvol. Obraz. Issledovania v oblasti mifopoeticheskogo* (Moscow: Progress-Kultura, 1995), 259–367.
40. "Konstantin Vaginov was an utterly phenomenal author and a true Peters-

burger. . . . [T]he fabric of Vaginov's works is like some old, disintegrating curtain, yeah? What especially attracts me in Vaginov's texts is this sensation of loose muscle. . . . You feel this constantly in both his composition and his intonation" (Volkov, *Dialogi s Iosifom Brodskim*, 289, 290).

41. Brodsky, *Less Than One*, 59.
42. The exceptions were special schools in which a number of subjects were taught in a foreign language; these schools were attended primarily by the children of the Party elite or the well-connected. Well-off parents could pay for private language or music lessons.
43. Brodsky, *Less Than One*, 20–21.
44. Katz, *Artists in Exile*, 48.
45. I am grateful to V. V. Gerasimov for collecting the materials on Brodsky's school days now housed in the National Library of Russia (NLR, file 2, folios 1–6).
46. Konstantin Vaginov, *Kozlinaya pesn* (Moscow: Sovremennik, 1991), 112. "Goat Song" is a literal translation of the Greek *tragoidia*. Among the many poems by Nikolay Zabolotsky that Brodsky admired, he especially liked "Obvodny Kanal" (1928; Volkov, *Dialogi s Iosifom Brodskim*, 288). The flea market that Zabolotsky describes was a fixture on the corner of Ligovsky Prospekt and Obvodny Kanal until the mid-1950s. Although in Brodsky's day horse-drawn carts had more or less disappeared from city streets, the rest of the picture he paints is reminiscent of Zabolotsky's description: "And all around—the factory castles, black, / just underneath a cloud, a factory whistle . . . / and plaintively the carts wail, / mud, exploding, splashes, / the cripples sleep by the canal, / propped up by empty bottles."
47. Brodsky, *Bolshaya kniga intervyu*, 418.
48. Brodsky, "MS," vol. 1, 142. Many people remember these unpublished verses. Brodsky often recited them at public readings, and they circulated in samizdat (see Anatoly Pikach, "I ot chego my bolshe daleki?" *Novoe literaturnoe obozrenie* 14 [1995], 181–187). Some other poems that fall into Brodsky's "jazz" period include "Mothers-of-God of the outskirts, holy fathers of the outskirts, holy infants of the outskirts" (Brodsky, "MS," vol. 1, 65–66) and parts of "July Intermezzo" (Brodsky, *SIB-2*, vol. 1, 68–78) and "From the outskirts to the center" (ibid., 201–204). For more on Brodsky's "poetics of jazz" see Petrushanskaya, *Muzykalny mir Iosifa Brodskogo*.
49. Gordin, *Pereklichka vo mrake*, 140.
50. Brodsky said more than once that he had never managed to finish school (see, for example, Volkov, *Dialogi s Iosifom Brodskim*, 25; Brodsky, *Bolshaya kniga intervyu*, 414), but in late 1963 he sent a letter to the editors of *Evening Leningrad* to refute some of the libelous charges against him, including the charge that he was a "dropout who had never even finished high school": "I received my secondary education at night school, since at age fifteen I went to work in a factory. I have a document attesting to that, a diploma, which I am willing to present this very minute" (cited in Gordin, *Pereklichka vo*

mrake, 168). Brodsky may have been talking about the certificate he received for attending night classes.

51. Sergeev, *Omnibus,* 436.
52. For statistics and related information see G. V. Kostyrenko, *Tainaya politika Stalina* (Moscow: Mezhdunarodnye otnosheniya, 2001), chapter 5; and also Aleksandr Solzhenitsyn, *Dvesti let vmeste, Chast II* (Moscow: Russkii put, 2002), 404–405.
53. Katz, *Artists in Exile,* 48.
54. Language and culture are extremely general categories, and the Soviet concept of nationality as applied to a single representative of an ethnic group is not particularly useful. Just as Brodsky had defined himself in more exact terms, the language and culture that formed his individual self might be more precisely called the language and culture of the twentieth-century Russian intelligentsia. We might also add "the Leningrad intelligentsia." On the other hand, language and culture are not the final determinants of the self: the parameters of the self are never entirely fixed. So Brodsky's "linguistic self" changed as his life changed: through his dealings with the "nonintellectual" segments of society, through his sojourn in a northern village, through intensive study of Polish and English, and, finally, through his creation of a language of his own as he consciously sought to find yet-unrealized possibilities within his native tongue.
55. *Iosif Brodsky: Trudy i dni,* 59. See also Bondarenko, "Vzbuntovavshiyisya pasynok russkoy kultury." This nationalistically (but not chauvinistically) inclined critic brings a rather convincing set of facts to bear as he makes the case that Brodsky was generally uninterested in the "Jewish question." Even Solzhenitsyn reproaches Brodsky for this (Solzhenitsyn, "Iosif Brodsky—izbrannye stikhi," 191).
56. Aleksandr Ivanovich Brodsky, the poet's father, told me this sometime between 1972 and 1975. Brodsky had apparently merged his great-grandfather's and grandfather's life stories when he said: "My grandfather was a kantonist, served twenty-five years in the military, and he had a little print shop" (Brodsky, *Bolshaya kniga intervyu,* 412). In the first half of the nineteenth century, the government regularly conscripted orphans or boys from poor families. These were the kantonists. This institution was abolished in 1858. So if his grandfather had indeed been a kantonist, he would have been at least sixty when the poet's father was born in 1903.
57. Brodsky, *Bolshaya kniga intervyu,* 328. Was Brodsky ever in Brody? I never heard of any trips he made to Galicia, and assumed that he had only seen it from a train window on his way to Odessa or the Crimea. However, in an undated postcard that he sent to his parents from Milan (now part of the collection of the Akhmatova Museum in Saint Petersburg), Brodsky tells them that he'd stopped to take a look at da Vinci's *Last Supper,* and adds: "I remember I saw my first depiction of this 'business dinner' in Mliny, in an orchard with marvelous yellow plums" (From a copy of the postcard in my

archive). Mlin, or "mill," is a common toponym in Ukraine, and there is a village by that name not far from Brody.

58. Brodsky, *Bolshaya kniga intervyu,* 656.
59. Ibid., 655–656.

CHAPTER TWO

1. *Daugava* 6 (2001): 101.
2. Sergeev, *Omnibus,* 426.
3. Okhotin, "Osvobozhdenie," 70. Brodsky talked frankly about dodging the Soviet draft by faking his physical: "I had a nice doctor that everyone in Leningrad visited who needed to avoid the draft. She said I was emotionally disturbed and put me on medication . . . Hungarian 'uppers.' A good part of the city took them" (*Iosif Brodsky: Trudy i dni,* 53). This made for a good story, but as it later became clear, he did indeed have heart disease. An earlier deferment, at age eighteen, was given on grounds of family hardship; Brodsky's father had recently suffered a heart attack.
4. See the second chapter of *Less Than One.*
5. In autumn 1963, in his response to the *Evening Leningrad* article accusing him of being a parasite, Brodsky parried that he "had taken part in geological expeditions to Yakutia, the White Sea coast, Tian Shan, and Kazakhstan. It's all recorded in my work documents" (quoted in Gordin, *Pereklichka vo mrake,* 171). In all, Brodsky participated in five expeditions: to the White Sea in 1957 and 1958; to eastern Siberia and Yakutia in 1959 and 1961; and to Kazakhstan in 1962.
6. Ivanov, "Literaturnye pokolenia," 548.
7. Vladimir Britanishsky, *Poiski* (Leningrad: Sovetskii pisatel, 1958), 20, 14–15.
8. Brodsky, *Bolshaya kniga intervyu,* 141; see also Volkov, *Dialogi s Iosifom Brodskim,* 34.
9. A five-volume authorized samizdat collection of Brodsky's works (referred to as "MS") was compiled between 1972 and 1974 by Vladimir Maramzin; it has served as the main source for subsequent publications of Brodsky's pre-1972 works.
10. Brodsky, "MS," vol. 1, 3.
11. Cited from a photocopy given to the Hoover Institute by Eleonora Larionova.
12. Volkov, *Dialogi s Iosifom Brodskim,* 29.
13. Polukhina, *Brodsky glazami sovremennikov,* 113 (from an interview with Valentina Polukhina in June or July 2004).
14. Volkov, *Dialogi s Iosifom Brodskim,* 85.
15. NLR, file 63, folio 63. D. V. Bobyshev recalls that Brodsky did similar work at the Baltiysky shipyards. His job was to crawl inside pipes to check the welds (Bobyshev, "Ya zdes," 79).
16. Okhotin, "Osvobozhdenie," 68.

17. From Mikhail Lukonin's poem "Workday," in *Russkaya sovetskaya poezia* (Moscow: Khudozhestvennaya literatura, 1954), 695.
18. Brodsky, *Bolshaya kniga intervyu*, 150. Earlier, on page 133, we read that "in Leningrad, any author who takes up the pen—however young and inexperienced he might be—one way or the other associates himself with what Aleksandr Pushkin dubbed 'the harmony school.'" "Harmony school" is the standard term for a group of early nineteenth-century Russian romantic poets; it included, among others, Vasily Zhukovsky, Konstantin Batyushkov, and Pushkin himself.
19. *Iosif Brodsky: Trudy i dni*, 21–24.
20. A first, less representative edition of *French Lyrical Poetry* was entitled *Ot romantikov do syurrealistov* (Leningrad: Vremya, 1934). Mirsky's name was nowhere to be found in his *Anthology*—he had been arrested the same year it was to come out (1937). Instead, a certain M. Gutner (one of the translators) was listed as editor. Mirsky's anthology was revered among Brodsky's friends, and his own copy was a 1963 birthday gift from Mikhail Meilakh (Meilakh, "Osvobozhdenie ot emotsionalnosti," 159).
21. Shults, "Iosif Brodsky v 1961–1964 godakh," 77.
22. Brodsky, *Bolshaya kniga intervyu*, 417.
23. Ibid., 325.
24. Brodsky's second trip to Poland is recounted in a book by Elżbieta Tosza, *Stan serca: Trzy dni z Josifem Brodskim* (Katowice: Książnica, 1993).
25. Influenced by Umansky and his circle, Brodsky was for a time interested in the occult; for example, he made a stab at reading *The Arcana of the Tarot*, a tract by the early twentieth-century Russian mystic V. Shmakov (see Meylakh, "Osvobozhdenie ot emotsionalnosti," 162). The appeal was short-lived but left its mark in "Isaac and Abraham." In later poems like "Two Hours in a Container" (1965) and "A Speech about Spilt Milk" (1967) the occult came in for rather acerbic comment.
26. Brodsky, *Less Than One*, 488.
27. Volkov, *Dialogi s Iosifom Brodskim*, 34.
28. Brodsky, *Age Ago*, 153, 154, 157, 158, 160, 162, 166, 170, 171, 165.
29. Gleb Semyonov, *Proshchanie s osennim sadom* (Leningrad: Sovetsky pisatel), 112.
30. Nikolay Ushakov, *Stikhotvorenia* (Moscow: GIKhL, 1958), 68–69.
31. Vadim Shefner, *Izbrannye proizvedenia* (Leningrad: Khudozhestvennaya literatura, 1975), vol. 1, 137.
32. Vadim Shefner, "O rukopisi Iosifa Brodskogo 'Zimnyaya pochta,'" *Russkaya mysl*, November 11, 1988 (Literary supplement no. 7).
33. Quoted in Stanislav Rassadin, *Tak nachinayut zhit stikhom* (Moscow: Detskaya literatura, 1967), 63. Sergey Orlov (Seryozha) went on to become a professional poet and mid-level literary functionary. His main claim to fame was a popular poem about a slain soldier ("They buried him in this

earthly globe"). For Brodsky's comments on Orlov, see Volkov, *Dialogi s Iosifom Brodskim*, 53.

34. "Readings by G. Gorbovsky, V. Sosnora, A. Morev, K. Kuzminsky, N. Rubtsov, and I. Brodsky were especially popular. This sort of poetry was sometimes called 'variety show' or 'vocal.' The visual and aural contact with the audience influenced the prosody—the instrumentation of sound and the organization of rhythm" (Ivanov, "Literaturnye pokoleniya," 548). We should also include Evgeniy Rein in the list of young Leningrad poets who in the 1950s and 1960s adopted this extravagant, declamatory style for their public readings. In Moscow, the trend was represented by Evgeniy Evtushenko, Andrey Voznesensky, and Bella Akhmadulina.
35. Gordin, *Pereklichka vo mrake*, 134.
36. Aleksandr Ginzburg later recalled what the typewritten *Sintaksis* physically looked like: "The whole issue was maybe ten stacks of two or three half-page sheets. Five poems by one poet would make up a stack, ten stacks would make up an issue" (*Russkaya mysl*, October 30, 1987). Here Ginzburg also mentions that Brodsky's poems were brought to him in Moscow by the engineer Igor Guberman, who later became a popular poet and humorist. Guberman was excited and enthusiastic about Brodsky's work.
37. Published on September 2, 1960; the author was Yury Ivashchenko.
38. Brodsky says: "They took me the first time when *Sintaksis* came out" (Volkov, *Dialogi s Iosifom Brodskim*, 64). "Took me" in this case meant interrogation and threats rather than arrest. Brodsky was actually arrested and jailed twice in the USSR. This is confirmed by one of his manuscripts, an unfinished poem that begins "Since it happened that both times / it was January when they jailed me" and later says: "Two times of course are not enough / to see some pattern in it / And way too few for prison" (NLR, file 63, folio 97).
39. Volkov, *Dialogi s Iosifom Brodskim*, 65.
40. For information on the Umansky circle I am greatly obliged to Georgy Voskov-Ginzburg. See also Shakhmatov, "'Grekhi molodosti.'"
41. Volkov, *Dialogi s Iosifom Brodskim*, 66.
42. According to Georgy Voskov-Ginzburg's recollections, this was a treatise on philosophy and politics, written in the form of a letter to President John F. Kennedy.
43. There is no mention of this episode in *Belli Looks at Life and Law in Russia* (Indianapolis: Bobbs-Merrill, 1963), a book written by Melvin Belli and his traveling companion, Danny Jones, about their trip to the USSR.
44. Volkov, *Dialogi s Iosifom Brodskim*, 66.
45. Shakhmatov, "'Grekhi molodosti.'"
46. Two years later, a report by the KGB officer Volkov read as follows: "Shakhmatov and Umansky were found guilty on May 25, 1962, of the charge of anti-Soviet agitation and sentenced to five years of incarceration apiece. Brodsky's participation in this [affair] took the following form.

"Brodsky became acquainted with Shakhmatov in late 1957, at the Leningrad editorial offices of *Smena*. During their conversation he learned that Shakhmatov was also writing. This is what brought them together. Later he became acquainted with Umansky, and he and Shakhmatov would spend time with him.

"In 1960, after serving out his sentence for hooliganism, Shakhmatov moved to Krasnoyarsk, and from there to Samarkand. He wrote Brodsky two letters, invited him to visit, said that life was good in Samarkand.

"In late December 1960, Brodsky set out to visit his friend. Umansky gave him a manuscript of 'Mr. President' and told him to pass it along to Shakhmatov, which Brodsky did. Subsequently they showed this manuscript to the American journalist Belli Melvin and inquired about the possibility of publishing it abroad. After receiving no clear answer from Melvin, they took back the manuscript and did not show it to anyone else.

"It has also been established that a conversation took place between Shakhmatov and Brodsky about hijacking an airplane and flying it across the border. Which one of them was the initiator of this conversation is unclear. They went to the Samarkand airport several times to study its layout, but in the end Brodsky suggested to Shakhmatov that they give up the whole thing and return to Leningrad.

"Umansky was a student of yoga, an opponent of Marxism. He laid out his anti-Marxist views in 'Supermonism' and other writings.

"As for Brodsky, Umansky testified that he had read Brodsky's poetry and been very critical of it. He considered Brodsky [just] a chatterbox. He learned of Shakhmatov and Brodsky's treasonous intentions only after they returned to Moscow. He did not attest to any conversations with Brodsky of an anti-Soviet nature. Brodsky was not charged in the Umansky-Shakhmatov case. The Leningrad regional branch of the KGB has worked with him to prevent future deviant behavior" (Published by O. Edelman, Radio Liberty, 2001, www.svoboda.org/programs/td/2001/td.060301.asp). As this document makes clear, the KGB officer had not the slightest idea who Melvin Belli was, let alone which name was his first or which was his last.

CHAPTER THREE

1. Brodsky, *SIB-1*, vol. 1, 20 (not included in *SIB-2*).
2. Ibid., 30 (not included in *SIB-2*).
3. Ibid., 35 (not included in *SIB-2*). In all likelihood, Brodsky's poem is a response to Slutsky's "Sleep": "Morning breaking / rain spattering down. / I'm lying in a corner at the station" (first published in *Znamya*, no. 7 [1956]). Beyond the shared motif of sleeping at the train station, there are some parodic moments: Slutsky writes that he accepts his fate "like a

planet or a star," while Brodsky writes that he sees "only one planet: / an orange clockface." In Slutsky's poem, Lenin descends from his pedestal at the train station and bears down on the author just as Mozart's Commendatore does in *Don Giovanni.* In Brodsky's version, the "blue-eyed Vologda cops" turn out the author's pockets in search of ten-ruble notes (bearing Lenin's portrait). On Brodsky's generally sympathetic but ironic take on Slutsky, see Sergeev, *Omnibus,* 439. The contemporary Russian reader may be somewhat put off by the tone of Brodsky's comments and those of his circle, but these young poets interpreted Slutsky's illusions about Communism as a sort of eccentric naïveté. For all their admiration of the elder poet, their skepticism toward him deepened when in 1958, torn between his "duty to the Party" and his own sense of decency, Slutsky added his voice to the official chorus condemning Pasternak.

4. Kuzminsky, "Laureat 'Eriki,'" 11. Kuzminsky mistakenly dates this to 1958.
5. First published in *Znamya,* no. 2 (1957).
6. Before 1972 this was expressed primarily in strikingly varied and original stanza forms. For a close reading, see Scherr, "Strofika Brodskogo."
7. Boris Slutsky, *Sobranie sochinenii* (Moscow: Khudozhestvennaya literatura, 1991), vol. 1, 71. By the way, in this poem Slutsky rhymes a preposition with a noun (*nemnogo ot—gospod*), a device that would become one of Brodsky's trademarks.
8. Joseph Brodsky, "Literature and War—a Symposium," *Times Literary Supplement,* May 17, 1985, 544.
9. David Dar (1910–1980) ran a literary circle at the "Labor Reserve" House of Culture but regularly sent his best pupils to Semyonov. For all practical purposes, these two writers were the mentors for the young miners group. See V. L. Britanishsky's memoir, "Pluto's Abduction of Proserpine," in *Pod voronikhinskimi svodami,* ed. V. A. Tsaritsyn (Saint Petersburg: Neva, 2003), 13–44.
10. Evgeniy Rein, *Izbrannoe* (Moscow: Tretya volna, 1992).
11. Ibid., 6.
12. Ludwig Wittgenstein, *Notebooks: 1914–1916* (Chicago: University of Chicago Press, 1979), 75.
13. Evgeniy Rein, "Chelovek v peyzazhe," *Arion* 3 (1996): 34. Rein was interviewing Brodsky for a documentary film that never came to be. The book that Brodsky refers to is Baratynsky's *Polnoe sobranie sochinenii* (Leningrad: Sovetsky pisatel, 1957). The theme of "Brodsky and Baratynsky" is developed in "Brodsky and the Art of the Elegy," an article by Efim Kurganov, in *Iosif Brodsky: Tvorchestvo, lichnost, sudba,* 166–185.
14. Brodsky, *Age Ago,* 159.
15. Rein, "Moy ekzemplyar 'Uranii,'" 73.
16. Volkov, *Dialogi s Brodskim,* 224.
17. See Loseff, "O lyubvi Akhmatovoy k 'Narodu.'"
18. Akhmatova, *Zapisnye knizhki,* 234, 390.

19. See, for example, Brodsky, *Bolshaya kniga intervyu,* 174.
20. Volkov, *Dialogi s Iosifom Brodskim,* 256.
21. Chukovskaya, *Zapiski ob Anne Akhmatovoy,* vol. 3, 208.
22. Volkov, *Dialogi s Iosifom Brodskim,* 256.
23. Nadezhda Mandelstam, *Vospominaniya* (New York: Chekhov, 1970), 205.
24. Akhmatova, *Zapisnye knizhki,* 523.
25. Ibid., 588, 601, 637.
26. Ibid., 724.
27. Ibid., 679.
28. Herman Melville's *Moby-Dick* was first translated into Russian by I. Bernshtein in 1961. As Georgy Voskov-Ginzburg remembers, Brodsky enthusiastically recommended the book. Allusions to *Moby-Dick* may be found in "Letter in a Bottle," "The New Jules Verne," and "Minefield Revisited."
29. V. G. Admoni (1909–1993), a Leningrad linguist and poetry translator was one of the witnesses for the defense in Brodsky's 1964 trial.
30. Akhmatova, *Zapisnye knizhki,* 667. On Akhmatova and "Hymn to the People," see Loseff, "O lyubvi Akhmatovoy k 'Narodu.'" "Levushka," the son of Akhmatova and Nikolay Gumilyov, was L. N. Gumilyov (1912–1992), a medieval historian. He was arrested in 1933 and again in 1935 and served time in the Gulag in 1938–1943 and 1948–1956. His relationship with Akhmatova was strained.
31. Brodsky, *Bolshaya kniga intervyu* 174.
32. Chukovskaya, *Zapiski ob Anne Akhmatovoy,* 73, 81.
33. See Gorbanevskaya, "Po ulitse Brodskogo," 16. See "Illustration," in Brodsky, *SIB-2,* vol. 2, 26.
34. As of this writing, the circumstances around the affair have become public knowledge, mainly thanks to Dmitriy Bobyshev's kiss-and-tell memoir (Bobyshev, "Ya zdes"). Brodsky had given interviewers nothing more than a general outline of the story (see, for example, Brodsky, *Bolshaya kniga intervyu,* 212).
35. Chukovskaya, *Zapiski ob Anne Akhmatovoy,* vol. 3, 141; Bobyshev, "Ya zdes."
36. Volkov, *Dialogi s Iosifom Brodskim,* 317.
37. Ibid.
38. In Brodsky, *SIB,* this is erroneously dated 1983. Although we do not have the exact date the poem was composed, it was most likely written in 1963 or 1964. Aside from the stylistic characteristics that place it in that period, the author put it at the very beginning of *New Stanzas to Augusta,* that is, within the "Songs of a Happy Winter" cycle.
39. Brodsky, *Bolshaya kniga intervyu,* 150.
40. The most frequently seen colors in Brodsky (including verbs like to "show" or "loom" white, and the noun "whiteness") are white and black; after them in diminishing but uneven order come red, gray, green, blue, brown, and dark blue (Patera, *Concordance,* book 6).

CHAPTER FOUR

1. See William Taubman, *Khrushchev: The Man and His Era* (New York: Norton, 2003), 591.
2. L. F. Ilyichev, "Fundamental Ideological Objectives in Party Work," *Plenum TsK KPSS 18–21 iyunya 1963. Stenografichesky otchet* (Moscow: Izdatelstvo politicheskoy literatury, 1964), 58–59.
3. Ibid., 36.
4. Ibid., 26.
5. Quoted in Yupp, "Osya Brodsky?"
6. Lurye, "Svoboda poslednego slova," 166, 167.
7. Lerner is described thus: "This is a man profoundly unhappy at working as a low-level manager and eager to move into a position of power; he saw the community patrols as his chance. He made connections within the militia, the prosecutor's office, among party functionaries and KGB investigators, and offered his valuable services to all. . . . He by nature likes nosing around, playing the provocateur. Mistrustful and ambitious" (Chukovskaya, "Delo Brodskogo" 159). According to I. M. Metter, a police-story writer who had friends among the top brass of the Leningrad militia, Yakov Lerner had been an informer for the NKVD, the KGB's immediate predecessor, in his youth in the 1930s (Gordin, "Delo Brodskogo," 149). Eventually Lerner went too far. He began dabbling in extortion and dropping the names of his official patrons in city government. Twice, in 1973 and 1984, he was tried for fraud, found guilty, and served time in prison. Brodsky's parents attended the first of these trials. Even after completing his second sentence, by which time Gorbachev's perestroika had begun, Lerner continued to publish the "truth about Brodsky" in extremist anti-Semitic publications.
8. Yakimchuk, *Kak sudili poeta,* 31.
9. *Literaturnaya gazeta,* June 4, 1997, 14.
10. Chukovskaya, *Zapiski ob Anne Akhmatovoy,* vol. 3, 385.
11. Ibid., 170.
12. Leningrad newspaper circles were relatively small, and Medvedev (Berman) and Ionin found themselves in a rather ticklish position, since the article they had put their name to would most likely send the son of their colleague Aleksandr Brodsky to prison. Both maintained that all they had done was edit Lerner's draft for publication, and that had they refused to do it, they would have lost their jobs.
13. Quoted in Gordin, *Pereklichka vo mrake,* 159, 163.
14. Ibid., 162.
15. Ibid., 163.
16. Six months later Ilyichev was to give his sanction to the case against Brodsky. In conversation with Aleksey Surkov he called the poet "scum" (Chukovskaya, *Zapiski ob Anne Akhmatovoy,* 217).

17. *Rodina* 12 (2006), http://www.istrodina.com/rodina_articul.php3?id=1999&n=105.
18. Gordin, *Pereklichka vo mrake,* 167–172.
19. See chapter VI, note 13.
20. Okhotin, "Osvobozhdenie," 70.
21. Gordin, *Pereklichka vo mrake,* 175. Efim Etkind claims that the actual author of the epigram was the poet Mikhail Dudin, who was soon to replace Prokofyev as head of the Leningrad Writers' Union (Etkind, *Zapiski nezagovorshchika,* 155).
22. Shneiderman, "Krugi na vode," 194. In February the Writers' Union sent a community prosecutor to Brodsky's trial. Since none of the more or less self-respecting writers was willing to play that particular role, the organization named the hack detective novelist E. V. Voevodin as its official representative.
23. Ibid., 196.
24. See Loseff, "On Hostile Ground."
25. Brodsky, *SIB-2,* vol. 2, 11.
26. Akhmatova, *Zapisnye knizhki,* 421. Aleksey Surkov (1899–1983), one of the leading Soviet propaganda versifiers and a powerful apparatchik, was a secret admirer and supporter of Akhmatova. See Roman Timenchik, *Anna Akhmatova v 1960-e gody* (Moscow: Vodoley Publishers; Toronto: University of Toronto, 2005), 327–328.
27. At his first court hearing, on February 18, 1964, Brodsky said that he had been discharged from the hospital on January 5 (Gordin, *Pereklichka vo mrake,* 182). This might have been Vigdorova's mistake, or Brodsky's, or a slip of the pen in his discharge papers, which were dated the 5th. But in fact Brodsky had arrived in Leningrad on the 3rd to confront Basmanova and Bobyshev. For an understandably subjective account of the affair see Bobyshev, "Ya zdes."
28. Chukovskaya, *Zapiski ob Anne Akhmatovoy,* vol. 1, 73, 81.
29. Brodsky, *SIB-2,* vol. 2, 21–22. "Letters to the Wall" has a quite specific location. The brick wall onto which the speaker's shadow falls is one of the walls of Kresty prison on Arsenal Embankment, close by the factory and the hospital where Brodsky worked as a teenager.
30. See Loseff, "Pervyi liricheskiy tsikl Iosifa Brodskogo," 68.
31. Gordin, "Delo Brodskogo," 150.
32. Ibid., 151.
33. Gordin, *Pereklichka vo mrake,* 181.
34. Ibid., 181, 182.
35. Brodsky's friend the poet Natalya Gorbanevskaya was one of those who would eventually go through "trial by psychiatry." On the punitive use of psychiatry by the Soviets see Sidney Bloch and Peter Reddaway, *Psychiatric Terror: How Soviet Psychiatry Is Used to Suppress Dissent* (New York: Basic

Books, 1977). On how Brodsky used his stay at Pryazhka as material for "Gorbunov and Gorchakov" see Loseff, "On Hostile Ground."

36. Gordin, *Pereklichka vo mrake,* 186.
37. See Etkind, *Zapiski nezagovorshchika,* 166.
38. Gordin, *Pereklichka vo mrake,* 184.
39. Gordin, "Delo Brodskogo," 153.
40. Chukovskaya, *Zapiski ob Anne Akhmatovoy,* 473. One of the witnesses, the Hermitage assistant maintenance director F. O. Logunov later regretted taking part in the trial: he had been called in by the Dzerzhinsky district Party office and felt that he could not refuse (Yakimchuk, *Kak sudili poeta,* 21).
41. Gordin, *Pereklichka vo mrake,* 159.
42. Ibid., 156.
43. Yakimchuk, *Kak sudili poeta,* 23.
44. Gordin, *Pereklichka vo mrake,* 187.
45. Quoted in Shneiderman, "Krugi na vode," 185.
46. Gordin, *Pereklichka vo mrake,* 183.
47. Ibid.
48. See Chukovskaya's diaries for a detailed account of the fight to save Brodsky (Chukovskaya, *Zapiski ob Anne Akhmatovoy,* passim).
49. Pascal Boulanger, *Une "action poétique" de 1950 à aujourd'hui* (Paris: Flammarion, 1998), 199, 200–201.
50. John Berryman, *The Dream Songs* (London: Faber and Faber, 1969), 199.
51. Before Brodsky's trial, the Western press had written a great deal about the harassment of the writer Valery Tarsis; soon after Brodsky's trial it would make much of the persecution of Andrey Sinyavsky and Yuly Daniel. Later it would take up the cause of Aleksandr Zinoviev and others. But their literary successes were short-lived. In the latter half of the twentieth century, only Brodsky and Solzhenitsyn were to find a place in world culture—even before either was awarded the Nobel Prize.
52. See Chaikovskaya, "Netochnye, nevernye zerkala."
53. A decidedly different image of Brodsky is projected in the person of Chigrashov, the poet-protagonist of Sergey Gandlevsky's novel *Illegible* (2002). Chigrashov has other prototypes, but the author endows him with some of Brodsky's traits, adds elements of Brodsky's biography, and, in giving examples of Chigrashov's work, paraphrases the final sonnet of "Twenty Sonnets to Mary Queen of Scots" and "Seven Strophes."
54. Etkind, *Zapiski nezagovorshchika,* 170.
55. Volkov, *Dialogi s Iosifom Brodskim,* 76.
56. In the history of the dissident movement of the 1960s–1970s the Brodsky case was the first big battle to be fought and won. Significantly, Raisa Orlova titles her essay about it "The Turning-Point Case." In this respect, Brodsky himself was merely the object of the struggle; its true heroes were Vigdorova and other defenders of the poet. About Vigdorova Orlova writes:

"She, too, was the accused; she was tried along with Brodsky." And: "Here Judge Savelyeva in alliance with the forces of darkness tried [not just Brodsky] but every member of the Soviet intelligentsia. *This is why* one cannot read the trial transcripts without being horrified" (quoted in Etkind, *Protsess Iosifa Brodskogo,* 93; emphasis added).

57. Gordin, "Delo Brodskogo," 153.
58. When first published, the poem had sixteen additional lines written a year later in a different cell, and the title was more ironic: "Chamber Music." In Russian, the adjective *kamerny* may refer either to a prison cell or to a musical ensemble.
59. Joseph Brodsky, "The Writer in Prison," *New York Times Book Review,* October 13, 1996, 24–25.
60. Volkov, *Dialogi s Iosifom Brodskim,* 82. In the fall of 1965, Yuly Daniel and Andrey Sinyavsky were indicted for publishing anti-Soviet materials in foreign presses. In early 1966, both were found guilty and sentenced to forced labor: Daniel for five years, Sinyavsky for seven.
61. This poem from the cycle "Sweetbriar in Blossom. From the Burnt Notebook" was written in July 1962, the period when Brodsky met with Akhmatova regularly. It is very likely that she read him this new poem.

CHAPTER FIVE

1. See, for example, Disch, review of *A Part of Speech;* Kirsch, "Art of the Contemporary," 40.
2. Coetzee's images of "a poet like himself" were no doubt gleaned from Solzhenitsyn's *One Day in the Life of Ivan Denisovich.*
3. J. M. Coetzee, *Youth: Scenes from Provincial Life II* (London: Secker and Warburg, 2002), 91. Brodsky had high praise for Coetzee's prose: "He is the only one who has a right to write prose after Beckett" (Brodsky, *On Grief and Reason,* 478). Brodsky was chagrined at the cool reception that Coetzee gave *On Grief and Reason* (J. M. Coetzee, "Speaking for Language," *New York Review of Books,* February 1, 1996). Although the article came out after his death, as a subscriber to *New York Review of Books,* Brodsky would have received the journal two or three weeks before the date shown on the front page.
4. Volkov, *Dialogi s Iosifom Brodskim,* 89.
5. What might seem just a modest little "nature sketch" provides a significant set of contrasts. The skywriting pilot suggests the author's childhood dreams of flying. Although the author never became a pilot, even jouncing atop a seeder, powdered by grit, he is "like Mozart." Brodsky paid less attention to the realities of farming: his seeder somehow turns into a harrow (although it may be that the tractor driver simply called the attachment by the same name). "Seeds turned and bristled" also sounds rather strange. This may be why he did not publish the poem: it was eventually included in his collected works.

6. Zabaluyev, "Konoshsky period poeta," 156.
7. Brodsky, *Bolshaya kniga intervyu,* 433.
8. Maksudov, "Komandirovka v Norinskuyu," 201–202.
9. Bobyshev, "Ya zdes," 73–75.
10. See Efimov, "Shag vpravo shag vlevo."
11. Solzhenitsyn, "Iosif Brodsky—izbrannye stikhi," 182.
12. Quoted in Gordin, *Pereklichka vo mrake,* 137.
13. Ibid.
14. Such poetics are also termed Acmeist. While Pasternak was never part of the day-to-day literary life of the Acmeist circle, his poetics were in principle very like Mandelstam's and Akhmatova's, especially in those features that Brodsky mentions in the letter quoted here. Yakov Gordin quotes remarks by Pasternak on the primacy of structure; these have much in common with Brodsky's thoughts on the matter (ibid., 138).
15. A very loose variation indeed. Brodsky recalled to friends that in Norenskaya he sometimes read and translated into Russian only the first and last lines of an English poem and then tried to "fill in the blanks."
16. It was in Oscar Williams's oft-reprinted *New Pocket Anthology of American Verse from Colonial Days to the Present* that Brodsky studied the "smallish black-and-white box[es]"—the portraits that he mentions in "To Please a Shadow."
17. See Brodsky, *Bolshaya kniga intervyu,* 154; Volkov, *Dialogi s Iosifom Brodskim,* 159–161.
18. Brodsky used the metaphor of parallel lines in "The End of a Beautiful Era" and a number of other poems.
19. See Brodsky's translation into Russian in *OVP;* see also G. Kruzhkov's fine translation in *Dzhon Donn: Izbrannoe* (Moscow: Moskovsky rabochii, 1994), 54–55.
20. On the fundamental resemblance of the "Futurist-raised" Mayakovsky and Pasternak to the English metaphysical poets see Dmitriy Svyatopolk-Mirsky's 1937 essay in D. Mirsky, *Statyi o literature* (Moscow: Khudozhestvennaya literatura, 1987), 35.
21. For a painstaking analysis of Brodsky's metaphors, see Polukhina, *Joseph Brodsky: A Poet for Our Time;* Polukhina and Pyarli, *Slovar tropov Brodskogo.*
22. L. N. Tolstoy, *Sobranie sochinenii v dvadtsati dvukh tomakh* (Moscow: Khudozhestvennaya literatura, 1983), vol. 15, 80.
23. I make these broad generalizations here solely in order to describe some of the essential differences between Russian and Anglo-American modernist lyric poetry. These are tendencies, not absolute facts. Subtexts that suggest "back stories" are characteristic of Akhmatova as well, and other Russian poets have also effectively spoken between the lines. The greatest Russian master of the unsaid, however, was not a poet but a prose writer—Anton Chekhov. For a discussion of the "Chekhovian" in Akhmatova and Brod-

sky, see Loseff, *Chekhovsky lirizm u Brodskogo,* and Loseff, "Iosif Brodsky: Erotika."

24. Volkov, *Dialogi s Iosifom Brodskim,* 98. Brodsky is not entirely accurate here. The action in Frost's poems does not always take place within four walls.
25. Ibid., 99, 101–102.
26. In his essay "On Grief and Reason," Brodsky mentions the influential American critic Lionel Trilling, who was perhaps the first to point out the darkness that underlies many of Frost's pastorales. Oddly enough, though, nowhere does Brodsky ever refer to an extended 1962 essay by Randall Jarrell, not only written on the same topic but also based on an analysis of the same poem Brodsky had chosen, "Home Burial." One explanation might be that Brodsky took offense at Jarrell's attacks on Auden's later poetry. Along the way we should note a mistake in the annotations to the Russian version of "On Grief and Reason" in *SIB-2:* Brodsky did not in fact attend Frost's reading in Leningrad in 1962. He was out of the city at the time of Frost's visit.
27. Brodsky, *Less Than One,* 361–363.
28. Ibid., 382. The reminder that life is finite ("since we have just one life"; his poem on Akhmatova's centenary) demonstrates the existentialist paradigm of Brodsky's thought: knowledge and the remembrance that life is finite determines the importance of the choices (true or false) that human beings make.
29. See Yakovich, "'Delo' Brodskogo na Staroy ploshchadi"; and Okhotin, "Osvobozhdenie."
30. Okhotin, "Osvobozhdenie," 70.
31. Ibid., 71.
32. Ibid.
33. See Chukovskaya, "Delo Brodskogo," 149.
34. Ibid., 154.
35. From a document presented to the Central Committee by KGB chairman Semichastny; in Yakovich, "'Delo' Brodskogo na Staroy Ploshchadi."

CHAPTER SIX

1. Sergeev, *Omnibus,* 440–441.
2. Rybakov, *Roman-vospominanie,* 370–372.
3. See Chukovskaya, *Zapiski ob Anne Akhmatovoy,* vol. 3, 206.
4. Ibid., 317. Brodsky said that Tvardovsky's comments on his poem were "very courteous" but that Tvardovsky himself was a "sad and ruined man" (Volkov, *Dialogi s Iosifom Brodskim,* 108).
5. Sergeev, *Omnibus,* 439.
6. Artistic and psychological implications of Aesopian language are discussed in my book Lev Loseff, *On the Beneficence of Censorship: Aesopian Language in Modern Russian Literature* (Münich: Sagner Verlag, 1986).

7. On the history of *Short Poems and Narratives,* see Kline, "Istoriya dvukh knig"; and Kuzminsky, "Iskusstvo vopreki."
8. For the reviews see "'*Zimnyaya pochta.*"
9. Ibid., iv.
10. Ibid., v.
11. Ibid.
12. Ibid., v–vi.
13. Elena Klepikova, a former editorial assistant at *Avrora,* a Leningrad youth magazine, describes one of Brodsky's last attempts at getting published in his homeland: "Brodsky radiated an almost superhuman charm. Even the chief editor, [Nina] Kosareva, a party functionary but a lady of a certain liberal bent, fell under the poet's spell; to be sure, she first reassured herself that the Regional Party Committee would support this. The Regional Committee examined the Brodsky selection and suggested, of course, some changes. Nothing too big, nothing too painful for the poet. Brodsky refused to make any at all but offered to replace some poems instead. This little game between the Regional Committee and Brodsky went on for a few rounds. And, finally, for the first time in Joseph's memory, a selection of his poems was approved by [Party] higher-ups and scheduled for inclusion in the upcoming issue of *Avrora.* . . . To make a long story short, the Regional Committee and the KGB had agreed to a compromise, but [in the end] it was a group of venerable and influential poets who resolutely, albeit privately, blocked publication. These senior editors—average age sixty-seven—held an emergency meeting late at night in the empty *Avrora* offices solely to discuss Brodsky's poems, which were about to go to press. And these overzealous mastodons killed the selection because of its 'inferior artistic quality and deliberate obfuscation of meaning'" (Klepikova, "Trizhdy nachinayushchiysya pisatel"). On Kosareva's role in Brodsky's exile and return see chapters IV and V of this book.
14. For the story of how *A Halt in the Desert* came to be published, see Kline, "Istoriya dvukh knig."
15. Ibid., 219.
16. Ibid., 222–223. Brodsky found seventy mistakes in the book; all were corrected in the 2000 edition.
17. Yury Ivask, "Iosif Brodsky, 'Ostanovka v pustyne,'" *Novy zhurnal* 102 (1971): 296.
18. Vyacheslav Zavalishin, "Podlinnyi Brodsky i mif o Brodskom," *Novoe russkoe slovo,* August 9, 1970.
19. G. Andreev, "Pod maskoi emigratsii," *Novoe russkoe slovo,* June 14, 1970. See also M. Koryakov, "Listki iz bloknota: Izdatelstvo im. Chekhova," *Novoe russkoe slovo,* June 25, 1970.
20. Edward Kline, letter to the editor, *Novoe russkoe slovo,* July 11, 1970.
21. Brodsky with Kline, "A Poet's Map of His Poem," 228.
22. Gorbanevskaya, "Po ulitse Brodskogo," 16.

23. Sergeev, *Omnibus*, 432.
24. Volkov, *Dialogi s Iosifom Brodskim*, 101. E. Petrushanskaya tentatively links the idea for the poem with Stravinsky's "Isaac and Abraham," a ballad for baritone and chamber orchestra. Stravinsky had traveled to the USSR in 1962, and there he mentioned that he was working on this new piece; Brodsky had long been interested in the composer (Petrushanskaya, *Muzykalnyi mir Iosifa Brodskogo*, 40–41).
25. Z. Bar-Sella, "Strakh i trepet. Iz knigi 'Iosif Brodsky. Opyty chteniya,'" *22*, no. 41 (1985): 213.
26. Polukhina, *Joseph Brodsky: A Poet for Our Time*, 264.
27. Sergeev, *Omnibus*, 428.
28. Volkov, *Dialogi s Iosifom Brodskim*, 195.
29. Brodsky, *Bolshaya kniga intervyu*, 279.
30. Patera, *Concordance;* Demetrius J. Koubourlis, ed., *A Concordance to the Poems of Osip Mandelstam* (Ithaca, NY: Cornell University Press, 1974). See also *Slovar yazyka Pushkina* (Moscow: Gosudarstvennoe izdatelstvo inostrannykh i natsionalnykh slovarey, 1957, 1961), vols. 2, 4.
31. Volkov, *Dialogi s Iosifom Brodskim*, 195.
32. See Proffer, "Stop in the Madhouse."
33. Vyacheslav Vs. Ivanov, "Khudozhestvennoe tvorchestvo, funktsionalnaya asimmetriya mozga i obraznye sposobnosti cheloveka," *Tekst i kultura. Trudy po znakovym sistemam XVI. Uchenye zapiski Tartuskogo gosudarstvennogo universiteta* 635 (1983): 12.
34. *Vladimir Nabokov: Selected Letters, 1940–1977*, ed. Dmitri Nabokov and Matthew J. Bruccoli (New York: Harcourt Brace Jovanovich 1989).
35. Brodsky, *Bolshaya kniga intervyu*, 567–568. The echo of Jung is easy enough to hear; the sea is his chief symbol of the unconscious, and here it plays an important role, especially in chapter 13 ("Conversations about the Sea").
36. M. M. Bakhtin, *Estetika slovesnogo tvorchestva* (Moscow: Iskusstvo, 1979), 288–289.
37. Cf. the end of "Nature Morte," in *The End of a Beautiful Era*, and comments in chapter VII.
38. Proffer, "Stop in the Madhouse," 348–349.
39. Father Aleksandr Shmeman, *Lent* (Paris: YMCA-Press, 1986), 91.
40. The same sense of the word "doctor" (teacher) comes through in Pasternak's choice of a Christ-like hero in *Doctor Zhivago*.
41. In "MS," the date for the first draft is given as May 1964: "Gorbunov was lying by the window / and Gorchakov was sprawling not too far away" (NLR, file 67, folio 57).
42. The date is sometimes given as May 10, but Brodsky recalled it as "a Friday evening" (Brodsky, *Bolshaya kniga intervyu*, 658). That year the second Friday in May was not the 10th but the 12th.
43. Ibid.

44. Brodsky himself suspected that his swift eviction had to do with the upcoming visit of U.S. president Richard Nixon: "Nixon was on his way, and the streets were being cleared" (ibid., 160; see also Volkov, *Dialogi s Iosifom Brodskim,* 125). As Evgeniy Evtushenko tells it, in April 1972, when he was called in for a talk with the chief officer of the KGB ideological department, F. D. Bobkov, he pleaded with Bobkov to stop harassing Brodsky and let him leave the country quietly. Brodsky never forgave Evtushenko, not for suggesting exile, but for keeping him in the dark about the conversation (Volkov, *Dialogi s Iosifom Brodskim,* 126–131).

CHAPTER SEVEN

1. On the fundamental impossibility of reducing Brodsky's philosophy to a coherent system, see Ranchin, "Filosofskaya traditsiya Iosifa Brodskogo."
2. Brumm, "Muse in Exile," 233.
3. While Brodsky was rather active in politics after he left the USSR, commentary on his political philosophy and political activity has been largely superficial. In contrast, his religious and philosophical views have been the subject of several serious studies: see Kelebay, *Poet v dome rebenka;* Plekhanova, *Metafizicheskaya misteriya Iosifa Brodskogo;* Radyshevsky, "Dzen poezii Brodskogo."
4. Brodsky, *Less Than One,* 368.
5. This very line is the reason that Auden cut "September 1, 1939" from his last collection: we are doomed to die no matter whether we follow the commandment to love one another or not (there was also a discarded variant—"We must love one another and die"). Brodsky reasoned as follows: "For the actual meaning of the line at the time was, of course, that 'We must love one another or kill.' Or 'We'll be killing one another in no time.' Since—after all, all he had was a voice and this wasn't heard or heeded" (Brodsky, *Less Than One,* 353). Brodsky's intuition here proves right in light of "Aubade," a late poem by Auden that Brodsky apparently did not know (or hadn't thought of) at the time he was writing his article. In "Aubade," Auden clarifies this thought: we live through human speech, through the act of communication: "Listen, Mortals, Lest Ye Die." In listening to the past and addressing the future, humankind is part of the continuum of being. On Auden's part, this was less a response to Horace than it was a reaction to the metaphysics of speech discussed in the works of Eugen Rosenstock-Huessy, an émigré Austrian-Jewish philosopher then teaching at Dartmouth College. Rosenstock-Huessy's views on the significance of dialogue were close to those of his friend Martin Buber as well as to those of Mikhail Bakhtin. Auden had read Rosenstock-Huessy's *Speech and Reality* quite closely: he understood the author's main point to be "Audi, ne moriamur" ("Listen, and you will not die"). See John Fuller, *W. H. Auden: A Commentary* (Princeton, NJ: Princeton University Press, 1998), 545.

6. Brodsky, *On Grief and Reason,* 44.
7. Brodsky, *Less Than One,* 115.
8. Ibid.
9. Ibid., 121. Brodsky died four years before the process of democratization in his native Russia was aborted, as the mechanism he describes here ground into action: the masses wanted stability; a virtual single-party system emerged; a generic leader took charge ("the drab, unspectacular appearance of [Party] leaders appeal[s] to the masses as their own reflection"; ibid., 116).
10. Chukovskaya, *Zapiski ob Anne Akhmatovoy,* 480.
11. "The Residence" (1983) was written with then General Secretary Yury Andropov in mind (see Rein, "Moy ekzemplyar 'Uranii,'" 194).
12. Quoted in Gordin, *Pereklichka vo mrake,* 219.
13. The metaphor of a "forest" of hands raised in unanimous approval of Party policy is a borrowing from Auden's "Spain": "The eager election of chairmen / By the sudden forest of hands." Brodsky uses this metaphor in the opposite, satirical, sense (see Anthony Hecht, *The Hidden Law: The Poetry of W. H. Auden* [Cambridge, MA: Harvard University Press, 1993], 129).
14. See Brodsky, "Says Poet Brodsky."
15. Brodsky, *Less Than One,* 385.
16. Volkov, *Dialogi s Iosifom Brodskim,* 182.
17. In everyday Soviet parlance, the word "individualism" was a synonym for selfishness. Brodsky was a thoroughgoing individualist; he was also an altruist. Therefore our use of the word "individualism" corresponds to his sense of it: intellectual independence and moral responsibility for one's actions, including any action by a group to which that individual belongs.
18. One odd coincidence: in the 1980s, Brodsky became part owner of a restaurant on Fifty-second Street. But it was hardly a dive.
19. Volkov, *Dialogi s Iosifom Brodskim,* 51. In the standard, two-volume edition of Tyutchev the lyric poems are concentrated in the first volume and the civic poems in the second.
20. Brodsky's initial acquaintance with Solovyov came from reading his articles in the Brokhaus-Efron encyclopedia, but later he was given the philosopher's collected works in a reprint edition brought by a friend from abroad.
21. For a more detailed discussion see Loseff, "Home and Abroad."
22. The Brodsky quotation is from Brodsky, *SIB-2,* vol. 2, 373.
23. Quoted in Boris Paramonov, "Sovetskoe evraziystvo," *Novoe russkoe slovo,* August 22, 1989.
24. "The modern philosopher sees Mohammedanism as the ultimate ideal: I believe in the one God Allah and his prophet Mohammed. He who does not acknowledge Mohammed or Allah is an unbeliever" (Lev Shestov, *Potestas Clavium* [Berlin: Skify, 1923], http://www.zhurnal.ru/magister/

library/philos/shestov/shest18.htm). For commentary on Shestov's and Brodsky's use of Islam as a metaphor see Kelebay, *Poet v dome rebenka,* 109.

25. Sergey Esenin, *Sobranie sochinenii* (Moscow: Khudozhestvennaya literatura, 1966), vol. 2, 119.
26. Osip Mandelstam, *Sochineniya* (Moscow: Khudozhestvennaya literatura, 1990), vol. 1, 177. See also fragments left from poems that were destroyed: "I returned, no—read: by force / I was brought back to Buddhist Moscow" and "You want to live, then look and smile / On milk that's Buddhist blue, / Cast an eye on Turkish drums" (ibid., 180–181).
27. Semen Frank, "The Ethic of Nihilism: A Characterization of the Russian Intelligentsia's Moral Outlook," in Boris Shragin and Albert Todd, eds., *Landmarks: A Collection of Essays on the Russian Intelligentsia, 1909* (New York: Karz Howard, 1977), 174.
28. Brodsky, *Bolshaya kniga intervyu,* 458–459.
29. In his famous poem "Panmongolism" (1894), Vladimir Solovyov admits that Russia is "the East" but asks what will it choose to become—"the East of Xerxes" or "the East of Christ."
30. Brodsky, "Why Milan Kundera Is Wrong about Dostoyevsky," 31, 33.
31. See Aist, "Iosif Brodsky—perevodchik s kitayskogo."
32. See Solzhenitsyn, "Iosif Brodsky—izbrannye stikhi," 192–193.
33. See Turoma, "Poet kak odinokii turist."
34. Birkerts, "Art of Poetry XXVIII," 110. When asked by a journalist whether the rumors about his official conversion to Christianity were true, Brodsky shot back that they were "stark, raving nonsense!" (Benedict, "Flight from Predictability," 21).
35. "Judases," *Kontinent* 43 (1985): 380–381. Brodsky is not the only "Judas" in this angry, incoherent letter; the editors of *Kontinent* are named as well.
36. "As far as faith is concerned, one shouldn't think that it has to be the product of suffering, and so on. I think that people can gain faith through happiness as well. It's quite possible. I've seen it happen" (Brodsky, *Bolshaya kniga intervyu,* 467).
37. Volkov, *Dialogi s Iosifom Brodskim,* 256.
38. Brodsky, *RS-2,* 68. Evgeniy Kelebay devotes an entire chapter to what I consider an overly literal interpretation of Brodsky's "Calvinism" (see Kelebay, *Poet v dome rebenka,* 270–286). Brodsky himself cautioned that he wasn't all that serious about the connection (ibid.).
39. Brodsky, *On Grief and Reason,* 214.
40. Shestov was Brodsky's favorite Russian thinker. More likely than not, Brodsky began reading Shestov in issues of *Sovremennye zapiski* belonging to Sergey Shults, but by the mid-1960s he owned several of Shestov's books, reprint editions published by YMCA-Press in Paris. Before leaving the USSR, Brodsky made me a gift of one of these—*Sola Fide.* In the West, a shared admiration for Shestov led to friendship between Brodsky and two other remarkable poets—Czesław Miłosz and Octavio Paz.

41. Brodsky, *Less Than One*, 66–67.
42. That is, if we exclude auxiliary words and pronouns, "soul" is number nineteen; more frequent are "one/alone," "life," "eye," "time," "here," "window," "person," "hand," "earth," "[to] know," "year," "[to] say," "night," "word," "face," "[to] see," and "light." The word "love" is twentieth. (See Patera, *Concordance*, book 6.)
43. Vladimir Maramzin, *Tyanitolkay* (Ann Arbor, MI: Ardis, 1981), 239.
44. First and foremost, Genrikh Sapgir, Stas Krasovitsky, and Mikhail Eryomin.
45. For the "other poems" see Brodsky, *SIB-2*, vol. 1, 26–27.
46. Brodsky, *Bolshaya kniga intervyu*, 513.
47. Albert Camus, *The Plague, The Fall, Exile and the Kingdom, and Selected Essays* (New York: Knopf, 2004), 538.
48. Ibid., 592.
49. There is no such episode in the Gospels. In all probability the idea came from Akhmatova's "Requiem," which also contains ten chapters, the last of which ("Crucifixion") abruptly shifts time and place and depicts two scenes from the Gospels. In the first of these Akhmatova quotes Christ's words to Mary "Do not weep for Me, O Mother" from the Easter Eve liturgy.
50. For a commentary on "Nature Morte," see also Loseff, "Joseph Brodsky's Poetics of Faith."
51. For detailed discussions of how some of Brodsky's themes relate to various philosophies, see Kelebay, *Poet v dome rebenka;* Ranchin, *Iosif Brodsky i russkaya poeziya;* Plekhanova, *Metafizicheskaya misteriya Iosifa Brodskogo;* and also Lakerbai, *Rannii Brodsky*.
52. Brodsky, *Bolshaya kniga intervyu*, 650.
53. See Ranchin, *Iosif Brodsky i russkaya poeziya*, 132.
54. Ibid., 133.
55. See Brodsky's "Isaiah Berlin at Eighty," first published in the *New York Review of Books*, August 17, 1989, 44–45.
56. On Brodsky and existentialism see Kelebay, *Poet v dome rebenka*, 106–218; Ranchin, *Iosif Brodsky i russkaya poeziya*, 146–174; and Plekhanova, *Metafizicheskaya misteriya Iosifa Brodskogo*, passim. When Brodsky declared that the French existentialists had played no part in the development of his worldview and immediately added that it was Shestov who had helped him articulate his own ideas (see Brodsky, *Bolshaya kniga intervyu*, 204–205), he probably simply wanted to say that he had never studied Sartre. Shestov's own vision of the world was very close to that of the French existentialists and may, to some degree, have influenced Camus and others.
57. In a conversation with David Bethea he said: "[T]he interesting thing about Shestov [is] that as a stylist, as a writer, he was indeed a product of Dostoevsky. . . . The only man . . . who developed Dostoevsky, in the first place in terms of style, . . . was indeed Shestov." I am indebted to Valentina

Polukhina for providing this quotation from the interview, which was published in Russian translation only.

58. Brodsky, *SIB-2,* vol. 2, 101. "Beginnings and endings" is an allusion to Shestov's book of the same name (*Nachala i kontsy*), published in 1908. Cf. a similar use of another Shestov title, "The Apotheosis of Groundlessness" ("Apofeoz bespochvennosti"), in "Homage to Yalta" and in "Going to Skiros": "the apotheosis of meaninglessness!" (*apofeoz bessmyslitsy*) and "the apotheosis of stoicism" (*apofeoz podvizhnichestva*).
59. Lev Shestov, *Apofeoz bespochvennosti* (Saint Petersburg: Shipovnik, 1911), 68.
60. Quoted from memory.
61. Nor did he hold with structuralism's cultural determinism as applied to ethics, or with postmodernist relativism.
62. For Brodsky's description of another great poet's widow see his "Nadezhda Mandelstam (1899–1980): An Obituary," in Brodsky, *Less Than One,* 145–156.
63. A brash enough joke but not the mere sign of hostility to the USSR that it is sometimes taken to be. It has more to do with one of Brodsky's constant themes—the "architectural" role played by the destruction of war. Cf. with "Rotterdam Diary": "Le Corbusier and the Luftwaffe have the following in common / they both worked very hard / on changing the face of Europe" (*Urania*).

CHAPTER EIGHT

1. This was a note to me, a postcard (with a panorama of Graben) written on the flight from Vienna to London.
2. Brodsky, *Less Than One,* 371. Brodsky is describing a portrait of Auden taken by Rollie MacKenna in New York in 1952. Auden is standing on the fire escape of his apartment on Seventh Avenue.
3. Ibid., 269.
4. The English cultural tradition, at least after Daniel Defoe, has defined the writer's trade in broader terms than has the Russian. The English tradition assumes that a writer can and often does work in a variety of genres—not just fiction or poetry. Among nineteenth-century Russian writers of the first rank, Nikolay Leskov was perhaps the only one who had the same attitude toward his trade.
5. From a letter to me dated August 2, 1972.
6. See Richard Davenport-Hines, *Auden* (New York: Pantheon, 1995), 325–341.
7. Charles Osborne, *W. H. Auden: The Life of a Poet* (New York: Harcourt Brace Jovanovich, 1979), 325. In all likelihood, Brodsky borrowed this comparison subconsciously as he was writing his 1984 memoir of Auden: "During those weeks in Austria he looked after my affairs with the diligence of a good mother hen" (Brodsky, *Less Than One,* 377).
8. In addition to his knowledge and love of the Russian classics, Auden also

had a "Russian side" to his life: he was friends with two Russian composers, Igor Stravinsky and Nikolay Nabokov (the writer's cousin), with the philosopher Isaiah Berlin, and with the New York physician and memoirist Vasily Yanovsky. At the request of another Russian friend, the poet and critic Yury Ivask, he had written a review of an English translation of Konstantin Leontyev's essays. Still, his close friend Isaiah Berlin remarked that "Auden, of course, knew perfectly well that [Brodsky] was a good poet who respected him a great deal, but Auden wasn't interested in Russian poetry, or in Russia. Not in the least. And not in France, either. It was all Germany. Italy to a certain extent, but mainly Germany. 'Yes, yes, I know I'm a German,' he would say to me. 'I'm a Kraut. What can you do, that's what I am, I'm German.'" (*Iosif Brodsky: Trudy i dni*, 103).

9. Brodsky, *Less Than One*, 382.
10. On this, see chapter V, in the sections devoted to Norenskaya and Brodsky's readings in Anglo-American poetry while in exile there. The overall topic of Brodsky and Auden is far too broad to be explored here, but it deserves serious research.
11. See Beinecke, Box 137, folder 3029.
12. Brodsky and George Kline were working on Brodsky's book soon to be published as *Selected Poems* (Harmondsworth, England: Penguin, 1973). The book was published in the United States at the end of the same year by Harper and Row.
13. *Iosif Brodsky. Trudy i dni*, 227.
14. See Volkov, *Dialogi s Iosifom Brodskim*, 107–108.
15. "Senegalskaya ballada" (1966), in Evgeniy Evtushenko, *Sobranie sochineii v trekh tomakh* (Moscow, Khudozhestvennaya literatura, 1984), vol. 2, 96.
16. Brodsky, *Bolshaya kniga intervyu*, 665 (see also 166–167 and 205).
17. Brodsky and Proffer had known each other for several years. In 1969 it was Proffer who managed to get the manuscript of "Gorbunov and Gorchakov" out to the United States.
18. Carl Proffer, *The Simile and Gogol's "Dead Souls"* (The Hague: Mouton, 1967); and Proffer, *Keys to Lolita* (Bloomington: Indiana University Press, 1968).
19. Beinecke, Box 123, folders 2772–2773.
20. Ardis was not the only "*tamizdat*" available to writers in the USSR. (*Tamizdat*, a play on *samizdat*, meant "publishing abroad" or "over there.") Long before Ardis came to exist, there were a number of émigré publishing houses scattered around the globe: Chekhov Publishing in the United States and YMCA-Press and Posev in Europe, plus several others. While Posev focused on social and political issues and YMCA-Press on religious and philosophical ones, Ardis was a purely literary endeavor. More important, it was not an émigré press as such; though based in the United States, it published works by contemporary writers still in the USSR—especially those in Moscow and Leningrad. What made this possible was Ardis's net-

work of "agents"—American and European students, professors, journalists, and even diplomats who, not without risk to themselves, sneaked manuscripts out of the country. The Russian authors of these manuscripts were of course at even greater risk.

21. Brodsky particularly liked the beginning of Sasha Sokolov's *School for Fools,* and he wanted to encourage the younger writer. Sokolov's subsequent works impressed him less (see Brodsky, *Bolshaya kniga intervyu,* 590).
22. Joseph Brodsky, "Poet's Round Table: 'A Common Language,'" *PN Review* 15, no. 4 (1989): 43.
23. Vladimir Nabokov, *Stikhi* (Ann Arbor, MI: Ardis, 1979), 267–268. It was perhaps owing to Nabokov's influence that the anapest was completely rehabilitated in the poetry of such 1970s poets as Sergey Gandlevsky, Bakhyt Kenzheev, Yury Kublanovsky, and Aleksey Tsvetkov.
24. Valery Bryusov, *Sobranie sochinenii* (Moscow: Khudozhestvennaya literatura, 1974), vol. 3, 488.
25. The majority of Balmont's poems featuring long anapestic lines are in one way or another related to the theme of antiquity. Perhaps Balmont thought that such lines sounded like Greek hexameter. We should note that in Brodsky's Leningrad milieu Balmont was regarded as a rather kitschy "decadent" poet and was not taken seriously. Still, the only written record of Brodsky's opinion about Balmont strikes a positive note. Lidiya Chukovskaya noted in her diary that at their first meeting in January 1963, Brodsky praised Balmont's translations from Shelley as superior to those done by her father, Korney Chukovsky. He said: "Balmont's translations from Shelley confirm that Balmont was a [real] poet" (Chukovskaya, *Zapiski ob Anne Akhmatovoy,* vol. 3, 71). This impertinent remark addressed to Chukovsky's daughter is curiously close to what Aleksandr Blok wrote in 1907 comparing Balmont and Chukovsky as translators of Shelley and Whitman: "Balmont's translations . . . are the work of a poet," implying that Chukovsky's are not, even if they are formally closer to the original texts. (Aleksandr Blok, *Sobranie sochinenii* [Moscow: Khudozhestvennaya literatura, 1962], vol. 5, 204.)
26. See examples in Brodsky, *SIB-2,* vol. 1, 68–78, 168, 180, 201–204, 210–211.
27. Efim Etkind, *Materiya stikha* (Paris: Institut d'Études Slaves, 1985), 114.
28. Brodsky, *Bolshaya kniga intervyu,* 643. No text by Leonidas of Tarent corresponds exactly to Brodsky's quotation; some fragments of his epigrams remotely resemble it.
29. My role was mainly technical, typesetting and proofreading, although Brodsky discussed the composition of the books and some stylistic nuances with me. On only one occasion did he follow my advice and make a significant change in a poem, "An autumn evening in the modest square." So I was surprised to see on the copyright pages of both books "Compiled

and edited by V. Maramzin and L. Loseff," a line that Brodsky asked Carl Proffer to add after I had finished my work.

30. Volkov, *Dialogi s Iosifom Brodskim,* 313.
31. Aleksandr Bakhrakh, "'Konets prekrasnoy epokhi,'" *Russkaya mysl,* November 24, 1977.
32. Byron Lindsey, *World Literature Today* 52, no. 1 (1978): 130.
33. Gifford, "Language of Loneliness," 903.
34. One literary encyclopedia, *Samizdat Leningrada* (Moscow: Novoe literaturnoe obozrenie, 2003), lists 343 "unofficial" writers, 109 of whom made their living by physical labor, 46 of them as stokers or gas boiler operators.
35. Brodsky's extended essays on Tsvetaeva, Mandelstam, Frost, Auden, Rilke, and others give some sense of these "slow readings."
36. Sven Birkerts, *My Sky Blue Trades: Growing Up Counter in Contrary Times* (New York: Viking, 2002), 226–228.
37. Aleksandr Minchin, *20 intervyu* (Moscow: Izografus EKSMO-PRESS, 2001), 35. We should note that these comments were made by someone who received a "C" in the course, so there may be an element of revenge at work here. But they clearly reflect how a young and ill-prepared student might react to Brodsky and his teaching style.
38. Loseff, "Poet na kafedre," 46.
39. Ibid., 49.
40. The quotation is from Updike, "Mandarins," 85.
41. See, for example, an interview with Maria Doria de Zuliani, who is featured at the beginning of *Watermark.* Her generally sour recollections of Brodsky include one outright lie, which was that in 1972 she "arranged a stay in Venice for him while he waited for his fate to be decided [that is, whether he would be permitted to emigrate to the United States]" (*Obshchaya gazeta,* April 3, 2002, 16). In fact, the first time Brodsky saw Venice was over the Christmas of 1972, after he had been a full six months in the United States.
42. In an article entitled "Poet kak odinokii turist" ("The Poet as a Lonely Tourist"), the Finnish scholar Sanna Turoma raises a rather artificial question: Is the speaker in Brodsky's travelogues an exile or a tourist? While displaying a great deal of erudition in history, sociology, and the semiotics of tourism, the author comes to a rather banal conclusion: Brodsky is a tourist because he visits places that tourists love. This means Venice above all other places, and its classical art and architecture above all else. The latter assertion is simply wrong. Brodsky's most intimate associations are not with the tourist sights in Venice but rather with the ordinary side streets and back streets of the city, with Venice out of season, with the apartment houses of San Pietro and the everyday life of its residents.
43. Shallcross, *Through the Poet's Eye.*
44. With certain provisos, we can add "December in Florence," "Elaborating Plato," and "In Italy" (all from *To Urania*) to this list of works in which

Brodsky looks at his native Leningrad through the prism of other real or imagined cities.

45. Volkov, *Dialogi s Iosifom Brodskim,* 170.
46. Joyce Purnick, "Koch Bested by a Loquacious Soviet Poet, Meets His Match," *New York Times,* December 13, 1987.
47. See *Iosif Brodsky. Trudy i dni,* 78–79.
48. In 1994, Farrar, Straus and Giroux was bought out by Georg von Holtzbrinck Publishing Group, a German firm that owns some eighty publishing houses throughout Europe and the United States. A condition of the sale was that Farrar, Straus and Giroux would retain its autonomy.
49. R. Z. Sheppard and Kathleen Brady, "Winning the Old-Fashioned Way," *Time,* February 8, 1988, http://www.time.com/time/magazine/article/0,9171,966662,,00.html.
50. I received support from the Guggenheim Foundation for work on this book.
51. Alexander Lieberman, *Campidoglio: Michelangelo's Roman Capital,* with an essay by Joseph Brodsky (New York: Random House, 1994).
52. The Liebermans virtually adopted one of Brodsky's friends, the talented and witty writer and dance critic Gennady Shmakov, who lived with them for some time. They also took in Eduard Limonov when he first came to New York. On the Liebermans, see Shtern, *Brodsky,* 179–195; and also Limonov, *Kniga mertvykh,* 99, 105, 111–115.
53. See Karabchievsky, *Voskresenie Mayakovskogo,* chap. 11.6 (Karabchievsky was still in the USSR at the time; his book was published by an émigré press and was not reviewed in the Soviet Union); and Kolker, "Neskolko nablyudenii." Karabchievsky and Kolker present interesting insights into Brodsky's work; Solzhenitsyn and Korzhavin are more subjective. Their criticism sheds more light on their own literary and aesthetic stance than it does on Brodsky's. During Brodsky's lifetime neither of the two published any specific remarks about him.
54. Brodsky, "Says Poet Brodsky."
55. An open letter by the artist Mikhail Shemyakin, quoted in Navrozov, "Russian Literature in Exile."
56. Ibid., 13.
57. Limonov, "Poet-bukhgalter," 135.
58. Brodsky, *SIB-2,* vol. 2, 155. Brodsky's barb was aimed at his former friend Dmitriy Bobyshev, but the juvenile eroticism of which he speaks is also characteristic of classic 1920s avant-garde (Kruchenykh, Dada, the Oberiuty) and later imitators like Limonov. On this see Igor Smirnov, "O nartsisticheskom tekste (Diakhroniya i psikhoanaliz)," *Wiener slawistischer Almanach* 12 (1983): 21–45.
59. "Hundreds" of Russian émigré poets is a hyperbole.
60. Limonov, *Kniga mertvykh,* 102. In this piece written after Brodsky's death, as the poet was being virtually canonized in his homeland, Limonov

softens his rhetoric. Now less sure of his own greatness, he admits that "Brodsky was one of the few writers in my own time that I saw as a true rival. The only one I might have wanted to talk and argue with, long and frankly, about life and the soul and all those planets and space in general. But he was afraid, he backed off. When he died, life became much more boring. I wish he had lived to see my latest victories, even if they have not been literary ones" (ibid.; also 110). When Limonov first arrived in the United States, Brodsky gave him help and support; he thought him talented. Later, he was put off by both Limonov's prose and his behavior, and when asked his opinion would simply answer, "*Shpana*" (a punk).

61. The rules of the MacArthur Foundation dictate that the older the recipient, the greater the prize. That year the twenty-four-year old physicist Stephen Wolfram received $24,000; the sixty-seven-year-old Robert Penn Warren received $60,000; the amount that forty-one-year-old Brodsky received fell somewhere in between.
62. Nabokov was not entirely apolitical. In both his prose and poetry he had always condemned totalitarianism; he took a public stand against persecution of dissidents in the USSR. See, for example, his telegram in defense of Vladimir Maramzin, quoted in Carl Proffer's letter to the editor in the *New York Review of Books,* March 6, 1975, http://www.nybooks.com/articles/9249.
63. Valentina Polukhina kindly provided the rough transcript.
64. *Vladimir Nabokov: Selected Letters, 1940–1977,* ed. Dmitri Nabokov and Matthew J. Bruccoli (New York: Harcourt Brace Jovanovich 1989), 461.
65. Ibid.
66. As Andrey Bitov tells it, Brodsky received a postcard from Nabokov in 1970: "I was pacing up and down [Nevsky Prospekt] because the store hadn't opened, it wasn't eleven yet. . . . I see Brodsky walking toward me. . . . 'What are you doing here so early?' 'Just submitted my novel.' 'What did you call it?' 'Pushkin House.' 'Sounds good. I got a postcard from Nabokov today.' 'So what did he have to say?' 'That 'Gorbunov and Gorbachov' was written in a rare and unusual style.' 'That's it?' (Bitov, "Azart, ili neizbezhnost nenapisannogo," 108–154).
67. For a detailed account of this meeting see Alexander Cockburn and James Ridgeway, "The Poles, the Left, and the Tumbrils of '84," *Village Voice,* February 10–16, 1982. The authors do not hide their feelings here.
68. Brodsky, *Bolshaya kniga intervyu,* 204.
69. Benedict, "Flight from Predictability," 10.
70. Ibid.
71. Gorbanevskaya, "Po ulitse Brodskogo."
72. Birkerts, "Art of Poetry XXVIII," 123.
73. Ibid.
74. Therefore it is irrelevant which particular political event Brodsky had

in mind. For an interesting analysis of other aspects of this poem, see "Joseph Brodsky, 'On the Talks in Kabul.'"

75. Brodsky, "Says Poet Brodsy" 80.
76. Brodsky, *Less Than One,* 390.
77. See Brodsky's essay entitled "The Condition We Call Exile" in Brodsky, *On Grief and Reason.*
78. Birkerts, "Art of Poetry XXVIII," 97–98. On the literary relations between the two writers see also Loseff, "Solzhenitsyn i Brodsky kak sosedi."
79. Brodsky, *Bolshaya kniga intervyu,* 650. Brodsky was talking with an old friend, the Polish journalist Adam Michnik, and so did not bother expressing himself more elegantly.
80. Ibid., 654.
81. Ibid.
82. Joseph Brodsky, review of *The Gulag Archipelago, Partisan Review* 44 (Winter 1977). The original Russian text, entitled "Geografiya zla" (The Geography of Evil) was first published by Viktor Kulle.
83. Beinecke, Box 14, folder 372. This letter is dated May 14, 1977, and was published in Loseff, "Solzhenitsyn i Brodsky kak sosedi," 94. If Solzhenitsyn had read everything that Brodsky had published outside the USSR, he would surely have been acquainted with the main body of the poet's work.
84. Solzhenitsyn, "Iosif Brodsky—izbrannye stikhi," 191–192, 188. For the polemic that followed, see Efimov, "Shag vpravo shag vlevo"; Loseff, "Solzhenitsyn i Brodsky kak sosedi"; Shtern, "Gigant protiv titana."
85. Brodsky, "Why Milan Kundera Is Wrong about Dostoyevsky," 31.
86. Ibid.

CHAPTER NINE

1. Solzhenitsyn, "Iosif Brodsky—izbrannye stikhi," 193.
2. Brodsky, "Pendulum's Song," in Brodsky, *Less Than One.*
3. *Michigan Today* 24 (December 1992): 7 (interview); *Michigan Today* 25 (March 1993): 14 (letter to the editor).
4. The only precedent for such subordination to a woman in Russian lyric poetry is to be found in Pasternak: "a poet's tracks are only tracks / along the road she's made, no more."
5. From a transcript of an interview with Ignatieff conducted by Valentina Polukhina, who kindly shared it with me.
6. Allan Bloom, *The Closing of the American Mind* (New York: Simon and Shuster, 1987), 132–133.
7. Brodsky, *On Grief and Reason,* 90–91.
8. Ibid., 91.
9. Limonov, "Poet-bukhgalter," 134–135.
10. From a letter to Professor Gleb Struve, November 27, 1964 (Gleb Struve archive, Hoover Institution).

11. We have to keep in mind that in Brodsky's poetic diction, the word "thing" is almost a pronoun. It might refer to an inanimate object ("Nature Morte"), to Jesus Christ ("Lithuanian Nocturne"), to the author himself, or, inter alia, to a woman. In this last case, the usage might have a positive or a negative connotation. An example of a positive connotation is "it was all quite alien to my Swedish thing" ("After a Journey, or Homage to Vertebrae," in Brodsky, *SIB-2*, vol. 6, 63); an example of a negative connotation is "You, guitar-shaped thing with a tangled web" (non-poetic; *Urania*).
12. Yu. Tynyanov, "Notebooks," *Zvezda*, no. 3 (1979): 70.
13. It was common for Brodsky to develop one and the same motif in opposite directions. In "Roman Elegy IX" we read: "Bosoms, ringlets of fleece: for effects, and for causes also. / Heaven-baked clay, fingertips' brave arena. / Flesh that renders eternity an anonymous torso." And later, "Hail the smooth abdomen, thighs as their hamstrings tighten!" He speaks here not of "female parts" but about the work of a sculptor who makes fleeting physical beauty into something eternal. The sculptor, of course, is a metaphorical one. He is both Goethe, the author of the original "Roman Elegies," and his imitator.
14. The contrast between "Angel" and "Invitation to a Journey" (*PSN*) is especially telling. The core images of these two short poems are the same: clothes left behind by a woman when she leaves. "A white pure-cotton angel / till this day hovering in my closet / on a metallic hanger" ("Angel") and "Scent of perfume—in the bedroom and the closet / but beyond some Dior rags there's nothing else" ("Invitation to a Journey"). In "Angel" the clothing left behind acts as the speaker's guardian angel, whereas in "Invitation" it is a fetish for masturbation. But what is most important in "Angel" is the leitmotif of limitless openness and amplification: "angels possess just color / and velocity. The latter explains their being / everywhere. That is why you are still / with me." And at the end of this poem Brodsky creates an amazing trope of pregnancy: he imagines the woman who has left him "letting the body burgeon / with happiness whose diameter lies somewhere in evergreen / California." In contrast to the openness and space in "Angel," the grotesque "Invitation" ends with coercion and constriction of space as the hero forces the woman's face into a pillow as he rapes her. On erotic and sexual motifs in Brodsky see Pilshchikov, "Coitus as a Cross Genre Motif in Brodsky's Poetry"; Loseff, "Iosif Brodsky: Erotika."
15. Joseph Conrad (Teodor Josef Konrad Korzeniowski, 1857–1924), a Pole born in Ukraine, spent his childhood in Vologda, not far from Cherepovets, the place of Brodsky's earliest memories. Conrad grew up speaking both Polish and Russian. His prose was renowned for the refinement of its style, but he never managed to shed the heavy Slavic accent that marked his speech.
16. Brodsky, *Bolshaya kniga intervyu*, 118.
17. Polukhina, "Brodsky through the Eyes of His Contemporaries," 317–318.
18. His English was often hard to understand. John le Carré marveled at the

quality of his prose, especially because he found Brodsky's conversational English so inarticulate. Perhaps it was less a matter of Brodsky's command of English than of his elliptical manner of speaking, even in his native language, especially when he was excited or carried away. He would leave out parts of sentences or simply not finish them, assuming that his train of thought was self-evident and that his listener would fill in the blanks.

19. *Ann Arbor News,* October 22, 1987.
20. Another peculiarity of Brodsky's English pronunciation was an exaggeratedly open *a.* So, for example, "I can" came out as "I caahn." This pronunciation is evinced in the rhyme "Now, that I am in *Paris,* / I wish I were where my *car is*" (quoted by Derek Walcott, who adds that Brodsky was very proud of this rhyme; Polukhina, *Brodsky glazami sovremennikov.* 408; quotation corrected). Probably he was unconsciously mimicking Auden, whose "ahhhs" sounded too open to the American ear. However, it is nearly impossible for a Russian to reproduce the subtle differences in the British and the American *a.*
21. This lecture was published as "Altra Ego." I have a similar recollection of Brodsky's speech at the Nobel banquet at the Stockholm City Hall and of his commencement address at Dartmouth College in 1989 ("In Praise of Boredom"). The audiences seemed to catch just bits and pieces.
22. Quoted in an article by Leigh Hafrey, "Love and the Analytic Poet," *New York Times Book Review,* July 13, 1983, 3. For a comparison of Brodsky's ideas on the influence of language on national mentality with Herder's and those of other eighteenth-century thinkers, and also with those current in modern ethnolinguistics and cultural studies, see Khayirov, "Esli bog dlya menya i sushchestvuet, to eto imenno yazyk'."
23. In the interest of objectivity, I should say that Brodsky harshly but rather arbitrarily rejected an opinion I first expressed in my article "Brodsky in English." An interviewer quoted: "One can be a writer only in one's native tongue, which is simply predetermined by geography. Even if you are fluent in two or more language from infancy, there is only one world which is yours, and you can be in conscious command of only one culture, one language, while all others remain alien. Even if you study them all your life, you still make blunders left and right" (Loseff, "Angliyskii Brodsky"). Brodsky replied with a harshness that was unprecedented in our longtime relationship: "That's a foolish statement. That is, not so much foolish, but I'd say it was extremely parochial, straight out of the shtetl. The fact is that in Russian literature it would be hard to find an example of a writer who was a writer in two cultures, but bilingualism was a norm, quite a real norm" (Brodsky, *Bolshaya kniga intervyu,* 117). He brought up Pushkin and Turgenev as examples. Of course, both had a perfect command of French, but neither wrote serious prose or poetry in that language. Turgenev the writer belonged to two cultures, perhaps, but not to two languages.
24. Polukhina, *Brodsky through the Eyes of His Contemporaries,* 317.

25. Myers, "Note on Joseph Brodsky," 35.
26. Plus the three above-mentioned books of essays. There are fourteen books in Polish, nine in Italian, and seven each in French and German. Other languages in which Brodsky's books were published during his lifetime include Dutch, Danish, Hebrew, Spanish, Korean, Mongolian, Norwegian, Serbo-Croatian, Finnish, Czech, and Swedish. In all, more than sixty books were published in languages other than Russian or English, one-third of which came out before 1987, when Brodsky received the Nobel Prize. Brodsky lived to see twenty-eight books published in his native Russian, not counting several published in extremely limited editions. Of the twenty-eight, seventeen were published in post-1991 Russia; the rest were published abroad. The first edition of his multivolume *Collected Works* (*SIB-1*) also came out during his lifetime.
27. Brodsky, *Elegy to John Donne.*
28. Among those omitted from *Selected Poems* were early poems like "Isaac and Abraham." Only one canto of "Gorbunov and Gorchakov" was translated ("On the Porch"), and one poem from "School Anthology" ("Albert Frolov").
29. See Brown, "The Best Russian Poetry Written Today"; Gifford, "Idioms in Interfusion"; Bethea, "Conjurer in Exile."
30. Quoted from the manuscript of an interview by Diana Abaeva-Meyers in *Iosif Brodsky. Trudy i dni*, 27; the beginning of this passage was cut.
31. One characteristic example of envy is an article by Richard Kostelanetz on *Less Than One* in which the author stoops to mimicking Brodsky's accent (Kostelanetz, review of Joseph Brodsky's *Less Than One*). Meanwhile, Brodsky's book was judged the best work of literary criticism for 1986.
32. Reid, "Great American Disaster."
33. Animosity toward Brodsky, or at least disapproval of him, was more typical of the English poetry establishment (Reid, Raine, Alvarez) than of others. After Larkin and Hughes, English poetry entered into a long, drawn-out crisis, and Brodsky's true English-language peers were Seamus Heaney and Paul Muldoon (Irish); Richard Wilbur, Anthony Hecht, Howard Moss, and Mark Strand (American); Les Murray (Australian); and Derek Walcott (a native of the Caribbean island of Saint Lucia).
34. This hysterical article did not go unnoticed in the English-language press. Michael Hofman wrote in the *Observer* about a "repellent and inept attack on Joseph Brodsky" and added that Raine "ought to feel ashamed of himself, though there's not much chance of that" (Hofman, "Raine, Raine, Go Away"). On the perception of Brodsky in the English-speaking world see Polukhina, "Poeticheskiy avtoportret Brodskogo"; Kyst, "Plokhoy poet Iosif Brodsky"; Lounsbery, "Iosif Brodsky kak amerikanskii poet-laureat"; Weissbort, "Something Like His Own Language."
35. Kirsch, "Art of the Contemporary," 42.
36. Ibid.

37. Heaney, "Brodsky's Nobel," 65.
38. It seems to me that there is little resemblance between Brodsky's prose and Mandelstam's, but any comparison goes far beyond the scope of this essay, let alone a footnote.
39. Here he also cleverly defines Rozanov as a "Russian thinker (or, more accurately, a tinker-thinker)" ["myslitel (tochney: razmyslitel)"] (Brodsky, *SIB-2*, vol. 5, 137).
40. Among these are two early essays—"A Writer Is a Lonely Traveler" (1972) and "Reflections on a Spawn of Hell" (1973)—written in Russian but intended for translation into English.
41. In an interview with Sven Birkerts, Brodsky said that when he wrote in English he thought "about Auden, what he would say—would he find it rubbish, or kind of entertaining." And then added: "Auden and Orwell" (Birkerts, "Art of Poetry XXVIII," 108).
42. T. V. Tsivyan, "Proza poetov o 'proze poeta,'" *Russian Literature* 41, no. 4 (1997): 429.
43. Bethea, "Conjurer in Exile," 3.
44. Once again I am grateful to Valentina Polukhina for sharing with me her transcript of her interview with Le Carré, which was published only in Russian translation.
45. Bayley, "Mastering Speech," 3.
46. Before Brodsky, it appears that the only writer who occasionally wrote in a second language for aesthetic rather than practical reasons was Samuel Beckett—one of Brodsky's idols. Their reasons, however, were different. Beckett wrote novels and plays in French in an effort to achieve a certain universality of tone. Brodsky chose English because he wanted to speak to Auden as an equal, as if to make up for his muteness at their meeting.
47. Updike, "Mandarins," 85.
48. See Polukhina, "Prose of Joseph Brodsky."
49. See Loseff, "Realnost zazerkalya," 235–236.
50. See, for example, Brodsky, *Bolshaya kniga intervyu,* 141.
51. Chukovskaya, *Zapiski ob Anne Akhmatovoy,* 307.
52. In 1989, Gunnar Jarring, the former Swedish ambassador to the USSR, recalled his attempts to persuade Anders Österling, permanent secretary of the Swedish Academy, that "a Nobel Prize to Paustovsky, bypassing Sholokhov, would hardly meet with appreciation in the Soviet Union. It would only give rise to new bitterness at a time when people are in the process of forgetting about the affront that the prize to Pasternak was regarded as implying" (quoted in Kjell Espmark, *The Nobel Prize in Literature: A Study of the Criteria behind the Choices* [Boston: G. K. Hall, 1991], 186). Usually the Nobel committee acted independently, without consulting politicians or diplomats, but in this case, on the heels of the Pasternak scandal, they were afraid of putting Paustovsky in jeopardy! The Swedish academicians and diplomats had no compass to make their way through the Byzantine

twists and turns of Soviet ideological policies. Nonetheless, when in 1970 Jarring advised the committee to take its time in awarding the prize to Solzhenitsyn, because giving it that year "would lead to difficulties for our relations with the Soviet Union," Österling replied, "Yes, that could well be so, but we are agreed that Solzhenitsyn is the most deserving candidate" (ibid., 113).

53. *Nobelpriset. The Nobel Prize. Translation of the Speeches at the Nobel Festival 1987* (Nobel Foundation, 1987), 27.
54. Quoted in Espmark, *Nobel Prize in Literature,* 110.
55. *Nobelpriset,* 28, 29.
56. Polukhina's transcript of her interview with Le Carré.
57. Ibid.
58. Brodsky, *On Grief and Reason,* 45–46.
59. Ibid., 55.
60. Cf. Wladimir Weidle's observation that Brodsky restores a literary succession interrupted by the Soviets (chapter I).
61. Brodsky, *On Grief and Reason,* 53. Brodsky's reasoning in his Nobel Lecture may have been influenced by his reading of eighteenth-century Russian poetry. On two facing pages in a volume of verse by M. N. Muravyov (1757–1807), a poet whom Brodsky read and admired, we find reflections on aesthetic education as a means of moral improvement, and thoughts on the necessity of education for all social estates that correspond to Brodsky's own belief that intellectual inequity has been Russia's downfall—that is, the society was split into the "people" and the "intelligentsia." Here, like Brodsky after him, Muravyov quotes Lord Shaftesbury. Brodsky's Nobel address at times seems a paraphrase of the following remarks by Muravyov: "He whose sensitive heart grasps the sufferings of Petrarch and shares the majestic sorrow of Phaedra and Dido, whose soul soars skyward at striking depictions by Corneille or fantastical scenes from Shakespeare, he who admires Lomonosov, the beauty of a poem, or the composition of a painting, is not capable of founding his own happiness on the misfortunes of others." Quoted in L. Kulakova, "Poeziya M. N. Muravyova" in M. N. Muravyov, *Stikhotvoreniya* (Leningrad: Sovetskii pisatel, 1967), 15.
62. Brodsky, *On Grief and Reason,* 49. It might appear that this aphorism contradicts Kierkegaard's assertion that ethics and faith are superior to aesthetics, but what Kierkegaard meant by "aesthetics" was hedonism.
63. Brodsky's habit of couching opinions and intuitions in quasi-logical form provoked skepticism on the part of some professional scholars (see chapter II). This is what an Oxford professor and noted scholar of Russian poetry, Gerald Smith, had to say: "It has something to do with fashion. For English people of my age, the kind of essays Brodsky wrote has an old-fashioned feel, especially from the stylistic point of view. Our men of letters went in for this sort of thing before the war, but now it's not done. . . . There's another important aspect of British intellectual life involved here as well, of

course, specialization, even *technologization*. For instance, nobody would write about Cavafy now if they don't know Modern Greek" (I am grateful to Professor Smith for providing the original text of this quotation).

64. Quoted in E. J. Czerwinski, "For Whom the Nobel Tolls: The Nationless," *World Literature Today* 62 (Spring 1988): 213. Brodsky also joked, "Such a small step for mankind, such a great step for me," paraphrasing Neil Armstrong's famous declaration on landing on the moon—"That's one small step for a man, one giant leap for mankind."
65. It is possible that the Soviet official was ironically quoting Brodsky himself, who had in one of his first post-prize interviews said that had he been on the Nobel committee, he would have given it to Naipaul. (See Brodsky, *Bolshaya kniga intervyu*, 275.)
66. *Moskovskie novosti*, November 8, 1987, 14.
67. *Literaturnaya gazeta*, November 18, 1987, 9.
68. *Literaturnaya gazeta*, November 25, 1987, 9.
69. Quoted in *Russkaya mysl*, October 30, 1987, 8.
70. Ibid., 10.
71. Aside from the "letters" there were "The New Jules Verne" and "An autumn evening in a modest square."

CHAPTER TEN

1. See Brodsky, *Bolshaya kniga intervyu*, 223; and *Newsday*, December 28, 1989, 57.
2. In 1990 the following were all published in the USSR: *Osennii krik yastreba* (The Hawk's Cry in Autumn) (Leningrad: IMA Press); *Stikhotvorenyia Iosifa Brodskogo* (The Poems of Joseph Brodsky) (Leningrad: SP Alga-fond); *Stikhotvoreniya* (Poems) (Moscow: Bibliotechka zhurnala *Poligrafia*); and, finally, a representative collection entitled *Chast rechi. Izbrannye stikhi 1962–1989* (A Part of Speech. Selected Poems, 1962–1969) (Moscow: Khudozhestvennaya literatura).
3. According to a yet incomplete bibliography, by the last year of Brodsky's life, critical works devoted to the poet numbered nearly a thousand (Lapidus, *Iosif Brodsky. Ukazatel*).
4. Tyurin, "Estetika—mat etiki."
5. Brodsky, *SIB-2*, vol. 7. English translations: *Granta* 30 (1993)—act 1; *Partisan Review* 60 (Spring 1993)—act 2.
6. In its time, one could also read "Anno Domini" as an account of a journey to the Soviet Republic of Lithuania reimagined as a province of the Roman empire. (See Venclova, "O stikhotvorenii Iosifa Brodskogo 'Litovskiy noktyurn.'")
7. Cf. his remarks to another interviewer: "I don't go to the theater at all. I read drama—it's fun for me to read, but to see it is always an embarrassment—the element of make-believe as such. I can't get rid of the notion of

the effort I have to make to believe it" (Henderson, interview with Brodsky, 52).

8. *Marbles:* Brodsky, *SIB-2,* vol. 7; the first English edition, *Marbles,* was translated by Alan Myers with the author (New York: Farrar, Straus and Giroux, 1989). "Tree": NLR, file 63, folios 139–155.
9. Brodsky, *Bolshaya kniga intervyu,* 486.
10. Brodsky, *Democracy! [Act 1],* 217, 216.
11. Brodsky, *Democracy! [Act 2],* 279. "When history ends . . ." continues the theme of the "end of history" discussed in act 1. The characters are reacting to Francis Fukuyama's famous essay "The End of History," first published in the summer of 1989. In it Fukuyama proclaimed that liberal democracy had finally triumphed worldwide.
12. Brodsky, *Democracy! [Act 1],* 226.
13. Aleksandr Goryanin, "Day ruku bratu svoemu! Dva pisma russkomu intelligentu ob Ukraine," *Russkaya mysl,* February 8–14, 1996.
14. Quoted in N. V. Izmaylov, *Ocherki tvorchestva Pushkina* (Leningrad: Nauka, 1975), 25.
15. After the poet's death an error-ridden transcript of the audiotape was published in a Kiev newspaper called *Stolitsa,* accompanied by a rebuke written in verse by a member of the Ukrainian National Academy of Sciences, Dr. Pavlo Kysly. Kysly enumerated Ukraine's historical grievances with Russia, and he addressed Brodsky: "You were a stinking hired goat / Not worth Taras's fingernail." But even in Ukraine opinions differed. "Of course we can take the poets' invectives as slurs, but they testify to the fact that the author is not indifferent. The author resorts to an archaic tradition of curses and spells peculiar to Ukrainian folklore. It is precisely from here, and from Shevchenko, that Brodsky draws his shattering barrage of words, his headlong denunciations. . . . Who is the poet addressing? Inarguably, the powers-that-be, the bearers of decline and discord. Yes, he identifies himself with the 'goats' [this is the clean-shaven Ukrainians' contemptuous term for the bearded Russians] and frankly condemns 'the seventy years' spent within the Soviet empire. But what he is condemning are not the polacks or the fritzies or the ukies but the forces of discord and enmity mystically set free by Chernobyl, the most crucial turn in a catastrophic series of events. I would like to note that Brodsky, as a discerning reader of [the eighteenth-century Ukrainian poet and philosopher Hryhorii (Grigory)] Skovoroda, whom he puts on the same plane as John Donne and Gavrila Derzhavin, subscribes to this wise man's chief tenet—'look into thyself.' This living call creates within Skovoroda's disciples a model for self-examination and exploration of the 'catacombs of the spirit.' Here is the foundation of the real Monument—Pure Logos—built by Horace, Derzhavin, and Pushkin" (Kravets, "Dvoynoe zaveshchanie Iosifa Brodskogo").
16. As Brodsky well knew—for he was widely read in classical literature—this

metaphor appears in Sophocles' *Oedipus the King*, where Jocasta compares the head of state to the helmsman of a ship caught in a storm at sea.

17. Brodsky, *Bolshaya kniga intervyu*, 653. This not just a pretty allegory worked up for interviews and other such occasions. Brodsky said much the same to me shortly after meeting Gorbachev: "He [Gorbachev] is saying something, but the something doesn't matter. It seems like History has just walked into the room."
18. Chukovskaya, *Zapiski ob Anne Akhmatovoy*, vol. 3, 410.
19. Sergeev, *Omnibus*, 464.
20. A preliminary study of Brodsky's 1979 notebooks and papers leads me to believe that although he *was* writing poetry that year, he was satisfied with none of it and thought all these texts needed further work.
21. Cf. the lines from "The End of a Beautiful Era": "Time's invented by death. It thrives on bodies and objects, / looking for properties of both in raw vegetables" (non-poetic).
22. Thomas Mann, *The Magic Mountain*, trans. John E. Woods (New York: Knopf, 1995), 456. See also Sergey Stratanovsky's interesting essay "Creativity and Illness: On Early Mandelstam," *Zvezda*, no. 2 (2004): 210–221.
23. Solzhenitsyn, "Iosif Brodsky—izbrannye stikhi," 190. I am referring not to those poems simply written around the Christmas season but rather to those in which the holy family and the birth of the child are the subject. The simply seasonal include "Christmas Romance" (1962), "New Year at Kanatchikov Dacha" (1964), "On the Departure of a Guest" (1964), "A Speech about Spilt Milk" (1967), "Anno Domini" (1968), "A second Christmas by the shore" (1971), and "Lagoon" (1973).
24. From a speech delivered at a memorial service for Carl Proffer (Beinecke, Box 123, folders 2772–2773).
25. According to Yuz Aleshkovsky, Brodsky used the words "we are them" when he related a dream that eventually led to the writing of "Letter to Horace." Brodsky thought highly of Aleshkovsky's metaphysical intuition and called him a "natural metaphysician" (Brodsky, *SIB-2*, vol. 7, 214).
26. Formally, "On the Centenary of Anna Akhmatova" commemorates a birthday, but its content makes it a typical "on the death of" poem.
27. Marcus Aurelius, *Meditations*, trans. Maxwell Staniforth (Harmondsworth, England: Penguin, 1964), 67–68. Brodsky had always been interested in the Stoics. In 1994 he wrote a long essay entitled "Homage to Marcus Aurelius," in which he talks of the posthumous peace to be found in the breakdown of matter. He had already, in his very early "A Jewish Cemetery near Leningrad," touched on this theme. In *PSN* there is another poem containing a textually similar passage, "In Front of Casa Marcello" (1995), where the Venetian air is redolent of the "scent of cells' liberation."
28. NLR, file 64, folio 54.
29. Lotman, "Poet i smert," 201–202.
30. Loman and Lotman, "Mezhdu veshchyu i pustotoy," 294.

31. Ibid., 295–296.
32. The book of Daniel (12:3) reads: "But they that are learned, shall shine as the brightness of the firmament: and they that instruct many to justice, as stars for all eternity." In Ovid's *Metamorphoses,* book XV, Julius Caesar becomes a star in the sky. Cf. Akhmatova's 1921 poem "The souls of all my dear ones are in the stars on high."
33. There is much in Brodsky's poetry to remind the reader of Mayakovsky, and this particular metaphor points to one of the most important similarities. Both poets were enthralled by the notion of the future and the problem of time. (See Kristina Pomorska, "Mayakovsky and Time: On the Chronotopical Myth of the Russian Avant-Garde," *Slavica Hierosolimitana* 5–6 [1981]: 341–353.) In this sense, Brodsky is no less a futurist than Mayakovsky, and Yury Karabchievsky is right when he finds a profound likeness between these two poets, both of whom he dislikes; he does concede, however, that Brodsky was "not merely better educated than Mayakovsky but also much smarter" (Karabchievsky, *Voskresenie Mayakovskogo,* 273). In a conversation with Tomas Venclova, Brodsky remarked that he had learned "a colossal number of tricks" from Mayakovsky, an admission all the more remarkable because in interviews and essays he scarcely even mentions the poet (Brodsky, *Bolshaya kniga intervyu,* 349).
34. Lotman, "Poet i smert," 189.
35. Ibid., 194.
36. A notorious example is the ego-futurist Vasilisk Gnedov's "Poem of the End" (1913), which consists of a title on an empty page. Whenever Gnedov gave public performances, he was invariably asked to *read it.* See Vladimir Markov, *Russian Futurism: A History* (Berkeley: University of California Press, 1968), 80.
37. In early Brodsky we find more traditional science-fiction or dystopian motifs as well, as in "To A. A. Akhmatova" and an unfinished long poem called "The Hundred Years' War."
38. This is connected to some more general features of Brodsky's poetics, a detailed discussion of which is beyond the scope of this essay: for a lyric poet, the actual "I" is relatively rare in his verse, and the presence of the "I" diminishes over time; in those cases where the "I" is present, it is most often somewhere on the margins, a passive observer rather than an active participant, watching from a café, sitting on a park bench, stranded in "a far province by the sea." The desire to "be lost in God" found in "Conversation with a Celestial Being" may be another variation on this theme.
39. Elena Petrushanskaya points out a comic parallel that might have served as a subconscious source: "scary stories" from children's folklore—as in "In a black black house in a black black coffin lies a black black corpse" (Petrushanskaya, *Muzykalnyi mir Iosifa Brodskogo,* 69).
40. It is quite possible that Brodsky himself experienced such panic attacks

in his youth. See his "In Mustard Wood," another poem that describes this groundless feeling of terror (Brodsky, *SIB-2*, vol. 1, 248–250).

41. Cf. Mikhail Bakhtin on death as a phenomenon outside personal experience: "All cemeteries are filled exclusively with others" (M. M. Bakhtin, *Estetika slovesnogo tvorchestva* [Moscow: Iskusstvo, 1979], 99).
42. In Ann Arbor in 1977 I told Brodsky that some linguists believe that the Russian sound *yi* (ы) is Mongol in origin. Also, Brodsky undoubtedly read Konstantin Batyushkov's 1811 essay "Something about the Poet and Poetry," where the great romantic humorously lamented the coarseness of the Russian language, starting with the letter *yi*. The popular lines from "Directive" (1927), a poem by the futurist Dmitriy Petrovsky, were another literary antecedent: "We will introduce suffixes to verbs, / Verbal adverbs to prepositions, / Lest the Mongols / Learn our language too soon." Brodsky repeats Petrovsky's rhyme, *glagol-mongol*. In one of his notebooks Brodsky had jotted down fragments of "The Hussar's Alphabet" from memory.
43. In a humorous 1974 epistle to Andrey Sergeev, Brodsky expressed a wish to be buried in Venice: "Though the insensate body / doesn't care where it decays, / deprived of native clay, / it doesn't mind rotting / in a silty Lombard valley. / It's still the native continent, the native worms. / Stravinsky rests in peace in San Michele" (Sergeev, *Omnibus*, 453).
44. Propertius, *Elegies*, book 4, VII. Brodsky's widow chose the inscription, knowing his fondness for Propertius and for this particular elegy, which is sometimes entitled "On the Death of Cynthia." This line is part of an epigraph to another elegy that Brodsky regarded highly, Konstantin Batyushkov's "On the Death of a Friend" (1814). Some echoes of Batyushkov's elegy can be found in Brodsky's poem "To Seamus Heaney" (*PSN*). Akhmatova may well have discussed the elegy with him when they talked at length in the fall of 1965, since that was the very time she was rereading the poem and declaring that "Propertius is the best of elegists" (Roman Timenchik, *Anna Akhmatova v 1960-e gody* [Moscow: Vodoley; Toronto: University of Toronto, 2005], 271).

SELECTED BIBLIOGRAPHY

ABBREVIATIONS

Beinecke	Joseph Brodsky Papers, Beinecke Rare Book and Manuscript Library, Yale University, New Haven, CT
ChR	Joseph Brodsky, *Chast rechi* (Ann Arbor, MI: Ardis, 1977)
KPE	Joseph Brodsky, *Konets prekrasnoy epokhi* (Ann Arbor, MI: Ardis, 1977)
"MS"	"Maramzinskoe sobranie" (Maramzin Collection): Samizdat edition of Brodsky's collected works compiled by Vladimir Maramzin in 1972–1974
NLR	Joseph Brodsky Papers, National Library of Russia
NSKA	Joseph Brodsky, *Novye stansy k Avguste* (Ann Arbor, MI: Ardis, 1983)
OVP	Joseph Brodsky, *Ostanovka v pustyne* (New York: Izdatelstvo imeni Chekhova, 1970)
PSN	Joseph Brodsky, *Peyzazh s navodneniyem* (Dana Point, CA: Ardis, 1996)
RS-2	Joseph Brodsky, *Rozhdestvenskie stikhi,* 2nd ed., expanded (Moscow: Nezavisimaya gazeta, 1996)
SIB-1	*Sochineniya Iosifa Brodskogo,* 1st ed., 5 vols. (Saint Petersburg: Pushkinsky fond, 1992–1995)
SIB-2	*Sochineniya Iosifa Brodskogo,* 2nd ed., 7 vols. (Saint Petersburg: Pushkinsky fond, 1997–2001)
Uncollected	Poems not included in the six books of poems compiled by Brodsky

SAMIZDAT AND ARCHIVAL SOURCES

Joseph Brodsky Papers, Beinecke Rare Book and Manuscript Library, Yale University, New Haven, CT. (Beinecke)

Joseph Brodsky Papers, Manuscript Department, National Library of Russia, Saint Petersburg (fond 1333). (NLR)

"Maramzinskoe sobranie" (Maramzin Collection): Samizdat edition of Brodsky's collected works compiled by Vladimir Maramzin in 1972–1974. ("MS")

WORKS BY JOSEPH BRODSKY

An Age Ago: A Selection of Nineteenth-Century Russian Poetry. Selected and translated by Alan Myers; with a foreword and biographical notes by Joseph Brodsky. New York: Farrar, Straus and Giroux, 1988.

Bolshaya kniga intervyu. Compiled by Valentina Polukhina. Moscow: Zakharov, 2000.

Chast rechi. Ann Arbor, MI: Ardis, 1977. (*ChR*)

Collected Poems in English. Edited by Ann Kjellberg. New York: Farrar, Straus and Giroux, 2000.

Democracy! [Act 1]. Granta 30 (Winter 1990).

Democracy! [Act 2]. Partisan Review 60 (Spring 1993).

Elegy to John Donne, and Other Poems. Selected, translated, and with an introduction by Nicholas Bethell. London: Longmans, 1967.

"Geografiya zla." *Literaturnoe obozrenie* 1 (1999): 4–8.

Interview with Rebekah Presson. *New Letters* 59, no. 1 (1992).

Konets prekrasnoy epokhi. Ann Arbor, MI: Ardis, 1977. (*KPE*)

Less Than One. New York: Farrar, Straus and Giroux, 1986.

Novye stansy k Avguste. Ann Arbor, MI: Ardis, 1983. (*NSKA*)

On Grief and Reason. New York: Farrar, Straus and Giroux, 1995.

Ostanovka v pustyne. New York: Izdatelstvo imeni Chekhova, 1970. (*OVP*)

Peresechyonnaya mestnost (Rough Terrain). Compiled and edited by Petr Vail. Moscow: Nezavisimaya gazeta, 1995.

Peyzazh s navodneniyem. Dana Point, CA: Ardis, 1996. (*PSN*)

"A Poet's Map of His Poem." With George Kline. *Vogue,* September 1973.

Rozhdestvenskie stikhi. 2nd ed., expanded. Moscow: Nezavisimaya gazeta, 1996. (*RS*-2)

"Says Poet Brodsky, Ex of the Soviet Union: 'A Writer Is a Lonely Traveler, and No One Is His Helper.'" *New York Times Magazine,* October 1, 1972.

Selected Poems. Harmondsworth, England: Penguin Books, 1973.

Sochineniya Iosifa Brodskogo. 1st ed. 5 vols. Saint Petersburg: Pushkinsky fond, 1992–1995. (SIB-1)

Sochineniya Iosifa Brodskogo. 2nd ed. 7 vols. Saint Petersburg: Pushkinsky fond, 1997–2001. (SIB-2)

Stikhotvoreniya i poemy. Washington, DC: Inter-Language Literary Associates, 1965.

To Urania. New York: Farrar, Straus and Giroux, 1988.

Uncollected: Poems not included in the six books of poems compiled by Brodsky.
Urania. Ann Arbor, MI: Ardis, 1987.
Watermark. New York: Farrar, Straus and Giroux, 1992.
"Why Milan Kundera Is Wrong about Dostoyevsky." *New York Times Review of Books,* February 17, 1985.

SECONDARY SOURCES

Aist, Tatyana. "Iosif Brodsky—perevodchik s kitayskogo." *Poberezhye,* no. 9 (2000).
Akhmatova, Anna. *Zapisnye knizhki Anny Akhmatovoy (1958–1966).* Moscow: Giulio Einaudi editore, 1996.
Bar-Sella, Zeev. "Tolkovaniya na . . ." *22,* no. 23 (1982).
Bayley, John. "Mastering Speech." *New York Review of Books,* June 12, 1986.
Benedict, Helen. "Flight from Predictability: Joseph Brodsky" (interview). *Antioch Review* 41 (Winter 1985).
Bethea, David. "Conjurer in Exile." *New York Times Book Review,* July 13, 1986.
———. *Joseph Brodsky and the Creation of Exile.* Princeton, NJ: Princeton University Press, 1994.
Birkerts, Sven. "The Art of Poetry XXVIII: Joseph Brodsky." *Paris Review* 83 (Spring 1982).
Bitov, Andrey. "Azart, ili neizbezhnost nenapisannogo." *Zvezda,* no. 7 (1997).
Bobyshev, Dmitriy. "Ya zdes." *Oktyabr,* no. 11 (2002).
Bondarenko, Vladimir. "Vzbuntovavshiysya pasynok russkoy kultury." *Den i noch. Literaturnyi zhurnal dlya semeynogo chteniya,* nos. 9–10 (2004).
Brown, Clarence. "The Best Russian Poetry Written Today." *New York Times Book Review,* September 7, 1980.
Brumm, Anne-Marie. "The Muse in Exile: Conversations with the Russian Poet Joseph Brodsky." *Mosaic: A Journal for the Comparative Study of Literature and Ideas* 8, no. 1 (1974).
Chaykovskaya, Olga. "Netochnye, nevernye zerkala." *Literaturnaya gazeta,* February 7–13, 2001.
Chukovskaya, Lidiya. "Delo Brodskogo po dnevniku Lidiyi Chukovskoy (dekabr 1963–dekabr 1964)." *Znamya,* no. 7 (1999).
Chukovskaya, Lidiya. *Zapiski ob Anne Akhmatovoy.* Vol. 2, *(1952–1962);* Vol. 3, *(1963–1966).* Moscow: Soglasie, 1997.
Disch, Thomas. Review of *A Part of Speech. Washington Post Book World,* August 24, 1980.
Efimov, Igor. "Shag vpravo shag vlevo." *Kolokol,* nos. 3–4 (2000).
Etkind, Efim. *Protsess Iosifa Brodskogo.* London: Overseas Interchange Publications, 1988.
———. *Zapiski nezagovorshchika.* London: Overseas Interchange Publications, 1977.
Gifford, Henry. "Idioms in Interfusion." *Times Literary Supplement,* October 17, 1980.

———. "The Language of Loneliness." *Times Literary Supplement,* August 11, 1978.

Gorbanevskaya, Natalya. "Po ulitse Brodskogo." *Russkaya mysl,* February 1–7, 1996.

Gordin, Yakov. "Delo Brodskogo: Istoriya odnoy raspravy." *Neva* 2 (1989).

———. *Pereklichka vo mrake.* Saint Petersburg: Izdatelstvo Pushkinskogo fonda, 2000.

Heaney, Seamus. "Brodsky's Nobel: What the Applause Was About." *New York Times Book Review,* November 8, 1987.

Henderson, Lisa. Interview with Joseph Brodsky. *Theatre,* Winter 1988.

Hofman, Michael. "Raine, Raine, Go Away." *Observer* (London), December 3, 2000.

Ignatieff, Michael. "V. Polukhina: Intervyu s Maiklom Ignatyevym (London 13 iyunya 1996 g.)." *Znamya,* no. 11 (1996).

Iosif Brodsky: Strategii chteniya. Materialy mezhdunarodnoy nauchnoy konferentsii 2–4 sentyabrya 2004 goda v Moskve. Moscow: Izdatelstvo Ippolitova, 2005.

Iosif Brodsky: Trudy i dni. Compiled by Lev Losev and Petr Vail. Moscow: Izdatelstvo "Nezavisimaya gazeta," 1998.

Iosif Brodsky: Tvorchestvo, lichnost, sudba. Itogi trekh konferentsii. Saint Petersburg: Zvezda, 1998.

Iosif Brodskij: Un crocevia fra culture (Joseph Brodsky: An Intersection of Cultures). Edited by Alessandro Niero and Sergio Pescatori. Milan: MG, 2002.

Ivanov, B. I. "Literaturnye pokoleniya v leningradskoy neofitsialnoy literature: 1950-e–1960-e gody." In *Samizdat Leningrada 1950-e–1980-e: Literaturnaya entsiklopediya,* edited by V. E. Dolinin et al. Moscow: Novoe literaturnoe obozrenie, 2003.

"Joseph Brodsky, 'On the Talks in Kabul': A Forum on Politics in Poetry" (participants: David Bethea, Catherine Ciepiela, Sarah Pratt, Stephanie Sandler, G. S. Smith, Katherine Tiernan O'Connor, Michael Wachtel). *Russian Review* 61 (April 2002): 186–219.

Karabchievsky, Yu. *Voskresenie Mayakovskogo.* Munich: Strana i mir, 1985.

Katz, Jane. *Artists in Exile.* New York: Stern and Day, 1983.

Kelebay, Evgeniy. *Poet v dome rebenka: Prolegomeny k filosofii tvorchestva Iosifa Brodskogo.* Moscow: Knizhnyi dom "Universitet," 2000.

Khayirov, Shamil. "'Esli bog dlya menya i sushchestvuet, to eto imenno yazyk': Yazykovaya refleksiya i lingvisticheskoe mifotvorchestvo Iosifa Brodskogo." *Novoe literaturnoe obozrenie* 67 (2004): 198–223.

Kirsch, Adam. "The Art of the Contemporary." *New Republic,* October 9, 2000.

Klepikova, Elena. "Trizhdy nachinayushchiysya pisatel," 2001, http://www.proza.ru/texts/2001/03/26–37.html. First published in *Novoe Russkoe Slovo,* March 17–18, 2001.

Kline, George L. Introduction to *Joseph Brodsky: Selected Poems,* by Joseph Brodsky. New York: Harper and Row, 1973.

Kline, George L. "Istoriya dvukh knig." In *Iosif Brodsky: Trudy i dni,* compiled by Lev Loseff and Petr Vail. Moscow: Izdatelstvo "Nezavisimaya gazeta," 1998.

Kolker, Yury. "Neskolko nablyudeniy (o stikhakh Iosifa Brodskogo)." *Grani,* no. 162 (1991).

Kostelanetz, Richard. Review of Joseph Brodsky's *Less Than One. Boston Review* 12 (August 1987).

Kravets, Viktor. "Dvoynoe zaveshchanie Iosifa Brodskogo." *Zerkalo nedeli,* August 1–September 1, 2001, http://www.zn.ua/3000/3680/31993/.

Kuzminsky, Konstantin. "Iskusstvo vopreki, ili intervyu s Kuzminskim." *Panorama,* January 21–27, 1998.

———. "Laureat 'Eriki.'" *Russkaya mysl,* no. 3697 (1987).

Kyst, Jon. "Plokhoy poet Iosif Brodsky: K istorii voprosa." *Novoe literaturnoe obozrenie* 45 (2000): 248–255.

Lakerbai, D. L. *Rannii Brodsky: Poetika i sudba.* Ivanovo: Izdatelstvo Ivanovskogo gosudarstvennogo universiteta, 2000.

Lapidus, A. Ya. *Iosif Brodsky: Ukazatel literatury na russkom yazyke za 1962–1995 gg.* 2nd ed., revised and expanded. Saint Petersburg: Rossiyskaya natsionalnaya biblioteka, 1999.

Limonov, Eduard. *Kniga mertvykh.* Saint Petersburg: Limbus Press, 2000.

———. "Poet-bukhgalter. (Neskolko yadovitykh nablyudeniy po povodu fenomena I. A. Brodskogo." *Muleta-A,* 1984.

Loseff, Lev. "Angliyskiy Brodsky." *Chast rechi* (New York), no. 1 (1980).

———. "Chekhovsky lirizm u Brodskogo." In *Poetika Brodskogo,* edited by Lev Loseff. Tenafly, NJ: Ermitazh, 1986.

———. "Home and Abroad in the Works of Brodsky." In *Under Eastern Eyes: The West as Reflected in Recent Russian Émigré Writing,* edited by Arnold McMillin. London: Macmillan, 1992.

———. "Iosif Brodskii: Erotica." *Russian Literature* 37, nos. 2–3 (1995): 289–301.

———. "Joseph Brodsky's Poetics of Faith." In *Aspects of Modern Russian and Czech Literature: Selected Papers of the Third World Congress for Soviet and East-European Studies,* edited by Arnold McMillin. Columbus, OH: Slavica, 1989.

———. "O lyubvi Akhmatovoy k 'Narodu.'" *Zvezda,* no. 1 (2002).

———. "On Hostile Ground: Madness and Madhouse in Joseph Brodsky's 'Gorbunov and Gorchakov.'" In *Madness and the Mad in Russian Culture,* edited by Angela Brintlinger and Ilya Vinitsky. Toronto: University of Toronto Press, 2008.

———. "Pervyi liricheskiy tsikl Iosifa Brodskogo." *Chast rechi* (New York), nos. 2–3 (1982).

———, ed. *Poetika Brodskogo* (Brodsky's Poetics). Tenafly, NJ: Ermitazh, 1986.

———. "Poet na kafedre." In *Iosif Brodsky: Trudy i dni,* compiled by Lev Loseff and Petr Vail. Moscow: Izdatelstvo "Nezavisimaya gazeta," 1998.

———. "Politics/Poetics." In *Brodsky's Poetics and Aesthetics,* edited by Lev Loseff and Valentina Polukhina. London: Macmillan Press, 1990.

———. "Realnost zazerkalya: Venetsiya Iosifa Brodskogo." *Inostrannaya literatura,* no. 5 (1996).
———. "Solzhenitsyn i Brodsky kak sosedi." *Zvezda,* no. 5 (2000).
Loseff, Lev, and Valentina Polukhina, eds. *Joseph Brodsky: The Art of a Poem.* Houndmills, UK: Macmillan 1999.
Lotman, M. "Poet i smert (iz zametok o poetike Brodskogo)." *Blokovskiy sbornik* 14. Tartu: Kirjastus, 1998.
Lotman, Yu., and M. Lotman. "Mezhdu veshchyu i pustotoy (Iz nablyudeniy nad poetikoy sbornika Iosifa Brodskogo 'Urania')." In *Izbrannye statyi,* vol. 3. Tallinn: Aleksandra, 1993.
Lounsbery, Anne. "Iosif Brodsky kak amerikanskii poet-laureat." *Novoe literaturnoe obozrenie* 56 (2002): 204–212.
Lurye, Samuil. "Svoboda poslednego slova." *Zvezda,* no. 8 (1990).
Maksudov, Sergey [A. Babyonyshev]. "Komandirovka v Norinskuyu [*sic*]." *Novoe literaturnoe obozrenie* 45 (2000): 199–207.
Meylakh, Mikhail. "Osvobozhdenie ot emotsionalnosti." In *Brodsky glazami sovremennikov: Kniga vtoraya,* by Valentina Polukhina. Saint Petersburg: Zvezda, 1997.
———. "Razgovor s Iosifom Brodskim letom 1991 goda." In *Iosif Brodsky: Strategii chteniya. Materialy mezhdunarodnoy nauchnoy konferentsii 2–4 sentyabrya 2004 goda v Moskve.* Moscow: Izdatelstvo Ippolitova, 2005.
Myers, Alan. "A Note on Joseph Brodsky." *Northern Review* 3 (Summer 1996).
Navrozov, Lev. "Russian Literature in Exile and the *New York Times.*" *Rockford Papers* 6 (January 1981).
Okhotin, N. G. "Osvobozhdenie." *Zvezda,* no. 5 (2000).
Patera, Tatyana. *A Concordance to the Poetry of Joseph Brodsky.* Books 1–6. Lewiston, NY: Edwin Mellen Press, 2002.
Petrushanskaya, Elena. *Muzykalnyi mir Iosifa Brodskogo.* Saint Petersburg: Zvezda, 2004.
Pilshchikov, Igor. "Coitus as a Cross Genre Motif in Brodsky's Poetry." *Russian Literature* 37, nos. 2–3 (1995): 339–350.
Plekhanova, I. I. *Metafizicheskaya misteriya Iosifa Brodskogo: Pod znakom beskonechnosti: estetica metafizicheskoy svobody protiv tragicheskoy realnosti.* Irkutsk: Izdatelstvo Irkutskogo gosudarstvennogo universiteta, 2001.
Polukhina, Valentina. *Brodsky glazami sovremennikov: Kniga vtoraya.* Saint Petersburg: Zvezda, 1997.
———. *Brodsky glazami sovremennikov. Kniga vtoraya (1996–2005).* Saint Petersburg: Zvezda, 2006.
———. *Brodsky through the Eyes of His Contemporaries.* London: Macmillan Press. New York: St. Martin's Press, 1992.
———. *Joseph Brodsky: A Poet for Our Time.* Cambridge: Cambridge University Press, 1989.
———. "Poeticheskiy avtoportret Brodskogo." In *Iosif Brodsky: Tvorchestvo, lichnost, sudba. Itogi trekh konferentsiy.* Saint Petersburg: Zvezda, 1998.

———. "The Prose of Joseph Brodsky: A Continuation of Poetry by Other Means." *Russian Literature* 41, no. 2 (1997): 223–240.

Polukhina, Valentina, and Yulle Pyarli. *Slovar tropov Brodskogo (na materiale sbornika "Chast rechi")*. Tartu: Izdatelstvo Tartuskogo universiteta, 1995.

Proffer, Carl. "Ostanovka v sumasshedshem dome: Poema Brodskogo 'Gorbunov i Gorchakov.'" In *Poetika Brodskogo,* edited by Lev Loseff. Tenafly, NJ: Ermitazh, 1986.

———. "A Stop in the Madhouse: Brodsky's *Gorbunov and Gorchakov.*" *Russian Literature Triquarterly* 1 (Fall 1971): 342–351.

Radyshevsky, Dmitriy. "Dzen poezii Brodskogo." *Novoe literaturnoe obozrenie* 27 (1997): 287–326.

Raine, Craig. "A Reputation Subject to Inflation." *Financial Times,* November 16–17, 1996.

Ranchin, A. "Filosofskaya traditsiya Iosifa Brodskogo." *Literaturnoe obozrenie* 3–4 (1993): 3–13.

Ranchin, A. M. *Iosif Brodsky i russkaya poeziya XVIII–XX vekov*. Moscow: MAKS Press, 2001.

Reid, Christopher. "Great American Disaster." *London Review of Books,* December 8, 1988.

Rein, Evgeniy. "Moy ekzemplyar 'Uranii.'" In *Mne skuchno bez Dovlatova.* Saint Petersburg: Limbus Press, 1997.

Rybakov, Anatoly. *Roman-vospominanie*. Moscow: Vagrius, 1997.

Scherr, Barry. "Strofika Brodskogo." In *Poetika Brodskogo,* edited by Lev Loseff. Tenafly, NJ: Ermitazh, 1986.

Sergeev, Andrey. *Omnibus*. Moscow: Novoe literaturnoe obozrenie, 1997.

Shakhmatov, O. "'Grekhi molodosti' skvoz prizmu let i mneniy." *Ponedelnik,* November 7–13, 1997.

Shallcross, Bożena. *Through the Poet's Eye: The Travels of Zagajewski, Herbert, and Brodsky*. Evanston, IL: Northwestern University Press, 2002.

Shneiderman, Eduard. "Krugi na vode. (Svideteli zashchity na sude nad Iosifom Brodskim pered sudom LO Soyuza pisateley RSFSR)." *Zvezda,* no. 5 (1998).

Shtern, Ludmila. *Brodsky: Osya, Iosif, Joseph*. Moscow: Izdatelstvo "Nezavisimaya gazeta," 2001.

———. "Gigant protiv titana, ili 'Izzhazhdannoe okunanye v khlyabi yazyka.'" In *Mir Iosifa Brodskogo: Putevoditel*. Saint Petersburg: Zvezda, 2003.

Shults, S. S. "Iosif Brodsky v 1961–1964 godakh." *Zvezda,* no. 5 (2000).

Smith, Gerald. "Intervyu Valentine Polukhinoy (Oksford, 27 iyunya 1996 g.)." *Znamya,* no. 11 (1996).

Solzhenitsyn, Aleksandr. "Iosif Brodsky—izbrannye stikhi." *Novyi mir,* no. 12 (1999).

Turoma, Sanna. "Poet kak odinokii turist." *Novoe literaturnoe obozrenie* 67 (2004): 164–180.

Tyurin, Arkady. "Estetika—mat etiki. Intervyu s Iosifom Brodskim." *Novoe russkoe slovo,* December 6, 1994.

Updike, John, "Mandarins." *New Yorker,* July 13, 1992.
Venclova, Tomas. "O stikhotvorenii Iosifa Brodskogo 'Litovskiy noktyurn: Tomasu Venclova.'" *Novoe literaturnoe obozrenie* 33 (1998): 205–222.
Volkov, Solomon. *Dialogi s Iosifom Brodskim.* 2nd ed., expanded. Moscow: Nezavisimaya gazeta, 2000.
Walcott, Derek. "Magic Industry." *New York Review of Books,* November 24, 1988.
Weissbort, Daniel. *From Russian with Love: Joseph Brodsky in English.* London: Anvil Press, 2004.
———. "'Something Like His Own Language': Brodsky in English." In *Iosif Brodskij: Un crocevia fra culture,* edited by Alessandro Niero and Sergio Pescatori. Milan: MG, 2002.
Yakimchuk, Nikolay. *Kak sudili poeta (delo I. Brodskogo).* Leningrad: Akvilon, 1990.
Yakovich, Elena. "'Delo' Brodskogo na Staroy ploshchadi." *Literaturnaya gazeta,* May 5, 1993.
Yupp, Mikhail. "Osya Brodsky? Legenda i fakty." *Literaturnaya Rossiya,* July 27, 2001, http://www.litrossia.ru/archive/51/history/1220.php.
Zabaluyev, A. "Konoshsky period poeta." In *Iosif Brodsky: Razmerom podlinnika,* edited by Gennady Komarov. Tallinn, 1990.
"'Zimnyaya pochta'—k dvadtsatiletiyu neizdaniya knigi Iosifa Brodskogo." *Russkaya mysl,* November 11, 1988 (Literary supplement no. 7).

INDEX